CONGRESSIONAL POLICIES, PRACTICES AND PROCEDURES

KEY CONGRESSIONAL REPORTS FOR MAY 2019

PART II

CONGRESSIONAL POLICIES, PRACTICES AND PROCEDURES

Additional books and e-books in this series can be found
on Nova's website under the Series tab.

CONGRESSIONAL POLICIES, PRACTICES AND PROCEDURES

KEY CONGRESSIONAL REPORTS FOR MAY 2019

PART II

PIOTR MEZA
EDITOR

Copyright © 2019 by Nova Science Publishers, Inc.

All rights reserved. No part of this book may be reproduced, stored in a retrieval system or transmitted in any form or by any means: electronic, electrostatic, magnetic, tape, mechanical photocopying, recording or otherwise without the written permission of the Publisher.

We have partnered with Copyright Clearance Center to make it easy for you to obtain permissions to reuse content from this publication. Simply navigate to this publication's page on Nova's website and locate the "Get Permission" button below the title description. This button is linked directly to the title's permission page on copyright.com. Alternatively, you can visit copyright.com and search by title, ISBN, or ISSN.

For further questions about using the service on copyright.com, please contact:
Copyright Clearance Center
Phone: +1-(978) 750-8400   Fax: +1-(978) 750-4470   E-mail: info@copyright.com.

NOTICE TO THE READER

The Publisher has taken reasonable care in the preparation of this book, but makes no expressed or implied warranty of any kind and assumes no responsibility for any errors or omissions. No liability is assumed for incidental or consequential damages in connection with or arising out of information contained in this book. The Publisher shall not be liable for any special, consequential, or exemplary damages resulting, in whole or in part, from the readers' use of, or reliance upon, this material. Any parts of this book based on government reports are so indicated and copyright is claimed for those parts to the extent applicable to compilations of such works.

Independent verification should be sought for any data, advice or recommendations contained in this book. In addition, no responsibility is assumed by the Publisher for any injury and/or damage to persons or property arising from any methods, products, instructions, ideas or otherwise contained in this publication.

This publication is designed to provide accurate and authoritative information with regard to the subject matter covered herein. It is sold with the clear understanding that the Publisher is not engaged in rendering legal or any other professional services. If legal or any other expert assistance is required, the services of a competent person should be sought. FROM A DECLARATION OF PARTICIPANTS JOINTLY ADOPTED BY A COMMITTEE OF THE AMERICAN BAR ASSOCIATION AND A COMMITTEE OF PUBLISHERS.

Additional color graphics may be available in the e-book version of this book.

Library of Congress Cataloging-in-Publication Data

ISBN: 978-1-53616-382-7

Published by Nova Science Publishers, Inc. † New York

CONTENTS

Preface		**vii**
Government Operations		**1**
Chapter 1	House Rules Changes Affecting Committee Procedure in the 116th Congress (2019-2020) *Jane A. Hudiburg*	**3**
Chapter 2	Federal Grants to State and Local Governments: A Historical Perspective on Contemporary Issues (Updated) *Robert Jay Dilger and Michael H. Cecire*	**23**
Chapter 3	Unfunded Mandates Reform Act: History, Impact, and Issues *Robert Jay Dilger*	**91**
Chapter 4	Military Pay: Key Questions and Answers *Lawrence Kapp and Barbara Salazar Torreon*	**179**
Homeland Security		**219**
Chapter 5	"Sanctuary" Jurisdictions: Federal, State, and Local Policies and Related Litigation *Sarah Herman Peck*	**221**

vi   *Contents*

Chapter 6   The H-2B Visa and the Statutory Cap:
                   In Brief (Updated)   **285**
                   Andorra Bruno

Index   **307**

Related Nova Publications   **321**

PREFACE

This book is a comprehensive compilation of all reports, testimony, correspondence and other publications issued by the Congressional Research Service during the month of May, grouped according to topics. This book is focused on the following topics:

- Government Operations
- Homeland Security

Chapter 1 - As agreed to in the House, H.Res. 6, a resolution adopting the rules of the House of Representatives, provided amendments to the rules, as well as separate orders, that affect committee procedure in the 116th Congress (2019-2020). Several of these changes apply to general committee procedure, while others concern specific committees, such as modifications to the names, jurisdiction, or procedures of certain House committees. The rules package also established, during the 116th Congress, two new select committees. H.Res. 6 made several changes to committee membership and organization. Most significantly, it removed the committee chair term limits that were in effect during each Congress from the 104th through the 115th Congresses (1995-2018), excluding the 111th Congress (2009-2010). H.Res. 6 added a provision to Rule XXIII that calls on any Member, Delegate, or the Resident Commissioner who has been indicted or formally charged with certain felony offenses to refrain from committee business. It clarified that Delegates and the Resident Commissioner may serve on joint committees, and it lengthened from 30 days to 60 days the period in which to adopt and publish committee rules at the start of a Congress. In a separate order, the 116th Congress rules package established a requirement that certain legislative measures must be reported and be subject to a committee hearing and markup prior to their consideration on the floor. This requirement applies, with some exceptions, to measures that are raised under the terms of a special rule reported from the Rules Committee. Another separate order requires most standing committees to hold a Member Day Hearing during the first session of the 116th Congress, affording any Member the opportunity to speak on proposed legislation within the committee's jurisdiction. H.Res. 6 clarified the notification requirement for committee markup meetings. As amended, clause 2 of Rule XI provides Members at least three *workdays* to prepare for an upcoming markup, as opposed to the less specific requirement that markups may not occur before the "third day" after a chair announces the meeting. H.Res. 6 altered procedures concerning committee oversight. The 115th Congress House rules requirement that committees prepare and submit "authorization and oversight plans" was replaced with the requirement that chairs develop oversight plans in consultation with the ranking member. In addition, a separate order now allows committee counsel to take depositions without the presence of a committee member. Amendments to the House standing rules changed two committees' names and clarified their jurisdictions. The Committee on Education and the Workforce became the Committee on Education and Labor, a name it held in some previous Congresses. As amended, Rule X specified that the committee's jurisdiction includes the general management of the Department of Education and the Department of Labor. The Committee on Oversight and Government Reform was re-designated the Committee on Oversight and Reform. The rules changes clarified that the Committee on Oversight and Reform's existing jurisdiction over the review and study of all government activities includes "the Executive Office of the President." A separate order directed the Committee on Ethics to empanel an investigative subcommittee to review allegations whenever a Member, Delegate, or the Resident Commissioner is indicted on a criminal charge. H.Res. 6 amended clause 3 of Rule XI to allow the Committee on Ethics, or an investigative subcommittee thereof, to consider trial evidence in ethics investigations of Members, Delegates, and the Resident Commissioner. Another separate order enabled the Committee on Financial Services to establish as many as seven subcommittees, as opposed to the six subcommittees allowed under the rules, while an amendment to clause 3 of Rule XIII exempted the Rules Committee from the requirement that committee reports must include recorded votes taken in committee. The rules changes also removed membership term limits to the Committee on the Budget. However, the rules of the Democratic Caucus and Republican Conference may continue to limit the number of terms that Members may serve on the Budget Committee. Finally, the rules package established, for the 116th Congress, the Select Committee on the Climate Crisis and the Select Committee on the Modernization of Congress. The committees are to "investigate, study, make findings, hold public hearings, and develop recommendations." By the end of the 116th Congress, they are to report their findings and policy recommendations to the relevant standing committees and publish them in a publicly available format.

Chapter 2 - The federal government is expected to provide state and local governments about $750 billion in federal grants in FY2019, funding a wide range of public policies, such as health care, transportation, income security, education, job training, social services, community development, and environmental protection. Federal grants account for about one-third of total state government funding, and more than half of state government funding for health care and public assistance. Congressional interest in federal grants to state and local governments has always been high given the central role Congress has in determining the scope and nature of the federal grant-in-aid system, the amount of funding involved, and disagreements over the appropriate role of the federal government in domestic policy generally and in its relationship with state and local governments. Federalism scholars agree that congressional decisions concerning the scope and nature of the federal grants-in-aid system are influenced by both internal and external factors. Internal factors include congressional party leadership and congressional procedures; the decentralized nature of the committee system; the backgrounds, personalities, and ideological preferences of individual Members; and the customs and traditions (norms) that govern congressional behavior. Major external factors include input provided by voter constituencies, organized interest groups, the President, and executive branch officials. Although not directly involved in the legislative process, the Supreme Court, through its rulings on federalism issues, also influences congressional decisions concerning the federal grants-in-aid system. Overarching all of these factors is the evolving nature of cultural norms and expectations concerning government's role in American society. Over time, the American public has become increasingly accepting of government activism in domestic affairs generally, and of federal government intervention in particular. Federalism scholars attribute this increased acceptance of, and sometimes demand for, government action as a reaction to the industrialization and urbanization of American society; technological innovations in communications, which have raised awareness of societal problems; and exponential growth in economic interdependencies brought about by an increasingly global economy. This chapter provides a historical synopsis of the evolving nature of the federal grants-in-aid system, focusing on the role Congress has played in defining the system's scope and nature. It begins with an overview of the contemporary federal grants-in-aid system and then examines its evolution over time, focusing on the internal and external factors that have influenced congressional decisions concerning the system's development. It concludes with an assessment of the scope and nature of the contemporary federal grants-in-aid system and raises several issues for congressional consideration, including possible ways to augment congressional capacity to provide effective oversight of this system.

Chapter 3 - The Unfunded Mandates Reform Act of 1995 (UMRA) culminated years of effort by state and local government officials and business interests to control, if not eliminate, the imposition of unfunded intergovernmental and private-sector federal mandates. Advocates argued the statute was needed to forestall federal legislation and regulations that imposed obligations on state and local governments or businesses that resulted in higher costs and inefficiencies. Opponents argued that federal mandates may be necessary to achieve national objectives in areas where voluntary action by state and local governments and business failed to achieve desired results. UMRA provides a framework for the Congressional Budget Office (CBO) to estimate the direct costs of mandates in legislative proposals to state and local governments and to the private sector, and for issuing agencies to estimate the direct costs of mandates in proposed regulations to regulated entities. Aside from these informational requirements, UMRA controls the imposition of mandates only through a procedural mechanism allowing Congress to decline to consider unfunded intergovernmental mandates in proposed legislation if they are estimated to cost more than specified threshold amounts. UMRA applies to any provision in legislation, statute, or regulation that would impose an enforceable duty upon state and local governments or the private sector. It does not apply to duties stemming from participation in voluntary federal programs; rules issued by independent regulatory agencies; rules issued without a general notice of proposed rulemaking; and rules and legislative provisions that cover individual constitutional rights, discrimination, emergency assistance, grant accounting and auditing procedures, national security, treaty obligations, and certain elements of Social Security. In most instances, UMRA also does not apply to conditions of federal assistance. State and local government officials argue that UMRA's coverage should be broadened, with special consideration given to including conditions of federal financial assistance. During the 116th Congress, H.R. 300, the Unfunded Mandates Information and Transparency Act of 2019, would broaden UMRA's coverage to include both direct and indirect costs, such as foregone profits and costs passed onto consumers, and, when requested by the chair or ranking member of a committee, the prospective costs of legislation that would change conditions of federal financial assistance. The bill also would make private-sector mandates subject to a substantive point of order and remove UMRA's exemption for rules issued by most independent agencies. The

House approved similar legislation during the 112th, 113th, 114th, and 115th Congresses. This chapter examines debates over what constitutes an unfunded federal mandate and UMRA's implementation. It focuses on UMRA's requirement that CBO issue written cost estimate statements for federal mandates in legislation, its procedures for raising points of order in the House and Senate concerning unfunded federal mandates in legislation, and its requirement that federal agencies prepare written cost estimate statements for federal mandates in rules. It also assesses UMRA's impact on federal mandates and arguments concerning UMRA's future, focusing on UMRA's definitions, exclusions, and exceptions that currently exempt many federal actions with potentially significant financial impacts on nonfederal entities. An examination of the rise of unfunded federal mandates as a national issue and a summary of UMRA's legislative history are provided in Appendix A. Citations to UMRA points of order raised in the House and Senate are provided in Appendix B.

Chapter 4 - From the earliest days of the republic, the federal government has compensated members of the Armed Forces for their services. While the original pay structure was fairly simple, over time a more complex system of compensation has evolved. The current military compensation system includes cash payments such as basic pay, special and incentive pays, and various allowances. Servicemembers also receive noncash benefits such as health care and access to commissaries and recreational facilities, and may qualify for deferred compensation in the form of retired pay and other retirement benefits. This chapter provides an overview of military compensation generally, but focuses on cash compensation for current servicemembers. Since the advent of the all-volunteer force in 1973, Congress has used military compensation to improve recruiting, retention, and the overall quality of the force. Congressional interest in sustaining the all-volunteer force during a time of sustained combat operations led to substantial increases in compensation in the decade following the attacks of September 11, 2001. Subsequently, in the earlier part of the 2010s, concerns over government spending generated congressional and executive branch interest in slowing the rate of growth in military compensation. Initiatives to slow compensation growth included presidentially directed increases in basic pay below the rate of increase for the Employment Cost Index (ECI) for 2014-2016 and statutory authority for the Department of Defense (DOD) to reduce Basic Allowance for Housing (BAH) payments by 1% of the national average monthly housing cost per year from 2015 to 2019 (for a maximum reduction of 5% under the national monthly average housing cost). Some have raised concerns about the impact of personnel costs on the overall defense budget, arguing that they decrease the amount of funds available for modernizing equipment and sustaining readiness. Others argue that robust compensation is essential to maintaining a high- quality force that is vigorous, well-trained, experienced, and able to function effectively in austere and volatile environments. The availability of funding to prosecute contingency operations in Iraq and Afghanistan mitigated the pressure to trade off personnel, readiness, and equipment costs, but the current budgetary environment appears to have brought these trade-offs to the fore again. DOD spends about $100,000-$110,000 per year to compensate the average active duty servicemember—to include cash, benefits, and contributions to retirement programs—although some estimates of compensation costs are substantially higher. However, gross compensation figures do not tell the full story, as military compensation *relative to* civilian compensation is a key factor in an individual's decision to join or stay in the military. Thus, the issue of comparability between military and civilian pay is an often-discussed topic. Some analysts and advocacy groups have argued that a substantial "pay gap" has existed for decades—with military personnel earning less than their civilian counterparts—although they generally concede that this gap is fairly small today. Others argue that the methodology behind this "pay gap" is flawed and does not provide a suitable estimate of pay comparability. Still others believe that military personnel, in general, are better compensated than their civilian counterparts. The Department of Defense takes a different approach to pay comparability. The 9th Quadrennial Review of Military Compensation (QRMC), published in 2002, argued that compensation for servicemembers should be around the 70th percentile of wages for civilian employees with similar education and experience. According to the 11th QRMC, published in 2012, regular military compensation for officers was at the 83rd percentile of wages for civilian employees with similar education and experience, and at the 90th percentile for enlisted personnel. A 2018 RAND report concluded that these overall percentiles were nearly the same in 2016.

Chapter 5 - There is no official or agreed-upon definition of what constitutes a "sanctuary" jurisdiction, and there has been debate as to whether the term applies to particular states and localities. Moreover, state and local jurisdictions have varied reasons for opting not to cooperate with federal immigration enforcement efforts, including reasons not necessarily motivated by disagreement with federal policies, such as concern about potential civil liability or the costs associated with assisting federal efforts. But traditional sanctuary policies are often described as falling under one of three categories. First, so-called "don't enforce" policies generally bar state or local police from assisting federal immigration authorities. Second, "don't ask" policies generally bar certain state or local officials from inquiring into a person's immigration status. Third, "don't tell" policies typically restrict information sharing between state or local law enforcement and federal immigration authorities. One legal question relevant to sanctuary policies is the extent to which states, as sovereign entities, may decline to assist in federal immigration enforcement, and the degree to which the federal government can stop state measures that undermine federal objectives. The Tenth Amendment preserves the states' broad police powers, and states have frequently enacted measures that, directly or indirectly, address aliens residing in their communities. Under the doctrine of preemption—derived from the Supremacy Clause— Congress may displace many state or local laws pertaining to immigration. But not every state or local law touching on immigration matters is necessarily preempted; the measure must interfere with, or be contrary to, federal law to be rendered unenforceable. Further, the anti-commandeering doctrine, rooted in the Constitution's allocation of powers between the federal government and the states, prohibits Congress from forcing state entities to perform regulatory functions on the federal government's behalf, including in the context of immigration. A series of Supreme Court cases

Preface xv

inform the boundaries of preemption and the anti-commandeering doctrine, with the Court most recently opining on the issue in *Murphy v. NCAA*. These dueling federal and state interests are front and center in numerous lawsuits challenging actions taken by the Trump Administration to curb states and localities from implementing sanctuary-type policies. Notably, Section 9(a) of Executive Order 13768, "Enhancing Public Safety in the Interior of the United States," directs the Secretary of Homeland Security and the Attorney General to withhold federal grants from jurisdictions that willfully refuse to comply with 8 U.S.C. § 1373—a statute that bars states and localities from prohibiting their employees from sharing with federal immigration authorities certain immigration-related information. The executive order further directs the Attorney General to take "appropriate enforcement action" against jurisdictions that violate Section 1373 or have policies that "prevent or hinder the enforcement of federal law." To implement the executive order, the Department of Justice added new eligibility conditions to the Edward Byrne Memorial Justice Assistance Grant (Byrne JAG) Program and grants administered by the Justice Department's Office of Community Oriented Policing Services (COPS). These conditions tied eligibility to compliance with Section 1373 and other federal immigration priorities, like granting federal authorities access to state and local detention facilities housing aliens and giving immigration authorities notice before releasing from custody an alien wanted for removal. Several lawsuits were filed challenging the constitutionality of the executive order and new grant conditions. So far the courts that have reviewed these challenges—principally contending that the executive order and grant conditions violate the separation of powers and anti-commandeering principles—generally agree that the Trump Administration acted unconstitutionally. For instance, the Ninth Circuit Court of Appeals upheld a permanent injunction blocking enforcement of Section 9(a) against California. Additionally, two separate district courts permanently enjoined the Byrne JAG conditions as applied to Chicago and Philadelphia. In doing so, these courts concluded that the Supreme Court's most recent formulation of the anti-commandeering doctrine in *Murphy* requires holding Section 1373 unconstitutional. These lawsuits notwithstanding, the courts still recognize the federal government's pervasive, nearly exclusive role in immigration enforcement. This can be seen in the federal government's lawsuit challenging three California measures governing the state's regulation of private and public actors' involvement in immigration enforcement within its border. Although a district court opined that several measures likely were lawful exercises of the state's police powers, it also concluded that two provisions regulating private employers are likely unlawful under the Supremacy Clause. This ruling was mostly upheld on appeal, in which the Ninth Circuit additionally opined that a provision requiring the California attorney general to review the circumstances surrounding detained aliens' apprehension and transfer to detention facilities within the state also violates the Supremacy Clause.

Chapter 6 - The Immigration and Nationality Act (INA) of 1952, as amended, enumerates categories of foreign nationals, known as nonimmigrants, who are admitted to the United States for a temporary period of time and a specific purpose. One of these nonimmigrant visa categories— known as the H-2B visa—is for temporary nonagricultural workers. The H-2B visa allows for the temporary admission of foreign workers to the United States to perform nonagricultural labor or services of a temporary nature if unemployed U.S. workers are not available. Common H-2B occupations include landscape laborer, housekeeper, and amusement park worker. The H-2B program is administered by the U.S. Department of Homeland Security's (DHS's) U.S. Citizenship and Immigration Services (USCIS) and the U.S. Department of Labor's (DOL's) Employment and Training Administration. DOL's Wage and Hour Division also has certain concurrent enforcement responsibilities. The H-2B program currently operates under regulations issued by DHS in 2008 on H-2B requirements, by DHS and DOL jointly in 2015 on H-2B employment, and by DHS and DOL jointly in 2015 on H-2B wages. Bringing workers into the United States under the H-2B program is a multiagency process involving DOL, DHS, and the Department of State (DOS). A prospective H-2B employer must apply to DOL for labor certification. Approval of a labor certification application reflects a finding by DOL that there are not sufficient U.S.

Preface

workers who are qualified and available to perform the work and that the employment of foreign workers will not adversely affect the wages and working conditions of U.S. workers who are similarly employed. If granted labor certification, an employer can file a petition with DHS to bring in the approved number of H-2B workers. If the petition is approved, a foreign worker overseas who the employer wants to employ can go to a U.S. embassy or consulate to apply for an H-2B nonimmigrant visa from DOS. If the visa application is approved, the worker is issued a visa that he or she can use to apply for admission to the United States at a port of entry. H-2B workers can be accompanied by eligible spouses and children. By law, the H-2B visa is subject to an annual numerical cap. Under the INA, the total number of individuals who may be issued H-2B visas or otherwise provided with H-2B nonimmigrant status in any fiscal year may not exceed 66,000. USCIS is responsible for implementing the H-2B cap, which it does at the petition receipt stage. Spouses and children accompanying H-2B workers are not counted against the H-2B cap. In addition, certain categories of H-2B workers are exempt from the cap. Among these categories are current H-2B workers who are seeking an extension of stay, change of employer, or change in the terms of their employment. Employer demand for H-2B workers has varied over the years. In recent years, demand has exceeded supply, and special provisions have been enacted to make additional H-2B visas available. For FY2016, a temporary statutory provision exempted certain H-2B workers from the cap. It applied to H-2B workers who had been counted against the cap in any one of the three prior fiscal years and would be returning as H-2B workers in FY2016. For FY2017, FY2018, and FY2019, a different type of H-2B cap-related provision authorized DHS to issue additional H-2B visas (above the cap) subject to specified conditions.

GOVERNMENT OPERATIONS

In: Key Congressional Reports for May 2019   ISBN: 978-1-53616-382-7
Editor: Piotr Meza   © 2019 Nova Science Publishers, Inc.

Chapter 1

HOUSE RULES CHANGES AFFECTING COMMITTEE PROCEDURE IN THE 116TH CONGRESS (2019-2020)[*]

Jane A. Hudiburg

ABSTRACT

As agreed to in the House, H.Res. 6, a resolution adopting the rules of the House of Representatives, provided amendments to the rules, as well as separate orders, that affect committee procedure in the 116th Congress (2019-2020). Several of these changes apply to general committee procedure, while others concern specific committees, such as modifications to the names, jurisdiction, or procedures of certain House committees. The rules package also established, during the 116th Congress, two new select committees.

---

[*] This is an edited, reformatted and augmented version of Congressional Research Service Publication No. R45731, dated May 21, 2019.

H.Res. 6 made several changes to committee membership and organization. Most significantly, it removed the committee chair term limits that were in effect during each Congress from the 104th through the 115th Congresses (1995-2018), excluding the 111th Congress (2009-2010). H.Res. 6 added a provision to Rule XXIII that calls on any Member, Delegate, or the Resident Commissioner who has been indicted or formally charged with certain felony offenses to refrain from committee business. It clarified that Delegates and the Resident Commissioner may serve on joint committees, and it lengthened from 30 days to 60 days the period in which to adopt and publish committee rules at the start of a Congress.

In a separate order, the 116th Congress rules package established a requirement that certain legislative measures must be reported and be subject to a committee hearing and markup prior to their consideration on the floor. This requirement applies, with some exceptions, to measures that are raised under the terms of a special rule reported from the Rules Committee. Another separate order requires most standing committees to hold a Member Day Hearing during the first session of the 116th Congress, affording any Member the opportunity to speak on proposed legislation within the committee's jurisdiction. H.Res. 6 clarified the notification requirement for committee markup meetings. As amended, clause 2 of Rule XI provides Members at least three *workdays* to prepare for an upcoming markup, as opposed to the less specific requirement that markups may not occur before the "third day" after a chair announces the meeting.

H.Res. 6 altered procedures concerning committee oversight. The 115th Congress House rules requirement that committees prepare and submit "authorization and oversight plans" was replaced with the requirement that chairs develop oversight plans in consultation with the ranking member. In addition, a separate order now allows committee counsel to take depositions without the presence of a committee member.

Amendments to the House standing rules changed two committees' names and clarified their jurisdictions. The Committee on Education and the Workforce became the Committee on Education and Labor, a name it held in some previous Congresses. As amended, Rule X specified that the committee's jurisdiction includes the general management of the Department of Education and the Department of Labor. The Committee on Oversight and Government Reform was re-designated the Committee on Oversight and Reform. The rules changes clarified that the Committee on Oversight and Reform's existing jurisdiction over the review and study of all government activities includes "the Executive Office of the President."

A separate order directed the Committee on Ethics to empanel an investigative subcommittee to review allegations whenever a Member, Delegate, or the Resident Commissioner is indicted on a criminal charge. H.Res. 6 amended clause 3 of Rule XI to allow the Committee on Ethics, or an investigative subcommittee thereof, to consider trial evidence in ethics investigations of Members, Delegates, and the Resident Commissioner.

Another separate order enabled the Committee on Financial Services to establish as many as seven subcommittees, as opposed to the six subcommittees allowed under the rules, while an amendment to clause 3 of Rule XIII exempted the Rules Committee from the requirement that committee reports must include recorded votes taken in committee. The rules changes also removed membership term limits to the Committee on the Budget. However, the rules of the Democratic Caucus and Republican Conference may continue to limit the number of terms that Members may serve on the Budget Committee.

Finally, the rules package established, for the 116th Congress, the Select Committee on the Climate Crisis and the Select Committee on the Modernization of Congress. The committees are to "investigate, study, make findings, hold public hearings, and develop recommendations." By the end of the 116th Congress, they are to report their findings and policy recommendations to the relevant standing committees and publish them in a publicly available format.

INTRODUCTION

In January 2019, the House agreed to H.Res. 6, a resolution "Adopting the Rules of the House of Representatives for the One Hundred Sixteenth Congress." This chapter summarizes amendments to House rules affecting committee procedure in the 116th Congress (2019-2020) as provided for in H.Res. 6.[1]

The report also describes separate orders contained in the resolution that relate to committee procedure, including the establishment of the Select Committee on the Climate Crisis and the Select Committee on the Modernization of Congress. Separate orders have the same force and effect

---

[1] This chapter does not consider changes related to the budget process, floor proceedings, or the administration of Congress (i.e., salaries, staff training, and membership requirements on boards and commissions). For more information about changes to House rules affecting floor procedure, see CRS Report R45787, *House Rules Changes Affecting Floor Proceedings in the 116th Congress (2019-2020)*, by Jane A. Hudiburg. For more information about budget process changes in the 116th Congress, see CRS Report R45552, *Changes to House Rules Affecting the Congressional Budget Process Included in H.Res. 6 (116th Congress)*, by James V. Saturno and Megan S. Lynch.

as House rules and are commonly included in the House rules package resolution.

In the 116th Congress, rules changes that affect all House committees concern committee membership and organization, hearings and markups, and committee oversight and investigations. Changes that affect specific committees include modifications to the names, jurisdiction, or procedure of certain House committees.[2]

GENERAL COMMITTEE PROCEDURE

Committee Chairs, Membership, and Organization

Committee Chairmanship Limits

In the 116th Congress, H.Res. 6 struck clause 5(c)(2) of Rule X, which stated that a Member could not serve as chair of the same standing committee or subcommittee for more than three consecutive Congresses (disregarding any service of less than a full session), except on the Committee on Rules.[3] This amendment enables Members to serve an unrestricted number of terms as chairs, as was the case before the 104th Congress (1995-1996) and during the 111th Congress (2009-2010).[4]

---

[2] Sources consulted include H.Res. 6 (116th Congress); U.S. Congress, House, *Rules of the House of Representatives, One Hundred Sixteenth Congress*, prepared by Karen L. Haas, Clerk of the House of Representatives, 116th Cong., 1st sess., 2019; U.S. Congress, House, *Constitution, Jefferson's Manual and the Rules of the House of Representatives of the United States One Hundred Fifteenth Congress* (hereinafter *House Manual*, 115th Congress), 114th Cong., 2nd sess., 2017, (Washington: GPO, 2017); U.S. Congress, House Committee on Rules, H.Res. 6 *Adopting the Rules for the 116th Congress, Section-by-Section Analysis* (hereinafter *Section-by-Section*), 116th Cong., 1st sess., 2019.

[3] *House Manual*, 115th Congress, §761, p. 518.

[4] The House first agreed to establish term limits for all standing committee chairs after the Republican Party assumed the chamber's majority in the 104th Congress (1995-1996). Under Republican leadership, the House maintained term limits for committee chairs during the 105th-109th Congresses (1997-2006) with a "Committee on Rules" exception added in the 109th Congress. Under Democratic majority, the House maintained term limits in the 110th Congress (2007-2008) but removed them at the start of the 111th Congress (2009-2010). During the 112th-115th Congresses (2011-2018), the House, under Republican control, restored and maintained the term limits provision.

Allowing Delegates and the Resident Commissioner to Serve on Joint Committees

H.Res. 6 amended clause 3(b) of Rule III to make clear that the Delegates and the Resident Commissioner from Puerto Rico may be appointed to joint committees.[5] The rule previously mentioned only service by the Delegates and the Resident Commissioner on select and conference committees.

House rules first afforded membership to standing committees to Delegates in 1871 and to the Resident Commissioner in 1904. House rules were amended in the 93rd Congress (1973-1974) to allow the Delegates and Resident Commissioner, effective in the subsequent Congress, to be appointed to conference committees on legislation reported from committees on which they served. Chamber rules were amended in 1979 (96th Congress) to authorize their appointment to select committees. In the 103rd Congress (1993-1994), the House expanded eligibility to encompass all conference committees.[6] The 116th Congress rules provide the Delegates and the Resident Commissioner with equal status as Members on standing, select, joint, and conference committees.[7]

Service of Indicted Members on Committees

H.Res. 6 amended clause 10 of Rule XXIII, adding a provision that calls on any Member, Delegate, or the Resident Commissioner who has been indicted or formally charged with a felony offense that is punishable by at least two years in prison to resign from committee assignments and party caucus or conference leadership positions. Such individuals should submit their resignations from any party leadership position and any type of House or joint committee or subcommittee thereof "unless or until" they are acquitted or the charges are dismissed or reduced to less than a felony.[8]

---

[5] Clause 3(b), Rule III, Rules of the House of Representatives, One Hundred Sixteenth Congress, p. 4.

[6] House Manual, 115th Congress, §676, p. 390.

[7] See CRS Report R40555, Delegates to the U.S. Congress: History and Current Status, by Christopher M. Davis.

[8] Clause 10(a), Rule XXIII, Rules of the House of Representatives, One Hundred Sixteenth Congress, p. 39.

Rule XXIII comprises the House's Code of Official Conduct, which was first adopted in 1968 by H.Res. 1099 (90th Congress). In the 116th Congress, the new language added to clause 10, subparagraph (b), supplements an existing provision written into the rule in 1975 (94th Congress) that states that a Member, Delegate, or Resident Commissioner should refrain from committee business if the individual is convicted of a crime and may be sentenced to imprisonment.[9]

Note that clause 10 language uses the word *should* as opposed to *shall* or *must*. The Democratic Caucus and Republican Conference could recommend the removal of a party member from a committee assignment if the Member does not voluntarily resign.[10] The House could then vote on a privileged resolution to remove the member.[11]

Rules of Committees

The rules package gave committees a longer period in which to adopt and publish committee rules of procedure. In the 116th Congress, each committee has 60 days, rather than 30 days, to "make its rules publicly available in electronic form and submit such rules for publication in the *Congressional Record*" after the chair is elected in an even-numbered year.[12] H.Res. 6 amended clause 2(a)(2) of Rule XI, striking the number 30 and replacing it with 60. According to the Rules Committee's summary of H.Res. 6, the "change is intended to grant committees adequate time to organize, as some committees do not have a full complement of members at the start of a Congress."[13]

---

[9] *House Manual*, 115th Congress, §1095, p. 958.

[10] House Republican Conference, "Conference Rules of the 116th Congress," 116th Cong., 1st sess., 2019; U.S. Congress, House Committee on Rules, *Compilation of Selected Rules of the Republican Conference and Democratic Caucus*, committee print, compiled by the Office of the Parliamentarian, 115th Cong., 1st sess., 2017, RCP 115-37 (Washington: GPO, 2017).

[11] Charles W. Johnson, John V. Sullivan, and Thomas J. Wickham Jr., *House Practice: A Guide to the Rules, Precedents, and Procedures of the House* (Washington: GPO, 2017), ch. 11, p. 247.

[12] Clause 2(a)(2), Rule XI, *Rules of the House of Representatives, One Hundred Sixteenth Congress*, p. 17.

[13] *Section-by-Section*, p. 3.

Hearing and Markup Procedure

Requiring Committee Hearing and Markup on Bills and Joint Resolutions

In a separate order, the rules package requires that, during the 116th Congress, after March 1, 2019, certain lawmaking measures must be reported and be subject to related committee hearings and a markup prior to floor consideration. Otherwise, "it shall not be in order" to consider them on the House floor. This requirement applies to bills and joint resolutions considered under the terms of a special rule reported by the Rules Committee—excluding measures that continue appropriations, contain an emergency designation, or are listed on the Consensus Calendar and are designated for consideration.

According to the separate order, a lawmaking measure is not to be considered "pursuant to a special order of business [special rule] reported by the Committee on Rules" if it has not been reported by a committee. If it has been reported, the committee report accompanying the bill or joint resolution is to include a list of related committee and subcommittee hearings and a designation of at least one such hearing that was used to develop or consider the measure.

Bills and joint resolutions brought to the House floor under the terms of a rule from the Rules Committee are generally measures that Members want to debate at length or amend on the floor due to their complexity, controversy, or policy importance. Measures considered under special rules include appropriations bills, tax legislation, and significant reauthorization bills.

Under the separate order, these types of bills and joint resolutions are to go through the committee hearing and markup process before being considered by the full chamber. However, special rules often include "waivers" for all or certain types of points of order against consideration of a bill.

Member Day Hearing Requirement

H.Res. 6 includes a separate order that requires standing committees to hold a "Member Day Hearing" during the first session of the 116th Congress. This new requirement does not apply to the Committee on Ethics, and it allows the Committee on Rules to hold its Member Day Hearing in the second session of the Congress "in order to receive testimony on proposed changes to the standing rules for the next Congress."[14] According to the Rules Committee summary of H.Res. 6, Member Day Hearings allow Members, Delegates, and the Resident Commissioner, "whether or not they are a member of the committee," to speak before a committee on proposed legislation within the committee's jurisdiction.[15]

Committee Markup Notice

H.Res. 6 amended clause 2(g) of Rule XI to modify the three-day notification requirement for committee markup meetings. Under paragraph (3)(A) of this clause, the chairs of committees "shall announce the date, place, and subject matter" to consider and markup legislation.[16]

As in previous Congresses, markups may not occur earlier than the third day on which Members have been given notice thereof. In the 116th Congress, subparagraph (3)(A)(ii) specifies that the third day is the "third *calendar* day," rather than the "third day," and that the notification period excludes "Saturdays, Sundays, or legal holidays except when the House is in session on such a day."[17] Thus, the revised provision is designed to guarantee Members at least three workdays' notice before a committee meets to markup legislation.

---

[14] Section-by-Section, p. 8.
[15] Section-by-Section, p. 8.
[16] *House Manual*, 115th Congress, §798, p. 570.
[17] Clause 2(g)(3)(A)(ii), Rule XI, Rules of the House of Representatives, One Hundred Sixteenth Congress, p. 18.

Committee Oversight, Activities and Investigations

Committee Oversight Plans

Oversight plans include a committee's intentions, during a Congress, to review federal laws, regulations, court decisions, programs, and agencies within their jurisdictions. From the 104th through the 114th Congresses (1995-2016), standing committees were required to adopt and submit an oversight plan. In the 115th Congress, House rules required committees to submit authorization and oversight plans.[18] H.Res. 6 amended clause 2(d) of Rule X to restore the previous requirement for committee oversight plans. The amendment also altered some procedures regarding oversight plans.

In the 115th Congress, each standing committee—except Appropriations, Ethics, and Rules—was required to hold an open meeting, not later than February 15th in odd-number years, in which the committee marked up and adopted an authorization and oversight plan. Each committee had to submit its plan to the Committees on Oversight and Government Reform (now Oversight and Reform), House Administration, and Appropriations. By March 31, the Committee on Oversight and Government Reform was to report the various plans to the House as well as any recommendations about them.

Under the rules change adopted in the 116th Congress, the same standing committees are required to submit oversight plans. In contrast to the 115th Congress, however, full committees do not mark up and adopt the plans in open meetings. Instead, the chair prepares the plan "in consultation with the ranking member." The chair then provides a copy to committee members "at least seven calendar days" before submitting it to the Committee on Oversight and Reform and the Committee on House Administration by March 1 of the first session of Congress, along with any "supplemental, minority, additional, or dissenting views submitted by a

---

[18] In addition to announcing a committee's intentions regarding oversight, in the 115th Congress an authorization and oversight plan was to include a list of certain programs and agencies that were operating under a lapsed or permanent authorization that could be subject to a review in the upcoming Congress. *House Manual*, 115th Congress, §743, p. 493.

member of the committee." The completed plans no longer must be submitted to the Appropriations Committee.

Pursuant to clause 2(d), the House Committee on Oversight and Reform shall, after consulting with the majority leader and the minority leader, "report to the House," by not later than April 15 in the first session, the various oversight plans. As in earlier Congresses, the Committee on Oversight and Reform is to also include "any recommendations ... to ensure the most effective coordination of oversight plans."

In sum, in the 116th Congress, chairs are given the prerogative to develop oversight plans, as opposed to the full standing committee, but are to include any dissenting views of committee members. The deadline is extended for submitting the plans to the Committee on Oversight and Reform and the Committee on House Administration (from February 15 to March 1) and for Oversight and Reform to report the plans to the full House (from March 1 to April 15). The resolution removed the role of the Appropriations Committee in the review of such plans.[19]

Activity Reports

The 116th rules package made a technical change to the list of items required to be included in the activity reports that committees must adopt by January 2 of each odd-numbered year. H.Res. 6 amended clause 1(d)(2) of Rule XI to remove authorization from the phrase *authorization and oversight plans*.[20]

In the 115th Congress, committee activity reports were required to summarize the authorization and oversight plans previously submitted by the committees. The amended clause brought the committee activity reports requirement in line with the 116th Congress requirement for oversight plans described in the previous section of this chapter.

---

[19] Clause 2(d), Rule XI, Rules of the House of Representatives, One Hundred Sixteenth Congress, p. 9.

[20] Clause 1(d)(2)(B) and (C), Rule XI, *Rules of the House of Representatives, One Hundred Sixteenth Congress*, p. 17.

Deposition Authority

The rules package included a separate order that authorized the chairs of all standing House committees, except for the Rules Committee, and the chair of the Select Intelligence Committee to order the "taking of depositions, including pursuant to subpoena, by a member or counsel of such committee." Depositions are to be ordered in consultation with the ranking minority member and are subject to regulations issued by the Committee on Rules and printed in the *Congressional Record.*

These provisions are identical to those of a separate order adopted in the 115th Congress, except the 116th Congress version does not include the requirement that "at least one member of the committee shall be present at each deposition" unless the witness or the committee waived the requirement.[21] Thus, according to the Rules Committee summary of H.Res. 6, "Members, Delegates, and the Resident Commissioner may participate in all such depositions, but their presence is not required."[22]

COMMITTEE ON OVERSIGHT AND REFORM

Designating Committee on Oversight and Reform

The 116th Congress rules package amended House rules to re-designate the Committee on Oversight and Government Reform as the Committee on Oversight and Reform. H.Res. 6 struck each occurrence of "Committee on Oversight and Government Reform" in the Rules and replaced it with "Committee on Oversight and Reform."

In previous Congresses, the committee operated under different names. In 1927, the committee was established as the Committee on Expenditures in the Executive Departments, consolidating 11 separate committees that investigated such expenditures. In 1953, the House changed its name to the

---

[21] H.Res. 5 (115th Congress).
[22] *Section-by-Section*, p. 8.

Committee on Government Operations.[23] Following a change in House majority to the Republican Party in 1995, the committee assumed the jurisdictions of the Committee on the Post Office and Civil Service and the Committee on the District of Columbia, which were abolished, and was designated the Committee on Government Reform and Oversight. Since then, it has also operated under the name Government Reform (106th-111th Congresses), Oversight and Government Reform (112th- 115th Congresses), and now Oversight and Reform (116th Congress).

Oversight over the Executive Office of the President

Clause 3 of Rule X assigns special oversight functions to some House committees. H.Res. 6 amended clause 3 of Rule X to include language emphasizing the Committee on Oversight and Reform's responsibility to oversee presidential activities. Clause 3(i) provides the committee's oversight mandate: "The Committee on Oversight and Reform shall review and study on a continuing basis the operation of Government activities at all levels." Previously, 3(i) concluded, "with a view to determining their economy and efficiency."

As amended by H.Res. 6, the clause 3 provision states that the committee is to review and study "Government activities at all levels, including the Executive Office of the President." According to the summary of the rules package issued by the Rules Committee, the amendment "clarifies the Committee on Oversight and Reform's existing special oversight authority over all operations of government."[24]

Oversight and Reform Committee Depositions

H.Res. 6 struck an existing provision from clause 4 of Rule X that required a member of the Committee on Oversight and Reform to be

---

[23] .S. Congress, House Committee on Government Reform, *Activities of the House Committee on Government Reform*, 106-1053, 106th Cong., 2nd sess. (GPO, Washington, DC, 2001).

[24] *Section-by-Section*, p. 2.

present when the committee takes a deposition unless the deponent waived the requirement. As amended, clause 4(c), now authorizes committee counsel to take a deposition without a committee member in attendance, a standard that was previously in force during the 111th Congress (2009-2010).

The deposition rules change is similar to the separate order described in the "Deposition Authority" section of this chapter. The separate order, however, applies to several committees, while the rules amendment affects only the Committee on Oversight and Reform. The amended rule will be printed in the *House Manual* for the 116th Congress. Separate orders are not printed in the *House Manual*.

COMMITTEE ON EDUCATION AND LABOR

Designating Committee on Education and Labor

The 116th rules package re-designated the Committee on Education and the Workforce, changing the committee's name to the Committee on Education and the Labor. H.Res. 6 strikes *Workforce* from clauses 1 and 3 of Rule X and inserts *Labor*.[25]

Since its establishment in 1867 (40th Congress), the committee has operated under several names: Education and Labor (40th-47th, 80th-103rd, 110th-111th, and 116th-present); Education (48th-79th); Economic and Educational Opportunities (104th); and Education and the Workforce (105th-109th and 112th-115th). In its recent history, the committee has been designated the Committee on Education and the Workforce under Republican leadership and the Committee on Education and Labor under Democratic leadership.

---

[25] Clause 1(e) and clause 3(d), Rule XI, Rules of the House of Representatives, One Hundred Sixteenth Congress, pp. 7, 10.

Education and Labor Jurisdiction Clarification

H.Res. 6 added two subparagraphs to clause 1(e) of Rule X to specify that the Committee on Education and Labor's jurisdiction includes the "organization, administration, and general management" of the Department of Education and the Department of Labor.[26] These subparagraphs were added to the existing provisions establishing the committee's jurisdiction over federal education and labor programs, standards, and disputes. According to the Rules Committee, the amendment clarifies the committee's "existing jurisdiction" concerning the departments' general management.[27]

COMMITTEE ON ETHICS

Empaneling Investigative Subcommittee of the Committee on Ethics

The 116th rules package includes a separate order directing the Committee on Ethics to form an investigative subcommittee in cases where a Member, Delegate, or the Resident Commissioner is indicted on a criminal charge. This separate order stated that the text of H.Res. 451 (110th Congress, 2007-2008) will apply in the 116th Congress. H.Res. 451 instructed the Ethics Committee (then called the Committee on Standards of Official Conduct) to empanel an investigative subcommittee to review the allegations whenever a Member of the House of Representatives, including a Delegate or Resident Commissioner to the Congress, is indicted or otherwise formally charged with criminal conduct in a court of the United States or any state not later than 30 days after the date of such indictment or charge. If the committee chooses not to empanel, it is to submit a report to the House describing the reasons for not empaneling an

---

[26] Clause 1(e)(14) and clause 1(e)(15), Rule X, Rules of the House of Representatives, One Hundred Sixteenth Congress, p. 7.

[27] Section-by-Section, p. 2.

investigative subcommittee as well as the actions, if any, the committee took in response to the allegations.[28]

Considering Criminal Trial Evidence in Ethics Investigation

H.Res. 6 amended clause 3(p) of Rule XI to allow the Committee on Ethics to consider certain criminal trial evidence in ethics investigations of Members, Delegates, and the Resident Commissioner. The new language authorizes the full committee or an investigative subcommittee thereof, if the respondent is convicted for a crime that "is related to the subject of the investigation," to "take into evidence the trial transcript or exhibits admitted into evidence at a criminal trial."[29] As referenced in the previous section of this chapter, "Empaneling Investigative Subcommittees of the Committee on Ethics," a 116th Congress separate order instructed the Committee on Ethics to form an investigative subcommittee in response to the criminal indictment or charging of a Member, Delegate, or the Resident Commissioner in federal or state court.[30] As amended, clause 3(p) enables investigative subcommittees formed under the terms of this separate order, or established in another manner, to consider trial evidence following a conviction. The full Ethics Committee may also receive trial evidence regarding a Member, Delegate, or Resident Commissioner under investigation.

COMMITTEE ON THE BUDGET

Committee Membership Limits

H.Res. 6 removed term limits for members of the Committee of the Budget. In previous Congresses, committee members could serve for a set

---

[28] .Res. 451 (110th Congress); CRS Report 98-15, House Committee on Ethics: A Brief History of Its Evolution and Jurisdiction, by Jacob R. Straus.

[29] Clause 3(p)(5)(E) and clause 3(p)(9), Rule XI, Rules of the House of Representatives, One Hundred Sixteenth Congress, p. 23.

[30] H.Res. 6 (116th Congress).

number of terms as specified in clause 5 of Rule X. In the 115th Congress, the limit was no more than "four Congresses in a period of six successive Congresses." That number could be extended if the Member served as the chair or ranking member of the committee.[31]

Now, under House rules, Members, Delegates, and the Resident Commissioner may serve as committee members or as the chair or ranking member regardless of the number of terms they have previously served in those positions. However, the rules of the Democratic Caucus, 116th Congress, state that no members of the caucus, with some exceptions, may serve as a member of the Budget Committee during more than three out of five successive Congresses.[32]

COMMITTEE ON RULES

Recorded Votes in Rules Committee Reports

The 116th rules package allows the Committee on Rules to file its committee reports without the inclusion of recorded votes taken in the committee. As stated in clause 3 of Rule XIII, committee reports are to include "the total number of votes cast for and against, and the names of members voting for and against" reporting a measure or amendments offered to a measure. In previous Congresses, clause 3(b) clarified that this requirement did not apply to the Committee on Ethics.[33] H.Res. 6 inserted an additional exception for the Committee on Rules: The requirement to include recorded vote information applies "only to the maximum extent

---

[31] *House Manual*, 115th Congress, §758, p. 512.

[32] The Democratic Caucus makes the following exceptions to the "three out of five successive Congresses" provision: any service performed for less than a full session in any Congress is disregarded; an incumbent chair, who has served on the committee for three Congress and not more than one Congress as chair, may serve an additional Congress as chair; and the limitation does not apply to members appointed to the committee by the Speaker. U.S. Congress, House Democratic Caucus, *Rules of the Democratic Caucus, 116th Congress*, 2018.

[33] *House Manual*, 115th Congress, §839, p. 645.

practicable to a report by the Committee on Rules on a rule, joint rule, or the order of business."[34]

According to the Rules Committee, the change reflects that committee's "constricted timeframe" for preparing written reports. Prior to the rules change, the reporting requirement in clause 3 could potentially delay the floor consideration of special orders of business (special rules) reported by the Rules Committee and, consequently, lead to the delay of the consideration of measures considered under the terms of special rules.[35]

COMMITTEE ON FINANCIAL SERVICES

Additional Subcommittee

H.Res. 6 included a separate order that provided the Committee on Financial Services with more flexibility to establish subcommittees. The separate order states that the committee can have "not more than seven subcommittees" during the 116th Congress.[36] Clause 5(d) of Rule X limits each committee to establishing not more than five subcommittees. Subsequent subdivisions of the rule, however, provide exceptions to this limit. For instance, a committee that has a Subcommittee on Oversight may have six subcommittees, the Appropriations Committee may have 13 subcommittees, and other named committees may have not more than seven subcommittees.[37]

Separate orders may provide additional exceptions for specific Congresses. The H.Res. 6 separate order also stated that the Committee on Agriculture may not have more six subcommittees. The Agriculture exception, however, existed in the previous two Congresses. The Financial Services exception is new to the 116th Congress.

---

[34] Clause 3(b), Rule XIII, *Rules of the House of Representatives, One Hundred Sixteenth Congress*, p. 26.

[35] *Section-by-Section*, p. 4.

[36] H.Res. 6 (116th Congress).

[37] *House Manual*, 115th Congress, §762, p. 519.

In the 115th Congress, the Financial Services had six subcommittees, including one on Oversight and Investigations. At the start of the 116th Congress, the committee re-established a Subcommittee on Oversight and Investigations, and it established a new Subcommittee on Diversity and Inclusion. Had it reestablished the five other subcommittees from the 115th Congress, Financial Services would have had seven subcommittees, necessitating an exception to clause 5 of Rule X. However, the committee combined the jurisdiction of two subcommittees from the previous Congress (Monetary Policy and Trade; Terrorism and Illicit Finance) to form a National Security, International Development and Monetary Policy Subcommittee. Accordingly, as of this writing, in the 116th Congress, Financial Services has established six subcommittees, although it is allowed seven subcommittees pursuant to the separate order.

SELECT COMMITTEE ON THE CLIMATE CRISIS

H.Res. 6 established a Select Committee on the Climate Crisis. The select committee's "sole authority" is to "investigate, study, make findings, and develop recommendations on policies, strategies, and innovations" to reduce pollution and "other activities that contribute to the climate crisis."[38] The select committee does not have the legislative authority to report bills or resolutions or the legal authority to issue subpoenas or take depositions. However, it can submit subpoena and deposition recommendations to relevant standing committees, hold public hearings in support of its investigative functions, and otherwise function under the rules governing standing committees.

The select committee shall be composed of 15 Members, Delegates, or the Resident Commissioner. The Speaker is to appoint the members, with six members selected at the recommendation of the minority leader. The Speaker is to designate a chair and, upon the minority leader's recommendation, a vice chair. The membership must possess certain

---

[38] H.Res. 6 (116th Congress).

attributes: At least two members are to be serving their first terms in Congress, at least two are to be members of the Committee on Rules, and at least two are to be members of the Committee on House Administration.

H.Res. 6 requires the select committee to submit policy recommendations to the relevant standing committees by March 31, 2020, and report to the House its investigations, detailed findings, and policy recommendations by December 31, 2020. The policy recommendations and report are to be made publicly available in "widely accessible formats" not later than 30 days following the March 31 and December 31, 2020, dates of completion.

SELECT COMMITTEE ON THE MODERNIZATION OF CONGRESS

Title II of H.Res. 6 establishes a Select Committee on the Modernization of Congress to recommend improvements to the work and operation of Congress. The select committee's "sole authority" is to "investigate, study, make findings, hold public hearings, and develop recommendations on modernizing Congress."[39] Such recommendations could include new rules to "promote a more modern and efficient Congress;" new scheduling procedures; policies to "develop the next generation of leaders;" policies to recruit, retain, and provide for a diverse staff; policies to make congressional administration more efficient; policies on technology and innovation; and new procedures regarding the House Commission on Congressional Mailing Standards (commonly known as the "Franking Commission").[40]

The select committee's membership is to include two Members, Delegates, or the Resident Commissioner appointed by the Speaker. At least two members must be serving in their first term, at least two members

---

[39] See CRS Report R45724, *House Select Committee on the Modernization of Congress: Structure and Procedures*, by Ida A. Brudnick and Mark J. Oleszek.

[40] H.Res. 6 (116th Congress).

must be members of the Committee on Rules, and at least two members must be members on the Committee of House Administration.

The select committee is bipartisan in composition. Half of the members are appointed on the recommendation of the minority leader. The Speaker designates the chair and, on the recommendation of the minority leader, the vice chair.

The select committee does not have legislative jurisdiction or authority to take legislative action on bills or resolutions, and it does not have subpoena or deposition authority. However, it may submit legislative, subpoena, and deposition recommendations to the relevant standing committees. And, like standing committees, the committee was required to have a Member Day hearing at the start of 116th Congress.

H.Res. 6 requires the select committee to provide an interim status report every 90 days. This interim report must include transcripts of committee proceedings, itemized expenditures, and a proposed plan of activity for the next 90 days. With the "votes of not fewer than 2/3 of its members," the select committee is also authorized to submit additional reports from "time to time" that provide the results of investigations, detailed findings, and policy recommendations.

The select committee is to submit its final report, with the "votes of not fewer than 2/3 of its members," at the end of the first session of the 116th Congress. This chapter is to include detailed findings and policy recommendations. The select committee is also to submit policy recommendations to the relevant standing committees. All committee reports are to be made available to the general public within 30 calendar days of their submittal to Congress or a committee.

The select committee is to terminate on February 1, 2020. Upon its termination, the select committee's records are to be transferred to relevant standing committees, as determined by the Speaker.

In: Key Congressional Reports for May 2019   ISBN: 978-1-53616-382-7
Editor: Piotr Meza   © 2019 Nova Science Publishers, Inc.

Chapter 2

FEDERAL GRANTS TO STATE AND LOCAL GOVERNMENTS: A HISTORICAL PERSPECTIVE ON CONTEMPORARY ISSUES (UPDATED)[*]

Robert Jay Dilger and Michael H. Cecire

ABSTRACT

The federal government is expected to provide state and local governments about $750 billion in federal grants in FY2019, funding a wide range of public policies, such as health care, transportation, income security, education, job training, social services, community development, and environmental protection. Federal grants account for about one-third of total state government funding, and more than half of state government funding for health care and public assistance.

Congressional interest in federal grants to state and local governments has always been high given the central role Congress has in

---

[*] This is an edited, reformatted and augmented version of a Congressional Research Service publication R40638, prepared for Members and Committees of Congress dated May 22, 2019.

determining the scope and nature of the federal grant-in-aid system, the amount of funding involved, and disagreements over the appropriate role of the federal government in domestic policy generally and in its relationship with state and local governments.

Federalism scholars agree that congressional decisions concerning the scope and nature of the federal grants-in-aid system are influenced by both internal and external factors. Internal factors include congressional party leadership and congressional procedures; the decentralized nature of the committee system; the backgrounds, personalities, and ideological preferences of individual Members; and the customs and traditions (norms) that govern congressional behavior. Major external factors include input provided by voter constituencies, organized interest groups, the President, and executive branch officials. Although not directly involved in the legislative process, the Supreme Court, through its rulings on federalism issues, also influences congressional decisions concerning the federal grants-in-aid system.

Overarching all of these factors is the evolving nature of cultural norms and expectations concerning government's role in American society. Over time, the American public has become increasingly accepting of government activism in domestic affairs generally, and of federal government intervention in particular. Federalism scholars attribute this increased acceptance of, and sometimes demand for, government action as a reaction to the industrialization and urbanization of American society; technological innovations in communications, which have raised awareness of societal problems; and exponential growth in economic interdependencies brought about by an increasingly global economy.

This chapter provides a historical synopsis of the evolving nature of the federal grants-in-aid system, focusing on the role Congress has played in defining the system's scope and nature. It begins with an overview of the contemporary federal grants-in-aid system and then examines its evolution over time, focusing on the internal and external factors that have influenced congressional decisions concerning the system's development. It concludes with an assessment of the scope and nature of the contemporary federal grants-in-aid system and raises several issues for congressional consideration, including possible ways to augment congressional capacity to provide effective oversight of this system.

THE CONGRESSIONAL ROLE

Over the years, the federal intergovernmental system of governance has been characterized by many scholars as becoming increasingly centralized and coercive, with the federal government using federal grants, federal mandates, and federal preemption of state authority to expand its influence in many policy areas previously viewed as being the traditional responsibility of state and local governments.[1] In FY2019, the federal government is expected to provide state and local governments about $750 billion in federal grants encompassing a wide range of public policy areas, such as health care, transportation, income security, education, job training, social services, community development, and environmental protection.[2] Federal grants account for just under one-third of total state government funding, and more than half of state government funding for health care and public assistance.[3]

Congress has a central role in determining the scope and nature of federal grant programs. In its legislative capacity, Congress first determines what it wants to accomplish and then decides whether a grant-in-aid program is the best means to achieve it. Congress then selects which of the six grant mechanisms to use (project categorical grant, formula categorical grant, formula-project categorical grant, open-end reimbursement categorical grant, block grant, or general revenue sharing), and crafts legislation to accomplish its purpose, incorporating the chosen grant instrument.[4] As with all legislation generally, Congress oversees the grant's implementation to ensure that the federal administrating agency is

---

[1] John Kincaid, "From Cooperative to Coercive Federalism," *The Annals of the American Academy of Political and Social Science*, vol. 509, no. 1 (1990), pp. 139-152. Note: the term *coercive* is often used in legal arguments to suggest that provisions of law related to federal grants-in-aid do not have constitutional standing. Federalism scholars use the term to describe, as Kincaid explained it (p. 139), the shift in emphasis "from fiscal tools to stimulate intergovernmental policy cooperation" to an increased reliance on "regulatory tools to ensure the supremacy of federal policy."

[2] U.S. Office of Management and Budget (OMB), *Budget of the United States Government, Fiscal Year 2020: Historical Tables*, Table 12.3, Total Outlays for Grants to State and Local Governments, at https://www.whitehouse.gov/wp-content/uploads/2019/03/hist-fy2020.pdf.

[3] National Association of State Budget Officers, *State Expenditure Report, Examining FY2016-2018 State Spending*, pp. 5, 8, 39, 53, at https://www.nasbo.org/mainsite/reports-data/state-expenditure-report.

[4] U.S. Advisory Commission on Intergovernmental Relations (ACIR), *Categorical Grants: Their Role and Design*, A 52, 1978, p. 61, at http://www.library.unt.edu/gpo/acir/ Reports/policy/a-52.pdf.

held accountable for making certain that congressional expectations concerning program performance are met.

Federalism scholars agree that congressional decisions concerning the scope and nature of the federal grants-in-aid system are influenced by both internal and external factors. Internal factors include congressional party leadership and congressional procedures; the decentralized nature of the committee system; the backgrounds, personalities, and ideological preferences of individual Members (especially those of party leaders and committee and subcommittee chairs and ranking minority Members); and the customs and traditions (norms) that govern congressional behavior. Major external factors include input provided by voter constituencies, organized interest groups (especially the National Governors Association, the National League of Cities, U.S. Conference of Mayors, and the National Association of Counties), the President, and executive branch officials.[5] Although not directly involved in the legislative process, the Supreme Court, through its rulings on federalism issues, also influences congressional decisions concerning federal grant-in-aid programs.

Overarching all of these factors is the evolving nature of cultural norms and expectations concerning government's role in American society. Over time, although the American public has become increasingly skeptical of government performance, they have also become increasingly accepting of government activism in domestic affairs generally, and of federal government activism in particular.[6] Federalism scholars attribute this increased acceptance of, and sometimes demand for, government action as a reaction to the industrialization and urbanization of American society; technological innovations in communications, which have raised awareness of societal problems; and exponential growth in economic interdependencies brought about by an increasingly global economy.[7]

---

[5] Ibid.

[6] For example, see Pew Research Center, "The Public, the Political System and American Democracy: Most say 'design and structure' of government need big changes," April 26, 2018, at https://www.people-press.org/2018/04/26/the-public-the-political-system-and-american-democracy/.

[7] Samuel H. Beer, "The Modernization of American Federalism," in *Toward '76 – The Federal Polity*, special issue of *Publius: The Journal of Federalism*, vol. 3, no 2 (fall 1973), pp. 49-

This chapter provides a historical synopsis of the evolving nature of the federal grants-in-aid system, focusing on the role Congress has played in defining the system's scope and nature. It begins with an overview of the contemporary federal grants-in-aid system and then examines its evolution over time, focusing on the internal and external factors that have influenced congressional decisions concerning the system's development. It concludes with an assessment of the scope and nature of the contemporary federal grants-in-aid system and raises several issues for congressional consideration, including possible ways to augment congressional capacity to provide effective oversight of this system.

FEDERAL GRANTS TO STATE AND LOCAL GOVERNMENTS

Different federal departments and agencies, including the U.S. Census Bureau, the Government Accountability Office (GAO), and the U.S. Office of Management and Budget (OMB), use different definitions to determine what counts as a federal grant-in-aid program. However, there is agreement on the general characteristics associated with each grant type.

The three general types of federal grants to state and local governments are categorical grants, block grants, and general revenue sharing (see Table 1). Categorical grants can be used only for a specifically aided program and usually are limited to narrowly defined activities. Block grants can be used only for a specifically aided set of programs and usually are not limited to narrowly defined activities. General revenue sharing can be used for any purpose not expressly prohibited by federal or state law and is not limited to narrowly defined activities.

The four types of categorical grants are project categorical grants, formula categorical grants, formula-project categorical grants, and open-end reimbursement categorical grants. Project categorical grants are awarded on a competitive basis through an application process specified by the federal agency making the grant.

95; and David B. Walker, *The Rebirth of Federalism*, 2nd Edition (NY: Chatham House Publishers, 2000), pp. 19-35.

Formula categorical grants are allocated among recipients according to factors specified within enabling legislation or administrative regulations (e.g., population, median household income, per capita income, poverty, and number of miles driven). Formula-project categorical grants use a mixture of fund allocation means, typically involving the use of a formula specified within enabling legislation or administrative regulations to allocate available funds among the states, followed by an application process specified by each recipient state to allocate available funds on a competitive basis among local governments or other eligible applicants. Open-end reimbursement categorical grants, often regarded as the equivalent of formula categorical grants, provide a reimbursement of a specified proportion of recipient program costs, eliminating competition among recipients as well as the need for an allocation formula.[8]

A Continuum of Federal Grant Administrative Conditions

Of the six grant types, project categorical grants typically impose the most restraint on recipients (see Table 1). Federal administrators have a high degree of control over who receives project categorical grants (recipients must apply to the appropriate federal agency for funding and compete against other potential recipients who also meet the program's specified eligibility criteria); recipients have relatively little discretion concerning aided activities (funds must be used for narrowly specified purposes); and there is a relatively high degree of federal administrative conditions attached to the grant, typically involving the imposition of federal standards for planning, project selection, fiscal management, administrative organization, and performance.

---

[8] ACIR, *Categorical Grants: Their Role and Design*, A-52, 1978, pp. 5, 61, at http://www.library.unt.edu/gpo/acir/ Reports/policy/a-52.pdf.

Federal Grants to State and Local Governments

General revenue sharing imposes the least restraint on recipients.[9] Federal administrators have a low degree of discretion over who receives general revenue sharing (funding is allocated automatically to recipients by a formula or formulas specified in legislation); recipients have broad discretion concerning aided activities; and there is a relatively low degree of federal administrative conditions attached to the grant, typically involving periodic reporting criteria and the application of standard government accounting procedures.

Table 1. Classification of Grant Types by Three Defining Traits

Federal Administrator's Funding Discretion		
Low	Medium	High
Formula Categorical Grant	Block Grant—Formula-Project Categorical Grant	Project Categorical Grant
Open-ended Reimbursement Categorical Grant		
General Revenue Sharing		
Range of Recipient's Discretion in Use of Funds		
Low	Medium	High
Project Categorical Grant	Block Grant	General Revenue Sharing
Formula-Project Categorical Grant		
Formula Categorical Grant		
Open-ended Reimbursement Categorical Grant		
Extent of Performance Conditions		
Low	Medium	High
General Revenue Sharing	Block Grant	Project Categorical Grant
		Formula Categorical Grant
		Formula-Project Categorical Grant
		Open-ended Reimbursement Categorical Grant

Source: U.S. Advisory Commission on Intergovernmental Relations, *Categorical Grants: Their Role and Design*, A-52 (Washington, DC: GPO, 1978), p. 7.

Block grants are at the midpoint in the continuum of recipient discretion. Federal administrators have a low degree of discretion over who receives block grants (after setting aside funding for administration and other specified activities, the remaining funds are typically allocated

---

[9] For further information and analysis concerning general revenue sharing, see CRS Report RL31936, *General Revenue Sharing: Background and Analysis*, by Steven Maguire.

automatically to recipients by a formula or formulas specified in legislation); recipients have some discretion concerning aided activities (typically, funds can be used for a specified range of activities within a single functional area); and there is a moderate degree of federal administrative conditions attached to the grant, typically involving more than periodic reporting criteria and the application of standard government accounting procedures, but with fewer conditions attached to the grant than project categorical grants.

OUTLAYS FOR FEDERAL GRANTS TO STATE AND LOCAL GOVERNMENTS

As indicated in Table 2, outlays for federal grants to state and local governments have generally increased over the years, with a relatively rapid increase from FY2008 through FY2010 due primarily to the enactment of P.L. 111-5, the American Recovery and Reinvestment Act of 2009 (ARRA). ARRA provided state and local governments $274.7 billion in grants, contracts, and loans combined.[10] State and local governments received $52.9 billion in ARRA grants, contracts, and loans in FY2009, $111.9 billion in FY2010, $68.8 billion in FY2011, $25.6 billion in FY2012, 11.8 billion in FY2013, and $1.6 billion in FY2014 to assist their recovery from the "Great Recession" (December 2007-June 2009).[11]

---

[10] The Recovery Accountability and Transparency Board, "Recovery.gov: State/Territory Totals by Award Type," at http://www.recovery.gov/arra/Transparency/RecoveryData/ Pages/ RecipientAwardSummarybyState.aspx.

[11] U.S. Government Accountability Office (GAO), "Following the Money: GAO's Oversight of the Recovery Act," at http://www.gao.gov/recovery/. ARRA provided additional funding for a wide range of federal grants to state and local governments, including Medicaid ($93 billion, primarily for a temporary increase in the Federal Medical Assistance Percentages reimbursement rate), a State Fiscal Stabilization Fund ($53.6 billion), Build America Bonds ($30 billion), Highways and Bridges ($27.5 billion), Title 1-A, elementary and secondary education for the disadvantaged, ($13 billion), Individuals with Disabilities Education Act ($12.2 billion), Public Transit ($8.4 billion), Intercity Passenger Rail Capital, Congestion, and Corridor Development grants ($8 billion), Temporary Assistance for Needy Families ($5 billion), and Weatherization Assistance Grants ($5 billion).

Federal Grants to State and Local Governments 31

As expected, after reaching $608.4 billion in FY2010, outlays for federal grants to state and local governments declined somewhat in FY2011 as ARRA funding began to unwind, and then declined further to $544.6 billion in FY2012 and to $546.2 billion in FY2013 as most of ARRA's funding expired. Outlays for federal grants to state and local governments have increased since then, primarily due to increased outlays for Medicaid.

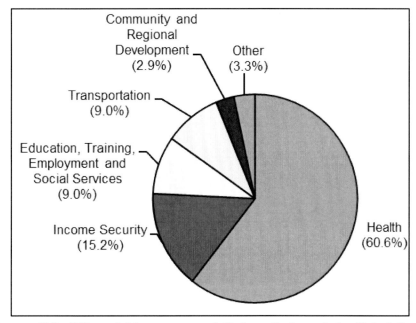

Source: U.S. Office of Management and Budget, *Budget of the United States Government, Fiscal Year 2020: Historical Tables*, Table 12.3, Total Outlays for Grants to State and Local Governments, at http://www.whitehouse.gov/ omb/ budget/Historicals.

Figure 1. Outlays for Federal Grants to State and Local Governments, by Function, FY2019 Estimate.

Table 2. Outlays for Federal Grants to State and Local Governments, by Function, Selected FY1902-FY2019 (nominal $ in millions)

Fiscal Year	Total	Health	Income Security	Education, Training, Employment and Social Services	Transportation	Community and Regional Development	Other
2019 est.	$749,554	$453,862	$114,169	$67,500	$67,211	$21,917	$24,895
2018	696,507	421,117	110,649	60,591	64,836	19,089	20,225
2017	674,700	406,946	107,400	61,553	64,783	14,797	19,221
2016	660,818	396,666	104,769	60,867	63,861	15,298	19,357
2015	624,354	368,026	101,082	60,527	60,831	14,357	19,531
2014	576,965	320,022	100,869	60,485	62,152	13,232	20,205
2013	546,171	283,036	102,190	62,690	60,518	16,781	20,956
2012	544,569	268,277	102,574	68,126	60,749	20,258	24,585
2011	606,766	292,847	113,625	89,147	60,986	20,002	30,159
2010	608,390	290,168	115,156	97,586	60,981	18,908	25,591
2000	285,874	124,843	68,653	36,672	32,222	8,665	14,819
1990	135,325	43,890	36,768	21,780	19,174	4,965	8,748
1980	91,385	15,758	18,495	21,862	13,022	6,486	15,762
1970	24,065	3,849	5,795	6,417	4,599	1,780	1,625
1960	7,019	214	2,635	525	2,999	109	537
1950	2,253	122	1,335	150	465	1	180
1940	872	22	341	28	165	0	316
1930	100	0	1	22	76	0	1
1922	118	0	1	7	92	0	18
1913	12	0	2	3	0	0	7
1902	7	0	1	1	0	0	5

Sources: U.S. Office of Management and Budget, *Budget of the United States Government, Fiscal Year 2020: Historical Tables*, Table 12.3, Total Outlays for Grants to State and Local Governments, at http://www.whitehouse.gov/omb/ budget/Historicals; and U.S. Department of Commerce, Bureau of the Census, *Historical Statistics of the United States, Colonial Times to 1970, Part 2*, pp. 1123, 1125, at http://www2.census.gov/prod2/statcomp/ documents/CT1970p2-12.pdf.

Federal Grants to State and Local Governments   33

As indicated in Table 2 and Figure 1, in FY2019 health care is anticipated to account for more than half of total outlays for federal grants to state and local governments (an estimated $453.9 billion in FY2019, or 60.6% of the total), followed by income security ($114.2 billion, or 15.2%), education, training, employment, and social services ($67.5 billion, or 9.0%), transportation ($67.2 billion, or 9.0%), community and regional development ($21.9 billion, or 2.9%), and all other ($24.9 billion, or 3.3%).

Medicaid, with $418.7 billion in expected federal outlays in FY2019, has, by far, the largest budget of any federal grant-in-aid program. Ten other federal grants to state and local governments are expected to have federal outlays in excess of $10 billion in FY2019: Federal-Aid Highways ($43.9 billion), Child Nutrition ($23.9 billion),[12] Tenant Based Rental Assistance— Section 8 vouchers ($22.3 billion), the Children's Health Insurance Fund ($18.4 billion), Accelerating Achievement and Ensuring Equity (Education for the Disadvantaged—$17.4 billion), Temporary Assistance for Needy Families ($16.5 billion), Special Education ($13.2 billion), State Children and Families Services Programs ($10.9 billion), Urban Mass Transportation Grants ($10.3 billion), and the Disaster Relief Fund ($10.2 billion).[13]

Table 3 provides data on outlays for federal grants to state and local governments in nominal and constant (inflation-adjusted) dollars, as a percentage of total federal outlays and as a percentage of national gross domestic product (GDP) for selected fiscal years since FY1960. It also indicates the percentage of these outlays that are payments for individuals, as opposed to payments for capital improvements and government operations.

---

[12] Child Nutrition includes the School Breakfast Program, the National School Lunch Program, and other nutrition programs.
[13] OMB, *Budget of the United States Government, Fiscal Year 2020: Historical Tables*, Table 12.3, Total Outlays for Grants to State and Local Governments, at http://www.white house.gov/omb/budget/Historicals.

Table 3. Outlays for Federal Grants to State and Local Governments, Percentage of Outlays for Individuals, in Constant Dollars, and as a Percentage of Total Federal Outlays and National Gross Domestic Product, Selected Fiscal Years, 1960-2019

Fiscal Year	Nominal $ (in millions)	% Outlays for Individuals	Constant $ (in billions, FY2012)	% of Total Federal Outlays	% of National GDP
2019 est.	$749,554	75.3%	$667.3	16.5%	3.5%
2018	696,507	75.5%	635.1	17.0%	3.4%
2017	674,712	75.3%	632.2	16.9%	3.5%
2016	660,833	75.0%	630.3	17.2%	3.6%
2015	624,357	74.2%	599.3	16.9%	3.5%
2014	576,978	71.5%	556.8	16.5%	3.3%
2013	546,178	69.4%	536.4	15.8%	3.3%
2012	544,573	66.9%	544.6	15.4%	3.4%
2011	606,700	64.7%	620.9	16.8%	3.9%
2010	608,390	64.3%	637.6	17.6%	4.1%
2005	428,018	65.1%	511.6	17.3%	3.3%
2000	285,874	65.2%	389.1	16.0%	2.8%
1995	224,991	64.7%	338.7	14.8%	3.0%
1990	135,325	57.2%	238.9	10.8%	2.3%
1985	105,852	47.9%	231.7	11.2%	2.5%
1980	91,385	36.2%	283.7	15.5%	3.3%
1975	49,791	34.4%	230.9	15.0%	3.1%
1970	24,065	37.7%	151.7	12.3%	2.3%
1965	10,910	35.9%	80.4	9.2%	1.5%
1960	7,019	37.4%	54.8	7.6%	1.3%

Source: U.S. Office of Management and Budget, *Budget of the United States Government, Fiscal Year 2020: Historical Tables*, Table 12.1, Summary Comparison of Total Outlays for Grants to State and Local Governments: 1940–2024 (in Current Dollars, as Percentages of Total Outlays, as Percentages of GDP, and in Constant (FY 2012) Dollars) at http://www.whitehouse.gov/omb/budget/Historicals.

As indicated in Table 3, total outlays for federal grants to state and local governments have generally increased since the 1960s.[14] However, the magnitude of those increases has varied over the years. For example, outlays for federal grants to state and local governments increased, in nominal dollars, 187.3% during the 1960s, 246.4% during the 1970s,

---

[14] Outlays for federal grants to state and local governments increased, in nominal dollars, in 51 of the 57 fiscal years from FY1960 through FY2017—the declines occurred in FY1982, FY1983, FY1987, FY2011, FY2012, and FY2013.

Federal Grants to State and Local Governments

33.4% during the 1980s, 98.0% during the 1990s, and 98.6% during the first decade of the 2000s.[15]

Outlay growth for federal grants to state and local governments has, in most years, exceeded inflation. However, as indicated in Table 3, those outlays, expressed in constant (FY2012) dollars, did not keep pace with inflation during the early 1980s and during the early 2010s.[16]

Federalism scholars have noted that since the 1980s, the focus of federal grants to state and local governments has shifted from providing assistance to places (e.g., to build public highways, support public education, criminal justice systems, economic development endeavors, and government administration) to people (e.g., providing health care benefits, social welfare income, housing assistance, and social services).[17] Much of this shift is attributed to Medicaid, which has experienced relatively large outlay growth over the past several decades. As shown in Table 3, during the 1960s and 1970s about one-third of total outlays for federal grants to state and local governments were for individuals, compared with more than 75% in FY2018.

NUMBER OF FEDERAL GRANTS TO STATE AND LOCAL GOVERNMENTS

In the past, the now-defunct U.S. Advisory Commission on Intergovernmental Relations (ACIR) and OMB used information contained

---

[15] OMB, *Budget of the United States Government, Fiscal Year 2010: Historical Tables*, pp. 239-240, at http://www.gpoaccess.gov/usbudget/fy10/pdf/hist.pdf. Note: The percentages were derived by dividing the difference between expenditures for the ninth year of the decade and the first year of the decade by expenditures for the first year of the decade.

[16] As will be discussed, the slowdown in federal grant funding during the early 1980s was largely due to the Reagan Administration's efforts to reduce the rate of growth in federal domestic expenditures and to reform federalism relationships. The slowdown in federal grant funding during the early 2010s was largely due to the expiration of temporary federal grant assistance provided by P.L. 111-5, the American Recovery and Reinvestment Act of 2009 (ARRA).

[17] John Kincaid, "Developments in Federal-State Relations, 1992-93," *The Book of the States, 1994-95* (Lexington, KY: The Council of State Governments, 1994), pp. 576-586; and John Kincaid, "Trends in Federalism, Continuity, Change and Polarization," *The Book of the States, 2004* (Lexington, KY: The Council of State Governments, 2004), pp. 21-27.

36 *Robert Jay Dilger and Michael H. Cecire*

in the Catalog of Federal Domestic Assistance (CFDA) to count the number of federal grants to state and local governments. The CFDA "is a government- wide compendium of Federal programs, projects, services, and activities that provide assistance or benefits to the American public."[18] It lists 15 categories of federal grants: formula grants (including formula categorical grants, formula-project categorical grants, and block grants); project grants; direct payments for specified uses to individuals and private firms; direct payments with unrestricted use to beneficiaries who meet federal eligibility requirements; direct loans; guaranteed/insured loans; insurance; sale, exchange, or donation of property and goods; use of property, facilities, and equipment; provision of specialized services; advisory services and counseling; dissemination of technical information; training; investigation of complaints; and federal employment. It lists all authorized federal grant programs, including grants that have not received an appropriation. Because the CFDA focuses on the needs of applicants, if a program uses a separate application or other delivery mechanism, the CFDA considers it a separate program. This complicates efforts to count federal grants to state and local governments.

ACIR periodically published counts of funded federal grants to state and local governments during the 1960s and then for Fiscal Years 1975, 1978, 1981, 1984, 1987, 1989, 1991, 1993, and 1995.[19] OMB provided

---

[18] U.S. General Services Administration (GSA), *2012 Catalog of Federal Domestic Assistance*, p. I, at https://www.cfda.gov/.

[19] ACIR, *A Catalog of Federal Grant-In-Aid Programs to State and Local Governments: Grants Funded FY 1975*, A-52a, 1977 at http://www.library.unt.edu/gpo/acir/Reports/policy/a-52a.pdf; ACIR, *A Catalog of Federal Grant-In-Aid Programs to State and Local Governments: Grants Funded FY 1978*, A-72, 1979 at http://www.library.unt.edu/gpo/ acir/ Reports/policy/a-52a.pdf; ACIR, *A Catalog of Federal Grant-In-Aid Programs to State and Local Governments: Grants Funded FY 1981*, M-133CAT, 1982 at http:// www.library.unt.edu/gpo/acir/Reports/information/M-133cat.pdf; ACIR, *A Catalog of Federal Grant-In-Aid Programs to State and Local Governments: Grants Funded FY 1984*, M-139, 1984 at http://www.library.unt.edu/gpo/acir/Reports/information/m-139.pdf; ACIR, *A Catalog of Federal Grant- In-Aid Programs to State and Local Governments: Grants Funded FY 1987*, M-153, 1987 at http://www.library.unt.edu/gpo/acir/ Reports/ information/m-153.pdf; ACIR, *A Catalog of Federal Grant-In-Aid Programs to State and Local Governments: Grants Funded FY 1989*, M-167, 1989 at http:// www.library.unt.edu/gpo/acir/Reports/ information/M-167.pdf; ACIR, *Characteristics of Federal Grant-In-Aid Programs to State and Local Governments: Grants Funded FY 1991*, M-182, 1992 at http://www.library.unt.edu/gpo/acir/Reports/information/M-182.pdf; ACIR, *Characteristics of Federal Grant-In-Aid Programs to State and Local Governments: Grants*

counts of funded grants to state and local governments for FY1980-FY2003.[20] Because they used a different methodology to determine which grant programs to include in their count, their results differed. OMB consistently identified fewer federal grants to state and local governments than ACIR. For example, in FY1995, OMB identified 608 funded federal grants to state and local governments compared to ACIR's count of 633.[21] No authoritative count of funded federal grants to state and local governments is known to have been issued in recent years.

ACIR included in its counts all direct cash grants to state or local governmental units, other public bodies established under state or local law, or their designee; payments for grants-in-kind, such as purchases of commodities distributed to state or local governmental institutions; payments to nongovernmental entities when such payments result in cash or in-kind services or products that are passed on to state or local governments; payments to state and local governments for research and development that is an integral part of their provision of services; and payments to regional commissions and organizations that are redistributed at the state or local level to provide public services.[22]

Funded FY1993, M-188, 1994 at http://www.library.unt.edu/gpo/ acir/Reports/ information/ M-188.pdf; and ACIR, *Characteristics of Federal Grant-In-Aid Programs to State and Local Governments: Grants Funded FY1995*, M-195, 1995 at http://www.library.unt.edu/ gpo/acir/Reports/information/M-195.pdf.

[20] OMB, "The Number of Federal Grant Programs to State and Local Governments: 1980-2003," February 18, 2004. Note: the GAO provided a count for FY1990; see U.S. General Accounting Office, *Federal Aid: Programs Available to State and Local Governments*, HRD 91-93FS, May 1991, at http://www.gao.gov/assets/90/89092.pdf.

[21] OMB, "The Number of Federal Grant Programs to State and Local Governments: 1980-2003," February 18, 2004.

[22] ACIR excluded grants directly to profit-making institutions, individuals, and nonprofit institutions (unless such payments result in cash or in-kind services or products that are passed on to state or local governments); payments for research and development not directly related to the provision of services to the general public; payments for services rendered; grants to cover administrative expenses for regional bodies; loans and loan guarantees; and shared revenues. See, ACIR, *Characteristics of Federal Grant-In-Aid Programs to State and Local Governments: Grants Funded FY 1995* (Washington, DC: GPO, 1995), pp. 26-28, at http://www.library.unt.edu/gpo/acir/Reports/information/M-195.pdf.

Table 4. Funded Federal Grants to State and Local Governments, by Type, Selected FY1902-FY2018

Fiscal Year	# of Funded Grants	Categorical	Block	General Revenue Sharing[a]
2018	1,274	1,253	21	0
2017	1,246	1,226	20	0
2016	1,216	1,196	20	0
2015	1,188	1,168	20	0
2014	1,099	1,078	21[b]	0
2013	1,052	1,030	22	0
2012	996	970	26	0
2009	953	929	24	0
1998	664	640	24	0
1995	633	618	15	0
1993	593	578	15	0
1991	557	543	14	0
1989	492	478	14	0
1987	435	422	13	0
1984	405	392	12	1
1981	541	534	6	1
1978	498	492	5	1
1975	448	442	5	1
1968	387	385	2	0
1965	327	327	0	0
1960	132	132	0	0
1950	68	68	0	0
1940	31	31	0	0
1930	15	15	0	0
1920	12	12	0	0
1902	5	5	0	0

Sources: FY1902, FY1920, FY1930, and FY1940: U.S. Advisory Commission on Intergovernmental Relations, *Periodic Congressional Reassessment of Federal Grants-in-Aid to State and Local Governments, June 1961*, pp. 44-49, at http://www.library.unt.edu/gpo/acir/Reports/policy/A-8.pdf; and U.S. Advisory Commission on Intergovernmental Relations, *Fiscal Balance in the American Federal System*, vol. 1, October 1967, pp. 140-141, 156-158, at http:// www.library.unt.edu/gpo/acir/ Reports/policy/a-31-1.pdf; FY1950, FY1960, FY1965, and FY1968: U.S. Advisory Commission on Intergovernmental Relations, *Fiscal Balance in the American Federal System*, vol. 1, October 1967, pp. 156-158, at http://www.library.unt.edu/ gpo/acir/Reports/policy/a-31-1.pdf; FY1975, FY1978, FY1981, FY1984: FY1987, FY1989, FY1991, FY1993, and FY1995: U.S. Advisory Commission on Intergovernmental Relations, *Characteristics of Federal Grant-In-Aid Programs to State and Local Governments: Grants Funded FY 1995*, p. 3, at http://www.library.unt.edu/ gpo/ acir/Reports/ information/M-195.pdf; FY1998: David B. Walker, *The Rebirth of* Federalism, 2nd Edition (NY: Chatham House Publishers, 2000), p. 7; and FY2009, FY2012- FY2018: CRS computation, U.S. General Services Administration, *The Catalog of Federal Domestic Assistance* at https://beta.sam.gov/.

Notes:

[a.] General revenue sharing distributed funds to states from 1972 to 1981 and to localities from 1972 to 1986.

[b.] For further analysis, see CRS Report R40486, *Block Grants: Perspectives and Controversies*, by Robert Jay Dilger and Eugene Boyd.

OMB counted only grants for traditional governmental operations, as defined in OMB Circular A-11. The definition covered only grants that "support State or local programs of government operations or provision of services to the public."[23] It excluded federal grants that went directly to individuals, fellowships, most grants to nongovernmental entities, and technical research grants.

A search of the CFDA's 2018 print edition and electronic version indicated that state governments, local governments, U.S. territories, and federally recognized tribal governments are eligible to apply for 1,616 federal grants (defined as authorized project grants, formula grants, cooperative agreements, direct payments for specified uses, and direct payments for unrestricted uses).[24] Of these grants, 141 were not currently funded, 160 were research or fellowship programs that were not targeted solely at either public institutions of higher education or other public agencies, and 41 had broad eligibility extending beyond state and local governments. Removing them from the list left 1,274 funded federal grants to state and local governments (see Table 4).

Because there is no consensus on the methodology used to count federal grants to state and local governments, the 1,274 count of federal grants to state and local governments listed in Table 4 should be viewed as illustrative, as opposed to definitive, of the current number of federal grants to state and local governments.

As the data in the table suggest, the number of federal grants to state and local governments increased slowly from 1902 to 1930. Then, partly in reaction to the Great Depression, Congress doubled the number of federal grants to state and local governments during the 1930s, and continued to

---

[23] OMB, "The Number of Federal Grant Programs to State and Local Governments: 1980-2003," February 18, 2004, p. 7.

[24] Search and analysis conducted May 1-7, 2019. The number of federal grants to state and local governments was determined by first examining all entries in the CFDA's print version and then cross-checking the findings against a search using the frequently updated CFDA's on-line search engine. Because the CFDA's on-line search engine includes subparts of programs, the following search terms were used to minimize this problem: assistance type (all types of formula grants, all types of project grants (except for fellowships), all types of cooperative agreements, all types of direct payments for specified uses, and direct payments for unrestricted uses) by beneficiary eligibility (state governments, local governments, U.S. territories, and federally recognized tribal governments).

increase the number of federal grants to state and local governments during the 1940s and 1950s.

During the mid-1960s, Congress increased the number of federal grants to state and local governments exponentially, primarily in response to national social movements concerning poverty and civil rights. Nine federal grants to state and local governments were added in 1961, 17 in 1962, 20 in 1963, 40 in 1964, 109 in 1965, 53 in 1966, 3 in 1967, and 4 in 1968.[25]

Congress continued to increase the number of federal grants to state and local governments during the 1970s, but at a relatively slow pace as it addressed budgetary constraints presented by "guns versus butter" issues associated with the Vietnam conflict. Then, at the urging of President Ronald Reagan in 1981, Congress approved the largest reduction in the number of federal grants to state and local governments in American history by creating 9 new block grants which consolidated 77 categorical grants and revised two earlier block grants. The Reagan Administration also eliminated funding for 62 categorical grants in 1981, mainly through authority provided under P.L. 97-35, the Omnibus Budget Reconciliation Act of 1981.[26]

The number of federal grants to state and local governments increased relatively slowly during the remainder of the 1980s, as Congress faced budgetary constraints presented by demographic changes in American society that led to escalating costs for several federal entitlement programs, especially for Social Security, Medicare and Medicaid, and by the Reagan Administration's general opposition to the expansion of the federal grants-in-aid system.

As the data in Table 4 indicate, the number of federal grants to state and local governments continued to increase during the 1990s, and has continued to do so, but more slowly in recent years.

---

[25] ACIR, *Fiscal Balance in the American Federal System,* vol. 1, October 1967, p. 157, at http://www.library.unt.edu/gpo/acir/Reports/policy/a-31-1.pdf.

[26] David B. Walker, Albert J. Richter, and Cynthia Cates Colella, "The First Ten Months: Grant-in-Aid, Regulatory, and Other Changes," *Intergovernmental Perspective* vol. 8, no. 1 (winter 1982): 5-22.

LAND GRANTS AND "DUAL FEDERALISM": 1776-1860

The relative influence of internal versus external factors on congressional decisions affecting the federal grants-in-aid system has varied, both over time and in each specific policy area. Prior to the Civil War, external factors, especially cultural norms and expectations concerning government's role in American society, restricted congressional options concerning enactment of federal grant-in-aid programs for state and local governments.

During this time period, America was primarily a rural nation of farmers. Travel conditions were, compared with today's standards, primitive. Many Americans rarely left their home state, and many others never set foot in another state. Government as we know it today, with regulations and spending programs affecting many aspects of American life, did not exist. Although ratification of the Articles of Confederation and Perpetual Union on March 1, 1781, formally established the United States of America, personal allegiance was still directed more toward the individual's home state than to the nation. It was an era of what federalism scholars have called "dual federalism," where states were expected to be the primary instrument of governance in domestic affairs.[27]

However, even before the Constitution's ratification, the federal government found ways to provide state and local governments with assistance to encourage them to pursue national policy objectives. For example, under the Articles of Confederation and Perpetual Union, Congress did not have the power to lay and collect taxes and relied heavily on state donations to fund the government. This lack of revenue, and

---

[27] Harry N. Scheiber, *The Condition of American Federalism: An Historian's View*, a study submitted by the Subcommittee on Intergovernmental Relations to the Committee on Government Operations, U.S. Senate, 89th Cong., 2nd sess., October 15, 1966; and Harry N. Scheiber, "Federalism and Legal Process: Historical and Contemporary Analyses of the American System," *Law & Civil Society Review*, vol. 14, no. 3 (spring 1980), pp. 669-683. Note: There were aspects of cooperative federalism during this time period as well. For example, state officials administered federal elections, state governments housed some federal prisoners, and state courts tried some federal court cases, see Daniel J. Elazar, *The American Partnership: Federal-State Cooperation in the Nineteenth Century United States* (Chicago, IL: University of Chicago Press, 1962).

expenses related to national defense, limited congressional spending options in domestic affairs. The Congress of the Confederation addressed that issue by adopting the Land Ordinance of 1785. The Ordinance generated revenue for the government by authorizing the sale of land acquired from Great Britain at the conclusion of the American Revolutionary War. The Ordinance also required every new township incorporated in those lands, called the Ohio Country, to be subdivided into 36 lots (or sections), each 1 mile square. Lots 8, 11, 26, and 29 were reserved for the United States.[28] The new townships were required to use Lot 16 "for the maintenance of public schools, within the said township."[29] Some schools are still located in lot 16 of their respective townships, although many of the school lots were sold to raise money for public education. These land grants for public education were reauthorized by Congress in the Northwest Ordinance of 1787.[30] Congress subsequently adopted similar legislation for all states admitted to the union from 1802 to 1910, with exceptions for Texas, which retained all of its public land, and Maine and West Virginia, which were formed from other states. From 1802 to 1848, one lot in each township was to be used for education, from 1848 to 1890 two lots, and from 1894 to 1910, with one exception, four lots.[31]

When the Framers met in Philadelphia in 1787 to rework the Articles of Confederation and Perpetual Union, the national economy was in recession, state governments were saddled with large debts left over from the Revolutionary War, the continental dollar was unstable and destined to be a national joke ("not worth a continental"), the navy could not protect

---

[28] *Journals of the Continental Congress, 1774-1789*, Volume XXVIII, May 20, 1785, p. 378. Note: Proceeds from the sale of the four lots set aside for the United States were intended to fund promised military officer pensions and claims for back pay for military service during the Revolutionary War. Soldiers were also eligible for grants of land as compensation for these purposes, see pp. 379-380.

[29] Ibid., p. 378.

[30] Note: The Northwest Ordinance of 1787 ended state claims to the Ohio Country, established a territorial government for the region, included civil rights provisions that served as a precursor for the Bill of Rights, mandated that new states could be formed out of the territory once an area in the region reached a population of 60,000, and prohibited slavery in the region.

[31] Matthias Nordberg Orfield, "Federal Land Grants to the States With Special Reference to Minnesota," *Bulletin of the University of Minnesota*, Minneapolis, MN, March 1915, p. 42.

Federal Grants to State and Local Governments 43

international shipping, and the army proved unable to protect its own arsenal during Shay's rebellion in 1786. To address these issues, Congress was provided 17 specific powers in Article 1, Section 8 of the U.S. Constitution, ratified in 1789, including the power to coin money, establish post offices, regulate copyright laws, declare war, regulate the Armed Forces, borrow money, and, importantly, lay and collect taxes.

The power to lay and collect taxes provided Congress the means to expand the federal government's role in domestic affairs. Moreover, the Supreme Court issued several rulings under Chief Justice John Marshall concerning congressional authority to regulate interstate commerce that effectively cleared the way for congressional activism in domestic policy.[32] However, the prevailing view in Congress at this time was that any power not explicitly provided to Congress in the Constitution was excluded purposively, suggesting that in the absence of specific, supporting constitutional language the exercise of governmental police powers (the regulation of private interests for the protection of public safety, health, and morals; the prevention of fraud and oppression; and the promotion of the general welfare) was either meant to be a state or local government responsibility, or outside the scope of governmental authority altogether.

Nevertheless, during the 1800s there were congressional efforts, primarily from representatives from western states, to adopt legislation to provide federal cash assistance for various types of internal improvement projects to encourage western migration and promote interstate commerce. Most of these efforts failed, primarily due to sectional divisions within Congress which, at that time, made it difficult to build coalitions large enough to adopt programs that targeted most of their assistance to western states. Some opposition came from Members of Congress who viewed

---

[32] For example, in *McCulloch v. Maryland*, 17 U.S. (4 Wheat.) 316 (1819), the Marshall Court established the doctrine of implied national powers, ruling that while federal powers were limited to those enumerated in the Constitution, the necessary and proper clause found in Article 1, Section 8, enlarged, rather than narrowed, congressional authority to act: "Let the end be legitimate, let it be within the scope of the Constitution, and all means which are appropriate, which are plainly adapted to that end, which are not prohibited, but consist with the letter and spirit of the Constitution are constitutional." For further analysis, see CRS Report RL30315, *Federalism, State Sovereignty, and the Constitution: Basis and Limits of Congressional Power*, by Kenneth R. Thomas.

reducing the national debt from the American Revolutionary War as a higher priority. Other Members opposed federal interventions as a matter of political philosophy. They viewed the provision of cash assistance for internal improvements, other than for post roads, which were specifically mentioned in the Constitution as a federal responsibility, a violation of states' rights, as articulated in the Tenth Amendment: "The powers not delegated to the United States by the Constitution, nor prohibited by it to the States, are reserved to the States respectively, or to the people."[33]

Given the prevailing views concerning the limited nature of the federal government's role in domestic affairs, Congress typically authorized federal land grants to states instead of authorizing direct cash assistance to states for internal improvements. For example, in 1823 Ohio received a federal land grant of 60,000 acres along the Maumee Road to raise revenue to improve that road. In 1827, Ohio received another federal land grant of 31,596 acres to raise revenue for the Columbus and Sandusky Turnpike.[34]

In 1841, nine states (Ohio, Indiana, Illinois, Alabama, Missouri, Mississippi, Louisiana, Arkansas, and Michigan) − and, with three exceptions, all subsequent newly admitted states− were designated land grant states and guaranteed at least 500,000 acres of federal land to be auctioned to support transportation projects, including roads, railroads, bridges, canals, and improvement of water courses, that expedited the transportation of United States mail, military personnel, and military munitions.[35] By 1900, over 3.2 million acres of federal land were donated to these states to support wagon road construction. Congress also authorized the donation of another 4.5 million acres of federal land to Illinois, Indiana, Michigan, Ohio, and Wisconsin to raise revenue for canal

---

[33] Constitution of the United States, text available on the National Archives website at http://www.archives.gov/exhibits/charters/bill_of_rights_transcript.html.

[34] Thomas Aquinas Burke, "Ohio Lands − A Short History," 8th ed. (Columbus, OH: State Auditor's Office, September 1996), at http://freepages.history.rootsweb.ancestry.com/~maggie/ohio-lands/ohl5.html#WROTLNDS.

[35] Benjamin Horace Hibbard, *A History of the Public Land Policies* (New York: The Macmillan Company, 1924), pp. 228-233. Note: Maine and West Virginia were not eligible for the guarantee because they were formed out of other states and Texas was ineligible because it was considered a sovereign nation when admitted to the Union. Also, five states, Wisconsin, Alabama, Iowa, Nevada and Oregon, subsequently were permitted to use their proceeds from federal land sales solely for public education.

Federal Grants to State and Local Governments   45

construction and 2.225 million acres to Alabama, Iowa, and Wisconsin to improve river navigation. In addition, states were provided 37.8 million acres for railroad improvements and 64 million acres for flood control.[36] States were provided wide latitude in project selection, and federal oversight and administrative regulations were minimal.

Although land grants were prevalent throughout the 1800s, given prevailing views concerning states' rights, land grants, as well as cash grants, were subject to opposition on constitutional grounds. For example, in 1854, Congress adopted legislation authorizing the donation of 10 million acres of federal land to states to be sold to provide for the indigent insane. President Franklin Pierce vetoed the legislation, claiming that

> I cannot find any authority in the Constitution making the federal government the great almoner of public charity throughout the United States. To do so would, in my judgment, be contrary to the letter and spirit of the Constitution, and subversive of the whole theory upon which the union of these States is founded.... I respectfully submit that, in a constitutional point of view, it is wholly immaterial whether the appropriation be in money, or in land.... should this bill become a law, ... the several States instead of bestowing their own means on the social wants of their own people, may themselves ... become humble supplicants for the bounty of the Federal Government, reversing the state's true relation to this Union.[37]

---

[36] Matthias Nordberg Orfield, *Federal Land Grants to the States With Special Reference to Minnesota* (Minneapolis, MN: Bulletin of the University of Minnesota, 1915), pp. 77-111, 115-118; Morton Grodzins, *The American System* (Chicago: Rand McNally, 1966), p. 35; Gary M. Anderson and Dolores T. Martin, "The Public Domain and Nineteenth Century Transfer Policy," *Cato Journal*, vol. 6, no. 3 (winter 1987): 908-910; John Bell Rae, "Federal Land Grants in Aid of Canals," *The Journal of Economic History*, vol. 4, no. 2 (November 1944): 167, 168; and U.S. Department of Transportation, Federal Highway Administration, *America's Highways, 1776/1976* (Washington, DC: GPO, 1976), 24. Note: 26 states received federal land grants during the 1800s.

[37] President Franklin Pierce, "Message from the President of the United States returning a bill entitled "An act making a grant of public lands to the several States for the benefit of indigent insane persons" with a statement of the objections which have required him to withhold from it his approval to the United States Senate," 33rd Cong., 1st sess., Exec. Doc. 56, May 3, 1854.

46   *Robert Jay Dilger and Michael H. Cecire*

One notable exception to the federal reluctance to provide cash grants to states occurred in 1837. The federal government used proceeds from western land sales to retire the federal debt in 1836. The Deposit Act of 1836 directed that, after reserving $5 million, any money in the federal Treasury on January 1, 1837, shall be distributed to states in proportion to their respective representation in the House and Senate. There were no restrictions placed on how states were to use the funds. About $30 million was distributed to states in three quarterly payments in 1837 before the banking crisis of 1837 led to a recession and payments were stopped. To avoid a promised veto from President Andrew Jackson, the legislation indicated that the funds were a deposit subject to recall, rather than an outright grant of cash.[38]

Overall, domestic policy in the United States prior to the Civil War was dominated by states. As a federalism scholar put it:

> With respect to the classic trinity of sovereign powers–taxation, the police power, and eminent domain–the states enjoyed broad autonomous authority, which they exercised vigorously. Indeed, property law, commercial law, corporation law, and many other aspects of law vital to the economy were left almost exclusively to the states.... Federalism thus provided a receptive structure for expressions of state autonomy and pursuit of state- oriented economic objectives, not only as a matter of constitutional theory and the distribution of formal authority but also as a matter of real power.[39]

THE ORIGINS OF THE MODERN GRANTS-IN-AID SYSTEM: 1860-1932

The Union's victory in the Civil War marked the beginning of a second evolutionary era in American federalism. It effectively put to an

---

[38] Henry Franklin Graff, editor, *The Presidents: A Reference History* (New York: Charles Scribner's Sons, 2002), pp. 118, 119; and Joseph A. Pechman, *Federal Tax Policy* (Washington, DC: The Brookings Institution, 1971), p. 290.

[39] Harry N. Scheiber, "State Law and 'Industrial Policy' in American Development, 1790-1987," *California Law Review*, vol. 75, no. 1 (January 1987), p. 419.

Federal Grants to State and Local Governments

end to the doctrine that the Constitution was a compact among sovereign states, each with the right to nullify an act of Congress that the state deemed unconstitutional, and each with the legal right to secede from the Union.[40] It also signaled the triumph of the northern states' commercialism over the southern states' agrarianism:

> Unimpeded by the political opposition of the southern slavocracy, the Republican coalition of north and west carried through a program of comprehensive changes that insured the expansion of industry, commerce, and free farming.... Instead of the policies of economic laissez faire that the slavocracy had demanded ... the Republicans substituted the doctrine that the federal government would provide assistance for business, industry, and farming; the protective tariff, homestead, land subsidies for agricultural colleges, transcontinental railroads and other internal improvements, national banks. When the defeated south came back into the Union, it had to accept the comprehensive alternation in government policy and economic institutions that historian Charles A. Beard was later to name the Second American Revolution.[41]

Following the war, three constitutional amendments—the Thirteenth adopted in 1865, the Fourteenth adopted in 1868, and the Fifteenth Amendment adopted in 1870—abolished slavery, prohibited states from denying due process or equal protection to any of their citizens, and banned racial restrictions on voting, respectively. In addition, Congress enacted the Reconstruction Acts of 1867 and 1868, which imposed military government on the formally secessionist states and required universal manhood suffrage.[42] Despite this active federal presence in domestic policy in the South following the Civil War, the concept of dual federalism and deference to states in domestic affairs remained a part of American culture. For example, several Supreme Court rulings during this time period limited congressional efforts to override state laws on civil rights, in effect leaving

---

[40] David B. Walker, *The Rebirth of Federalism*, 2nd ed. (New York: Chatham House Publishers, 2000), p. 74.

[41] Robert A. Dahl, *Pluralist Democracy in the United States: Conflict and Consent* (Chicago: Rand McNally, 1967), pp. 318-319.

[42] 15 Stat. 2 ff; 15 Stat. 14 ff; and 15 Stat. 41.

civil and voting rights matters to states until the 1950s and 1960s.[43] The Supreme Court also limited congressional efforts to regulate interstate commerce by limiting the Interstate Commerce Commission's authority.[44]

Reflecting prevailing views concerning dual federalism, and limited federal fiscal resources, the first on-going, federal cash grant to states, other than for the support of the National Guard, was not adopted until 1879. P.L. 45-186, the Federal Act to Promote the Education of the Blind, appropriated $250,000 to create a perpetual source of income for the purchase of teaching materials for the blind. It marked the beginning of the modern federal grants-in-aid system. The funds were used to purchase interest bearing bonds. The interest was used to purchase teaching materials for the blind. These teaching materials were then distributed among the states (and the District of Columbia) annually, with each state applying for assistance receiving a share of the available teaching materials based on the state's share of the total number of pupils enrolled in public schools of education for the blind. The second federal cash grant to states was authorized by the Hatch Act of 1887. It provided each state an annual cash grant of $15,000 to establish agricultural experiment stations. In 1888, an annual grant of $25,000 was appropriated for the care of disabled veterans in state hospitals. States were provided $100 per disabled veteran.[45] In 1890, funding was provided to subsidize resident instruction in the land grant colleges made possible by the Morrill Act of 1862, which provided each existing and future state with 60,000 acres of federal land, plus an additional 30,000 acres for each of its congressional representatives, to be sold for the endowment, support, and maintenance of

---

[43] David B. Walker, *The Rebirth of Federalism*, 2nd ed. (New York: Chatham House Publishers, 2000), p. 75. The most famous civil rights case during this time period was *Plessy v. Ferguson* 163 U.S. 537 (1896) which upheld the constitutionality of state-imposed racial segregation.

[44] Cynthia Cates Colella, "The United States Supreme Court and Intergovernmental Relations," in *American Intergovernmental Relations Today: Perspectives and Controversies*, ed. Robert Jay Dilger (Englewood Cliffs, NJ: Prentice-Hall, Inc., 1986), p. 43. Note: In *Interstate Commerce Commission v. Brimson* 154 U.S. 447 (1894), the Court curtailed the ICC's hearing capacity and in *Interstate Commerce Commission v. Cincinnati, New Orleans and Texas Pacific Railway Company,* 167 U.S. 479 (1897) it ruled against the ICC's authority to fix rates.

[45] Morton Grodzins, *The American System* (Chicago: Rand McNally, 1966), pp. 35, 37.

at least one college where the leading subject was agriculture and the mechanic arts.[46]

In 1902, there were five federal grants to states and local governments (in addition to funding for the National Guard): teaching materials for the blind, agricultural experiment stations, the care of disabled veterans, resident instruction in the land grant colleges, and funding to the District of Columbia. Outlays for these grants were about $7 million in FY1902, or about 1% of total federal outlays. State and local government total outlays at that time were slightly over $1 billion, evidence of the relatively limited nature of federal involvement in domestic policy at that time.

An important difference between land grants and cash grants had emerged, even at this early date. Because federal grants were funded from the federal treasury, many in Congress felt that they had an obligation to ensure that the funds were spent by states in an appropriate manner. As a result, Congress began to attach an increasing number of administrative requirements to these grant programs. For example, in 1889, states were required to match federal funding for the care of disabled veterans or lose it. The Morrill Act of 1890 authorized the Secretary of the Interior to withhold payments, pending an appeal to Congress, from states that failed to meet conditions specified in the act. In 1895, expenditures authorized by the Hatch Act for agricultural experiment stations were conditioned by annual audits. In 1911, funding authorized by the Weeks Act to support state efforts to prevent forest fires was conditioned by advance approval of state plans for the funds' use, annual audits and inspections, and a state matching requirement.[47]

The Sixteenth Amendment's ratification in 1913 provided Congress the authority to lay and collect taxes on income. Although the federal income tax initially generated only modest amounts, it provided Congress an opportunity to shift from land grants to cash grants to encourage state and local governments to provide additional attention to policy areas Congress considered of national interest. Between 1913 and 1923,

---

[46] Ibid., p. 34.

[47] ACIR, *Categorical Grants: Their Role and Design*, A-52, 1978, pp. 15, 16, at http://www.library.unt.edu/gpo/acir/ Reports/policy/a-52.pdf.

Congress adopted new federal grant-in-aid programs for highway construction, vocational education, public health, and maternity care. Outlays for federal grants to state and local governments increased from $12 million in FY1913 to $118 million in FY1922.

In 1923, Massachusetts brought suit against the Secretary of the Treasury, Andrew Mellon, claiming that the maternal care grants authorized by the Sheppard-Towner Act of 1921 were unconstitutional infringements on states' rights. The Supreme Court dismissed the case on the grounds that it lacked jurisdiction. Nonetheless, Justice George Sutherland, writing on behalf of the unanimous Court, indicated that, in his view, this form of congressional spending was not unconstitutional because federal grants to state and local governments were optional and, as such, were not coercive instruments.[48] As a result, although few new federal grants to state and local governments were adopted during the remainder of the 1920s, those grants were now accepted as a legal means for Congress to encourage state and local governments to pursue national goals.

THE NEW DEAL AND THE RISE OF "COOPERATIVE FEDERALISM": 1932-1960

Political scientists contend that about once in every generation partisan affiliations realign across the nation, typically taking a few years to materialize but often becoming apparent during a "critical" presidential election. Critical elections typically result in relatively dramatic and lasting changes in the partisan composition within Congress and state governments. They also usually signal the coming to power of a new partisan coalition that dominates congressional decisionmaking for a relatively long period of time. For example, the election of 1896 ended the political stalemate between the Democratic and Republican parties and solidified the Republican Party's position as the majority party for the next

---

[48] Cynthia Cates Colella, "The United States Supreme Court and Intergovernmental Relations," in *American Intergovernmental Relations Today: Perspectives and Controversies*, ed. Robert Jay Dilger (Englewood Cliffs, NJ: Prentice-Hall, Inc., 1986), p. 47.

Federal Grants to State and Local Governments

51

36 years. The election of 1932 signaled a new period of Democratic Party dominance, particularly in the "Solid South," that lasted until the 1970s, when partisan attachments began to weaken, southern states became increasingly Republican, and the two major political parties became increasingly competitive, each seemingly on the verge of achieving majority party status at various times, but unable to retain that status permanently.[49]

The 1932-1960 period also saw the emergence of the "congressional conservative coalition," the unofficial title given to the shifting political alliances of southern, conservative Democrats and Republican Members. The conservative coalition became an increasingly important counter-balance to large Democratic majorities in both houses of Congress. Members of the conservative coalition generally advocated balanced budgets and states' rights, especially in civil rights legislation. They used congressional procedures, such as the filibuster or threat of a filibuster, to win concessions from the Democratic majority, and, in some instances, to prevent legislation they opposed from becoming law. They also benefitted from the congressional seniority system, which, during this time period, allocated committee chairmanships according to seniority. Because many of the congressional districts in the "solid south" were noncompetitive seats, southern representatives held a disproportionate number of committee chairmanships in the House, further strengthening the conservative coalition's influence on congressional policymaking.

The conservative coalition prevented civil rights legislation from being enacted during this time period, but it could not prevent Democratic majorities in the House and Senate from expanding the federal government's presence in domestic policy. However, throughout this time period, the conservative coalition actively sought concessions to ensure that any new federal programs, including any new grants to state and local governments, respected state rights. As a result, the grant-in-aid programs

---

[49] Valdimer Orlando Key, "A Theory of Critical Elections," *The Journal of Politics*, vol. 17, no. 1 (February 1955), pp. 3-18; Walter Dean Burnham, *Critical Elections and the Mainsprings of American Politics* (New York: W.W. Norton & Company, 1970); and David R. Mayhew, *Electoral Realignments: A Critique of an American Genre* (New Haven: Yale University Press, 2002).

adopted during this time period tended to be in policy areas where state and local governments were already active, such as in education, health care, and highway construction, or where additional federal assistance was welcomed, such as job creation. Also, federal administrative conditions attached to these grants during this era focused on the prevention of corruption and fraudulent expenditures as opposed to encouraging states to move in new policy directions. As a result, federalism scholars have labeled this time period as an era of "cooperative federalism," where intergovernmental tensions were relatively minor and state and local governments were provided flexibility in project selection.

Faced with unprecedented national unemployment and economic hardship, President Franklin Delano Roosevelt advocated a dramatic expansion of the federal government's role in domestic affairs during his presidency, including an expansion of federal grant-in-aid programs as a means to help state and local governments combat poverty and create jobs. Congress approved 16 new, continuing federal grants to state and local governments from 1933 to 1938, and increased funding for federal grants to states and local governments from $214 million in FY1932 to $790 million in FY1938.[50]

Congress also enacted several temporary, emergency relief grant-in-aid programs that distributed federal funds to states according to the state's fiscal capacity. Congress devised mathematical formulas, based on a variety of economic and business measures, to allocate funding to each state, resulting in the share of relief funds varying among states based on the formula's assessment of need. At their peak, in 1935, emergency relief measures provided states nearly $1.9 billion to create jobs and provide emergency assistance for the unemployed. The emergency relief programs were terminated during the 1940s, but they established a precedent for extensive federal involvement with state and local governments in areas of national concern and for the use of mathematical formulas for distributing federal assistance.[51]

---

[50] ACIR, *Categorical Grants: Their Role and Design*, A-52, 1978, pp. 18-19, at http://www.library.unt.edu/gpo/acir/ Reports/policy/a-52.pdf.
[51] Ibid., p. 18.

The Social Security Act of 1935 (SSA) was, arguably, the most significant legislative enactment of the New Deal period. It established a federal presence in social welfare policy. New federal grant-in-aid programs were established for old age assistance, aid to the blind, aid to dependent children, unemployment compensation, maternal and child health, crippled children, and child welfare. The act also enhanced federal oversight of grants to state and local governments as auditing requirements were now required in almost all grant programs. In addition, in 1939, state employees administering SSA programs were required to be selected by merit system procedures, a major advancement for the development of professional state and local government administration and a signal of the declining influence of state and local party bosses in American society. In 1940, the Hatch Act restricted the political activities of state and local government employees paid with federal funds.[52]

Legally, New Deal legislation was based on an expanded interpretation of congressional authority to spend through grant-in-aid programs to promote the nation's welfare under Article 1, Section 8, clause 1 of the Constitution, often referred to as the congressional "spending power." Federal expenditures through grant-in-aid programs during the New Deal were made in several functional areas, including some, such as social welfare, that were traditionally viewed as state responsibilities. Opponents of an expanded role for the federal government in domestic policy argued that New Deal grant programs precluded state action in these traditionally state functional areas and, as such, violated the Constitution's Tenth Amendment. Advocates of an expansion of federal involvement in domestic affairs argued that the power of Congress to spend is more extensive than, rather than concurrent with, enumerated or even implied law-making powers. This disagreement led to a number of Supreme Court cases, a full discussion of which is beyond the scope of this chapter. The Supreme Court rejected the New Deal's expansion of federal authority in 8 of the first 10 cases that it decided. Then, after President Roosevelt's failed legislative proposal to "pack the Court" in 1937, the Supreme Court upheld

---

[52] Ibid., p. 20.

54 *Robert Jay Dilger and Michael H. Cecire*

the constitutionality of several New Deal laws, including the Social Security Act.[53] As a federalism scholar noted,

> A new era of judicial construction had been launched. The commerce power was given broad interpretation in cases upholding the Labor Relations Act. The older distinction between direct and indirect effects of commercial activity was abandoned and the more realistic "stream-of-commerce" concept adopted. The scope of Federal taxing power was also broadened expansively. In sanctioning the Social Security Act, the unemployment excise tax on employers was upheld as a legitimate use of the tax power, and the grants to the states were viewed as examples of Federal-state collaboration, not Federal coercion. The act's old-age and benefit provisions were deemed to be proper because "Congress may spend money in aid of general welfare." When combined, these decisions obviously amounted to last rites for judicial dual federalism.[54]

Although the Supreme Court was no longer viewed as a major obstacle for the expansion of the federal grants-in-aid system, external factors led to a reduction in outlays for federal grants to state and local governments from FY1939 to FY1946 as Congress focused on defense-related issues during World War II. For example, outlays for federal grants to state and local governments averaged $947 million from FY1939 through FY1946, less than half of the New Deal's peak. Following the war, the number of federal grants to state and local governments began to increase at a somewhat accelerated pace, reaching 68 grants in 1950 and 132 grants in 1960. Outlays for federal grants to state and local governments also accelerated, from $859 million in FY1945, to $2.3 billion in FY1950, to $3.2 billion in FY1955, and to $7 billion in 1960.[55] A new development was increased outlays targeted at urban areas, such as grants for airport

---

[53] David B. Walker, *The Rebirth of Federalism*, 2nd ed. (New York: Chatham House Publishers, 2000), p. 91. Note: President Roosevelt proposed that he be given the authority to appoint another judge for each one who had served 1 0 years or more and had not retired within six months of their 70th birthday. A maximum of 50 such appointments were to be permitted, and the Supreme Court's size was to be increased to 15.

[54] Ibid., p. 92.

[55] OMB, *Budget of the United States Government, Fiscal Year 2014: Historical Tables*, p. 257, at http://www.whitehouse.gov/sites/default/files/omb/budget/fy2014/assets/hist.pdf.

construction (1946), urban renewal (1949), and urban planning (1954).[56] The most significant federal grant-in-aid program enacted during the 1950s was the $25 billion, 13-year Federal-Aid Highway Act of 1956, which authorized the construction of the then-41,000 mile National System of Interstate and Defense Highways, with a 1972 target completion date. For the next 35 years, federal surface transportation policy focused on the completion of the interstate system.[57]

THE GREAT SOCIETY AND THE RISE OF "COERCIVE FEDERALISM": 1960-1980

The 1960s was a turbulent decade, marked by both political and social upheaval of historic proportions. Three leading public figures were assassinated: President John F. Kennedy in 1963, civil rights leader the Reverend Martin Luther King Jr. in 1968, and President Kennedy's brother, presidential candidate and Senator Robert Kennedy, in 1968. The civil rights movement, led by the Reverend King, was often met with violent resistance, with bombings of black churches, murders of civil rights workers, and televised police beatings of civil rights demonstrators. One of the defining moments of the civil rights movement was the march on Washington, DC, in August 1963, where the Reverend King made his famous "I Have A Dream" speech. Congress responded to the social turmoil by adopting the Civil Rights Act of 1964, which superseded state civil rights laws by prohibiting discrimination based on race, color, religion, or national origin; the Voting Rights Act of 1965, which superseded state election laws by outlawing literacy tests, poll taxes, and other means to discourage minority voting; and the Civil Rights Act of 1968, which superseded state civil rights laws by prohibiting

---

[56] ACIR, *Categorical Grants: Their Role and Design*, A-52, 1978, p. 23, at http://www.library.unt.edu/gpo/acir/ Reports/policy/a-52.pdf.
[57] For further analysis, see CRS Report R40431, *Federalism Issues in Surface Transportation Policy: A Historical Perspective*, by Robert Jay Dilger; and CRS Report R40053, *Surface Transportation Program Reauthorization Issues for the 111th Congress*, coordinated by John W. Fischer.

discrimination in the sale, rental, and financing of housing. Nonetheless, race riots took place in several urban areas in 1965 and in 1967.[58]

During the latter half of the decade, the civil rights movement was joined by what has been called the hippie movement, where young people rebelled against the conservative norms of the time and disassociated themselves from mainstream liberalism and materialism. This "counterculture" movement began in the United States and sparked a social revolution throughout much of the Western world. It began as a reaction against the conservatism and social conformity of the 1950s, and the U.S. government's military intervention in Vietnam. These groups questioned authority and government, and demanded more freedom and rights for women, gays, and minorities, as well as greater awareness of the need to protect the environment and address poverty.

The social movements and social unrest that swept across the nation during the 1960s had a strong impact on Congress. Reflecting the growing public demand for congressional action to address civil rights, poverty, and the environment, in 1961 the House approved, 217-212, a proposal by Speaker Sam Rayburn to enlarge the House Rules Committee from 12 to 15 Members. Prior to the change, the House Rules Committee was divided, 6 to 6, along ideological lines. Because a majority vote is necessary for the issuance of a legislative rule, the House Rules Committee served as an institutional barrier to the passage of legislation that the committee's more conservative Members believed infringed on states' rights, including civil rights legislation.[59]

The enlargement of the House Rules Committee in 1961 signaled the weakening of the conservative coalition's influence within Congress and enabled the large Democratic majorities elected during the early 1960s in the House and Senate to adopt a succession of civil rights laws, highlighted by the previously mentioned Civil Rights Act of 1964. It also enabled

---

[58] David B. Walker, *The Rebirth of Federalism: Slouching Toward Washington* (Chatham, NJ: Chatham House Publishers, Inc., 1995), p. 125; and Theodore H. White, *America In Search of Itself* (New York: Harper & Row, Publishers, 1982), p. 108.

[59] David W. Rohde, "Committee Reform in the House of Representatives and the Subcommittee Bill of Rights," *Annals of the American Academy of Political and Social Science*, vol. 411, no. 1 (January 1974): 40, 41.

Federal Grants to State and Local Governments

Congress to expand the federal grants-in-aid system, focusing on grants designed to protect the environment and address poverty, both directly through public assistance and job training programs and indirectly through education, housing, nutrition, and health care programs.

These legislative efforts were both supported and encouraged by President Lyndon Baines Johnson. For example, during his commencement address at the University of Michigan on May 22, 1964, President Johnson announced that he would establish working groups to prepare a series of White House conferences and meetings to develop legislative proposals to revitalize urban America, address environmental problems, and improve educational opportunities "to begin to set our course toward the Great Society" which "demands an end to poverty and racial injustice, to which we are totally committed."[60] The term "The Great Society" came to symbolize legislative efforts during the 1960s to address poverty and racial injustice.

In concert with President Johnson's Great Society initiatives, Congress nearly tripled the number of federal grants to state and local governments during the 1960s, from 132 in 1960 to 387 in 1968. In 1965 alone, 109 federal grants to state and local governments were adopted, including Medicaid, which now has, by far, the largest budget of any federal grant-in-aid program. Outlays for federal grants to state and local governments also increased, from $7 billion in FY1960 to $20 billion in FY1969. Functionally, federal grants for health care increased from $214 million in FY1960 to $3.8 billion in FY1970, for income security from $2.6 billion to $5.7 billion, for education, training, employment, and social services from $525 million to $6.4 billion, for transportation from $3 billion to $4.6 billion, and for community and regional development from $109 million to $1.7 billion.[61]

---

[60] President Lyndon Baines Johnson, "Remarks at the University of Michigan, May 22, 1964," Lyndon Baines Johnson Library and Museum, Austin, TX, at http://www.lbjlib.utexas.edu/johnson/archives.hom/speeches.hom/640522.asp.

[61] U.S. Department of Commerce, Bureau of the Census, *Historical Statistics of the United States, Colonial Times to 1970, Part 2*, pp. 1123, 1125, at http://www2.census.gov/prod2/statcomp/documents/CT1970p2-12.pdf.

For the most part, these legislative efforts were not opposed by state and local government officials and their affiliated public interest groups (e.g., National Governors Association, National League of Cities, U.S. Conference of Mayors, and National Association of Counties), primarily because federal grants are voluntary and, in many instances, provided funding for activities that had broad public support. However, the new grants had a number of innovative features that distinguished them from their predecessors. Previously, most federal grants to state and local governments supplemented existing state efforts and, generally, did not intrude on state and local government prerogatives. Most of the federal grants created during the 1960s, on the other hand, were designed purposively by Congress to encourage state and local governments to move into new policy areas, or to expand efforts in areas identified by Congress as national priorities, especially in environmental protection and water treatment, education, public assistance, and urban renewal.[62]

In addition, there was an increased emphasis on narrowly focused project, categorical grants to ensure that state and local governments were addressing national needs. Most of the new grants had relatively low, or no, matching requirements, to encourage state and local government participation. New incentive grants encouraged states to move into new policy areas and to diversify eligible grant recipients, including individuals, nonprofit organizations, and specialized public institutions, such as universities. A greater emphasis also was on grants to urban areas. For example, outlays for federal grants targeted at metropolitan areas more than tripled during the 1960s, and grew to include about 70% of total federal grant-in-aid funding, up from about 55% at the beginning of the decade. There was also a greater emphasis on mandated planning requirements.[63]

---

[62] ACIR, *An Agenda for American Federalism: Restoring Confidence and Competence,* A-86, 1981, pp. 1-3, at http://www.library.unt.edu/gpo/acir/Reports/policy/a-86.pdf; and James Sundquist, *Making Federalism Work* (Washington, DC: The Brookings Institution, 1969), p. 3.

[63] ACIR, *Fiscal Balance in the American Federal System, Volume 1: Basic Structure of Fiscal Federalism,* A-31, 1967, pp. 150-184, at http://www.library.unt.edu/gpo/acir/ Reports/policy/a-31-1.pdf.

Although most of the federal grants adopted during the 1960s were narrowly focused project, categorical grants, the first two block grants were enacted during this time period. P.L. 89-749, the Comprehensive Health Planning and Public Health Services Amendments of 1966, later known as the Partnership for Public Health Act, created a block grant for comprehensive health care services (now the Preventive Health and Health Services Block Grant). It replaced nine formula categorical grants.[64] Two years later, Congress created the second block grant, the Law Enforcement Assistance Administration's Grants for Law Enforcement program (sometimes referred to as the "Crime Control" or "Safe Streets" block grant) in the Omnibus Crime Control and Safe Streets Act of 1968.[65] Unlike the health care services block grant, it was created *de novo*, and did not consolidate any existing categorical grants.[66]

The rapid expansion of federal grants to state and local governments during the 1960s led to a growing concern that the intergovernmental grant-in-aid system had become dysfunctional and needed to be reformed. For example, ACIR argued that along with the expansion of the federal grant system came "a rising chorus of complaints from state and local government officials" concerning the inflexibility of fiscal and administrative requirements attached to the grants.[67] It suggested that state and local government officials were subjected to an information gap because they found it difficult to keep up with the host of new programs and administrative requirements. It also cited the need for improved coordination among programs, noting that many state and local

---

[64] David B. Walker, *The Rebirth of Federalism: Slouching Toward Washington* (Chatham, NJ: Chatham House Publishers, Inc., 1995), pp. 70-71; and Kenneth T. Palmer, "The Evolution of Grant Policies," in *The Changing Politics of Federal Grants*, eds. Lawrence D. Brown, James W. Fossett and Kenneth T. Palmer (Washington, DC: The Brookings Institution Press, 1984), pp. 18-20.

[65] Carl W. Stenberg, "Block Grants and Devolution: A Future Tool?" in *Intergovernmental Management for the 21st Century*, eds. Timothy J. Conlan and Paul L. Posner (Washington, DC: Brookings Institution Press, 2008), p. 266.

[66] ACIR, *The Future of Federalism in the 1980s*, M-126, July 1980, p. 51, at http://www.library.unt.edu/gpo/acir/ Reports/information/M-126.pdf.

[67] ACIR, *Categorical Grants: Their Role and Design*, A-52, 1978, p. 29, at http://www.library.unt.edu/gpo/acir/Reports/policy/a-52.pdf.

government officials were reporting administrative difficulties dealing with federal agencies and those agencies' regional offices:

> Between 1962 and 1965 four new systems of regional offices were established as a consequence of grants-in-aid legislation. Adding these bodies to the separate, already existing regional structures brought the total number of regional systems to 12. Regional boundaries and field office locations varied widely. Kentucky, to cite the most extreme case, had to deal with federal agencies in ten different cities. This confusion imposed burdens on the recipients of grants and also made the task of coordinating operations by federal agencies in pursuit of national objectives more difficult.[68]

During the 1970s, President Richard Nixon and his successor, President Gerald R. Ford, argued that the intergovernmental grant-in-aid system was dysfunctional and advocated the sorting out of governmental responsibilities, with the federal government taking the lead in some functional areas and states in others. They also advocated a shift from narrowly focused categorical grants, especially project categorical grants, toward block grants and revenue sharing. They argued that block grants and general revenue sharing provided state and local governments additional flexibility in project selection and promoted program efficiency by reducing administrative costs. They, and others, believed that state and local governments should be provided additional flexibility in project selection and relief from federal administrative requirements because

- greater reliance on state and local governments promotes a sense of state and local community responsibility and self-reliance;
- state and local government officials are closer to the people than federal administrators and, as a result, are better positioned to discern and adapt public programs to state and local needs and conditions;

---

[68] Ibid., and ACIR, *Fiscal Balance in the American Federal System, Vol. 1*, A-31,1967, pp. 181-184, at http://www.library.unt.edu/gpo/acir/Reports/policy/a-31-1.pdf.

Federal Grants to State and Local Governments 61

- state and local governments encourage participation and civic responsibility by allowing more people to become involved in public questions;
- active state and local governments encourage experimentation and innovation in public policy design and implementation;
- active state and local governments reduce administrative workload on the federal government, which creates program efficiencies; and
- active state and local governments reduce the political turmoil that sometimes results from single policies that govern the entire nation.[69]

Opponents of a shift from categorical grants to block grants and revenue sharing presented several arguments, including

- because funding comes from the federal Treasury, Congress has both the right and an obligation to determine how that money is spent;
- many state and local governments lack the fiscal resources to provide levels of government services necessary to provide the poor and disadvantaged a minimum standard of living and equal access to governmental services, such as education and health care, which are essential to economic success. Therefore, Congress must act to ensure uniform levels of essential governmental services throughout the nation;
- state and local governments that have the fiscal resources to provide levels of government services necessary to provide the poor and disadvantaged a minimum standard of living and equal access to governmental services essential to economic success are often unable to do so because they compete with other state and local governments for business and taxpaying residents. As a result, state and local governments tend to focus available

---

[69] Thomas R. Dye, *Understanding Public Policy*, 6th ed. (Englewood Cliffs, NJ: Prentice-Hall, Inc., 1987), p. 301.

resources on programs designed to attract business investment and taxpaying residents to their communities and states rather than on programs assisting the poor and disadvantaged. Therefore, Congress must act to ensure uniform levels of essential governmental services throughout the nation;

- Congress has both the right and the obligation to ensure through the carrot of grant-in-aid programs and the stick of federal requirements that certain national goals, such as civil rights, equal employment opportunities, protection for the environment, and care for the poor and aged, are met because it is difficult to achieve change when reform-minded citizens must deal with 50 state governments and more than 79,000 local governments; and

- some governmental services have either costs or benefits that spill over onto other localities or states. Water and air pollution controls, for example, benefit not only the local community that pays for the air or water pollution controls, but all of the communities that are located downwind or downstream from that community. Because state and local taxpayers are generally reluctant to pay for programs whose benefits go to others, state and local governments often underfund programs with significant spillover effects. Therefore, Congress must act to ensure that these programs are funded at logical levels.[70]

Opponents also asserted that the arguments presented by advocates for a shift in emphasis to block grants and revenue sharing were actually a "smoke screen" masking their true intent which, allegedly, was to shift federal resources to their core constituencies. As mentioned previously, most federal grant-in-aid funding during the 1960s and 1970s was targeted to metropolitan areas, which, at that time, were considered Democratic Party strongholds. Many observers believed that shifting from project

---

[70] ACIR, *Categorical Grants: Their Role and Design*, A-52 (Washington, DC: GPO, 1978), pp. 50-58; Claude E. Barfield, *Rethinking Federalism: Block Grants and Federal, State, and Local Responsibilities* (Washington, DC: American Enterprise Institute for Public Policy Research, 1981), pp. 4-8; and Thomas R. Dye, *Understanding Public Policy*, 6th ed. (Englewood Cliffs, NJ: Prentice-Hall, Inc., 1987), p. 300.

Federal Grants to State and Local Governments 63

categorical grants to block grants or general revenue sharing would result in less money for metropolitan areas and more money for suburban and rural areas, areas that were more likely to be populated by Republicans than Democrats. This shift would occur because project categorical grants are awarded on a competitive basis by federal administrators while block grant and revenue sharing funding is allocated according to pre-determined formula, often with minimum funding guarantees for each state and with a portion of the funding determined by either population or per capita income. Because block grant and revenue sharing funding tends to be more geographically dispersed than project categorical grants, congressional debates over which grant mechanism was best had partisan overtones that often transcended discussions over which grant mechanism would improve grant performance.

Some federalism scholars have also suggested that Congress tends to prefer categorical grants over block grants and revenue sharing because Members take pride in the authorship of sponsored programs. They argue that categorical grants provide more opportunities for sponsorship, and more opportunities for receiving political credit for that sponsorship, than block grants or revenue sharing. In their view, constituents are more interested in a Member's ability to serve in a material way than in their competence in broad policymaking or in "the rightness of positions on issues of principle, form or structure."[71] As a result, they argue that Members are more likely to be recognized for sponsoring or supporting specific, narrowly focused categorical grants than by championing a more general block grant or revenue sharing approach. For example, they assert that Members are more likely to receive recognition and political credit from constituents for sponsoring and supporting legislation to prevent lead-based paint poisoning among children than for legislation covering the broad area of preventive health services.[72]

---

[71] Roger H. Davidson, "Representation and Congressional Committees," *The Annals of the American Academy of Political and Social Science*, vol. 411, no. 1 (January 1974), p. 50.

[72] ACIR, *Categorical Grants: Their Role and Design*, A-52, 1978, p. 65, at http:// www.library.unt.edu/gpo/acir/ Reports/policy/a-52.pdf; and David Mayhew, "Congressional Elections: The Case of the Vanishing Marginals," *Polity*, vol. VI, no. 3 (spring 1974), pp. 295-317.

64   *Robert Jay Dilger and Michael H. Cecire*

Presidents Nixon's and Ford's efforts to gain congressional approval for a shift in emphasis from categorical grants to block grants and revenue sharing were only partially successful. For example, in his 1971 State of the Union speech, President Nixon announced a plan to consolidate 129 federal grant programs in six functional areas—33 in education, 26 in transportation, 12 in urban community development, 17 in manpower training, 39 in rural community development, and 2 in law enforcement—into what he called six "special revenue sharing" programs. Unlike the categorical grants they would replace, the proposed special revenue sharing programs had no state matching requirements and relatively few auditing or oversight requirements, and the funds were distributed automatically by formula without prior federal approval of plans for their use.[73]

The education, transportation, rural community development, and law enforcement proposals failed to gain congressional approval, primarily because they generated opposition from interest groups affiliated with the programs who worried that the programs' future funding would be compromised.[74] However, three block grants, the first signed by President Nixon and the remaining two signed by President Ford, were approved.

The Comprehensive Employment and Training Assistance Block Grant program, created by the Comprehensive Employment and Training Act of 1973, merged 17 existing manpower training categorical grant programs. The Community Development Block Grant program (CDBG), created by the Housing and Community Development Act of 1974, consolidated six existing community and economic development categorical grant programs.[75] Title XX social services, later renamed the Social Services Block Grant program, was created *de novo* and, therefore, did not consolidate any existing categorical grant programs. It was authorized by

---

[73] Claude E. Barfield, *Rethinking Federalism: Block Grants and Federal, State, and Local Responsibilities* (Washington, DC: American Enterprise Institute for Public Policy Research, 1981), p. 3.

[74] Timothy Conlan, *From New Federalism to Devolution: Twenty-Five Years of Intergovernmental Reform* (Washington, DC: The Brookings Institution, 1998), p. 62.

[75] Note: Most sources indicate that CDBG merged 7 categorical grant programs. However, one of the categorical grant programs initially designated for consolidation, the Section 312 Housing Rehabilitation Loan program, was retained as a separate program. See ACIR, *Block Grants: A Comparative Analysis*, A-60, 1977, p. 7, at http://www.library.unt.edu/gpo/acir/Reports/policy/A-60.pdf.

Federal Grants to State and Local Governments

the 1974 amendments of the Social Security Act, which was signed into law on January 4, 1975.[76] Also, in 1972, general revenue sharing was approved by Congress. General revenue sharing distributed funds to states from 1972 to 1981 and to localities from 1972 to 1986.

Nevertheless, Congress retained an emphasis on the use of categorical grants. On December 31, 1980, there were 534 categorical grant programs, 5 block grant programs, and 1 general revenue sharing program. Of the categorical grant programs, 361 were project categorical grants, 42 were project, formula categorical grants, 111 were formula categorical grants, and 20 were open-ended reimbursement categorical grants.[77] Overall, categorical grants accounted for 79.3% of the $91.3 billion in outlays for federal grants to state and local governments that year, block grants accounted for 11.3%, and general revenue sharing 9.4%.[78]

Efforts to sort out governmental responsibilities were also met with resistance in Congress. For example, President Nixon's six special revenue sharing proposals would have provided state and local governments the leading role in decisionmaking in those six functional areas. Also, his proposed Family Assistance Plan would have replaced several public assistance categorical grant programs with a national public assistance system covering all low-income families with children. Although his Family Assistance Plan was not adopted, Congress did nationalize several adult-age public assistance grant-in-aid programs in 1972, including old-

---

[76] Carl W. Stenberg, "Block Grants and Devolution: A Future Tool?" in *Intergovernmental Management for the 21st Century*, eds. Timothy J. Conlan and Paul L. Posner (Washington, DC: Brookings Institution Press, 2008), p. 266; ACIR, *In Respect to Realities: A Report on Federalism in 1975*, M-103, April 1976, pp. 16-20, at http://www.library.unt.edu/gpo/ acir/Reports/information/m-103.pdf; and ACIR, *Block Grants: A Comparative Analysis*, A-60, 1977, pp. 15-40, at http://www.library.unt.edu/gpo/acir/Reports/policy/A-60.pdf. Note: Title XX initially had all of the characteristics of a block grant and ACIR counted it as a block grant since its inception, but it was not formally called a block grant program until 1981.

[77] ACIR, *A Catalog of Federal Grant-In-Aid Programs to State and Local Governments: Grants Funded FY 1981*, M-133, 1982, pp. 1-3, at http://www.library.unt.edu/gpo/acir/ Reports/information/M-133cat.pdf.

[78] OMB, *Special Analyses: Budget of the United States Government, FY 1984*, p. H-20.

66 *Robert Jay Dilger and Michael H. Cecire*

age assistance, aid to the blind, and aid to the permanently and totally disabled.[79]

Another Related Development: Federal Mandates

Another related, new development during the 1960s and 1970s was the imposition by Congress of numerous federal mandates on state and local government officials. The concept of mandates covers a broad range of policy actions with centralizing effects on the intergovernmental system, including statutory direct-order mandates, both total and partial statutory preemption of state and local government law, federal tax policies affecting state and local tax bases, and regulatory action taken by federal courts and agencies. Many federalism scholars also consider program-specific and crosscutting federal grant administrative conditions mandates, even though the grants themselves are voluntary.[80]

Crosscutting requirements are, perhaps, the most widely recognized mandate. They are a condition of federal assistance that applies across-the-board to all, or most, federal grants to advance a national social or economic goal. Title VI of the Civil Rights Act of 1964 was the first post-World War II statute to use a crosscutting requirement. It specifies that

> No person in the United States shall, on the ground of race, color, or national origin, be excluded from participation in, be denied the benefits of, or be subjected to discrimination under any program receiving Federal financial assistance.[81]

---

[79] David B. Walker, *The Rebirth of Federalism*, 2nd ed. (New York: Chatham House Publishers, 2000), p. 127.

[80] Paul L. Posner, "Mandates: The Politics of Coercive Federalism," in *Intergovernmental Management for the 21st Century*, eds. Timothy J. Conlan and Paul L. Posner (Washington, DC: Brookings Institution Press, 2008), p. 287.

[81] 42 U.S.C. 2000d cited in ACIR, *Regulatory Federalism: Policy, Process, Impact, and Reform*, A-95, 1984, p. 71, at http://www.library.unt.edu/gpo/acir/Reports/policy/a-95.pdf.

Federal Grants to State and Local Governments 67

In 1980, OMB counted 59 crosscutting requirements intended to further national social or economic goals in a variety of functional areas, including education and the environment.[82]

Some of the statutory direct-order mandates adopted during this era included the Equal Employment Opportunity Act of 1972, which extended the prohibitions against discrimination in employment contained in the Civil Rights Act of 1964 to state and local government employment; the Fair Labor Standards Act Amendments of 1974, which extended the prohibitions against age discrimination in the Age Discrimination in Employment Act of 1967 to state and local government employment; and the Public Utilities Regulatory Policy Act of 1978, which established federal requirements concerning the pricing of electricity and natural gas.[83]

ACIR suggested that the expansion of federal intergovernmental regulatory activity during the 1960s and 1970s fundamentally changed the nature of intergovernmental relations in the United States:

> During the 1960s and 1970s, state and local governments for the first time were brought under extensive federal regulatory controls.... Over this period, national controls have been adopted affecting public functions and services ranging from automobile inspection, animal preservation and college athletics to waste treatment and waste disposal. In field after field the power to set standards and determine methods of compliance has shifted from the states and localities to Washington.[84]

The continued emphasis on categorical grants, the increased emphasis on provisions encouraging states to move in new policy directions, and, especially, the increased imposition of federal mandates on state and local governments during the 1960s and 1970s led some federalism scholars to label the 1960s and 1970s as the beginnings of a shift toward "coercive federalism."[85] Cooperative features were still present, but congressional

---

[82] ACIR, *Regulatory Federalism: Policy, Process, Impact, and Reform*, A-95, 1984, p. 71, at http://www.library.unt.edu/gpo/acir/Reports/policy/a-95.pdf.

[83] Ibid., p. 88.

[84] Ibid., p. 246.

[85] John Kincaid, "From Cooperative to Coercive Federalism," *The Annals of the American Academy of Political and Social Science*, vol. 509, no. 1 (1990), pp. 139-152. Note: the term

68   *Robert Jay Dilger and Michael H. Cecire*

deference to state and local government prerogatives seen in previous eras was no longer in force. Instead of focusing primarily on the "carrot" of federal assistance to encourage state and local governments to pursue policies that aligned with national goals, Congress increasingly relied on the "stick" of federal mandates.

CONGRESS ASSERTS ITS AUTHORITY: THE DEVOLUTION REVOLUTION THAT WASN'T, 1980-2000

By the end of the 1970s, the social turmoil that marked the previous two decades had receded. Into the 1980s, the United States and most of the Western world experienced a revival of conservative politics, the advancement of free market solutions to improve government efficiency and solve social problems, and a renewed emphasis on materialism and the possession of consumer goods.[86] Yet, at the same time, social change continued to affect American lifestyles, as women became fixtures in the workplace, the gay rights movement become more active, environmental concerns intensified, and rock concerts featuring the leading rock bands and performers of the era were televised to millions of viewers across the nation and the world to raise money for various social causes, such as famine relief, support for family farms, and AIDS prevention and treatment.

The seemingly contradictory societal trends of self-promotion and altruism that swept across American society during the 1980s and 1990s were reflected in responses to national public opinion polls concerning politics and government. These polls evidenced a growing public hostility toward government intrusion and government performance, especially the

---

coercive is often used in legal arguments to suggest that provisions of law related to federal grants-in-aid do not have constitutional standing. Federalism scholars use the term to describe, as Kincaid explained it (p. 139), the shift in emphasis "from fiscal tools to stimulate intergovernmental policy cooperation" to an increased reliance on "regulatory tools to ensure the supremacy of federal policy."

[86] David Harvey, *A Brief History of Neoliberalism* (New York: Oxford University Press, 2005); and Milton Friedman, *Free to Choose* (New York: Harcourt Brace Jovanovich, 1980).

Federal Grants to State and Local Governments 69

federal government's performance, despite growing support for specific programs and regulations that represented the polar opposite of these attitudes.[87] Perhaps reflecting these seemingly contradictory trends, during this era the public tended to elect a President of one political party and a Congress of another. Moreover, nationally, the two-party political system became more competitive as the once solid Democratic South turned increasing Republican. The Republican Party's resurgence was evidenced by its winning the presidency from 1981 to 1993, and its achieving majority status in the Senate from 1981 to 1987, and in both houses of Congress from 1995 to 2001.

President Ronald Reagan's election in 1980, coupled with the Republican Party's resurgence, especially its winning majority party status in the Senate that year, signaled for some the potential for a "devolution revolution" in American federalism, where unfunded federal mandates would be rescinded, "burdensome" administrative federal grant-in-aid conditions removed, and the cooperative features of the federal grants-in-aid system enhanced. This belief was based on President Reagan's commitment to reducing the federal budget deficit. Because he was convinced that it was necessary to increase defense spending, President Reagan concluded that the only way to reduce the federal budget deficit was to increase revenue by encouraging economic growth through tax reduction and regulatory relief, and limiting the growth of federal domestic expenditures. As a former governor, he trusted state and local governments' ability to provide essential government services. As a result, he advocated a sorting out of governmental responsibilities that would reduce the federal government's role in domestic affairs, increase the emphasis on block grants to provide state and local government officials

---

[87] Richard L. Cole and John Kincaid, "Public Opinion and American Federalism: Perspectives on Taxes, Spending, and Trust: An ACIR Update," *Publius: The Journal of Federalism*, vol. 30, no. 1 (winter 2000), pp. 197-198; William G. Jacoby, "Issue Framing and Public Opinion on Government Spending," *American Journal of Political Science*, vol. 44, no. 4 (October 2000), pp. 752-758; and David B. Walker, *The Rebirth of Federalism*, 2nd ed. (New York: Chatham House Publishers, 2000), p. 341.

greater flexibility in determining how the program's funds are spent, and impose fiscal restraint on all federal grant-in- aid programs.[88]

For example, on February 18, 1981, President Reagan addressed a joint session of Congress and proposed the consolidation of 84 existing categorical grants into 6 new block grants and requested significant funding reductions for a number of income maintenance categorical grants, including housing (rental) assistance, food stamps (now Supplemental Nutrition Assistance Program), Medicaid, and job training. Congress subsequently approved P.L. 97-35, the Omnibus Budget Reconciliation Act of 1981, which consolidated 77 categorical grants and two earlier block grants into the following nine new block grants:

- Elementary and Secondary Education (37 categorical grants),
- Alcohol, Drug Abuse, and Mental Health Services (10 categorical grants),
- Maternal and Child Health Services (9 categorical grants),
- Preventive Health and Human Services Block Grant (merged 6 categorical grants with the Health Incentive Grants for Comprehensive Health Services Block Grant),
- Primary Care (2 categorical grants),
- Community Services (7 categorical grants),
- Social Services (one categorical grant and the Social Services for Low Income and Public Assistance Recipients Block Grant),
- Low-Income Home Energy Assistance (1 categorical grant), and
- a revised Community Development Block Grant program (adding an existing discretionary grant and 3 categorical grants).[89]

Overall, funding for the categorical grants bundled into these block grants was reduced 12%, about $1 billion, from their combined funding

---

[88] Timothy J. Conlan and David B. Walker, "Reagan's New Federalism: Design, Debate and Discord," *Intergovernmental Perspective*, vol. 8, no. 4 (winter 1983), pp. 6-15, 18-22.

[89] David B. Walker, Albert J. Richter, and Cynthia Colella, "The First Ten Months: Grant-In-Aid, Regulatory, and Other Changes," *Intergovernmental Perspective*, vol. 8, no. 1 (winter 1982), pp. 5-11.

Federal Grants to State and Local Governments 71

level the previous year.[90] President Reagan argued that the funding reductions would not result in the loss of services for recipients because the reductions would be offset by administrative efficiencies. In addition, the Reagan Administration eliminated funding for 62 categorical grants in 1981, mainly through authority provided under the Omnibus Budget Reconciliation Act of 1981.[91]

Some observers were convinced that the adoption of the Omnibus Budget Reconciliation Act of 1981 was proof of the coming devolution revolution. The number of federal grants to state and local governments was reduced and outlays for federal grants to state and local governments fell for the first time since World War II, from $94.7 billion in FY1981 to $88.1 billion in FY1982.[92] However, in retrospect, federalism scholars now consider the 1981 block grants as more "historical accidents than carefully conceived restructurings of categorical programs" because they were contained in a lengthy bill that was primarily designed to reduce the budget deficit, not to reform federalism relationships. The bill was adopted under special parliamentary rules requiring a straight up or down vote without the possibility of amendment, and it was not considered and approved by authorizing committees of jurisdiction.[93] Nonetheless, largely due to the Omnibus Budget and Reconciliation Act of 1981, in 1984 there were 12

---

[90] GAO, *Block Grants: Characteristics, Experience and Lessons Learned*, GAO/HEHS-95-74, February 9, 1995, p. 2, at http://www.gao.gov/assets/230/220911.pdf. Note: funding changes ranged from a $159 million, or 30%, reduction in the Community Services Block Grant to a $94 million, or 10%, increase in funding for the Community Development Block Grant program.

[91] David B. Walker, Albert J. Richter, and Cynthia Cates Colella, "The First Ten Months: Grant-in-Aid, Regulatory, and Other Changes," *Intergovernmental Perspective* vol. 8, no. 1 (winter 1982): 5-22.

[92] OMB, *Budget of the United States Government, Fiscal Year 2014: Historical Tables*, p. 257, at http://www.whitehouse.gov/sites/default/files/omb/budget/fy2014/assets/hist.pdf.

[93] Carl W. Stenberg, "Block Grants and Devolution: A Future Tool?" in *Intergovernmental Management for the 21ˢᵗ Century*, eds. Timothy J. Conlan and Paul L. Posner (Washington, DC: Brookings Institution Press, 2008), p. 267; and Timothy Conlan, *From New Federalism to Devolution: Twenty-Five Years of Intergovernmental Reform* (Washington, DC: The Brookings Institution, 1998), pp. 110-121.

72 *Robert Jay Dilger and Michael H. Cecire*

block grants in operation (compared to 392 categorical grants), accounting for about 15% of total grants-in-aid funding.[94]

During the remainder of his presidency, President Ronald Reagan submitted 26 block grant proposals to Congress, with only one, the Federal Transit Capital and Operating Assistance Block Grant, added in 1982. In addition, Congress approved the Job Training Partnership Act of 1982, which created a new block grant for job training to replace the block grant contained in the Comprehensive Employment and Training Act of 1973.[95]

Federalism scholars generally agree that President Reagan had unprecedented success in achieving congressional approval for block grants in 1981. However, they also note that most of President Reagan's subsequent block grant proposals failed to gain congressional approval, primarily because they were opposed by organizations that feared, if enacted, the block grants would result in less funding for the affected programs. For example, in 1982, President Reagan proposed, but could not get congressional approval for, a $20 billion "swap" in which the federal government would return to states full responsibility for funding Aid to Families With Dependent Children (AFDC) (now Temporary Assistance for Needy Families) and food stamps (now Supplemental Nutrition Assistance Program) in exchange for federal assumption of state contributions for Medicaid. As part of the deal, he also proposed a temporary $28 billion trust fund or "super revenue sharing program" to replace 43 other federal grant programs, including 19 social, health, and nutrition services programs, 11 transportation programs, 6 community development and facilities programs, 5 education and training programs, Low Income Home Energy Assistance, and general revenue sharing. The trust fund, and federal taxes supporting it, would begin phasing out after four years, leaving states the option of replacing federal tax support with

---

[94] ACIR, *A Catalog of Federal Grant-In-Aid Programs to State and Local Governments: Grants Funded FY1984*, M-139, 1984, pp. 1-3, at http://www.library.unt.edu/gpo/ acir/Reports/ information/m-139.pdf.

[95] Ibid., p. 3; Timothy Conlan, *From New Federalism to Devolution: Twenty-Five Years of Intergovernmental Reform* (Washington, DC: The Brookings Institution, 1998), p. 142; and out-of-print CRS Report 87-845, *Block Grants: Inventory and Funding History*, Sandra S. Osbourn, November 21, 1986, available to congressional clients by request.

Their own funds to continue the programs or allowing the programs to expire.[96]

Both the swap proposal and the proposed devolution of 43 federal grants failed to gain congressional approval, primarily because they were opposed by organizations and Members who feared that, if enacted, the proposals would result in less funding for the affected programs. For example, the National Governors Association supported the federal takeover of Medicaid, but objected to assuming the costs for AFDC and food stamps. The economy was weakening at that time and governors worried that they would not have the fiscal capacity necessary to support the programs without continued federal assistance.[97]

Evidence of a coming devolution revolution proved elusive as the upward trend in outlays for federal grants to state and local programs resumed in FY1983, although at a somewhat lower rate of increase than during the previous two decades. As shown in Table 2, outlays for federal grants to state and local governments increased from $91.4 billion in FY1980 to $135.3 billion in FY1990 and $285.9 billion in FY2000. Medicaid accounted for much of that revenue growth, increasing from $13.9 billion in FY1980 to $41.1 billion in FY1990 and $117.9 billion in FY2000.[98]

Functionally, as shown in Table 2, outlays for federal grants to state and local governments for health care increased from $15.8 billion in FY1980 to $124.8 billion in FY2000. Also, outlays for federal grants to state and local governments for income security increased from $18.5 billion in FY1980 to $68.7 billion in FY2000; for education, training, employment, and social services from $21.9 billion to $36.7 billion; for transportation from $13.0 billion to $32.2 billion; and for community and regional development from $6.5 billion to $8.7 billion.

---

[96] Timothy J. Conlan and David B. Walker, "Reagan's New Federalism: Design, Debate and Discord," *Intergovernmental Perspective*, vol. 8, no. 4 (winter 1983), p. 9. Note: The cost of the proposed trust fund was later estimated at $34.4 billion.

[97] Ibid., pp. 6-15, 18-22; and Timothy Conlan, *New Federalism: Intergovernmental Reform From Nixon to Reagan* (Washington, DC: The Brookings Institution, 1988), pp. 182-198.

[98] OMB, *Historical Tables: Budget of the United States Government, Fiscal Year 2009*, pp. 262, 268, 276, at http://www.whitehouse.gov/sites/default/files/omb/budget/fy2009/pdf/hist.pdf.

74   *Robert Jay Dilger and Michael H. Cecire*

The number of federal grants to state and local governments fell at the beginning of this era, from 541 in 1981 to an era low of 405 in 1984, but then resumed an upward trend. As indicated in Table 4, there were 541 grants to state and local governments in 1981, 405 in 1984, 435 in 1987, 492 in 1989, 557 in 1991, 593 in 1993, 633 in 1995, and 664 in 1998. Moreover, the number of intergovernmental mandates continued to increase throughout the era. ACIR, for example, identified 36 significant federal mandates affecting state and local governments in 1980. In 1990, it identified 63.[99] ACIR concluded that "despite efforts to constrain the growth of intergovernmental regulation, the 1980s remained an era of regulatory expansion rather than contraction."[100] It offered the following explanation for the increased number of federal mandates during the 1980s:

> The causes of this continued regulatory growth are complex and varied. Many regulations address important and well documented problems from pollution to health care to civil rights. The goals associated with these programs are popular not only with the general public but with state and local government officials as well. But, whereas the Congress in the past might have responded to emerging needs with a new federal aid program, the scarcity of federal funds during a decade of historic deficits has made the alternative of federal mandates look increasingly attractive to federal policymakers.[101]

Some observers believed that the anticipated devolution revolution might be realized following the 1994 congressional elections, which resulted in the Republican Party gaining majority status in both the House and Senate. As evidence of the potential for a devolution revolution they pointed to the Unfunded Mandate Reform Act of 1995 (UMRA). Its intent

---

[99] ACIR, *Regulatory Federalism: Policy, Process, Impact, and Reform*, A-95, 1984, pp. 246-249, at http://www.library.unt.edu/gpo/acir/Reports/policy/a-95.pdf; and Timothy J. Conlan and David R. Beam, "Federal Mandates: The Record of Reform and Future Prospects," *Intergovernmental Perspective*, vol. 18, no. 4 (Fall 1992), p. 7.

[100] Timothy J. Conlan and David R. Beam, "Federal Mandates: The Record of Reform and Future Prospects," *Intergovernmental Perspective*, vol. 18, no. 4 (Fall 1992), p. 8.

[101] Ibid., p. 11.

Federal Grants to State and Local Governments 75

was to limit the federal government's ability to impose costs on state and local governments or on the private sector through unfunded mandates. Providing relief from unfunded mandates was one of the stated goals of the Republican Party's 1994 Contract With America.[102]

Under UMRA, congressional committees have the initial responsibility to identify certain federal mandates in measures under consideration. If the measure contains a federal mandate, the authorizing committee must provide the measure to the Congressional Budget Office (CBO). It reports back to the committee an estimate of the mandate's costs. The office must prepare full quantitative estimates for each reported measure with mandate costs over pre-determined thresholds in any of the first five fiscal years the legislation would be in effect. CBO's cost estimates include the direct costs of the federal mandates contained in the measure, or in any necessary implementing regulations; and the amount of new or existing federal funding the legislation authorizes to pay these costs. The thresholds triggering a full CBO cost estimate are adjusted annually for inflation. They were originally $50 million for intergovernmental mandates and $100 million for private sector mandates. The thresholds in 2019 are $82 million for intergovernmental mandates and $164 million for private sector mandates. CBO must prepare brief statements of cost estimates for those mandates that have estimated costs below these thresholds.[103]

Members can raise a point of order if the measure containing the mandate lacks a CBO cost estimate, either because the committee failed to publish the CBO's cost estimate in its report or in the *Congressional Record*, or CBO determined that no reasonable estimate of the mandate's cost was feasible. Members can also raise a point of order if the measure has an intergovernmental cost estimate that exceeds the annually adjusted

---

[102] Richard P. Nathan, "The 'Devolution Revolution' An Overview," *Rockefeller Institute Bulletin* (Albany, NY: The Nelson A. Rockefeller Institute of Government, 1996), pp. 5-13; John Kincaid, "The Devolution Tortoise and the Centralization Hare," *New England Economic Review* (May/June 1998), pp. 36-38; and Chung-Lae Cho and Deil S. Wright, "The Devolution Revolution in Intergovernmental Relations in the 1990s: Changes in Cooperative and Coercive State–National Relations as Perceived by State Administrators," *Journal of Public Administration Research and Theory*, vol. 14, no. 4 (2004), pp. 447-467.

[103] For further analysis, see CRS Report R40957, *Unfunded Mandates Reform Act: History, Impact, and Issues*, by Robert Jay Dilger and Richard S. Beth.

76 *Robert Jay Dilger and Michael H. Cecire*

cost threshold in any of the first five fiscal years the mandate would be in effect.

UMRA's impact on unfunded mandates has been relatively limited. For example, from 1996 to May 2019, 62 points of order were raised in the House and 4 in the Senate. One point of order, concerning a 1996 minimum wage bill, was sustained in the House and two points of order, concerning amendments relating to an increase in the minimum wage in 2005, were sustained in the Senate.[104] In addition, UMRA covers only certain types of unfunded federal mandates. As a federalism scholar argued,

> UMRA primarily covers only statutory direct orders, excluding most grant conditions and preemptions whose fiscal effects fall below the threshold. Statutory direct orders dealing with constitutional rights, prohibition of discrimination, national security, and Social Security are among those excluded from coverage. Moreover, analytic and procedure requirements do not apply to appropriations bills, floor amendments or conference reports–those tools of "unorthodox lawmaking" that have become increasingly prevalent in the Congress.[105]

Moreover, another federalism scholar noted that the overall record of the 104th Congress, expected by some to decentralize and devolve federalism relationships, was more status quo than devolutionary:

> Shifting back to the overall record of the 104th Congress, it is appropriate here to note the various proposed devolutionary bills that were defeated. Chief among these was the proposed Medicaid block grant with a $163 billion cut in funding over five years. Both a public housing blocking proposal and the big regulatory reform measure that would have seriously limited the Federal government's power to issue rules affecting health, safety, and the environment were scuttled. Extension of the Clean

---

[104] CRS Report R40957, *Unfunded Mandates Reform Act: History, Impact, and Issues*, by Robert Jay Dilger and Richard S. Beth; and U.S. Government Accountability Office, *Unfunded Mandates: Analysis of Reform Act Coverage,* GAO-04-637 (Washington, DC: GPO, 2004), p. 7.

[105] Paul Posner, "The Politics of Coercive Federalism in the Bush Era," *Publius: The Journal of Federalism*, vol. 37, no. 3 (Summer 2007), p. 403.

Water Act, enactment of a consolidation of eighty-odd manpower training programs, and passage of a revised Endangered Species Act, which eliminated the Federal authority to restrict threatening activities, were all successfully resisted. A rollback of affirmative action, a conservative shift in the Superfund's program and rules, and the proposed Product Liability Legal Reform Act of 1996 were also scuttled. Of the nine here, two died because of Senate rejection; three, because of a presidential veto or the threat of one; two others failed because neither chamber dared take either one up; and the last two died because of a deadlocked Conference Committee and a lack of time to consider a Conference Report.[106]

The devolution revolution never fully materialized during this era, despite growing public hostility toward the federal government. The emphasis on categorical grants and the issuance of federal mandates continued. Yet, some decentralization of decisionmaking authority did take place during the era. For example, in 1980, there were four block grants in operation. In 2000, there were 24 block grants, including the Surface Transportation Program (1991) and the Temporary Assistance for Needy Families (TANF) program (1996). Funded at $16.7 billion annually, TANF rivaled the Surface Transportation Program during this era for the largest budget of all the block grants. In addition, Congress authorized state waivers for Medicaid starting in 1981, and for child welfare assistance programs starting in 1994.[107]

The seemingly contradictory trends of centralization and decentralization that took place in the federal intergovernmental system during the 1980s and 1990s perhaps reflected the contradictory societal trends that swept across America at the time. As mentioned previously, national public opinion polls indicated that the public was increasingly dissatisfied with the performance of government, especially the federal government's performance, and expressed a growing hostility toward

---

[106] David B. Walker, *The Rebirth of Federalism*, 2nd ed. (New York: Chatham House Publishers, 2000), p. 165.

[107] For additional analysis, see CRS Report RS22448, *Medicaid's Home and Community-Based Services State Plan Option: Section 6086 of the Deficit Reduction Act*, by Cliff Binder; and CRS Report RL31082, *Child Welfare Financing: Issues and Options*, by Karen Spar and Christine M. Devere.

government (and Congress) as a whole. It could be argued that these views suggest that the public wanted Congress to devolve federal grant-in-aid programs to state and local governments or, at least, provide state and local governments greater flexibility in determining how the grants' funding should be spent. Yet, at the same time, the public also expressed relatively strong support for individual federal government programs (and individual Members of Congress).[108] It could be argued that these views suggest that the public wanted Congress to maintain federal government control over these programs, and expressed approval of their individual Members for doing so.

Another possible explanation for the continued focus on categorical grants and the imposition of federal mandates during this era is that federalism issues tend to be a second order priority for many federal policymakers. For example, it could be argued that President Reagan's commitment to strengthening federalism through program decentralization and devolution was unrivaled in the modern era. Yet, in an analysis of the Reagan Administration's federalism policies, a leading federalism scholar concluded that "devolutionary policies consistent with the president's definition of federalism reform ... consistently lost out in the Reagan Administration when they ... conflicted with the sometimes competing goals of reducing the federal deficit, deregulating the private sector, and advancing the conservative social agenda."[109] For example, this scholar noted that President Reagan opposed the expansion of General Revenue Sharing, advocated the elimination of the deductibility of state and local taxes, supported the preemption of state laws regulating double-trailer trucks and establishing minimum drinking ages, overrode state objections to increased off-shore oil drilling and increased use of nuclear power, and supported efforts to require states to establish workfare programs for public

---

[108] Richard F. Fenno, "If, as Ralph Nader Says, Congress Is "The Broken Branch," How Come We Love Our Congressmen So Much?" in *Congress in Change: Evolution and Reform*, Norman J. Ornstein, ed. (New York: Praeger Publishers, 1975), pp. 277-287.

[109] Timothy J. Conlan, "Federalism and Competing Values in the Reagan Administration," *Publius: The Journal of Federalism*, vol. 16, no. 1 (Winter 1986), p. 30.

assistance recipients and suing localities which sought to retain aggressive affirmative action hiring policies.[110]

FEDERAL GRANTS TO STATE AND LOCAL GOVERNMENTS IN THE 21ST CENTURY

Some observers thought that the number of federal grants to state and local governments and outlays for federal grants to state and local governments might fall during George W. Bush's presidency (2001-2009), given federal budgetary pressures created by what many called the "war on terror" following 9/11, President Bush's commitment to reducing the annual federal budget deficit and addressing the federal debt, and the Republican Party's winning majority status in the House of Representatives from 2001 to 2007 and in the Senate for portions of 2001 and 2002, and from 2003 to 2007. Yet, outlays for federal grants to state and local governments increased during his presidency, from $285.8 billion in FY2000 to $461.3 billion in FY2008.

Others thought that the "the ascendancy of George W. Bush to the presidency, in concert with a remarkably unified Republican control of the Congress, presaged a period of unified government ... [that would lead to] the arrest and even reversal of federal policy centralization."[111] For example, President Bush used his authority to grant state waivers to increase state flexibility in the use of Medicaid funds and, in his second term, in complying with No Child Left Behind requirements. He also proposed grant consolidations of community development programs, state control of the Head Start program, and waivers of regulations in many low-income programs (called superwaivers).[112] However, despite these efforts, federalism scholars argue that the federal government continued to further centralize its authority in many policy areas during his presidency, often

---

[110] Ibid.

[111] Paul Posner, "The Politics of Coercive Federalism in the Bush Era," *Publius: The Journal of Federalism*, vol. 37, no. 3 (summer 2007), p. 390.

[112] Ibid., p. 392.

with President Bush's approval. For example, President Bush supported the extension of "federal goals and standards to such areas as education testing, sales tax collection, emergency management, infrastructure, and elections administration"[113] and the imposition of restrictions on partial-birth abortions, new work requirements for TANF recipients, and new standards for issuing secure driver's licenses. President Bush also supported legislative efforts to prohibit same-sex marriage.[114]

The expansion and centralization of the federal grants-in-aid system continued under President Barack Obama and has continued, albeit counter to his recommendations, under President Trump. As shown in Table 2, outlays for federal grants to state and local governments has continued to increase in recent years (from $660.8 billion in FY2016 to $674.7 billion in FY2017, and to an anticipated $728.0 billion in FY2018), largely due to increased outlays for Medicaid (increasing from $368.3 billion in FY2016 to $374.7 billion in FY2017, and to an anticipated $400.4 billion in FY2018). However, outlays for federal grants to state and local governments has increased in other policy areas as well.[115]

As shown in Table 4, the number of federal grants to state and local governments has also increased, from 664 in 1998, to 953 in 2009, 996 in 2012, 1,188 in 2015, and 1,274 in 2018. In addition, the emphasis on categorical grants has been retained, as 1,253 of the 1,274 funded federal grants to state and local governments in 2018 were categorical grants, and 21 were block grants.

Also, despite UMRA, unfunded federal mandates have continued to be issued in many policy areas. For example, CBO reports that from January 1, 2006, to December 31, 2018, 217 laws were enacted with at least one intergovernmental mandate as defined under UMRA. These laws imposed 443 mandates on state and local governments, with 16 of these mandates exceeding UMRA's threshold, 14 with estimated costs that could not be

---

[113] Ibid., pp. 390-391.

[114] Tim Conlan and John Dinan, "Federalism, the Bush Administration, and the Transformation of American Conservatism," *Publius: The Journal of Federalism*, vol. 37, no. 3 (Summer 2007), pp. 279-303.

[115] OMB, *Budget of the United States Government, Fiscal Year 2019: Historical Tables*, Table 12.3, Total Outlays for Grants to State and Local Governments, at http:// www.whitehouse. gov/omb/budget/Historicals.

determined, and 413 with estimated costs below the threshold.[116] CBO reported that hundreds of other laws had an effect on state and local government budgets, but those laws did not meet UMRA's definition of a federal mandate.[117]

Grant conditions, historically the predominant means used to impose federal control over state and local government actions, have also continued to be used to promote national goals. For example, many observers consider the adoption of the No Child Left Behind Act of 2001, signed into law on January 8, 2002, to be President George W. Bush's signature federalism achievement. Although the act allows states to define the standards used for testing, it imposed federal testing, teaching, and accountability standards on states and school districts that, overall, significantly increased federal influence on public elementary and secondary education throughout the nation.[118] In addition, during his presidency, the Help America Vote Act of 2002 instituted "sweeping new federal standards, along with new funding, that regulated significant features of state and local election processes."[119]

---

[116] CBO, *Laws Enacted Between 2006 and 2018 That Contain Mandates*, at https://www.cbo.gov/publication/51335; and CBO, "Laws That Contain Mandates," at https://www.cbo.gov/umra-search/law.

[117] CBO, *A Review of CBO's Activities in 2008 Under the Unfunded Mandates Reform Act*, March 2009, p. 48, at http://www.cbo.gov/ftpdocs/100xx/doc10058/03-31-UMRA.pdf; CBO, *A Review of CBO's Activities in 2010 Under the Unfunded Mandates Reform Act*, March 2011, p. 5, at http://www.cbo.gov/ftpdocs/121xx/doc12117/03-31- UMRA.pdf; CBO, *A Review of CBO's Activities in 2011 Under the Unfunded Mandates Reform Act*, March 2012, pp. 5-7, at http://www.cbo.gov/sites/default/files/cbofiles/attachments/03-30-UMRA.pdf; CBO, *A Review of CBO's Activities in 2012 Under the Unfunded Mandates Reform Act*, March 2013, pp. 5-9, at http://www.cbo.gov/sites/default/files/cbofiles/attachments/ 44032_UMRA.pdf; CBO, *A Review of CBO's Activities in 2013 Under the Unfunded Mandates Reform Act*, March 2014, p. 5, at http://www.cbo.gov/sites/default/files/cbofiles/attachments/45209- UMRA.pdf; CBO, *A Review of CBO's Activities in 2014 Under the Unfunded Mandates Reform Act*, March 2015, p. 5, at http://www.cbo.gov/sites/default/files/cbofiles/attachments/50051-UMRA.pdf; and CBO, *Laws Enacted Between 2006 and 2016 That Contain Mandates*, at https://www.cbo.gov/publication/51335.

[118] For further analysis, see CRS Report RL33960, *The Elementary and Secondary Education Act, as Amended by the No Child Left Behind Act: A Primer*, by Rebecca R. Skinner.

[119] Paul Posner, "The Politics of Coercive Federalism in the Bush Era," *Publius: The Journal of Federalism*, vol. 37, no. 3 (Summer 2007), p. 395. For further information and analysis of the Help America Vote Act, see CRS Report RL32685, *Election Reform: The Help America Vote Act and Issues for Congress*, by Eric A. Fischer and Kevin J. Coleman.

President Obama did not issue a formal federalism plan and did not formally advocate a major shift in funding priorities within functional categories. Instead, the Obama Administration attempted to cultivate

> a place-based approach, customizing support for communities based on their specific assets and challenges. This new approach seeks out communities' plans or vision for addressing a set of challenges and then works across agency and program silos to support those communities in implementing their plans.[120]

However, the expansion of Medicaid eligibility under P.L. 111-148, the Patient Protection and Affordable Care Act (ACA), which President Obama strongly endorsed, increased health care's position as the leading category of federal assistance to state and local governments. The ACA also either authorized or amended 71 federal categorical grants to state and local governments, further enhancing the role of categorical grants in the intergovernmental grant-in-aid system.[121]

The Obama Administration did not formally advocate a major shift in funding priorities from categorical grants to block grants, or from block grants to categorical grants. However, the number of funded block grants declined somewhat during the Obama Administration, from 24 in 2009 to 20 in 2016. Also, although the Obama Administration did support ARRA's funding for two relatively significant temporary block grants (the $53.6 billion Government Services State Fiscal Stabilization Fund for public education; and the $3.2 billion Energy Efficiency and Conservation Block Grant for energy efficiency and conservation programs) and ARRA's provision of additional, temporary funding to TANF ($5 billion), the Child Care and Development Block Grant ($2 billion), the Community Development Block Grant ($1 billion), the Community Services Block Grant ($1 billion), and the Native American Housing Block Grant ($510

---

[120] OMB, *Budget of the United States Government, Fiscal Year 2017, Analytical Perspectives: Special Topics, Aid to State and Local Governments*, p. 269, at https://www.whitehouse.gov/sites/default/files/omb/budget/fy2017/assets/ap_15_state_and_local.pdf.

[121] U.S. General Services Administration, "Catalog of Federal Domestic Assistance," at https://www.cfda.gov/.

million) programs, the Obama Administration generally advocated enactment of new competitive categorical grant programs (e.g., TIGER surface transportation grants and Race to the Top education grants) rather than the expansion of existing block grants or the creation of new ones.[122] However, the Obama Administration did advocate the consolidation of categorical grant programs in several functional areas as a means to reduce duplication and promote program efficiency. For example, the Obama Administration supported the consolidation of dozens of surface transportation categorical grant programs into other surface transportation categorical grant programs in P.L. 112-141, the Moving Ahead for Progress in the 21st Century Act of 2012 (MAP-21).[123] The Obama Administration also advocated the merging of categorical grant programs in the Department of Homeland Security as a means to "better target these funds."[124]

The Trump Administration indicated in its FY2018 budget request that it intended to refocus federal grants on "the highest priority areas," provide "a greater role for state and local governments," "slow the growth of grant spending over the 10-year budget window," and "rein in the growth of Medicaid."[125]

---

[122] For additional information concerning TIGER grants see CRS Report R43464, *Federal Support for Streetcars: Frequently Asked Questions*, by William J. Mallett. For additional information concerning Race to the Top grants see CRS Report R41355, *Administration's Proposal to Reauthorize the Elementary and Secondary Education Act: Comparison to Current Law*, by Rebecca R. Skinner et al.; and CRS Report R41267, *Elementary and Secondary School Teachers: Policy Context, Federal Programs, and ESEA Reauthorization Issues*, by Jeffrey J. Kuenzi.

[123] For additional information concerning MAP-21 see CRS Report R42762, *Surface Transportation Funding and Programs Under MAP-21: Moving Ahead for Progress in the 21st Century Act (P.L. 112-141)*, coordinated by Robert S. Kirk.

[124] OMB, *Budget of the United States Government, Fiscal Year 2015: Analytical Perspectives*, p. 248, at http://www.whitehouse.gov/sites/default/files/omb/budget/fy2015/assets/spec.pdf. For additional information concerning the merging of categorical grant programs in the Department of Homeland Security into a proposed National Preparedness Grant Program see CRS Report R42985, *Issues in Homeland Security Policy for the 113th Congress*, coordinated by William L. Painter.

[125] OMB, *Budget of the United States Government, Fiscal Year 2018, Analytical Perspectives: Special Topics, Aid to State and Local Governments*, p. 171, at https:// www.whitehouse.gov/sites/whitehouse.gov/files/omb/budget/fy2018/ spec.pdf.

This budget proposes to cap federal funding for the Medicaid program, to establish a state matching requirement for the Supplemental Nutrition Assistance Program, to eliminate the Community Development Block Grant and Social Services Block Grant programs, and to make other reductions that reestablish an appropriate federal-state fiscal relationship and contribute to achieve a balanced federal budget by 2027. Among other grant initiatives, the budget proposes to establish a 25% non-federal cost match for FEMA [Federal Emergency Management Agency] preparedness grant awards that currently require no cost match ... authorizes a new Federal Emergency Response Fund to rapidly respond to public health outbreaks ... reforms the Centers for Disease Control and Prevention through a new $500 million block grant to increase state flexibility and focus on the leading public health challenges specific to each state ... [and] includes $200 billion in budget authority related to the [Trump Administration's] infrastructure initiative.[126]

The Trump Administration continued to advocate for these objectives in its FY2019 and FY2020 budget requests. For example, the Administration indicated in its FY2019 budget request that

Over many decades, the increasing number of grants and size of grants has created overlap between programs, and complexity for grantees, and has made it difficult to compare program performance and conduct oversight. The multiple layers of grants administration can increase the cost of administration and create inefficiencies and duplication. Less Federal control gives State and local recipients more flexibility to use their knowledge of local conditions and need to administer programs and projects more efficiently. The 2019 Budget takes steps toward limiting the Federal role, and reducing spending.

This budget slows the growth of grant spending over the 10-year budget window and, in particular, starts to rein in the growth of Medicaid ... The Budget provides $749 billion in outlays for aid to State and local governments in 2019, an increase of 3% from 2018. The increase is entirely due to spending for the Administration's infrastructure initiative;

---

[126] Ibid.

all grant spending other than Medicaid and the infrastructure initiative will decline by 11% in 2019.[127]

The Trump Administration repeated its intent to slow the growth of federal aid to state and local governments in its FY2020 budget request:

> This budget slows the growth of grant spending over the 10-year budget window and, in particular, starts to rein in the growth of Medicaid, which accounts for 56 percent of total grant spending to State and local governments. The Budget provides $751 billion in outlays for aid to State and local governments in 2020, an increase of less than one percent from spending in 2019.[128]

Among its proposals to slow the growth of federal aid to state and local governments and improve federal grant performance, the Administration recommended that

- Medicaid be converted to a block grant or be subject to a per capita spending cap indexed to the Consumer Price Index "to support States as they transition to more sustainable health care programs and encourage them to pursue innovative ideas to that aim to curb costs moving forward."[129]
- states be provided "maximum flexibility over their Medicaid programs" to place the program "on a sound fiscal path."[130]
- funding be eliminated for "lower priority grant programs," such as the Sea Grant, Coastal Zone Management Grants, and the Pacific Coastal Salmon Recovery Fund.[131]

---

[127] OMB, *Budget of the United States Government, Fiscal Year 2019, Analytical Perspectives: Special Topics, Aid to State and Local Governments*, pp. 197, 198, at https:// www.gpo.gov/fdsys/pkg/BUDGET-2019-PER/pdf/BUDGET-2019-PER-7-1.pdf.

[128] OMB, *Budget of the United States Government, Fiscal Year 2020, Analytical Perspectives: Special Topics, Aid to State and Local Governments*, p. 231, at https:// www.whitehouse. gov/omb/analytical-perspectives/.

[129] Ibid., p. 235.

[130] Ibid.

[131] Ibid., p. 233.

- funding be eliminated for Community Development Block Grants and the Economic Development Administration.[132]

In addition, the Trump Administration noted that its President's Management Agenda, released in March 2018, included a cross-agency priority goal of achieving results-oriented accountability for federal grants funding. The Administration's goal is to ensure that federal grants to state and local governments are "delivered to intended recipients as efficiently as possible" by standardizing the grants management process and data, building shared IT infrastructure, managing risk, and achieving program goals and objectives.[133] The Administration also included proposals "to require able-bodied adults participating in the Supplemental Nutrition Assistance Program (SNAP) enter and re-enter the job market and work toward self-sufficiency."[134]

CONGRESSIONAL ISSUES

As the data in Table 2, Table 3, and Table 4 attest, outlays for federal grants to state and local governments, in both nominal and constant dollars, and the number of federal grants to state and local governments have continued to increase since the mid-1980s. Given its increased size and cost, providing effective congressional oversight of federal grants to state and local governments can be a daunting task. Given the decentralized nature of the congressional committee system, Congress is well positioned to provide effective oversight of individual federal grants to state and local governments. However, it could be argued that the decentralized nature of the congressional committee system is not optimally conducive to providing effective oversight of the interactive effects of multiple federal grants to state and local governments, or of the potential interactive effects of federal grants to state and local governments and federal tax policy.

---

[132] Ibid., p. 234.
[133] Ibid., p. 233.
[134] Ibid., p. 236.

Federal Grants to State and Local Governments 87

In the past, the independent, bipartisan ACIR, which operated from 1959 to 1996, provided Congress and others a series of authoritative reports on the status and operation of intergovernmental grants, both as individual programs and as a collective system. GAO has published several reports over the years on federal grants that have helped to fill the informational and analytic void left by ACIR's demise.[135] However, it could be argued that Congress may wish to examine whether a reconstituted ACIR, perhaps one that focuses on the structure and operation of the intergovernmental system as a whole, might prove useful as an additional source of information and analysis as it conducts oversight of the federal grants to state and local governments. For example, such an organization could provide an accepted methodology for counting federal grants to state and local governments, and provide Congress periodic assessments of the intergovernmental grant system's overall performance.

CONCLUDING REMARKS

It could be argued that the recent upward trend in outlays for federal grants to state and local governments is about to end because there is a general consensus that anticipated growth in federal discretionary spending, which includes outlays for federal grants to state and local governments, may be targeted for reductions as part of an effort to address the federal deficit and debt. However, Congress's historical tendency to use federal grants to state and local governments as a means to create jobs and promote national economic growth suggests that the upward trend in federal grant outlays and federal grant numbers that has been experienced

---

[135] ACIR's funding was withdrawn following the release for public comment and a hearing on a draft ACIR report on federal mandates. ACIR was required by UMRA to conduct the study, and to make recommendations for mitigating the effect mandates have on state and local governments. The draft report recommended the elimination of a number of federal mandates which had strong support in Congress. ACIR's commission members killed the report in a party-line vote. Many observers concluded that the draft report led to ACIR's losing its funding. See, John Kincaid, "Review of 'The Politics of Unfunded Mandates: Whither Federalism?' by Paul L. Posner," *The Academy of Political Science*, vol. 114, no. 2 (Summer 1999), pp. 322-323.

over the past several decades may continue, although at a slower pace. President Trump's FY2020 budget request estimates that total outlays for federal grants to state and local governments will increase from $696.5 billion in FY2018 to an anticipated $749.5 billion in FY2019 and $750.7 billion in FY2020.[136]

In retrospect, with the exception of the early 1980s, federal grant funding, the number of federal grants, and the issuance of federal mandates have increased under both Democratic and Republican Congresses and Presidents. Historically, there have been notable differences between the two parties' approaches toward federalism. Although both parties have generally opposed unfunded federal mandates, the Republican Party has done so more aggressively, as evidenced by its 1994 Contract With America, sponsorship of UMRA, and recent legislative efforts to broaden UMRA's coverage to include, when requested by the chair or ranking Member of a committee, the prospective costs of legislation that would change conditions of federal financial assistance.[137] The Republican Party has also advocated the devolution of certain federal grant-in- aid programs to state and local governments while the Democratic Party has generally opposed devolution. The Republican Party has also been more aggressive in its support of the decentralization of grants-in-aid decisionmaking to state and local governments through the consolidation of categorical grants into block grants, for revenue sharing, and administrative relief from various grant conditions. But, overall, the historical record suggests that for most Members of both political parties, regardless of their personal ideological preferences, federalism principles are often subordinated to other policy goals, such as reducing the federal budget deficit, promoting social values or environmental protection, and guaranteeing equal treatment and opportunity for the disadvantaged. As long at this continues to be the case, and the public continues to express support for specific

---

[136] OMB, *Budget of the United States Government, Fiscal Year 2020: Historical Tables*, Table 12.1, Summary Comparison of Total Outlays for Grants to State and Local Governments: 1940–2024 (in Current Dollars, as Percentages of Total Outlays, as Percentages of GDP, and in Constant (FY 2012) Dollars) at http://www.whitehouse.gov/omb/budget/Historicals.

[137] For additional information and analysis, see CRS Report R40957, *Unfunded Mandates Reform Act: History, Impact, and Issues*, by Robert Jay Dilger and Richard S. Beth.

Federal Grants to State and Local Governments

government programs– even if they generally oppose "big" government as a whole there is little evidence to suggest that the general historical trends of increasing numbers of federal grants to state and local governments, increasing outlays for those grants, an emphasis on categorical grants, and continued enactment of federal mandates, both funded and unfunded, are likely to change.

In: Key Congressional Reports for May 2019   ISBN: 978-1-53616-382-7
Editor: Piotr Meza   © 2019 Nova Science Publishers, Inc.

Chapter 3

UNFUNDED MANDATES REFORM ACT: HISTORY, IMPACT, AND ISSUES[*]

Robert Jay Dilger

ABSTRACT

The Unfunded Mandates Reform Act of 1995 (UMRA) culminated years of effort by state and local government officials and business interests to control, if not eliminate, the imposition of unfunded intergovernmental and private-sector federal mandates. Advocates argued the statute was needed to forestall federal legislation and regulations that imposed obligations on state and local governments or businesses that resulted in higher costs and inefficiencies. Opponents argued that federal mandates may be necessary to achieve national objectives in areas where voluntary action by state and local governments and business failed to achieve desired results.

UMRA provides a framework for the Congressional Budget Office (CBO) to estimate the direct costs of mandates in legislative proposals to state and local governments and to the private sector, and for issuing agencies to estimate the direct costs of mandates in proposed regulations

---

[*] This is an edited, reformatted and augmented version of Congressional Research Service, Publication No. R40957, dated May 22, 2019.

to regulated entities. Aside from these informational requirements, UMRA controls the imposition of mandates only through a procedural mechanism allowing Congress to decline to consider unfunded intergovernmental mandates in proposed legislation if they are estimated to cost more than specified threshold amounts. UMRA applies to any provision in legislation, statute, or regulation that would impose an enforceable duty upon state and local governments or the private sector. It does not apply to duties stemming from participation in voluntary federal programs; rules issued by independent regulatory agencies; rules issued without a general notice of proposed rulemaking; and rules and legislative provisions that cover individual constitutional rights, discrimination, emergency assistance, grant accounting and auditing procedures, national security, treaty obligations, and certain elements of Social Security. In most instances, UMRA also does not apply to conditions of federal assistance.

State and local government officials argue that UMRA's coverage should be broadened, with special consideration given to including conditions of federal financial assistance. During the 116th Congress, H.R. 300, the Unfunded Mandates Information and Transparency Act of 2019, would broaden UMRA's coverage to include both direct and indirect costs, such as foregone profits and costs passed onto consumers, and, when requested by the chair or ranking member of a committee, the prospective costs of legislation that would change conditions of federal financial assistance. The bill also would make private-sector mandates subject to a substantive point of order and remove UMRA's exemption for rules issued by most independent agencies. The House approved similar legislation during the 112th, 113th, 114th, and 115th Congresses.

This chapter examines debates over what constitutes an unfunded federal mandate and UMRA's implementation. It focuses on UMRA's requirement that CBO issue written cost estimate statements for federal mandates in legislation, its procedures for raising points of order in the House and Senate concerning unfunded federal mandates in legislation, and its requirement that federal agencies prepare written cost estimate statements for federal mandates in rules. It also assesses UMRA's impact on federal mandates and arguments concerning UMRA's future, focusing on UMRA's definitions, exclusions, and exceptions that currently exempt many federal actions with potentially significant financial impacts on nonfederal entities. An examination of the rise of unfunded federal mandates as a national issue and a summary of UMRA's legislative history are provided in Appendix A. Citations to UMRA points of order raised in the House and Senate are provided in Appendix B.

AN OVERVIEW OF UMRA, ITS ORIGINS, AND PROVISIONS

Overview

The Unfunded Mandates Reform Act of 1995 (UMRA) established requirements for enacting certain legislation and issuing certain regulations that would impose enforceable duties on state, local, or tribal governments or on the private sector.[1] UMRA refers to obligations imposed by such legislation and regulations as "mandates" (either "intergovernmental" or "private sector," depending on the entities affected). The direct cost to affected entities of meeting these obligations are referred to as "mandate costs," and when the federal government does not provide funding to cover these costs, the mandate is termed "unfunded."

UMRA incorporates numerous definitions, exclusions, and exceptions that specify what forms and types of mandates are subject to its requirements, termed "covered mandates." Covered mandates do not include many federal actions with potentially significant financial impacts on nonfederal entities. This chapter's primary purpose is to describe the kinds of legislative and regulatory provisions that are subject to UMRA's requirements, and, on this basis, to assess UMRA's impact on federal mandates. The report also examines debates that occurred, both before and since UMRA's enactment, concerning what kinds of provisions UMRA ought to cover, and considers the implications of experience under UMRA for possible future revisions of its scope of coverage.

This chapter also describes the requirements UMRA imposes on congressional and agency actions to establish covered mandates. For most legislation and regulations covered by UMRA, these requirements are only informational. For reported legislation that would impose covered mandates on the intergovernmental or private sectors, UMRA requires the Congressional Budget Office (CBO) to provide an estimate of mandate costs. Similarly, for regulations that would impose covered mandates on

---

[1] P.L. 104-4; 109 Stat. 48 *et seq.*; and 2 U.S.C. §§602, 632, 653, 658-658(g), 1501-1504, 1511-1516, 1531-1538, 1551-1556, and 1571.

the intergovernmental or private sectors, UMRA requires that the issuing agency provide an estimate of mandate costs (although the specifics of the estimates required for legislation and for regulations differ somewhat). Also, solely for legislation that would impose covered intergovernmental mandates, UMRA establishes a point of order in each house of Congress through which the chamber can decline to consider the legislation. This chapter examines UMRA's implementation, focusing on the respective requirements for mandate cost estimates on legislation and regulations, and on the point of order procedure for legislation proposing unfunded intergovernmental mandates.

Origin

The concept of unfunded mandates rose to national prominence during the 1970s and 1980s primarily through the response of state and local government officials to changes in the nature of federal intergovernmental grant-in-aid programs and to regulations affecting state and local governments. Before then, the federal government had traditionally relied on the provision of voluntary grant-in-aid funding to encourage state and local governments to perform particular activities or provide particular services that were deemed to be in the national interest. These arrangements were viewed as reflecting, at least in part, the constitutional protections afforded state and local governments as separate, sovereign entities. During the 1970s and 1980s, however, state and local government advocates argued that a "dramatic shift" occurred in the way the federal government dealt with states and localities. Instead of relying on the technique of subsidization to achieve its goals, the federal government was increasingly relying on "new, more intrusive, and more compulsory" programs and regulations that required compliance under the threat of civil or criminal penalties, imposed federal fiscal sanctions for failure to comply with the programs' requirements, or preempted state and local government authority to act in the area.[2] These new, more intrusive and compulsory programs and regulations came to be referred to as "unfunded mandates" on states and localities.

State and local government advocates viewed these unfunded federal intergovernmental mandates as inconsistent with the traditional view of American federalism, which was based on cooperation, not compulsion. They argued that a federal statute was needed to forestall federal legislation and regulations that imposed obligations on state and local governments that resulted in higher costs and inefficiencies. UMRA's enactment in 1995 culminated years of effort by state and local government officials to control, if not eliminate, the imposition of unfunded federal mandates.

Advocates of regulatory reform adapted the concept of unfunded mandates to their view that federal regulations often impose financial burdens on private enterprise. Critics of government regulation of business argued that these regulations impose unfunded mandates on the private sector, just as federal programs and regulations impose fiscal obligations on state and local governments. As a result, various business organizations subject to increased federal regulation came to support state and local government efforts to enact federal legislation to control unfunded federal intergovernmental mandates. Private-sector advocates argued that they, too, should be provided relief from what they viewed as burdensome federal regulations that hinder economic growth.[3] Subsequently, proposals to control unfunded mandates that were developed in the early 1990s contained provisions addressing not only federal intergovernmental mandates, but federal private-sector mandates as well.

During floor debate on legislation that became UMRA, sponsors of the measure emphasized its role in bringing "our system of federalism back

---

[2] U.S. Advisory Commission on Intergovernmental Relations (ACIR), *Regulatory Federalism: Policy, Process, Impact, and Reform*, A-95 (Washington, DC: ACIR, 1984), pp. 1-18.

[3] Mary McElvenn, "The Federal Impact on Business," *Nation's Business*, vol. 79, no. 1 (January 1991), pp. 23-26; David Warner, "Regulations' Staggering Costs," *Nation's Business*, vol. 80, no. 6 (June 1992), pp. 50-53; Michael Barrier, "Taxing the Man Behind the Tree," *Nation's Business*, vol. 81, no. 9 (September 1993), pp. 31, 32; and Michael Barrier, "Mandates Foes Smell a Victory," *Nation's Business*, vol. 82, no. 9 (September 1994), p. 50.

into balance, by serving as a check against the easy imposition of unfunded mandates."[4] Opponents argued that federal mandates may be necessary to achieve national objectives in areas where voluntary action by state and local governments or business failed to achieve desired results. See Appendix A for a more detailed examination of the rise of unfunded federal mandates as a national issue and of UMRA's legislative history.[5]

SUMMARY OF UMRA'S PROVISIONS

The congressional commitment to reshaping intergovernmental relations through UMRA is reflected in its eight statutory purposes:

1) to strengthen the partnership between the Federal Government and State, local, and tribal governments;
2) to end the imposition, in the absence of full consideration by Congress, of Federal mandates on State, local, and tribal governments without adequate Federal funding, in a manner that may displace other essential State, local, and tribal governmental priorities;
3) to assist Congress in its consideration of proposed legislation establishing or revising Federal programs containing Federal mandates affecting State, local, and tribal governments, and the private sector by—(A) providing for the development of information about the nature and size of mandates in proposed legislation; and (B) establishing a mechanism to bring such information to the attention of the Senate and the House of Representatives before the Senate and the House of Representatives vote on proposed legislation;

---

[4] Senator Dirk Kempthorne, "Unfunded Mandate Reform Act," remarks in the Senate, *Congressional Record*, vol. 141, part 1 (January 12, 1995), p. 1166.
[5] Senator Frank Lautenberg, "Unfunded Mandate Reform Act," remarks in the Senate, *Congressional Record*, vol. 141, part 1 (January 12, 1995), p. 1193.

Unfunded Mandates Reform Act

4) to promote informed and deliberate decisions by Congress on the appropriateness of Federal mandates in any particular instance;

5) to require that Congress consider whether to provide funding to assist State, local, and tribal governments in complying with Federal mandates, to require analyses of the impact of private sector mandates, and through the dissemination of that information provide informed and deliberate decisions by Congress and Federal agencies and retain competitive balance between the public and private sectors;

6) to establish a point-of-order vote on the consideration in the Senate and House of Representatives of legislation containing significant Federal intergovernmental mandates without providing adequate funding to comply with such mandates;

7) to assist Federal agencies in their consideration of proposed regulations affecting State, local, and tribal governments, by—(A) requiring that Federal agencies develop a process to enable the elected and other officials of State, local, and tribal governments to provide input when Federal agencies are developing regulations; and (B) requiring that Federal agencies prepare and consider estimates of the budgetary impact of regulations containing Federal mandates upon State, local, and tribal governments and the private sector before adopting such regulations, and ensuring that small governments are given special consideration in that process; and

8) to begin consideration of the effect of previously imposed Federal mandates, including the impact on State, local, and tribal governments of Federal court interpretations of Federal statutes and regulations that impose Federal intergovernmental mandates.[6]

---

[6] 2 U.S.C. §1501.

To achieve its purposes, UMRA's Title I established a procedural framework to shape congressional deliberations concerning covered unfunded intergovernmental and private-sector mandates. This framework requires CBO to estimate the direct mandate costs of intergovernmental mandates exceeding $50 million and of private-sector mandates exceeding $100 million (in any fiscal year) proposed in any measure reported from committee. It also establishes a point of order against consideration of legislation that contained intergovernmental mandates with mandate costs estimated to exceed the threshold amount. In addition, Title II requires federal administrative agencies, unless otherwise prohibited by law, to assess the effects on state and local governments and the private sector of proposed and final federal rules and to prepare a written statement of estimated costs and benefits for any mandate requiring an expenditure exceeding $100 million in any given year. All threshold amounts under these provisions are adjusted annually for inflation.[7] In 2019, the threshold amounts are $82 million for intergovernmental mandates and $164 million for private sector mandates.

In general, the requirements of Titles I and II apply to any provision in legislation, statute, or regulation that would impose an enforceable duty upon state and local governments or the private sector. However, UMRA does not apply to duties stemming from participation in voluntary federal programs, rules issued by independent regulatory agencies, or rules issued without a general notice of proposed rulemaking. Exceptions also exist for rules and legislative provisions that cover individual constitutional rights, discrimination, emergency assistance, grant accounting and auditing procedures, national security, treaty obligations, and certain elements of Social Security legislation. In most instances, UMRA also does not apply to conditions of federal assistance.[8]

UMRA's Title III also called for a review of federal intergovernmental mandates to be completed by the now-defunct U.S. Advisory Commission on Intergovernmental Relations (ACIR) within 18 months of enactment.[9]

---

[7] 2 U.S.C. §658; and 2 U.S.C. §1532.
[8] 2 U.S.C. 658(5)(A), (7)(A) and (10), and 2 U.S.C. §1503.
[9] 2 U.S.C. §§1551-1553.

ACIR completed a preliminary report on federal intergovernmental mandates in January 1996, but the final report was not released.[10] Finally, UMRA's Title IV authorizes judicial review of federal agency compliance with Title II provisions.[11]

WHAT IS AN UNFUNDED FEDERAL MANDATE?

One of the first issues Congress faced when considering unfunded federal mandate legislation was how to define the concept. For example, during a November 3, 1993, congressional hearing on unfunded mandate legislation, Senator Judd Gregg argued,

> Any bill reported out this committee [Governmental Affairs] should precisely define what constitutes an unfunded federal mandate... An appropriate definition is crucial because it will drive almost everything else that occurs. Without a precise definition, endless litigation would likely ensue over what is and what is not an unfunded federal mandate. A true solution to the problem cannot allow it to become more cost-effective to pay the bills than to seek payment. Furthermore, the definition cannot be too restrictive. It would solve nothing to cut off one particular type of unfunded mandate, only to prompt Congressional use of another to accelerate.[12]

---

[10] ACIR funding was withdrawn following the release for public comment and a hearing on the draft report on federal mandates. ACIR was required by UMRA to conduct the study and to make recommendations for mitigating the effect mandates have on state and local governments. The draft report recommended the elimination of a number of federal mandates which had strong support in Congress. ACIR's commission members decided not to release the report in a party-line vote. Most observers concluded that the draft report was a contributing factor in ACIR's losing its funding. See, John Kincaid, "Review of 'The Politics of Unfunded Mandates: Whither Federalism?' by Paul L. Posner," *Political Science Quarterly*, vol. 114, no. 2 (Summer 1999), pp. 322-323.

[11] 2 U.S.C. §1571.

[12] U.S. Congress, Senate Committee on Governmental Affairs, *Federal Mandates on State and Local Governments*, 103rd Cong., 1st sess., November 3, 1993, S.Hrg. 103-405 (Washington: GPO, 1994), p. 66.

The difficulty Congress faced in defining the concept was that there were strong disagreements, among academics, practitioners, and elected officials, over how to define it. These disagreements appear motivated by concerns about which classes of costs incurred by state and local governments (or the private sector) should be identified and controlled for in the legislative or regulatory process. They have typically been conducted, however, as disputes about which classes of such costs are properly considered as obligatory requirements on the affected entities. The resulting focus on whether or not particular kinds of costs are "mandatory" has tended to obscure consideration of the core policy question concerning what kinds of costs should be subjected to informational requirements or procedural restrictions such as those that UMRA establishes.

Competing Definitions

In 1979, one set of federalism scholars defined unfunded federal intergovernmental mandates broadly as including "any responsibility, action, procedure, or anything else that is imposed by constitutional, administrative, executive, or judicial action as a direct order or that is required as a condition of aid."[13] In 1984, ACIR offered a rationale for defining unfunded federal intergovernmental mandates which excluded conditions of aid. ACIR argued that defining unfunded federal intergovernmental mandates was difficult because federal grant-in-aid programs typically include both incentives and mandates backed by sanctions or penalties:

> Few federal programs affecting state and local governments are pure types Every grant-in-aid program, including General Revenue Sharing,

---

[13] Catherine H. Lovell, Max Neiman, Robert Kneisel, Adam Rose, and Charles Tobin, *Federal and State Mandating on Local Governments: Report to the National Science Foundation* (Riverside, CA: University of California, June 1979), p. 32.

the least restrictive form of aid, comes with federal "strings" attached. Here, as in other areas, there is no such thing as a free lunch....

In the intergovernmental sphere, then, [mandates] and subsidy are less like different parts of a dichotomy than opposing ends of a continuum. At one extreme is the general support grant with just a few associated conditions or rules; at the other is the costly, but wholly unfunded, national "mandate." In between are many programs combining subsidy and [mandate] approaches, in varying degrees and in various ways.[14]

ACIR argued that because federal grant-in-aid programs typically combine subsidy and mandate approaches, grant-in-aid programs should be classified according to their degree of compulsion. It argued that conditions of grant aid should not be classified as a mandate because "one of the most important features of the grant-in-aid is that its acceptance is still viewed legally as entirely voluntary" and "although it is difficult for many jurisdictions to forego substantial financial benefits, this option remains real."[15] ACIR also argued that most grant conditions affect only the administration of those activities funded by the program, and "grants-in-aid generally provide significant benefits to the recipient jurisdiction."[16]

ACIR argued that federal grant-in-aid programs that "cannot be side-stepped, without incurring some federal sanction, by the simple expedient of refusing to participate in a single federal assistance program" should be considered mandates.[17] ACIR provided four examples of federal activities that, in the absence of sufficient compensatory funding, could be an unfunded intergovernmental mandate: (1) direct legal orders that must be complied with under the threat of civil or criminal penalties; (2)

---

[14] ACIR, *Regulatory Federalism: Policy, Process, Impact, and Reform*, A-95 (Washington, DC: ACIR, 1984), p. 4.

[15] Ibid. The Supreme Court has emphasized the voluntary nature of federal grant programs and the fact that states and private parties remain free to accept or reject the offer of federal funds and thus avoid the attached conditions. "This Court has repeatedly upheld against constitutional challenge the use of this technique to induce governments and private parties to cooperate voluntarily with federal policy." Fullilove v. Klutznick, 448 U.S. 448, 474 (1980) (Chief Justice Burger announcing judgment of the Court); see also South Dakota v. Dole, 483 U.S. 203 (1987).

[16] Ibid.

[17] Ibid., p. 7.

102 Robert Jay Dilger

crosscutting or generally applicable requirements imposed on grants across the board to further national social and economic policies; (3) programs that impose federal fiscal sanctions in one program area or activity to influence state and local government policy in another area; and (4) federal preemption of state and local government law.[18]

In 1994, several organizations representing state and local governments issued a set of unfunded mandate principles which defined unfunded federal intergovernmental mandates as

- any federal requirement that compels state or local activities resulting in additional state or local expenditures;
- any federal requirement that imposes additional conditions or increases the level of state and local expenditures needed to maintain eligibility for existing federal grants;
- any reduction in the rate of federal matching for existing grants; and
- any federal requirement that reduces the productivity of existing state or local taxes and fees and/or that increases the cost of raising state and local revenue (including the costs of borrowing).[19]

Also in 1994, ACIR introduced the term "federally induced costs" to replace what it described as "the pejorative and definitional baggage associated with the term 'mandates.'"[20] ACIR identified the following types of federal activities that expose states and localities to additional costs:

- statutory direct orders;
- total and partial statutory preemptions;

---

[18] Ibid., pp. 7-10.

[19] National Conference of State Legislatures, "Unfunded Mandate Principles," Washington, DC, 1994, p. 1, cited in CRS Report 95-62, *Mandates and the Congress*, by Sandra S. Osbourn (out of print; available to congressional clients by request).

[20] ACIR, *Federally Induced Costs Affecting State and Local Governments*, M-193 (Washington, DC: ACIR, 1994), p. 3.

- grant-in-aid conditions on spending and administration, including matching requirements;
- federal income tax provisions;
- federal court decisions; and
- administrative rules issued by federal agencies, including regulatory delays and nonenforcement.[21]

ACIR defended its inclusion of grant-in-aid conditions in its list of "federally induced costs," which it had excluded from its definition of federal mandates a decade earlier, by asserting that although the option of refusing to accept federal grants "seemed plausible when federal aid constituted a small and highly compartmentalized part of state and local revenues, it overlooks current realities. Many grant conditions have become far more integral to state and local activities—and far less subject to voluntary forbearance—than originally suggested by the contractual model."[22]

On April 28, 1994, John Kincaid, ACIR's executive director, testified at a congressional hearing that legislation concerning unfunded mandates "should recognize that unfunded Federal mandates include, in reality, a range of Federally-induced costs for which reimbursements may be legitimate considerations."[23] State and local government officials generally advocated the inclusion of ACIR's "federally induced costs" in legislation placing conditions on the imposition of unfunded intergovernmental mandates. However, organizations representing various environmental and social groups, such as the Committee on the Appointment of People With Disabilities, the Natural Resources Defense Council, the American Federation of State, County, and Municipal Employees, and the Service Employees International Union, argued that ACIR's definition was too

---

[21] Ibid., p. 19. ACIR also included laws that expose state and local governments to liability lawsuits, which, at the time, affected such programs as the Superfund toxic wastes cleanup program.

[22] Ibid., p. 20.

[23] U.S. Congress, Senate Committee on Governmental Affairs, *Federal Mandate Reform Legislation*, 103rd Cong., 2nd sess., April 28, 1994, S.Hrg. 103-1019 (Washington: GPO, 1995), p. 56.

104 *Robert Jay Dilger*

broad. These groups testified at various congressional hearings that some federal mandates, particularly those involving the environment and constitutional rights, should be retained, even if they were unfunded.[24]

Statutory Direct Orders

With respect to definitions, there was, and continues to be, a general consensus among federalism scholars, state and local government officials, and other organizations that federal policies which impose unavoidable costs on state and local governments or business are, in the absence of sufficient compensatory funding, unfunded federal mandates. Because statutory direct orders, such as the Equal Employment Opportunity Act of 1972, which bars employment discrimination on the basis of race, color, religion, sex, and national origin, are compulsory, they are considered federal mandates. In the absence of sufficient compensatory funding, they are unfunded federal mandates. However, there was, and continues to be, a general consensus that some statutory direct orders, particularly those involving the guarantee of constitutional rights, should be exempt from legislation placing conditions on the imposition of unfunded federal mandates.[25] For example, on April 28, 1994, then-Governor (and later Senator) Benjamin Nelson, testifying on behalf of the National Governors Association at a congressional hearing on unfunded mandate legislation, argued,

> At the outset, Mr. Chairman, I want to make it absolutely crystal clear that the Governors' position opposing unfunded environmental mandates must not be interpreted as an effort to discontinue environmental legislation and regulations or oppose any individual's civil

---

[24] Ibid., pp. 53-55, 57-63, 68-70, 162-185, 200-230 and 247-249; U.S. Congress, Senate Committee on Governmental Affairs and Senate Committee on the Budget; U.S. Congress, Senate Committee on Governmental Affairs, *Federal Mandates on State and Local Governments*, 103rd Cong., 1st sess., November 3, 1993, S.Hrg. 103-405 (Washington: GPO, 1994), pp. 241-245; and U.S. Congress, Senate Committee on Governmental Affairs, *S.1–Unfunded Mandates*, 104th Cong., 1st sess., January 5, 1995, S.Hrg. 104-392 (Washington: GPO, 1995), pp. 90-107.

[25] U.S. Government Accountability Office (GAO), *Unfunded Mandates: Views Vary About Reform Act's Strengths, Weaknesses, and Options for Improvement*, GAO-05-454, March 31, 2005, pp. 9, 13, 14, at http://www.gao.gov/ new.items/d05454.pdf.

or constitutional rights. The Governors consider the protection of public health and State natural resources as among the most important responsibilities of our office. We all take an oath of office to protect the health and safety of our citizens. In addition, we have worked with Congress over the years to enact strong Federal environmental laws.[26]

Total and Partial Statutory Preemptions

Total and partial preemptions of state and local spending and regulatory authority by the federal government are compulsory, but there was, and continues to be, disagreement concerning whether they should be considered federal mandates, or whether they should be included in legislation designed to provide relief from unfunded federal mandates. Total preemptions in the intergovernmental arena prevent state and local government officials from implementing their own programs in a policy area. For example, states have been "stripped of their powers to engage in economic regulation of airlines, bus, and trucking companies, to establish a compulsory retirement age for their employees other than specified state policymakers and judges, or to regulate bankruptcies with the exception of the establishment of a homestead exemption."[27]

Partial preemption typically is a joint enterprise, "whereby the federal government exerts its constitutional authority to preempt a field and establish minimum national standards, but allows regulatory administration to be delegated to the states if they adopt standards at least as strict as the federal rules."[28] Legally, the state decision to administer a partial preemption program is voluntary. States that do not have a program in a particular area or do not wish to assume the costs of administration and enforcement can opt out and allow the federal government to enforce the standards.[29] Nonetheless, the federal standards apply.

---

[26] U.S. Congress, Senate Committee on Governmental Affairs, *Federal Mandate Reform Legislation*, 103rd Cong., 2nd sess., April 28, 1994, S.Hrg. 103-1019 (Washington: GPO, 1995), p. 7.

[27] Joseph F. Zimmerman, "National-State Relations: Cooperative Federalism in the Twentieth Century," *Publius: The Journal of Federalism*, vol. 31, no. 2 (Spring 2001), p. 23.

[28] ACIR, *Federally Induced Costs Affecting State and Local Governments*, M-193 (Washington, DC: ACIR, 1994), p. 22.

[29] Ibid., p. 23.

106 *Robert Jay Dilger*

Total and partial statutory preemptions are distinct from unfunded federal intergovernmental mandates because they do not necessarily impose costs or require state and local governments to take action. Nonetheless, some federalism scholars and state and local government officials have argued that total and partial statutory preemptions should be included in legislation placing conditions on the imposition of unfunded federal mandates because they can have similar adverse effects on state and local government flexibilities and, in some instances, resources.[30] A leading federalism scholar identified 557 federal preemption statutes as of 2005.[31]

Others argue that total and partial preemptions are distinct from unfunded federal mandates and, therefore, should not be included in legislation placing conditions on the imposition of unfunded federal mandates. In addition, some business organizations oppose including preemptions in any law or definition involving unfunded federal mandates because federal preemptions can result in the standardization of regulation across state and local jurisdictions, an outcome favored by some business interests, particularly those with interstate and global operations.[32]

Grant-in-Aid Conditions

Conditions of grants-in-aid are generally not considered unfunded mandates because the costs they impose on state and local governments can be avoided by refusing the grant. However, federalism scholars and state and local government officials have argued that, in the absence of sufficient compensatory funding, grant conditions should be considered unfunded federal intergovernmental mandates, even though the grants

---

[30] GAO, *Unfunded Mandates: Views Vary About Reform Act's Strengths, Weaknesses, and Options for Improvement*, GAO-05-454, March 31, 2005, pp. 5, 11, 12, 23, 38, 39, 43, 47, 48, at http://www.gao.gov/new.items/d05454.pdf.

[31] Joseph F. Zimmerman, "Congressional Preemption During the George W. Bush Administration," *Publius: The Journal of Federalism*, vol. 37, no. 3 (Summer 2007), p. 436.

[32] GAO, *Unfunded Mandates: Views Vary About Reform Act's Strengths, Weaknesses, and Options for Improvement*, GAO-05-454, March 31, 2005, p. 12, at http://www.gao.gov/new.items/d05454.pdf; and Paul L. Posner, "The Politics of Preemption: Prospects for the States," *PS* (July 2005), p. 372.

themselves are voluntary.[33] In their view, federal "grants often require major commitments of state resources, changes in state laws, and even constitutional provisions to conform to a host of federal policy and administrative requirements" and that some grant programs, such as Medicaid, are "too large for state and local governments to voluntarily turn down, or when new and onerous conditions are added some time after state and local governments have become dependent on the program."[34] For example, on April 28, 1994, Patrick Sweeney, a Democratic Member of Ohio's state House of Representatives testifying on behalf of the National Conference of State Legislatures (NCSL), asserted at a congressional hearing on unfunded mandate legislation that

> A great majority of the current problem can be attributed to Federal entitlements that are defined but then not adequately funded, and the proliferation of a mandatory requirement for what previously were voluntary programs. Programs like Medicaid are voluntary in theory only. A State cannot unilaterally opt out of Medicaid at any time it wishes, once it is in the program, without having to obtain a Federal waiver or face certain lawsuits.[35]

Federal Tax Provisions

Federalism scholars and state and local government officials argue that federal tax policies that preempt state and local authority to tax specific activities or entities are unfunded mandates, and should be covered under legislation placing restrictions on unfunded mandates, because the fiscal

---

[33] Paul L. Posner, "Mandates: The Politics of Coercive Federalism," in *Intergovernmental Management for the 21st Century*, eds. Timothy J. Conlan and Paul L. Posner (Washington, DC: Brookings Institution Press, 2008), p. 287; and Paul L. Posner, *The Politics of Unfunded Mandates: Whither Federalism?* (Washington, DC: Georgetown University Press, 1998), pp. 4, 12-14.

[34] Paul L. Posner, *The Politics of Unfunded Mandates: Whither Federalism?* (Washington, DC: Georgetown University Press, 1998), pp. 12, 13. See also, Joseph F. Zimmerman, "Federally Induced State and Local Government Costs," paper delivered at the 1991 Annual Meeting of the American Political Science Association, Washington, DC, September 1, 1991, p. 4.

[35] U.S. Congress, Senate Committee on Governmental Affairs, *Federal Mandate Reform Legislation*, 103rd Cong., 2nd sess., April 28, 1994, S.Hrg. 103-1019 (Washington: GPO, 1995), p. 11.

108 *Robert Jay Dilger*

impact of preempting state or local government revenue sources cannot be avoided and "can be every bit as costly" as mandates ordering state or local government action.[36] For example, P.L. 105-277, the Omnibus Consolidated and Emergency Supplemental Appropriations Act, 1999 (Title XI, Internet Tax Freedom Act) created a three-year moratorium preventing state and local governments from taxing internet access, or imposing multiple or discriminatory taxes on electronic commerce.[37] A grandfather clause allowed states that had already imposed and collected a tax on internet access before October 1, 1998, to continue implementing those taxes. The moratorium on internet access taxation was extended eight times and made permanent by P.L. 114-125, the Trade Facilitation and Trade Enforcement Act of 2015. The grandfather clause was temporarily extended through June 30, 2020. The NCSL has cited research suggesting that states could receive an additional $6.5 billion annually in state sales tax revenue if the moratorium was lifted.[38]

In addition, because most state and local income taxes have been designed purposively to conform to federal tax law, changes in federal tax policy can impact state and local government finances. For example, federal tax cuts adopted in 2001 and 2003 affecting depreciation, dividends, and estate taxes "forced states to acquiesce and accept their consequences or decouple from the federal tax base."[39] Yet, federal tax changes are generally considered not to be unfunded mandates because

---

[36] National Conference of State Legislatures, "Policy Position on Federal Mandate Relief," effective through August 2011, at http://www.ncsl.org/Default.aspx?TabID=773 &tabs=855,20,632#FederalMandate; and Paul L. Posner, "Mandates: The Politics of Coercive Federalism," in *Intergovernmental Management for the 21st Century*, eds. Timothy J. Conlan and Paul L. Posner (Washington, DC: Brookings Institution Press, 2008), pp. 287, 292, 293.

[37] For additional information and analysis concerning the Internet Tax Freedom Act see CRS Report R43772, *The Internet Tax Freedom Act: In Brief*, by Jeffrey M. Stupak, and CRS Report R41853, *State Taxation of Internet Transactions*, by Steven Maguire.

[38] Michael Mazerov, "Congress Should End—Not Extend—the Ban on State and Local Taxation of Internet Access Subscriptions," Center on Budget and Policy Priorities, Washington, DC, July 10, 2014, Table 2, at http://www.cbpp.org/cms/?fa=view&id=4161; and Michael Mazerov, "State Implications of a Permanent Internet Tax Freedom Act," Presentation to the NCSL Executive Committee Task Force on State and Local Taxation, January 8, 2016, at http://www.ncsl.org/documents/task_forces/ITFA_Presentation_Final.pdf.

[39] Paul L. Posner, "Mandates: The Politics of Coercive Federalism," in *Intergovernmental Management for the 21st Century*, eds. Timothy J. Conlan and Paul L. Posner (Washington, DC: Brookings Institution Press, 2008), p. 292.

states and localities can avoid their costs by decoupling their income tax from the federal income tax. Nevertheless, because federal tax changes can affect state and local government tax bases, most state and local government officials advocate their inclusion in federal legislation placing conditions on the imposition of unfunded federal mandates.

Federal Court Decisions; Administrative Rules Issued by Federal Agencies; and Regulatory Delays and Nonenforcement

Federalism scholars, state and local government officials, and other organizations argue that, in the absence of sufficient compensatory funding, court decisions and regulatory actions taken by federal agencies, including regulatory delays and nonenforcement, are unfunded mandates and should be included in legislation placing conditions on the imposition of unfunded mandates because these actions can impose costs on state and local governments that cannot be avoided. UMRA's provisions concerning administrative rules are discussed in greater detail later in this chapter (see the section on "UMRA and Federal Rulemaking (Title II)").

UMRA's Definition of an Unfunded Federal Mandate

After taking various definitions into consideration, Congress defined federal mandates in UMRA more narrowly than state and local government officials had hoped. Federal intergovernmental mandates were defined as any provision in legislation, statute, or regulation that "would impose an enforceable duty upon State, local, or tribal governments" or "reduce or eliminate the amount" of federal funding authorized to cover the costs of an existing mandate.[40] Provisions in legislation, statute, or regulation that "would increase the stringency of conditions of assistance" or "would place caps upon, or otherwise decrease" federal funding for existing intergovernmental grants with annual entitlement authority of $500 million or more could also be considered a federal intergovernmental mandate, but

---

[40] 2 U.S.C. §658(5)(A).

only if the state, local, or tribal government "lack authority under that program to amend their financial or programmatic responsibilities to continue providing required services that are affected by the legislation, statute, or regulation."[41]

Private-sector mandates were defined as "any provision in legislation, statute, or regulation that would impose an enforceable duty upon the private sector" or "reduce or eliminate the amount" of federal funding authorized "for the purposes of ensuring compliance with such duty."[42]

Key words in both definitions are "enforceable duty." Because statutory direct orders, total and partial preemptions, federal tax policies that preempt specific state and local tax policies, and administrative rules issued by federal agencies cannot be avoided, they are enforceable duties and are covered under UMRA. In contrast, because federal grants are voluntary, grant conditions are not considered enforceable duties and, therefore, are not covered under UMRA. Federal tax policies that impose costs on state and local governments that can be avoided by decoupling the state or local government's affected income tax provision from the federal income tax code are not enforceable duties, and, therefore, also are not covered under UMRA.

UMRA considers a mandate unfunded unless the legislation authorizing the mandate fully meets its estimated direct costs by either (1) providing new budget authority (direct spending authority or entitlement authority) or (2) authorizing appropriations. If appropriations are authorized, the mandate is still considered unfunded unless the legislation ensures that in any fiscal year, either (1) the actual costs of the mandate are estimated not to exceed the appropriations actually provided; (2) the terms of the mandate will be revised so that it can be carried out with the funds appropriated; (3) the mandate will be abolished; or (4) Congress will enact new legislation to continue the mandate as an unfunded mandate.[43] This mechanism for reviewing and revising mandates on the basis of their actual costs, which was introduced into UMRA in the "Byrd look- back

---

[41] 2 U.S.C. §658(5)(B).

[42] 2 U.S.C. §658(7)(A) and 2 U.S.C. §658(7)(B).

[43] 2 U.S.C. §658d(a)(2); §425 of the Congressional Budget and Impoundment Control Act of 1974, as amended, P.L. 93-344, 88 Stat. 297, 2 U.S.C. §658 *et seq.*

Unfunded Mandates Reform Act

amendment" (as described in Appendix A), applies only to intergovernmental mandates enacted in legislation as funded through appropriations.

Exemptions and Exclusions

UMRA generally excluded preexisting federal mandates from its provisions, but, as mentioned previously, it did include any provision in legislation, statute, or regulation that "would increase the stringency of conditions of assistance" or "would place caps upon, or otherwise decrease" federal funding for existing intergovernmental grants with annual entitlement authority of $500 million or more.[44] However, this provision applies "only if the state or locality lacks authority to amend its financial or programmatic responsibilities to continue providing the required services."[45]

On June 28, 2012, the Supreme Court ruled in *National Federation of Independent Business (NFIB) v. Sebelius* that the withdrawal of all Medicaid funds from the states for failure to comply with Medicaid's expansion under health care reform (P.L. 111-148; the Patient Protection and Affordable Care Act) violated the Tenth Amendment. Prior to that ruling, CBO determined that large intergovernmental entitlement grant programs, such as Medicaid and Temporary Assistance to Needy Families, "allow states significant flexibility to alter their programs and accommodate new requirements," and, as a result, it determined that UMRA provisions generally did not apply to these programs.[46] Subsequent to the Supreme Court's ruling, CBO has indicated that UMRA's provisions may apply to changes in "the stringency of conditions" or reductions in

---

[44] 2 U.S.C. §658(5)(B).

[45] U.S. Congress, Senate Committee on Finance, *Work, Opportunity, and Responsibility for Kids Act*, report to accompany H.R. 4737, 107th Cong., 2nd sess., July 25, 2002, S.Rept. 107-221 (Washington: GPO, 2002), p. 61; and 2 U.S.C. §658(5)(B).

[46] U.S. Congress, Senate Committee on Finance, *Work, Opportunity, and Responsibility for Kids Act*, report to accompany H.R. 4737, 107th Cong., 2nd sess., July 25, 2002, S.Rept. 107-221 (Washington: GPO, 2002), p. 61. For additional information and analysis concerning National Federation of Independent Business (NFIB) v. Sebelius, see CRS Report R42367, *Medicaid and Federal Grant Conditions After NFIB v. Sebelius: Constitutional Issues and Analysis*, by Kenneth R. Thomas.

112 *Robert Jay Dilger*

funding for "certain large mandatory programs ... if the affected governments lack the flexibility to alter the programs."[47]

Otherwise, UMRA's Title I does not apply to conditions of federal assistance; duties stemming from participation in voluntary federal programs; and legislative provisions that cover individual constitutional rights, discrimination, emergency assistance, grant accounting and auditing procedures, national security, treaty obligations, and certain parts of Social Security relating to the old-age, survivors, and disability insurance program under title II of the Social Security Act.[48]

UMRA did not indicate that these exempted provisions and rules were not federal mandates. Instead, it established that their costs would not be subject to its provisions requiring written cost estimate statements, or to its provisions permitting a point of order to be raised against the consideration of reported legislation in which they appear. The Senate Committee on Governmental Affairs report accompanying S. 1, The Unfunded Mandates Reform Act of 1995, provided its reasoning for adopting the exempted provisions and rules:

> A number of these exemptions are standard in many pieces of legislation in order to recognize the domain of the President in foreign affairs and as Commander-in-Chief as well as to ensure that Congress's and the Executive Branch's hands are not tied with procedural requirements in times of national emergencies. Further, the Committee thinks that Federal auditing, accounting and other similar requirements designed to protect Federal funds from potential waste, fraud, and abuse should be exempt from the Act.
>
> The Committee recognizes the special circumstances and history surrounding the enactment and enforcement of Federal civil rights laws. During the middle part of the 20th century, the arguments of those who opposed the national, uniform extension of basic equal rights, protection, and opportunity to all individuals were based on a States rights philosophy. With the passage of the Civil Rights Acts of 1957 and 1964 and the Voting Rights Act of 1965, Congress rejected that argument out

---

[47] CBO, "CBO's Activities Under the Unfunded Mandates Reform Act," at https://www.cbo.gov/publication/51335.

[48] 2 U.S.C. §658a.

Unfunded Mandates Reform Act

of hand as designed to thwart equal opportunity and to protect discriminatory, unjust and unfair practices in the treatment of individuals in certain parts of the country. The Committee therefore exempts Federal civil rights laws from the requirements of this Act.[49]

In addition, as will be discussed in the next section, UMRA does not require all legislative provisions that contain federal mandates, even those that contain mandates that meet UMRA's definition, to have a CBO written cost estimate statement. In some instances, CBO may determine that cost estimates may not be feasible or complete. In addition, UMRA only requires estimates of direct costs imposed by the legislation. Estimates of indirect, secondary costs, such as effects on prices and wages when the costs of a mandate imposed on one party are passed on to others, such as customers or employees, are not required.[50]

UMRA AND CONGRESSIONAL PROCEDURE (TITLE I)

UMRA's Procedures

Under Title I, which took effect on January 1, 1996, CBO was directed, to the extent practicable, to assist congressional committees, upon their request, in analyzing the budgetary and financial impact of any proposed legislation that may have (1) a significant budgetary impact on state, local, and tribal governments; (2) a significant financial impact on the private sector; or (3) a significant employment impact on the private sector. In addition, CBO was directed, if asked by a committee chair or committee ranking minority member, to conduct a study, to the extent practicable, of the budgetary and financial impact of proposed legislation containing a federal mandate. If reasonably feasible, the study is to include

---

[49] U.S. Congress, Senate Committee on Governmental Affairs, *Unfunded Mandate Reform Act of 1995*, report to accompany S. 1, 104th Cong., 1st sess., January 11, 1995, S.Rept. 104-1 (Washington: GPO, 1995), p. 12.

[50] U.S. General Accounting Office, *Unfunded Mandates: Analysis of Reform Act Coverage*, GAO-04-637, May 12, 2004, pp. 11-17, at http://www.gao.gov/new.items/d04637.pdf.

estimates of the future direct costs of the federal mandate "to the extent that such costs significantly differ from or extend beyond the 5- year period after the mandate is first effective."[51]

Although the actions noted above are technically discretionary, UMRA does contain mandatory directives. When an authorizing committee reports a public bill or joint resolution containing a federal mandate, UMRA requires the committee to provide the measure to CBO for budgetary analysis.[52] CBO is required to provide the committee a cost estimate statement of a mandate's direct costs if those costs are estimated to equal or exceed predetermined amounts, adjusted for inflation, in any of the first five fiscal years the legislation would be in effect. In 2019, those threshold amounts are $82 million for intergovernmental mandates and $164 million for private- sector mandates. CBO is also required to inform the committee if the mandate has estimated direct costs below these thresholds and briefly explain the basis of the estimate.

CBO must also identify any increase in federal appropriations or other spending that has been provided to fund the mandate.[53] The federal mandate is considered unfunded unless estimated costs are fully funded. As described above, under "UMRA's Definition of an Unfunded Federal Mandate," UMRA provides that mandate costs be considered as funded only if the legislation covers the mandate costs either by providing new direct spending or entitlement authority or by authorizing appropriations and incorporating a mechanism to provide for the mandate to be revised or abolished if the requisite appropriations are not provided.

Direct costs for intergovernmental mandates are defined as "the aggregate estimated amounts that all State, local and tribal governments would be required to spend or would be prohibited from raising in revenues in order to comply with the Federal intergovernmental mandate."[54] Direct costs for private-sector mandates are defined as "the

---

[51] 2 U.S.C. §602.
[52] 2 U.S.C. §658b.
[53] 2 U.S.C. §658c.
[54] 2 U.S.C. §658 (3)(A)(i).

aggregate estimated amounts that the private sector will be required to spend in order to comply with the Federal private sector mandate."[55]

To accomplish these tasks, CBO created the State and Local Government Cost Estimates Unit within its Budget Analysis Division to prepare intergovernmental mandate cost estimate statements as well as other studies on the budgetary effects of mandates. It also added new staff to its program analysis divisions to prepare private-sector mandate cost estimate statements.[56]

A congressional committee is required to include the CBO estimate of mandate costs in its report on the bill. If the mandate cost estimate is not available, or if the report is not expected to be in print before the legislation reaches the floor for consideration, the committee is to publish the mandate cost estimate in the *Congressional Record* in advance of floor consideration. In addition to identifying direct costs, the committee's report must also assess the likely costs and benefits of any mandates in the legislation, describe how they affect the competitive balance between the private and public sectors, state the extent to which the legislation would preempt state, local, or tribal law, and explain the effect of any preemption. For intergovernmental mandates alone, the committee is to describe in its report the extent to which the legislation authorizes federal funding for direct costs of the mandate, and detail whether and how funding is to be provided.[57]

CBO Cost Estimate Statements

CBO submitted 13,310 estimates of mandate costs to Congress from January 1, 1996, when UMRA's Title I became effective, to May 20, 2019 (see Table 1).

---

[55] 2 U.S.C. §658 (3)(B).
[56] Theresa A. Gullo and Janet M. Kelly, "Federal Unfunded Mandate Reform: A First-Year Retrospective," *Public Administration Review*, vol. 58, no. 5 (September/October 1998), p. 381. The State and Local Government Cost Estimates Unit is now named the State, Local, and Tribal Government Cost Estimates Unit.
[57] 2 U.S.C. §658c(a).

Table 1. CBO Estimates of costs of intergovernmental mandates, 104th -116th Congresses

Congress	Cost Estimate Statements Transmitted	Statements With Identified Intergovernmental Mandates	Intergovernmental Mandate Costs Exceeding the Threshold	CBO Unable to Determine Mandate Costs
104th (1996)	718	69	11	6
105th (1997-1998)	1,062	128	14	14
106th (1999-2000)	1,279	158	7	1
107th (2001-2002)	1,038	110	10	8
108th (2003-2004)	1,172	152	16	7
109th (2005-2006)	978	171	18	6
110th (2007-2008)	1,382	168	7	6
111th (2009-2010)	893	134	11	19
112th (2011-2012)	862	124	4	8
113th (2013-2014)	976	86	5	0
114th (2015-2016)	1,227	110	8	2
115th (2017-2018)	1,582	118	3	2
116th (1/1/2019-5/20/2019)	141	9	1	0
Total	13,310	1,537	115	79

Sources: U.S. Congressional Budget Office (CBO), A Review of CBO's Activities Under the Unfunded Mandates Reform Act, 1996 to 2005, March 2006, p. 4; CBO, A Review of CBO's Activities in 2008 Under the Unfunded Mandates Reform Act, March 2009, p. 21; CBO, A Review of CBO's Activities in 2010 Under the Unfunded Mandates Reform Act, March 2011, p. 6: CBO, A Review of CBO's Activities in 2012 Under the Unfunded Mandates Reform Act, March 2013, p. 4; CBO, A Review of CBO's Activities in 2014 Under the Unfunded Mandates Reform Act, March 2015, p. 4; CBO, "Mandate Statements Transmitted by CBO, 2007 to 2018," at https://www.cbo.gov/publication/51335, and CBO, "Cost Estimates," May 22, 2019, at http://www.cbo.gov/search/ce_sitesearch.cfm.

Notes: CBO began preparing mandate statements in January 1996. The figures for the 104th Congress reflect bills on the legislative calendar in January 1996 and bills reported by authorizing committees thereafter.

Each of these statements examined the mandate costs imposed on the private sector or state, local, and tribal governments by provisions in a specific bill, amendment, or conference report.

Table 2. CBO estimate of costs of private-sector mandates, 104th-116th Congresses

Congress	Cost Estimate Statements Transmitted	Statements With Identified Private-Sector Mandates	Private-Sector Mandate Costs Exceeding Threshold	CBO Unable to Determine Mandate Costs
104th (1996)	673	91	38	2
105th (1997-1998)	1,023	140	36	14
106th (1999-2000)	1,253	191	26	20
107th (2001-2002)	1,034	139	37	22
108th (2003-2004)	1,168	171	38	28
109th (2005-2006)	974	184	45	32
110th (2007-2008)	1,382	256	67	49
111th (2009-2010)	893	190	41	50
112th (2011-2012)	862	147	40	35
113th (2013-2014)	976	124	22	13
114th (2015-2016)	1,226	162	14	14
115th (2017-2018)	1,582	207	17	17
116th (1/1/2019-5/20/2019)	141	20	6	3
Total	13,187	2,022	427	299

Sources: CBO, A Review of CBO's Activities Under the Unfunded Mandates Reform Act, 1996 to 2005, March 2006, p. 4; CBO, A Review of CBO's Activities in 2008 Under the Unfunded Mandates Reform Act, March 2009, p. 21; CBO, A Review of CBO's Activities in 2010 Under the Unfunded Mandates Reform Act, March 2011, p. 6: CBO, A Review of CBO's Activities in 2012 Under the Unfunded Mandates Reform Act, March 2013, p. 4; CBO, A Review of CBO's Activities in 2014 Under the Unfunded Mandates Reform Act, March 2015, p. 4; CBO, "Mandate Statements Transmitted by CBO, 2007 to 2018," at https://www.cbo.gov/publication/51335, and CBO, "Cost Estimates," May 22, 2019, at http://www.cbo.gov/search/ce_sitesearch.cfm.

Notes: CBO began preparing mandate statements in January 1996. The figures for the 104th Congress reflect bills on the legislative calendar in January 1996 and bills reported by authorizing committees thereafter. In some years, CBO transmitted more cost estimate statements for intergovernmental mandates than private-sector mandates because sometimes CBO was asked to review a specific bill, amendment, or conference report solely for intergovernmental mandates.

About 11.5% of these cost estimate statements (1,537 of 13,310 cost estimate statements) identified costs imposed by intergovernmental mandates, and less than 1.0% of them (115 of 13,310 cost estimate statements) identified intergovernmental mandates that exceeded UMRA's threshold. CBO was unable to determine costs imposed by intergovernmental mandates in 79 bills, amendments, or conference reports. CBO has submitted 13,187 estimates to Congress that examined private-sector mandate costs imposed by provisions in a specific bill, amendment, or conference report from January 1, 1996, when UMRA's Title I became effective, to May 20, 2019 (see Table 2). The number of statements transmitted to Congress shown in Table 2 is less than the number shown in Table 1 because CBO is sometimes asked to review a specific bill, amendment, or conference report solely for intergovernmental mandates.

About 15.3% of these private-sector estimates (2,022 of 13,187 cost estimate statements) identified costs imposed by mandates, and about 3.2% of them (427 of 13,187 cost estimate statements) identified costs that exceeded UMRA's threshold. CBO was unable to determine costs imposed by private-sector mandates in 299 bills, amendments, or conference reports.

Points of Order for Initial Consideration

UMRA provides for the enforcement of its informational requirements on legislation by establishing a point of order in each chamber against consideration of a measure on which the reporting committee has not published the required estimate of mandate costs. This point of order applies only to measures reported by committees (for which CBO estimates of mandate costs are required), but it applies for both intergovernmental and private-sector mandates. In addition, however, if the informational requirement is met, a point of order against consideration of a measure may still be raised, if, for any fiscal year, the estimated total mandate cost of unfunded intergovernmental mandates in the measure exceeds UMRA's threshold amount ($82 million in 2019). This point of order may be raised also if CBO reported that no reasonable estimate of the cost of intergovernmental mandates was feasible.[58]

---

[58] 2 U.S.C. §658d(a); and 2 U.S.C. §658c(b)(3).

Unfunded Mandates Reform Act

Uniquely among the requirements established by UMRA, this substantive point of order addressing intergovernmental mandates contained in legislation constitutes a potential means of control over the actual imposition of mandate costs. Even in this case, however, the mechanisms established by UMRA provide a means of controlling mandates only on the basis of estimates of the costs that will be incurred in subsequent fiscal years. The only provision of UMRA that offers a possibility of controls based on costs actually incurred by affected entities is the requirement, mentioned earlier, that a mandate can be considered funded through appropriations only if it directs that, if insufficient appropriations are made, the mandate must be revised, abolished, or reenacted as unfunded.

In several respects, the applicability of the substantive point of order differs from that of the informational point of order. First, it applies to any measure coming to the floor for consideration, whether or not reported by a committee, and also to conference reports. For a measure that has been reported, this point of order applies to the measure in the form reported, including, for example, to a committee amendment in the nature of a substitute. In addition, this point of order applies against an amendment or motion (such as a motion to recommit with amendatory instructions), and does so on the basis not that the mandate costs of the amendment or motion itself exceeds the threshold, but that the amendment or motion would cause the total mandate costs in the measure to do so. Finally, however, this point of order applies only against intergovernmental mandates. UMRA imposes no comparable control in relation to private-sector mandates.

Because federal mandates are created through authorization bills, the UMRA points of order generally do not apply to bills reported by the House and Senate Committees on Appropriations. However, if an appropriation bill, resolution, amendment, or conference report contains legislative provisions that would either increase the direct costs of a federal intergovernmental mandate that exceeds the threshold, or cause those costs to exceed the threshold, a point of order may be raised against the

120   *Robert Jay Dilger*

provisions themselves. In the Senate, if this point of order is sustained, the provisions are stricken from the bill.[59]

In the House, the chair does not rule on a point of order raised under these provisions. Instead, the House, by majority vote, determines whether to consider the measure despite the point of order.

To prevent dilatory use of the point of order, the chair need not put the question of consideration to a vote unless the Member making the point of order meets the "threshold burden" of identifying specific language that is claimed to contain the unfunded mandate. Also, if several points of order could be raised against the same measure, House practices under UMRA allow all of them to be disposed of at once by a single vote on consideration. If the Committee on Rules proposes a special rule for considering the measure that waives the point of order, UMRA subjects the special rule itself to a point of order, which is disposed of by the same mechanism.[60]

In the Senate, if questions are raised challenging the applicability of an UMRA point of order (e.g., to prevent its use for dilatory purposes), the presiding officer, to the extent practicable, consults with the Committee on Homeland Security and Governmental Affairs to determine if the measure contains an intergovernmental mandate and with the Senate Committee on the Budget to determine if the mandate's direct costs meet UMRA's threshold for allowing a point of order to be raised. The Senate Committee on the Budget may draw for this purpose on CBO cost estimate statements. If there are no such challenges, or the presiding officer rules against the challenge, the Senate determines whether to consider the measure despite the point of order. It may do so by voting on a motion to waive the point of order.[61]

Initially, a majority vote was sufficient to waive the point of order in the Senate.[62] In 2005, the Senate increased its threshold to waive an UMRA point of order to three-fifths of Senators duly chosen and sworn (normally 60 votes), as was already required of many other Budget Act

---

[59] 2 U.S.C. §658d(c).

[60] 2 U.S.C. §658e(a); and 2 U.S.C. §658e(b)(3).

[61] 2 U.S.C. §658d(d); and 2 U.S.C. §658d(e).

[62] 2 U.S.C. §558d(a); §403(b)(1) of H.Con.Res. 95, adopted April 28, 2005.

Unfunded Mandates Reform Act

points of order. Two UMRA points of order were raised in the Senate that year, and both were sustained, defeating two amendments to an appropriations bill that would have increased the minimum wage (see Table 3). In 2007, the Senate returned its threshold for waiving an UMRA point of order to a majority vote.[63]

On April 2, 2009, the Senate approved, by unanimous consent, an amendment (S.Amdt. 819) to S.Con.Res. 13, the concurrent budget resolution for FY2010, which would have again increased the vote necessary in the Senate to waive an UMRA point of order to three-fifths of Senators duly chosen and sworn (normally 60 votes). The amendment was subsequently dropped in the final version of the concurrent budget resolution for FY2010.

On March 23, 2013, the Senate agreed, by voice vote, to an amendment (S.Amdt. 538) to S.Con.Res. 8, the concurrent budget resolution for FY2014. It would have restored the requirement for waiving an UMRA point of order in the Senate to three-fifths of the full Senate (normally 60 votes). S.Con.Res. 8 was received in the House on April 15, 2013, and held at the desk. Because the House did not act on the measure, and no other legislation on the matter was approved by Congress, the simple majority requirement for appealing or waiving UMRA points of order in the Senate remained in effect.

On May 5, 2015, the Senate agreed to the conference report on S.Con.Res. 11, the concurrent budget resolution for FY2016, which the House had previously agreed to on April 30, 2015. The resolution included a provision that restored the requirement for waiving an UMRA point of order in the Senate to three-fifths of Senators duly chosen and sworn (normally 60 votes).

Prior to the Senate's increasing the threshold necessary to waive an UMRA point of order, a scholar familiar with UMRA argued that, inasmuch as the general floor procedures of the Senate already allows Senators to force a majority vote on a mandate by moving to strike it from the bill, UMRA's enforcement procedure of waiving a point of order by

---

[63] 2 U.S.C. §558d(a).

122   *Robert Jay Dilger*

majority vote meant that UMRA mattered only in the House.[64] As evidence of this, the scholar noted that during UMRA's first 10 years of operation, when the threshold to waive an UMRA point of order was a majority vote in both the House and Senate, 13 UMRA points of order were raised, all in the House (see Table 3).

Table 3. UMRA points of order in the House and Senate, by Congress

Congress	Points of Order Raised in the House	Points of Order Sustained in the House	Points of Order Raised in the Senate	Points of Order Sustained in the Senate
104th (1996)	3	1	0	0
105th (1997-1998)	4	0	0	0
106th (1999-2000)	4	0	0	0
107th (2001-2002)	2	0	0	0
108th (2003-2004)	0	0	0	0
109th (2005-2006)	6	0	2	2
110th (2007-2008)	8	0	0	0
111th (2009-2010)	13	0	1	0
112th (2011-2012)	10	0	0	0
113th (2013-2014)	6	0	0	0
114th (2015-2016)	5	0	1	0
115th (2017-2018)	1	0	0	0
116th (1/1/2019-5/20/2019)	0	0	0	0
Total	62	1	4	2

Source: *Congressional Record*, various years. A list of UMRA points of order raised to date is provided in Appendix B.

As indicated in Table 3, 62 UMRA points of order have been raised in the House. Only one of these points of order, the first one, which was raised on March 28, 1996, in opposition to a proposal to add a minimum wage increase to the Contract With America Advancement Act of 1996, resulted in the House voting to reject consideration of a proposed provision. During the 111th-114th Congresses, UMRA points of order in the House were often raised not to challenge unfunded federal mandates *per*

---

[64] Elizabeth Garrett, "Framework Legislation and Federalism," *Notre Dame Law Review*, vol. 83, no. 4 (2008), p. 1502.

se, but to use the 10 minutes of debate allowed each House Member initiating an UMRA point of order to challenge the pace of legislative consideration, limitations on the offering of amendments to appropriations bills, or the inclusion of earmarks in legislation.[65]

Also, as indicated in Table 3, UMRA points of order have been raised in the Senate four times. In 2005, points of order were raised against two amendments relating to an increase in the minimum wage. In each case the Senate declined to waive the point of order, and the chair ruled that the amendment was out of order because it contained unfunded intergovernmental mandates in excess of the threshold.[66] In 2009, an UMRA point of order was raised against intergovernmental mandates in a health care reform bill.[67] The Senate voted to waive the point of order, 55-44.[68] The Senate subsequently approved the bill with the mandates.[69] In 2016, an UMRA point of order was raised against intergovernmental mandates in a bill designed to assist Puerto Rico in addressing its debt.[70] The Senate voted to waive the point of order, 85-13.[71] The Senate subsequently approved the bill with the mandates.[72]

---

[65] Based on CRS review of the 34 points of order raised in the House during the 111th-114th Congresses.

[66] "Transportation, Treasury, Housing and Urban Development, the Judiciary, the District of Columbia, and Independent Agencies Appropriations Act, 2006," proceedings in the Senate, *Congressional Record*, daily edition, vol. 151 (October 19, 2005), pp. S11526, S11547-S11548.

[67] Senator Robert Corker, "H.R. 3590, the Service Members Home Ownership Tax Act of 2009," remarks in the Senate, *Congressional Record*, daily edition, vol. 155, no. 199 (December 23, 2009), pp. S13803, S13804.

[68] "Consideration of H.R. 3590, the Service Members Home Ownership Tax Act of 2009, Senate Rollcall Vote No. 390," *Congressional Record*, daily edition, vol. 155, no. 199 (December 23, 2009), p. S13831.

[69] "Consideration of H.R. 3590, the Patient Protection and Affordable Care Act, Senate Rollcall Vote No. 396," *Congressional Record*, daily edition, vol. 155, no. 201 (December 24, 2009), p. S13831.

[70] Senator Bernie Sanders, "National Sea Grant College Program Amendments of 2015 (Puerto Rico Oversight, Management, and Economic Stability Act–PROMESA)," Senate debate on S. 2328, *Congressional Record*, vol. 162, no. 105 (June 29, 2016), pp. S4691-S4702.

[71] "Motion to Concur, Senate Rollcall Vote No. 115," *Congressional Record*, daily edition, vol. 162, no. 105 (June 29, 2016), p. S4702.

[72] "Vote on Motion to Concur, Senate Rollcall Vote No. 116," *Congressional Record*, daily edition, vol. 162, no. 105 (June 29, 2016), p. S4702.

124   *Robert Jay Dilger*

Impact on the Enactment of Statutory Intergovernmental and Private-Sector Mandates

Although UMRA points of order have been sustained just three times, most state and local government officials assert that UMRA has reduced "the number of unfunded federal mandates by acting as a deterrent to their enactment."[73] For example, in 2001, Raymond Scheppach, then- NGA's executive director, testified before a House subcommittee that UMRA had slowed the growth of unfunded mandates and improved communications between federal policymakers and state and local government officials:

> Direct mandates have declined sharply in the wake of the Act. But I would venture that UMRA has had an even greater intangible benefit. As Congressman Portman once told us, he was certain this would be one of those bills that he could frame and hang on his wall, and it would become just another relic of history. But, to his surprise, the Act has led— time and again—to members asking his advice: "Do you think this bill will cause an UMRA problem? With whom should I work?" The very threat of a CBO report has engendered efforts to reach out to state and local leaders before the fact—instead of after. It has changed the nature of our intergovernmental discussion in a very positive way.[74]

More recently, NCSL has argued that UMRA has brought increased attention to the fiscal effects of federal legislation on state and local governments, improved federal accountability, and enhanced consultation.[75] In addition, there have been documented instances in which either sponsors of legislation have modified provisions to avoid a CBO

---

[73] GAO, *Unfunded Mandates: Views Vary About Reform Act's Strengths, Weaknesses, and Options for Improvement*, GAO-05-454, March 31, 2005, p. 15, at http://www.gao.gov/new.items/d05454.pdf.

[74] Joint Hearing, U.S. Congress, House Committee on Government Reform, Subcommittee on Energy Policy, Natural Resources and Regulatory Affairs, and House Committee on Rules, Subcommittee on Technology and the House, *Unfunded Mandates: A Five Year Review and Recommendations for Change*, hearing on the Unfunded Mandates Reform Act of 1995, 107th Cong., 1st sess., May 24, 2001, H. Hrg. 107-19 (Washington: GPO, 2001), p. 61.

[75] National Conference of State Legislatures, "State and Federal Budgeting: Federal Mandate Relief," at http://www.ncsl.org/state-federal-committees.aspx?tabs=855,20,632.

Unfunded Mandates Reform Act 125

statement that unfunded intergovernmental mandate costs exceeded the threshold, or measures with such costs estimated to exceed the threshold were altered prior to floor consideration to reduce their costs below the threshold.[76]

As mentioned previously, since UMRA's Title I became effective in 1996, CBO has submitted 13,310 written cost estimate statements to Congress that examined the costs imposed by provisions in a specific bill, amendment, or conference report on the private sector and/or state and local governments. It identified intergovernmental mandates in 1,537 of them (11.5%). CBO reports that, as of December 31, 2018, 15 laws (containing 21 intergovernmental mandates) have been enacted since UMRA became effective in 1996 that have costs estimated to exceed the statutory threshold.[77] Those laws are as follows:

- Two increases in the minimum wage. P.L. 104-188, the Small Business Job Protection Act of 1996, enacted in 1996, was estimated to cost state and local governments more than $1 billion during the first five years that it was in effect. P.L. 110-28, the U.S. Troop Readiness, Veterans' Care, Katrina Recovery, and Iraq Accountability Appropriations Act, 2007, enacted in 2007, was estimated to cost state and local governments slightly less than $1 billion during the first five years that it was in effect.

- A reduction in federal funding for administering the food stamp program, now the Supplemental Nutrition Assistance Program, in P.L. 105-185, the Agricultural Research, Extension, and Education Reform Act of 1998, enacted in 1998, was estimated to cost states between $200 million and $300 million annually.

---

[76] Paul L. Posner, "Unfunded Mandates Reform Act: 1996 and Beyond," *Publius: The Journal of Federalism*, vol. 27, no. 2 (Spring 1997), pp. 57-59; U.S. General Accounting Office, *Unfunded Mandates: Analysis of Reform Act Coverage*, GAO-04-637, May 12, 2004, p. 19, at http://www.gao.gov/new.items/d04637.pdf; and GAO, *Unfunded Mandates: Views Vary About Reform Act's Strengths, Weaknesses, and Options for Improvement*, GAO-05-454, March 31, 2005, p. 15, at http://www.gao.gov/new.items/d05454.pdf.

[77] CBO, *Enacted Intergovernmental Mandates With Estimated Costs That Exceed the Statutory Threshold, 1996 to 2018*, at https://www.cbo.gov/publication/51335; and CBO, "Laws That Contain Mandates," at https://www.cbo.gov/umra-search/law/intergovernmental?f%5B0%5D=field_state_local_costs_of_manda%3Ayes.

- Preemption of state taxes on premiums for certain prescription drug plans in P.L. 108-73, the Family Farmer Bankruptcy Relief Act of 2003, enacted in 2003, was estimated to cost states $70 million in revenue in 2006, the first year it was in effect, and increase to about $95 million annually by 2010.
- The temporary preemption of states' authority to tax certain internet services and transactions in P.L. 108-435, the Internet Tax Nondiscrimination Act, enacted in 2004, was estimated to reduce state and local government tax revenue by at least $300 million. The extension of this preemption in P.L. 110-108, the Internet Tax Freedom Act Amendments Act of 2007, enacted in 2007, was estimated to reduce state and local government tax revenue by about $80 million annually. Making the moratorium permanent (while allowing state and local governments that had been collecting such taxes prior to October 1, 1998 to continue to collect such taxes, but only through June 2020) in P.L. 114-125, the Trade Facilitation and Trade Enforcement Act of 2015, enacted in 2016, was estimated to cost state and local governments more than $100 million in the final three months of fiscal year 2020 (July through September) and more than several hundred million dollars annually thereafter.
- The requirement that state and local governments meet certain standards for issuing driver's licenses, identification cards, and vital statistics documents in P.L. 108-458, the Intelligence Reform and Terrorism Prevention Act of 2004, enacted in 2004, was estimated to cost state and local governments more than $100 million over 2005-2009, with costs exceeding the threshold in at least one of those years.
- The elimination of matching federal payments for some child support spending in P.L. 109-171, the Deficit Reduction Act of 2005, enacted in 2006, was estimated to cost states more than $100 million annually beginning in 2008.
- The requirement that state and local governments withhold taxes on certain payments for property and services in P.L. 109-222, the

Tax Increase Prevention and Reconciliation Act of 2005, enacted in 2006, was estimated to cost state and local governments more than $70 million annually beginning in 2011.

- Requirements on rail and transit owners and operators to train workers and submit reports to the Department of Homeland Security in P.L. 110-53, the Implementing Recommendations of the 9/11 Commission Act of 2007, enacted in 2007, was estimated to cost state and local governments more than UMRA's threshold in at least one of the first five years following enactment.

- The requirement that commuter railroads install train-control technology in P.L. 110-432, the Railroad Safety Enhancement Act of 2008, enacted in 2008, was estimated to cost state and local governments more than UMRA's threshold in at least one of the first five years following enactment.

- The requirement that public entities that handle health insurance information comply with new regulations; health insurance plans pay an annual fee based on average number of people covered by the policy; public employers pay an excise tax on employer-sponsored health insurance coverage defined as having high costs; health insurance plans comply with new standards for extending coverage; and public entities must comply with new notice and reporting requirements on health insurance plans in P.L. 111-148, the Patient Protection and Affordable Care Act, enacted in 2010, was estimated to have costs for state and local governments that would greatly exceed UMRA's thresholds in each of the first five years following enactment.

- The requirement that schools provide meals that comply with new standards for menu planning and nutrition and with nutrition standards for all food sold in schools in P.L. 111-296, the Healthy, Hunger-Free Kids Act of 2010, enacted in 2010, was estimated to have costs for state and local governments that would exceed

UMRA's threshold beginning the first year that the mandates take effect.[78]

- The aggregate cost of requiring Puerto Rico and its instrumentalities to comply with the directives and processes of a federal oversight board tasked with overseeing the territory's fiscal affairs and to pay for the costs of the oversight board's staff and operating expenses in P.L. 114-187, the Puerto Rico Oversight, Management, and Economic Stability Act (PROMESA), enacted in 2016, was estimated to exceed UMRA's threshold.

State and local government interest groups argue that these statistics confirm UMRA's effectiveness in serving as a deterrent to the enactment of new unfunded mandates that exceed UMRA's threshold and meet UMRA's definition of a federal mandate. However, they also argue that many mandates with costs below UMRA's threshold, or that do not meet UMRA's definition of a federal mandate, have been adopted since UMRA's enactment.[79]

CBO also reports that from January 1, 2006, to December 31, 2018, 217 laws were enacted with at least one intergovernmental mandate as defined under UMRA. These laws imposed 443 mandates on state and local governments, with 16 of these mandates exceeding UMRA's threshold, 14 with estimated costs that could not be determined, and 413 with estimated costs below the threshold.[80] CBO reported that hundreds of

---

[78] CBO, *A Review of CBO's Activities in 2014 Under the Unfunded Mandates Reform Act*, March 2015, pp. 5, 40, at https://www.cbo.gov/sites/default/files/114th-congress-2015-2016/reports/50051-UMRA2_0.pdf; CBO, *Selected CBO Publications Related to Health Care Legislation, 2009-2010*, December 2010, pp. 17, 18, 148, 166, at http://www.cbo.gov/ftpdocs/120xx/doc12033/12-23-SelectedHealthcarePublications.pdf; and S.Rept. 111-178, Healthy, Hunger-Free Kids Act of 2010, Estimated Costs and Unfunded Mandates.

[79] National Conference of State Legislatures, "State and Federal Budgeting: Federal Mandate Relief," at http://www.ncsl.org/Default.aspx?TabID=773&tabs=855,20,632#Federal Mandate.

[80] CBO, *Laws Enacted Between 2006 and 2018 That Contain Mandates*, at https://www.cbo.gov/publication/51335; and CBO, "Laws That Contain Mandates," at https://www.cbo.gov/umra-search/law.

other laws had an effect on state and local government budgets, but those laws did not meet UMRA's definition of a federal mandate.[81]

As mentioned previously, CBO has submitted 13,187 cost estimate statements to Congress that examined the costs imposed by provisions in a specific bill, amendment, or conference report that might impact the private sector. It identified private-sector mandates in 2,022 of them (15.3%). CBO reports that from January 1, 2006, to December 31, 2018, 330 laws were enacted with at least one private-sector mandate as defined under UMRA. These laws imposed 836 mandates on the private sector, with 128 of these mandates exceeding UMRA's threshold, 96 with estimated costs that could not be determined, and 612 with estimated costs below the threshold.[82]

Congressional Issues for Title I

Exemptions and Exclusions

State and local government officials argue that UMRA's exemptions and exclusions reduce its effectiveness in limiting the enactment of unfunded federal intergovernmental mandates. They argue that federal programs in the exempted and excluded areas can still result in the imposition of costs on state, local, and tribal governments. Also, because

---

[81] CBO, *A Review of CBO's Activities in 2008 Under the Unfunded Mandates Reform Act*, March 2009, p. 48, at http://www.cbo.gov/ftpdocs/100xx/doc10058/03-31-UMRA.pdf; CBO, *A Review of CBO's Activities in 2010 Under the Unfunded Mandates Reform Act*, March 2011, p. 5, at http://www.cbo.gov/ftpdocs/121xx/doc12117/03-31- UMRA.pdf; CBO, *A Review of CBO's Activities in 2011 Under the Unfunded Mandates Reform Act*, March 2012, pp. 5-7, at http://www.cbo.gov/sites/default/files/cbofiles/attachments/03-30-UMRA.pdf; CBO, *A Review of CBO's Activities in 2012 Under the Unfunded Mandates Reform Act*, March 2013, pp. 5-9, at http://www.cbo.gov/sites/default/ files/ cbofiles/attachments/44032_UMRA.pdf; CBO, *A Review of CBO's Activities in 2013 Under the Unfunded Mandates Reform Act*, March 2014, p. 5, at http://www.cbo.gov/ sites/default/files/cbofiles/attachments/45209- UMRA.pdf; CBO, *A Review of CBO's Activities in 2014 Under the Unfunded Mandates Reform Act*, March 2015, p. 5, at http://www.cbo.gov/sites/default/files/cbofiles/attachments/50051-UMRA. pdf; and CBO, *Laws Enacted Between 2006 and 2016 That Contain Mandates*, at https://www.cbo.gov/publication/51335.

[82] CBO, *Enacted Private-Sector Mandates With Estimated Costs That Exceed the Statutory Threshold, 1996 to 2018*, at https://www.cbo.gov/publication/51335; and CBO, "Laws That Contain Mandates," at https://www.cbo.gov/umra- search/law.

UMRA does not include these costs as "mandates," they are exempt even from the requirement for CBO to estimate these costs. For example, in 2008, NCSL asserted that "although fewer than a dozen mandates have been enacted that exceed the threshold established in UMRA, Congress has shifted at least $131 billion in costs to states over the past five years" and that during the 110th Congress at least $31 billion in additional costs were imposed on states through new mandates.[83]

To reduce these costs, NCSL has recommended that UMRA's provisions on points of order and requirements for written cost estimate statements also apply to (1) all open-ended entitlement grant-in-aid programs, such as Medicaid, and legislative provisions that would cap or enforce a ceiling on the cost of federal participation in any entitlement or mandatory spending program; (2) new conditions of federal funding for existing federal grants and programs; (3) legislative provisions that reduce state revenues, especially when changes to the federal tax code are retroactive or otherwise provide states with little or no opportunity to prospectively address the impact of a change in federal law on state revenues; and (4) mandates that fail to exceed the statutory threshold only because they do not affect all states.[84]

For the most part, business interests have generally supported state and local government officials in their efforts to broaden UMRA's coverage of federal intergovernmental mandates. In perhaps the most extensive effort to obtain various viewpoints on UMRA, in 2005, the Government Accountability Office (GAO) held group meetings, individual interviews, and received written responses from 52 individuals and organizations, including academic centers and think tanks, businesses, federal agencies, public interest advocacy groups, and state and local governments,

---

[83] National Conference of State Legislatures, *Mandate Monitor*, vol. 6, no. 1 (April 8, 2008), p. 1.

[84] NCSL also advocates a revision of the definition of direct costs to capture and more accurately reflect the true costs to state governments of particular federal actions; requiring that mandate statements accompany appropriations bills; enactment of legislation that would require federal reimbursement, as long as the mandate exists, to state and local governments for costs imposed on them by any new federal mandates; restrictions regarding the preemption of state laws; repeal or modification of certain existing mandates; and a review of UMRA's existing exclusions. See National Conference of State Legislatures, "State and Federal Budgeting: Federal Mandate Relief," at http://www.ncsl.org/ Default.aspx? TabID=773&tabs=855,20,632#FederalMandate.

Unfunded Mandates Reform Act 131

concerning unfunded mandates. GAO reported that UMRA's coverage was the issue most frequently commented on by parties from all five sectors, including business, and that most of the parties representing business viewed UMRA's relatively narrow coverage as a major weakness that leaves out many federal actions with potentially significant financial impacts on nonfederal parties.[85] However, GAO also found that the business sector has "generally been in favor of federal preemptions for reasons such as standardizing regulation across state and local jurisdictions."[86]

Although GAO found that most of the parties it contacted viewed UMRA's coverage of intergovernmental mandates as being too narrow, it also reported that some of the participants opposed an expansion of UMRA's coverage:

> A few parties from the public interest sector and academic/think tank sectors considered some of the existing exclusions important or identified UMRA's narrow scope as one of the act's strengths Specifically, these parties argued in favor of maintaining UMRA's exclusions or expanding them to include federal actions regarding public health, safety, environmental protection, workers' rights, and the disabled [They also] focused on the importance of the existing exclusions, particularly those dealing with constitutional and statutory rights, such as those barring discrimination against various groups.[87]

With respect to private-sector mandates in legislation, UMRA allows a point of order to be raised only if UMRA's informational requirements are not met; that is, only if the committee reporting the measure fails to publish a CBO cost estimate statement of the private-sector mandate's costs. Over the years, various business organizations, including the U.S. Chamber of Commerce, have advocated the extension of UMRA's substantive point of order for intergovernmental mandates to the private sector, permitting a

---

[85] GAO, *Unfunded Mandates: Views Vary About Reform Act's Strengths, Weaknesses, and Options for Improvement*, GAO-05-454, March 31, 2005, p. 9, at http://www.gao.gov/new.items/d05454.pdf.

[86] Ibid., p. 12.

[87] Ibid., pp. 9, 13-14.

132   *Robert Jay Dilger*

point of order to be raised against consideration of legislation that includes private-sector mandates with costs that exceed UMRA's threshold.[88]

The GAO report also noted that "parties primarily from the academic/think tank and state and local governments sectors ... noted that while much attention has been focused on the actual (direct) costs of mandates, it is important to consider the broader implications on affected nonfederal entities beyond direct costs, including indirect costs such as opportunity costs, forgone revenues, shifting priorities, and fiscal trade-offs."[89]

During the 114th Congress, H.R. 50, the Unfunded Mandates Information and Transparency Act of 2015, passed by the House on February 4, 2015, and its Senate companion bill, S. 189, would have broadened UMRA's coverage to include both direct and indirect costs, such as foregone profits and costs passed onto consumers, and, when requested by the chair or ranking member of a committee, the prospective costs of legislation that would change conditions of federal financial assistance. The bills also would have made private-sector mandates subject to a substantive point of order and remove UMRA's exemption for rules issued by most independent agencies.

H.R. 50, and its Senate companion bill, S. 1523, were reintroduced in the 115th Congress as the Unfunded Mandates Information and Transparency Act of 2017.[90] The House passed H.R. 50 on July 13, 2018. The House also passed similar legislation during the 112th Congress (H.R. 4078, the Red Tape Reduction and Small Business Job Creation Act: Title IV, the Unfunded Mandates Information and Transparency Act of 2012),

---

[88] U.S. Congress, Senate Committee on Government Reform, *S. 389–The Unfunded Mandates Information Act*, hearing on S. 389, 105th Cong., 2nd sess., June 3, 1998, S.Hrg. 105-664 (Washington: GPO, 1998), pp. 28-35.

[89] GAO, *Unfunded Mandates: Views Vary About Reform Act's Strengths, Weaknesses, and Options for Improvement*, GAO-05-454, March 31, 2005, pp. 22, 23, at http://www.gao.gov/new.items/d05454.pdf. GAO also found that "parties across the sectors suggested that various forms of retrospective analysis are needed for evaluating federal mandates after they are implemented" and "parties in the academic/think tank sector suggested analyzing the benefits of federal mandates, when appropriate, not just costs."

[90] In addition, S. 686, the Unfunded Mandates Accountability Act of 2017, would, among other provisions, broaden UMRA's coverage to include both direct and any reasonably foreseeable indirect costs and remove UMRA's exemption for rules issued by most independent agencies.

the 113th Congress (H.R. 899, the Unfunded Mandates Information and Transparency Act of 2014; and H.R. 4, the Jobs for America Act: Division III, the Unfunded Mandates Information and Transparency Act of 2014), and, as just mentioned, during the 114th Congress (H.R. 50, the Unfunded Mandates Information and Transparency Act of 2015).

During the 116th Congress, H.R. 300, the Unfunded Mandates Information and Transparency Act of 2019, was introduced on January 8, 2019.

UMRA AND FEDERAL RULEMAKING (TITLE II)

UMRA's Title II, which became effective on March 22, 1995, generally requires federal agencies, unless otherwise prohibited by law, to prepare written statements that identify costs and benefits of a federal mandate to be imposed through the rulemaking process that may result in the expenditure by state, local, and tribal governments, in the aggregate, or by the private sector, of $100 million or more (adjusted annually for inflation) in any one year, before "promulgating any general notice of proposed rulemaking."[91] In 2019, the threshold for preparing a written statement is $164 million. These informational requirements for regulations, like the Title I cost estimate requirements for legislation, apply to both intergovernmental and private-sector mandates. Title II establishes no equivalent to the point of order mechanism in Title I through which either house can decline to consider legislation proposing covered unfunded intergovernmental mandates above the applicable threshold level.

The written assessments that federal agencies are to prepare for their regulations must identify the law authorizing the rule and include a qualitative and quantitative assessment of anticipated costs and benefits, the share of costs to be borne by the federal government, and the disproportionate budgetary effects upon particular regions, state, local, or

---

[91] 2 U.S.C. §1532.

tribal governments, or particular segments of the private sector. Assessments must also include estimates of the effect on the national economy, descriptions of consultations with nonfederal government officials, and a summary of the evaluation of comments and concerns obtained throughout the promulgation process.[92] Impacts of "any regulatory requirements" on small governments must be identified, notice must be given to those governments, and technical assistance must be provided.[93] Also, federal agencies are required, to the extent permitted in law, to develop an "effective process to permit elected officers of State, local, and tribal governments (or their designated employees with authority to act on their behalf) to provide meaningful and timely input in the development of regulatory proposals containing significant Federal intergovernmental mandates."[94] UMRA also requires federal agencies to consider "a reasonable number" of regulatory alternatives and select the "least costly, most cost-effective or least burdensome alternative" that achieves the objectives of the rule.[95]

UMRA requires the Office of Management and Budget's (OMB's) director to collect the executive branch agencies' written cost estimate statements and periodically forward copies to CBO's director. It also directs OMB to establish pilot programs in at least two federal agencies to test innovative regulatory approaches to reduce regulatory burdens on small governments, and provide Congress a written annual report detailing compliance with the act by each agency for the preceding reporting period.[96] OMB's director has delegated these responsibilities to its Office of Information and Regulatory Affairs (OIRA).

Most of these provisions were already in place when UMRA was adopted. For example, Executive Order 12866, issued in September 1993, required agencies to provide OIRA with assessments of the costs and benefits of all economically significant proposed rules (defined as having an annual impact on the economy of $100 million or more), including

---

[92] Ibid.
[93] 2 U.S.C. §1533.
[94] 2 U.S.C. §1534.
[95] 2 U.S.C. §1535.
[96] 2 U.S.C. §§1536-1538.

Unfunded Mandates Reform Act

some rules that were not mandates; identify regulatory alternatives and explain why the planned regulatory action is preferable to other alternatives; issue regulations that were cost-effective and impose the least burden on society; and seek the views of state, local, and tribal officials before imposing regulatory requirements that might significantly or uniquely affect them.[97]

Title II's Exemptions and Exclusions

UMRA's requirement for federal agencies to issue written cost estimate statements for mandates issued through the rulemaking process that may result in expenditures of $100 million or more (adjusted annually for inflation) by state and local governments, in the aggregate, or by the private sector, in any one year, is subject to the exemptions and exclusions that apply to legislative provisions (e.g., conditions of federal assistance, duties arising from participation in a voluntary federal program, and constitutional rights of individuals). UMRA's requirements also do not apply (1) to provisions in rules issued by independent regulatory agencies; (2) if the agency is "otherwise prohibited by law" from considering estimates of costs in adopting the rule (e.g., under the Clean Air Act the primary air quality standards are health-based and the courts have affirmed that the U.S. Environmental Protection Agency is not to consider costs in determining air quality standards for ozone and particulate matter); or (3) to any rule for which the agency does not publish a general notice of proposed rulemaking in the *Federal Register*.[98]

---

[97] U.S. General Accounting Office, *Unfunded Mandates: Reform Act Has Had Little Effect on Agencies' Rulemaking Actions*, GAO-GDD-98-30, February 4, 1998, p. 29, at http://www.gao.gov/assets/230/225165.pdf; and GAO, *Unfunded Mandates: Views Vary About Reform Act's Strengths, Weaknesses, and Options for Improvement*, GAO-05- 454, March 31, 2005, p. 27, at http://www.gao.gov/new.items/d05454.pdf. For further analysis concerning OIRA, see CRS Report RL32397, *Federal Rulemaking: The Role of the Office of Information and Regulatory Affairs*, coordinated by Maeve P. Carey.

[98] GAO, *Unfunded Mandates: Views Vary About Reform Act's Strengths, Weaknesses, and Options for Improvement*, GAO-05-454, March 31, 2005, pp. 26, 27, at http://www.gao.gov/new.items/d05454.pdf; and U.S. Office of Management and Budget (OMB), Office of Information and Regulatory Affairs, *2008 Report to Congress on the*

GAO has found that about half of all final rules published in the *Federal Register* are published without a general notice of proposed rulemaking, including some rules with impacts over $100 million annually.[99]

In addition, UMRA's threshold for federal mandates in rules is limited to expenditures, in contrast to the thresholds in Title I which refer to direct costs. As a result, a federal rule's estimated annual effect on direct costs might meet Title I's threshold, but might not meet Title II's threshold if the rule does not compel nonfederal entities to spend that amount. For example, under Title I, direct costs include any amounts that state and local governments are prohibited from raising in revenue to comply with the mandate. These costs are not considered when determining whether a mandate meets Title II's threshold because funds not received are not expenditures.[100]

Also, in contrast to Title I, Title II does not require the agencies issuing regulations to address the question of whether federal funding is available to cover the costs to the private sector of mandates imposed by regulations. In general, agencies lack authority to provide such funding, which could be provided only by legislative action. Title II addresses the funding only of intergovernmental mandates, and only by requiring that agencies identify the extent to which federal resources may be available to carry out those mandates.[101] The differences in the coverage of Title I and Title II may reflect a compromise reached with congressional Members who opposed using UMRA as a vehicle to address broader regulatory reform advocated by business interests.

Benefits and Costs of Federal Regulations and Unfunded Mandates on State, Local, and Tribal Entities, 2008, p. 25.

[99] U.S. General Accounting Office, *Federal Rulemaking: Agencies Often Published Final Actions Without Proposed Rules*, GAO/GGD-98-126, August 31, 1998, pp. 1, 2, at http://www.gao.gov/assets/230/226214.pdf; and GAO, *Federal Rulemaking: Past Reviews and Emerging Trends Suggest Issues That Merit Congressional Attention*, GAO-06-228T, November 1, 2005, pp. 8-10, at http://www.gao.gov/assets/120/112501.pdf.

[100] GAO, *Unfunded Mandates: Views Vary About Reform Act's Strengths, Weaknesses, and Options for Improvement*, GAO-05-454, March 31, 2005, p. 27, at http://www.gao.gov/new.items/d05454.pdf.

[101] 2 U.S.C. §1532 (a)(2).

Unfunded Mandates Reform Act

For example, Senator John Glenn argued in the Senate Committee on Governmental Affairs' committee report on UMRA:

> Another problematic change from S. 993 is the expansion of the "regulatory accountability and reform" provisions of Title 2 to go beyond intergovernmental mandates to address any and all regulatory effects on the private sector. The intended purpose of S. 1 is to control unfunded Federal mandates on State and local governments. I have always supported that goal. Moreover, I believe that if we keep the bill sharply focused on that purpose, we can get the legislation passed quickly and signed into law. If, however, we let the bill be stretched to cover other issues, we hurt prospects for enactment and we break our pledge to our friends in the State and local governments I believe that the bill should be brought back to its original purpose by limiting regulatory analysis to intergovernmental mandates.... In short, I support using this legislation to control intergovernmental regulatory costs. I oppose using this bill to address broader regulatory reform issues.[102]

Federal Agency Cost Estimate Statements in Major Federal Rules

From March 22, 1995, when UMRA's Title II became effective, to the end of FY2016, OMB reviewed 1,060 final rules with estimated benefits and/or costs exceeding $100 million annually.[103] Most (73.6%) of those

---

[102] U.S. Congress, Senate Committee on Governmental Affairs, *Unfunded Mandate Reform Act of 1995*, report to accompany S. 1, 104th Cong., 1st sess., January 11, 1995, S.Rept. 104-1 (Washington: GPO, 1995), p. 28.

[103] U.S. General Accounting Office, *Unfunded Mandates: Reform Act Has Had Little Effect on Agencies' Rulemaking Actions*, GAO-GDD-98-30, February 4, 1998, p. 16, at http://www.gao.gov/assets/230/225165.pdf; OMB, *1997 Report to Congress on the Costs and Benefits of Regulations*, September 1997, chapter 3; OMB, *1998 Report to Congress on the Costs and Benefits of Regulations*, January 1999, p. 44; OMB, *2000 Report to Congress on the Costs and Benefits of Regulations*, June 2000, pp. 37, 38; OMB, *Making Sense of Regulation: 2001 Report to Congress on the Costs and Benefits of Regulations and Unfunded Mandates on State, Local, and Tribal Entities*, December 2001, pp. 20, 21; OMB, *Stimulating Smarter Regulation: 2002 Report to Congress on the Costs and Benefits of Regulations and Unfunded Mandates on State, Local, and Tribal Entities*, December 2002, pp. 46, 47; OMB, *Informing Regulatory Decisions: 2003Report to Congress on the Costs*

"major" rules (780) did not contain provisions meeting UMRA's definition of a mandate.

Whereas, as Table 1 and Table 2 show, CBO identified slightly more private-sector mandates than intergovernmental mandates, Table 4 shows that most of the mandates identified in regulations have been directed at the private sector. This emphasis appears consistent with the original concern of business advocates to extend the concept of mandates to the area of regulatory reform.

As indicated in Table 4, during the time period covered, 280 major rules met UMRA's definition of a mandate on the private sector and, therefore, were issued an UMRA cost estimate statement and 15 met UMRA's definition of a mandate on state, local, and tribal governments and, therefore, were issued an UMRA cost estimate statement.

---

and Benefits of Regulations and Unfunded Mandates on State, Local, and Tribal Entities, September 2003, p. 10; OMB, Progress in Regulatory Reform: 2004 Report to Congress on the Costs and Benefits of Regulations and Unfunded Mandates on State, Local, and Tribal Entities, December 2004, p. 12; OMB, Validating Regulatory Analysis: 2005 Report to Congress on the Costs and Benefits of Regulations and Unfunded Mandates on State, Local, and Tribal Entities, December 2005, p. 11; OMB, 2006 Report to Congress on the Costs and Benefits of Regulations and Unfunded Mandates on State, Local, and Tribal Entities, January 2007, p. 6; OMB, 2007 Report to Congress on the Costs and Benefits of Regulations and Unfunded Mandates on State, Local, and Tribal Entities, June 2008, p. 7; OMB, 2008 Report to Congress on the Costs and Benefits of Regulations and Unfunded Mandates on State, Local, and Tribal Entities, January 2009, p. 8; OMB, 2009 Report to Congress on the Benefits and Costs of Federal Regulations and Unfunded Mandates on State, Local, and Tribal Entities, January 2010, p. 3; OMB, 2010 Report to Congress on the Benefits and Costs of Federal Regulations and Unfunded Mandates on State, Local, and Tribal Entities, July 2010, p. 3; OMB, 2011 Report to Congress on the Benefits and Costs of Federal Regulations and Unfunded Mandates on State, Local, and Tribal Entities, June 2011, p. 3; OMB, 2012 Report to Congress on the Benefits and Costs of Federal Regulations and Unfunded Mandates on State, Local, and Tribal Entities, April 2013, p. 3; OMB, 2013 Report to Congress on the Benefits and Costs of Federal Regulations and Unfunded Mandates on State, Local, and Tribal Entities, May 2014, p. 4; OMB, 2014 Report to Congress on the Benefits and Costs of Federal Regulations and Unfunded Mandates on State, Local, and Tribal Entities, June 2015, p. 2; OMB, 2015 Report to Congress on the Benefits and Costs of Federal Regulations and Unfunded Mandates on State, Local, and Tribal Entities, March 2016, p. 2; OMB, 2016 Draft Report to Congress on the Benefits and Costs of Federal Regulations and Agency Compliance with the Unfunded Mandates Reform Act, December 23, 2016, p. 2; and OMB, 2017 Draft Report to Congress on the Benefits and Costs of Federal Regulations and Agency Compliance with the Unfunded Mandates Reform Act, February 23, 2018, p. 2.

Table 4. UMRA written mandate cost estimate statements issued by federal agencies in final rules, 1995-2015

Time Period	Private-Sector Mandates	Public-Sector Mandates	Total
June 1995-May 2000	76	4	80
June 2000-May 2001	16	2	18
May 2001-October 2001	4	0	4
October 2001-September 2002	5	0	5
October 2002-September 2003	17	0	17
October 2003-September 2004	10	0	10
October 2004-September 2005	3	1	4
October 2005-September 2006	9	1	10
October 2006-September 2007	11	0	11
October 2007-September 2008	8	0	8
October 2008-September 2009	11	1	12
October 2009-September 2010	13	0	13
October 2010-September 2011	13	0	13
October 2011-September 2012	9	2	11
October 2012-September 2013	10	2	12
October 2013-September 2014	10	1	11
October 2014-September 2015	12	1	13
October 2015-September 2016	28	0	28
Total	265	15	280

Sources: Joint Hearing, U.S. Congress, House Committee on Government Reform, Subcommittee on Energy Policy, Natural Resources and Regulatory Affairs, and House Committee on Rules, Subcommittee on Technology and the House, *Unfunded Mandates: A Five Year Review and Recommendations for Change*, hearing on the Unfunded Mandates Reform Act of 1995, 107th Congress, 1st session, May 24, 2001, H. Hrg. 107-19 (Washington: GPO, 2001), p. 40; U.S. Office of Management and Budget (OMB), *Making Sense of Regulation: 2001 Report to Congress on the Costs and Benefits of Regulations and Unfunded Mandates on State, Local, and Tribal Entities*, December 2001, pp. 189-195; OMB, *Stimulating Smarter Regulation: 2002 Report to Congress on the Costs and Benefits of Regulations and Unfunded Mandates on State, Local, and Tribal Entities*, December 2002, pp. 161, 162; OMB, *Informing Regulatory Decisions: 2003 Report to Congress on the Costs and Benefits of Regulations and Unfunded Mandates on State, Local, and Tribal Entities*, September 2003, pp. 202-204; OMB, *Progress in Regulatory Reform: 2004 Report to Congress on the Costs and Benefits of Regulations and Unfunded Mandates on State, Local, and Tribal Entities*, December 2004, pp. 225-234; OMB, *Validating Regulatory Analysis: 2005 Report to Congress on the Costs and Benefits of Regulations and Unfunded Mandates on State, Local, and Tribal Entities*, December 2005, pp. 143-148; OMB, *2006 Report to Congress on the Costs and Benefits of Regulations and Unfunded Mandates on State, Local, and Tribal Entities*, January 2007, pp. 141-143; OMB, *2007 Report to Congress on the Costs and Benefits of Regulations and Unfunded Mandates on State, Local, and Tribal Entities*, June 2008, pp. 76-81; OMB, *2008 Report to Congress on the Costs and Benefits of Regulations and Unfunded Mandates on State, Local, and Tribal Entities*, January 2009, pp. 77-

Table 4. (Continued)

81; OMB, *2009 Report to Congress on the Benefits and Costs of Federal Regulations and Unfunded Mandates on State, Local, and Tribal Entities*, January 27, 2010, pp. 62-65; OMB, *2010 Report to Congress on the Benefits and Costs of Federal Regulations and Unfunded Mandates on State, Local, and Tribal Entities*, July 20, 2010, pp. 73-79; OMB, *2011 Report to Congress on the Benefits and Costs of Federal Regulations and Unfunded Mandates on State, Local, and Tribal Entities*, June 24, 2011, pp. 94-98; OMB, *2012 Report to Congress on the Benefits and Costs of Federal Regulations and Unfunded Mandates on State, Local, and Tribal Entities*, April 2013, pp. 101-104; OMB, *2013 Report to Congress on the Benefits and Costs of Federal Regulations and Unfunded Mandates on State, Local, and Tribal Entities*, May 2014, pp. 79-83; OMB, *2014 Report to Congress on the Benefits and Costs of Federal Regulations and Unfunded Mandates on State, Local, and Tribal Entities*, June 2015, pp. 73-77; OMB, *2015 Report to Congress on the Benefits and Costs of Federal Regulations and Unfunded Mandates on State, Local, and Tribal Entities*, March 2016, pp. 73-76; OMB, *2016 Draft Report to Congress on the Benefits and Costs of Federal Regulations and Agency Compliance with the Unfunded Mandates Reform Act*, December 23, 2016, pp. 56-60; and OMB, *2017 Draft Report to Congress on the Benefits and Costs of Federal Regulations and Agency Compliance with the Unfunded Mandates Reform Act, February* 23, 2018, pp. 56-62.

The 15 intergovernmental rules, 9 issued by the U.S. Environmental Protection Agency (EPA), were as follows:

- EPA's Rule on Standards of Performance for Municipal Waste Combustors and Emissions Guidelines (1995), with estimated costs of $320 million annually;[104]
- EPA's Standards of Performance for New Stationary Sources and Guidelines for Control of Existing Sources: Municipal Solid Waste Landfills (1996), with estimated costs of $110 million annually;[105]
- EPA's National Primary Drinking Water Regulations: Disinfectants and Disinfection Byproducts (1998), with estimated costs of $700 million annually;[106]
- EPA's National Primary Drinking Water Regulations: Interim Enhanced Surface Water Treatment (1998), with estimated costs of $300 million annually;[107]

---

[104] OMB, *2006 Report to Congress on the Costs and Benefits of Regulations and Unfunded Mandates on State, Local, and Tribal Entities*, January 2007, pp. 18-19.

[105] Ibid., p. 19.

[106] Ibid.

Unfunded Mandates Reform Act

- EPA's National Pollutant Discharge Elimination: System B Regulations for Revision of the Water Pollution Control Program Addressing Storm Water Discharges (1999), with estimated costs of $803.1 million annually;[108]
- EPA's National Primary Drinking Water Regulations; Arsenic and Clarifications to Compliance and New Source Contaminants Monitoring (2001), with estimated costs of $189 million to $216 million annually;[109]
- EPA's National Primary Drinking Water Regulations: Long Term 2 Enhanced Surface Water Treatment (2005), with estimated costs between $80 million and $130 million per year;[110]
- EPA's National Primary Drinking Water Regulations: Stage 2 Disinfection Byproducts Rule (2006), with estimated costs of at least $100 million annually;[111]
- U.S. Department of Health and Human Services' (DHHS's) Health Insurance Reform; Modifications to the Health Insurance Portability and Accountability Act (HIPAA) Electronic Transaction Standards (2009), with estimated costs of $1.1 billion per year;[112]
- EPA's National Emission Standards for Hazardous Air Pollutants from Coal- and Oil-Fired Electric Utility Steam Generating Units and Standards for Performance for Electric Utility Steam Generating Units (2011), with estimated costs of $9.6 billion annually;[113]

---

[107] Ibid.

[108] Ibid., p. 20.

[109] OMB, *2011 Report to Congress on the Benefits and Costs of Federal Regulations and Unfunded Mandates on State, Local, and Tribal Entities*, June 24, 2011, p. 33.

[110] Ibid.

[111] OMB, *2016 Draft Report to Congress on the Benefits and Costs of Federal Regulations and Agency Compliance with the Unfunded Mandates Reform Act*, December 23, 2016, pp. 34-35.

[112] OMB, *2010 Report to Congress on the Benefits and Costs of Federal Regulations and Unfunded Mandates on State, Local, and Tribal Entities*, July 2010, pp. 77-78.

[113] OMB, *2016 Draft Report to Congress on the Benefits and Costs of Federal Regulations and Agency Compliance with the Unfunded Mandates Reform Act*, December 23, 2016, p. 35.

- U.S. Department of Agriculture's (USDA's) Nutrition Standards in the National School Lunch and School Breakfast Programs (2012), with estimated costs of $479 million annually;[114]
- DHHS's Patient Protection and Affordable Care Act; Benefit and Payment Parameters for 2014 (issued FY2013), 2015 (issued FY2014), 2016 (issued FY2015), and 2017 (issued FY2016). Although DHHS was unable to quantify the user fees that will be associated with these three rules, CBO found that the combined administrative cost and user fee impact for each of them may be high enough to constitute a state, local, or tribal government mandate under UMRA; and
- U.S. Department of Labor's Defining and Delimiting the Exemptions for Executive, Administrative, Professional, Outside Sales and Computer Employees (2016) revised and indexed for inflation salary thresholds for determining overtime requirements for salaried workers. CBO found that employee enumeration impacts and compliance costs were estimated to be well over $100 million annually and that, in addition to private sector industries, some local government entities will be substantially affected by the rule.[115]

---

[114] Ibid.

[115] OMB, *2016 Draft Report to Congress on the Benefits and Costs of Federal Regulations and Agency Compliance with the Unfunded Mandates Reform Act,* December 23, 2016, p. 36. Note: The rule on Standards for Privacy of Individually Available Health Information, issued in 2001 by the Department of Health and Human Services, was identified as costing state and local governments $240 million annually, but the rule was later determined not to be an enforceable duty as defined under UMRA. The Department of Homeland Security's (DHS) Chemical Facility Anti- Terrorism Standards Rule, issued in 2007, was identified as having the potential to require certain municipalities that own and/or operate power generating facilities to purchase security enhancements. However, DHS was unable to determine whether the rule would impose an enforceable duty on state and local governments of $100 million or more (adjusted for inflation) in any one year. OMB includes the rule as a state and local government mandate meeting UMRA's requirements "for the sake of completeness."

Impact on the Rulemaking Process

In 1997, Senators Fred Thompson and John Glenn, chair and ranking minority member of the Senate Committee on Governmental Affairs, respectively, asked GAO to review federal agencies' implementation of UMRA's Title II. On February 4, 1998, GAO issued its report, concluding that "our review of federal agencies' implementation of Title II of UMRA indicates that this title of the act has had little direct effect on agencies' rulemaking actions during the first 2 years of its implementation."[116]

GAO concluded that Title II had limited impact on agencies' rulemaking primarily because of its limited coverage. For example, GAO noted that written mandate cost estimate statements were not on file at CBO for 80 of the 110 economically significant rules published in the *Federal Register* between March 22, 1995, and March 22, 1997. GAO examined the 80 economically significant rules that lacked a written mandate cost estimate statement and concluded that UMRA did not require a written mandate cost estimate statement for 78 of them because the rule either did not have an associated notice of proposed rulemaking (18 instances); did not impose an enforceable duty (3 instances); imposed such a duty but only as a condition of federal assistance (33 instances); imposed such a duty but only as part of a voluntary program (11 instances); did not involve an expenditure of $100 million in any single year by the private sector or by state, local, and tribal governments (12 instances); or incorporated requirements specifically set forth in law (1 instance). GAO concluded that written mandate cost estimate statements should have been filed at CBO for two of the rules that lacked one, but, in both instances, the rules appeared to satisfy UMRA's written statement requirements.[117]

Even where UMRA applied, GAO concluded that the act did not appear to have had much effect on federal agencies' rulemaking actions because UMRA does not require agencies to take the actions required in

---

[116] U.S. General Accounting Office, *Unfunded Mandates: Reform Act Has Had Little Effect on Agencies' Rulemaking Actions*, GAO-GDD-98-30, February 4, 1998, p. 29, at http://www.gao.gov/assets/230/225165.pdf.

[117] Ibid., pp. 12-16.

144   *Robert Jay Dilger*

the statute if the agencies determine that the actions are duplicative of other actions or that accurate estimates of the rule's future compliance costs are not feasible.[118] Because federal agencies' rules commonly contain an estimate of compliance costs, GAO found that most agencies rarely prepared a separate UMRA written cost estimate statement. Moreover, Executive Order 12866, which was issued more than a year before UMRA's enactment, already required federal agencies to provide OIRA with assessments of the costs and benefits of all economically significant rules. GAO also concluded that UMRA did not substantially change agencies' intergovernmental consultation processes.[119]

In 2001, OMB's director, Mitchell L. Daniels Jr., acknowledged at a House hearing coinciding with UMRA's fifth anniversary that UMRA's Title II had not resulted in major changes in federal agency rulemaking. He noted that, according to OMB's five annual reports to Congress on the implementation of Title II, 80 rules had required the preparation of a separate written mandate cost estimate statement (see Table 4). He said that "it was hard to believe that only 80 regulations had significant impacts on state, local, or tribal governments, or the private sector. In fact, it appears that agencies have attempted to limit their consultative processes, and ignored potential alternative remedies, by aggressively utilizing the exemptions outlined by the Act."[120] He added that "when agencies fail to solicit or consider the views of states and localities, they deny themselves the benefit of state and local innovation and experience. This will not be accepted practice in this [George W. Bush] Administration."[121]

In 2004, GAO released a second study of UMRA's implementation of Title II (and the first for Title I), focusing on statutes enacted and rules published during 2001 and 2002. GAO found that 5 of 377 statutes enacted and 9 of 122 major or economically significant final rules issued in 2001 or

---

[118] Ibid., p. 28.

[119] Ibid., pp. 21, 22.

[120] Joint Hearing, U.S. Congress, House Committee on Government Reform, Subcommittee on Energy Policy, Natural Resources and Regulatory Affairs, and House Committee on Rules, Subcommittee on Technology and the House, *Unfunded Mandates: A Five Year Review and Recommendations for Change*, hearing on the Unfunded Mandates Reform Act of 1995, 107th Cong., 1st sess., May 24, 2001, H. Hrg. 107-19 (Washington: GPO, 2001), p. 40.

[121] Ibid.

2002 were identified as containing federal mandates at or above UMRA's thresholds.[122] GAO concluded its report by stating that "the findings raise the question of whether UMRA's procedures, definitions, and exclusions adequately capture and subject to scrutiny federal statutory and regulatory actions that might impose significant financial burdens on affected nonfederal parties."[123]

As noted earlier, in 2005, GAO sought and received input from participating parties about UMRA's strengths and weaknesses and potential options for reinforcing the strengths or addressing the weaknesses. It also held a symposium on federal mandates to examine those identified strengths and weaknesses in more depth.[124] Although the symposium's participants viewed UMRA's coverage as its most significant issue, GAO reported that comments received concerning federal agency consultation with state and local governments under Title II "focused on the quality of consultations across agencies, which was viewed as inconsistent" and that "a few parties commented that UMRA had improved consultation and collaboration between federal agencies and nonfederal levels of government."[125]

At a Senate hearing held on April 14, 2005, OIRA's director, John Graham, testified that OMB includes summaries of agency consultations with state and local government officials in its annual report to Congress and that "this year's report shows an increased level of engagement."[126] He added that there were "some very good examples of consultation that are documented in that report at the Department of Education, the Environmental Protection Agency and so forth, but I think that it would be

---

[122] U.S. General Accounting Office, *Unfunded Mandates: Analysis of Reform Act Coverage*, GAO-04-637, May 12, 2004, pp. 4, 28-33, at http://www.gao.gov/new.items/d04637.pdf.

[123] Ibid., pp. 36, 37.

[124] GAO, *Unfunded Mandates: Views Vary About Reform Act's Strengths, Weaknesses, and Options for Improvement*, GAO-05-454, March 31, 2005, pp. 3, 4, at http://www.gao.gov/new.items/d05454.pdf.

[125] Ibid., p. 20.

[126] U.S. Congress, Senate Committee on Homeland Security and Governmental Affairs, Subcommittee on Oversight of Government Management, the Federal Workforce, and the District of Columbia, *Passing the Buck: A Review of the Unfunded Mandates Reform Act*, hearing on the Unfunded Mandates Reform Act, 109th Cong., 1st sess., April 14, 2005, S. Hrg. 109-82 (Washington: GPO, 2005), p. 52.

146   *Robert Jay Dilger*

fair to say that those best practices are not necessarily uniform across the federal government or across any particular agency."[127] State and local government officials testifying at the hearing stated that federal agency consultation had improved somewhat, but remained "sporadic."[128]

Congressional Issues for Title II

Exemptions and Exclusions

State and local government public interest groups continue to advocate a broadening of Title II's coverage. For example, as mentioned previously, they advocate a broader definition of what UMRA considers a mandate, under the presumption that a broader definition would subject more rules to Title II. An alternative approach would be to separate debates concerning the definition of "mandate" and UMRA's coverage, and, instead, apply Title II's information requirements to whatever classes of federally induced costs Congress deems appropriate to cover. This approach might be implemented by incorporating coverage of various kinds of "federally induced costs," adopting the terminology proposed earlier by ACIR. In either case, inasmuch as Title II's requirements are informational only, their extension to new classes of regulations, or to new kinds of federally induced costs, would not affect the authority of agencies to issue regulations or the substance of the regulations that could be issued.

As mentioned previously, UMRA's threshold for federal mandates in rules is limited to expenditures, in contrast to the thresholds in Title I that refer to direct costs. Introduced during the 116th Congress, H.R. 300, the Unfunded Mandates Information and Transparency Act of 2019, would broaden UMRA's coverage to include both direct and indirect costs, such as foregone profits and costs passed onto consumers, and, when requested

---

[127] Ibid., p. 16.
[128] Ibid., pp. 22, 23, 27.

by the chair or ranking member of a committee, the prospective costs of legislation that would change conditions of federal financial assistance.[129]

State and local government advocacy groups have also argued that Title II should apply to rules issued by independent regulatory agencies.[130] Although OMB does not review rules issued by independent regulatory agencies, in recent years it has included information concerning independent regulatory agency rules in its annual UMRA report to Congress. According to those reports, independent regulatory agencies issued 271 major rules from FY1997 through FY2016.[131] H.R. 300 would remove UMRA's exemption for rules issued by most independent agencies.[132]

The National Association of Counties (NACO) and other state and local government public interest groups have also advocated a strengthening of OMB's role in the enforcement of Title II to ensure consistent application of UMRA's provisions across federal agencies.[133] For example, NCSL's current policy statement on unfunded mandates

---

[129] As mentioned previously, the House passed similar legislation during the 112th Congress (H.R. 4078, the Red Tape Reduction and Small Business Job Creation Act: Title IV, the Unfunded Mandates Information and Transparency Act of 2012), the 113th Congress (H.R. 899, the Unfunded Mandates Information and Transparency Act of 2014, and H.R. 4, the Jobs for America Act: Division III, the Unfunded Mandates Information and Transparency Act of 2014), the 114th Congress (H.R. 50, the Unfunded Mandates Information and Transparency Act of 2015), and the 115th Congress (H.R. 50, the Unfunded Mandates Information and Transparency Act of 2017).

[130] U.S. Congress, Senate Committee on Homeland Security and Governmental Affairs, Subcommittee on Oversight of Government Management, the Federal Workforce, and the District of Columbia, *Passing the Buck: A Review of the Unfunded Mandates Reform Act*, hearing on the Unfunded Mandates Reform Act, 109th Cong., 1st sess., April 14, 2005, S. Hrg. 109-82 (Washington: GPO, 2005), pp. 112-126, 167-174.

[131] OMB, *2007 Report to Congress on the Costs and Benefits of Regulations and Unfunded Mandates on State, Local, and Tribal Entities*, June 2008, p. 16; OMB, *2014 Report to Congress on the Benefits and Costs of Federal Regulations*, June 2015, p. 106; OMB, *2017 Draft Report to Congress on the Benefits and Costs of Federal Regulations and Agency Compliance with the Unfunded Mandates Reform Act*, February 23, 2018, pp. 90, 91.

[132] Both bills would retain the exemption for rules that concern monetary policy proposed or implemented by the Board of Governors of the Federal Reserve System, the Federal Open Market Committee, or the Bureau of Consumer Financial Protection.

[133] U.S. Congress, Senate Committee on Homeland Security and Governmental Affairs, Subcommittee on Oversight of Government Management, the Federal Workforce, and the District of Columbia, *Passing the Buck: A Review of the Unfunded Mandates Reform Act*, hearing on the Unfunded Mandates Reform Act, 109th Cong., 1st sess., April 14, 2005, S. Hrg. 109-82 (Washington: GPO, 2005), p. 124.

148   *Robert Jay Dilger*

recommends that UMRA be amended to include "the creation of an office within the Office of Management and Budget that is analogous to the State and Local Government Cost Estimates Unit at the Congressional Budget Office."[134] Business organizations, led by the U.S. Chamber of Commerce, also have advocated an independent review of federal agency cost estimates, recommending that the reviews be conducted by OMB or GAO. They also have advocated the permitting of early judicial challenges to an agency's failure to complete an UMRA cost estimate statement or for completing one that is deficient.[135]

During the 112th Congress, H.R. 214, the Congressional Office of Regulatory Analysis Creation and Sunset and Review Act of 2011, would have created a Congressional Office of Regulatory Analysis.[136] The bill included a provision that would have transferred from CBO's director to the director of the proposed Congressional Office of Regulatory Analysis the responsibility to compare federal agency estimates of the cost of regulations implementing an act containing a federal mandate with the CBO's estimate of those costs. The Congressional Office of Regulatory Analysis would also have received federal agency statements that accompany significant regulatory actions.

As mentioned previously, organizations representing various environmental and social groups have argued that UMRA has achieved its stated goals of strengthening the partnership between the federal government and state, local, and tribal governments by promoting

---

[134] National Conference of State Legislatures, "State and Federal Budgeting: Federal Mandate Relief," at http://www.ncsl.org/Default.aspx?TabID=773&tabs=855,20,632#Federal Mandate.

[135] Joint Hearing, U.S. Congress, House Committee on Government Reform, Subcommittee on Energy Policy, Natural Resources and Regulatory Affairs, and House Committee on Rules, Subcommittee on Technology and the House, *Unfunded Mandates: A Five Year Review and Recommendations for Change*, hearing on the Unfunded Mandates Reform Act of 1995, 107th Cong., 1st sess., May 24, 2001, H. Hrg. 107-19 (Washington: GPO, 2001), pp. 80, 88, 89.

[136] H.R. 214, the Congressional Office of Regulatory Analysis Creation and Sunset and Review Act of 2011, was introduced on January 7, 2011, and referred to the House Committee on the Judiciary and House Committee on Oversight and Government Reform. The bill was later referred to the House Committee on the Judiciary's Subcommittee on Courts, Commercial and Administrative Law and the House Committee on Oversight and Government Reform's Subcommittee on Regulatory Affairs, Stimulus Oversight and Government Spending.

informed and deliberate decisions by Congress on the appropriateness of federal mandates. In their view, broadening UMRA's coverage would dilute its impact. For example, a participant at GAO's 2005 symposium on federal mandates argued that eliminating any of UMRA's exclusions and exemptions might make the identification of mandates less meaningful, saying "The more red flags run up, the less important the red flag becomes."[137] Also, some of the participants at the symposium from the academic, policy research institute, and public interest advocacy sectors argued that it was essential that some of the existing exclusions, such as those dealing with constitutional and statutory rights barring discrimination against various groups, be retained.

They also advocated additional exclusions to include federal actions regarding public health, safety, environmental protection, workers' rights, and the disabled.[138]

Federal Agency Consultation Requirements

State and local government public interest groups assert that enhanced requirements for federal agency consultation with state and local government officials during the rulemaking process are needed.[139] For example, the NCSL has asserted that federal agency "consultation with state and local governments in the construction of these rules is haphazard."[140] It recommends that Title II be amended to include "enhanced requirements for federal agencies to consult with state and local governments."[141]

---

[137] GAO, *Unfunded Mandates: Views Vary About Reform Act's Strengths, Weaknesses, and Options for Improvement*, GAO-05-454, March 31, 2005, p. 13, at http://www.gao.gov/new.items/d05454.pdf.

[138] Ibid.

[139] National Conference of State Legislatures, "State and Federal Budgeting: Federal Mandate Relief," at http://www.ncsl.org/Default.aspx?TabID=773&tabs=855,20,632#Federal Mandate.

[140] National Conference of State Legislatures, "Policy Position on Federal Mandate Relief," effective through August 2011.

[141] National Conference of State Legislatures, "State and Federal Budgeting: Federal Mandate Relief," at http://www.ncsl.org/Default.aspx?TabID=773&tabs=855,20,632#Federal Mandate.

150   *Robert Jay Dilger*

OMB asserts that "federal agencies have been actively consulting with states, localities, and tribal governments in order to ensure that regulatory activities were conducted consistent with the requirements of UMRA."[142] In addition, OMB notes that it has had guidelines in place since September 21, 1995, to assist federal agencies in complying with the act.[143] The current guidelines suggest that (1) intergovernmental consultations should take place as early as possible, beginning before issuance of a proposed rule and continuing through the final rule stage, and be integrated explicitly into the rulemaking process; (2) agencies should consult with a wide variety of state, local, and tribal officials; (3) agencies should estimate direct benefits and costs to assist with these consultations; (4) the scope of consultation should reflect the cost and significance of the mandate being considered; (5) effective consultation requires trust and significant and sustained attention so that all who participate can enjoy frank discussion and focus on key priorities; and (6) agencies should seek out state, local, and tribal views on costs, benefits, risks, and alternative methods of compliance, and whether the federal rule will harmonize with and not duplicate similar laws in other levels of government.[144]

OMB often includes summaries of selected consultation activities by agencies whose actions affect state, local, and tribal governments in its annual draft and final UMRA reports to Congress. OMB has argued that the summaries are an indication that federal agencies are complying with the act. For example, in OMB's final 2015 UMRA report to Congress, OMB wrote in the introduction to these summaries:

> Four agencies subject to UMRA (the Departments of Energy, Health and Human Services, Interior, and Labor) provided examples of consultation activities that involved State, local, and tribal governments not only in their regulatory processes, but also in their program planning

---

[142] OMB, *2011 Report to Congress on the Benefits and Costs of Federal Regulations and Unfunded Mandates on State, Local, and Tribal Entities*, June 24, 2011, p. 93.

[143] OMB, *Agency Compliance with Title II of the Unfunded Mandates Reform Act of 1995: 4th Annual Report to Congress from the Director of the Office of Management and Budget*, October 1999, p. 2.

[144] OMB, *2015 Report to Congress on the Costs and Benefits of Regulations and Unfunded Mandates on State, Local, and Tribal Entities*, March 2016, p. 73.

Unfunded Mandates Reform Act

and implementation phases. These agencies have worked to enhance the regulatory environment by improving the way in which the Federal Government relates to its intergovernmental partners. Many of the departments and agencies not listed here (i.e., the Departments of Justice, State, Treasury, and Veterans Affairs, the Small Business Administration, and the General Services Administration) do not often impose mandates upon States, localities, or tribes, and thus have fewer occasions to consult with these governments. Other agencies, such as the National Archives and Records Administration, are exempt from UMRA's reporting requirements, but may nonetheless engage in consultation where their activities would affect State, local, and Tribal governments.

As the following descriptions indicate, Federal agencies conduct a wide range of consultations. Agency consultations sometimes involve multiple levels of government, depending on the agency's understanding of the scope and impact of its rule or policy.[145]

As mentioned previously, H.R. 300, the Unfunded Mandates Information and Transparency Act of 2019, would require federal agencies to enhance their consultation with UMRA stakeholders.

CONCLUSION

In 1995, UMRA's enactment was considered an historic, milestone event in the history of American intergovernmental relations. For example, when signing UMRA, President Bill Clinton said,

> Today, we are making history. We are working to find the right balance for the 21st century. We are recognizing that the pendulum had swung too far, and that we have to rely on the initiative, the creativity, the determination, and the decisionmaking of people at the State and local level to carry much of the load for America as we move into the 21st century.[146]

---

[145] Ibid., p. 99.

[146] President Bill Clinton, "Remarks on Signing the Unfunded Mandates Reform Act of 1995," *Weekly Compilation of Presidential Documents*, vol. 31, no. 12 (March 22, 1995), p. 455.

Since UMRA's enactment, parties participating in its implementation and researchers in the academic community, policy research institutes, and nonpartisan government agencies have reached different conclusions concerning the extent of UMRA's impact on intergovernmental relations and whether UMRA should be amended. State and local government officials and federalism scholars generally view UMRA as having a limited, though positive, impact on intergovernmental relations. In their view, the federal government has continued to expand its authority through the "carrots" of increased federal assistance and the "sticks" of grant conditions, preemptions, mandates, and administrative rulemaking. Facing what they view as a seemingly ever growing federal influence in American governance, they generally advocate a broadening of UMRA's coverage to enhance its impact, emphasizing the need to include conditions of grant assistance and a broader range of federal agency rulemaking, including rules issued by independent regulatory agencies.

Other organizations, representing various environmental and social groups, argue that UMRA's coverage does not need to be broadened. In their view, UMRA has accomplished its goals of fostering improved intergovernmental relations and ensuring that when Congress votes on major federal mandates it is aware of the costs imposed by the legislation. They assert that UMRA's current limits on coverage should be maintained or reinforced by adding exclusions for mandates regarding public health, safety, workers' rights, environmental protection, and the disabled.[147]

During the 111th Congress, UMRA received increased attention as Congress considered various proposals to reform health care. Governors, for example, expressed opposition to proposals that would have required states to contribute toward the cost of expanding Medicaid eligibility, asserting that the expansion could inflate state deficits and impose on states what Tennessee Governor Philip Bredesen reportedly described as the "mother of all unfunded mandates."[148] As mentioned previously, at that

---

[147] GAO, *Unfunded Mandates: Views Vary About Reform Act's Strengths, Weaknesses, and Options for Improvement*, GAO-05-454, March 31, 2005, pp. 5-7, 9-14, at http://www.gao.gov/new.items/d05454.pdf.

[148] Robert Pear and David M. Herszenhorn, "Senators Hear Concerns Over Costs of Health Proposal," *The New York Times*, August 6, 2009, at http://www.nytimes.com/2009/

time, CBO had determined that UMRA provisions did not apply to Medicaid's conditions of federal assistance because, in its view, states had "significant flexibility to make programmatic adjustments in their Medicaid programs to accommodate" new federal requirements.[149] Following the Supreme Court's ruling in *National Federation of Independent Business (NFIB) v. Sebelius* (June 28, 2012), CBO indicated that UMRA's provisions may apply to changes in "the stringency of conditions" or reductions in funding for "certain large mandatory programs … if the affected governments lack the flexibility to alter the programs."[150]

As discussed previously, H.R. 300, the Unfunded Mandates Information and Transparency Act of 2019, would

- require CBO to assess the prospective costs of changes in conditions of federal financial assistance when requested by the chair or ranking member of a committee;
- broaden UMRA's coverage to include assessments of indirect as well as direct costs by amending the definition of direct costs to include forgone profits, costs passed onto consumers or other entities, and, to the extent practicable, behavioral changes;
- expand the scope of reporting requirements to include regulations imposed by most independent regulatory agencies;
- make private-sector mandates subject to a substantive point of order;
- establish principles for federal agencies to follow when assessing the effects of regulations on state and local governments and the private sector, including requiring the agency to identify the

---

08/07/health/policy/07health.html?hpw; Clifford Krauss, Governors Fear Added Costs in Health Care Overhaul, *The New York Times*, August 6, 2009, at http://www.nytimes.com/2009/08/07/business/07medicaid.html; and Chas Sisk, "Tennessee Gov. Bredesen takes lead role in fight over health costs," *The Tennessean*, August 18, 2009, at http://www.tennessean.com/article/20090818/NEWS02/908180357/1009/NEWS02/Tennessee+Gov.+Bredesen+takes+lead+role+in+fight+over+health+costs.

[149] CBO, "Cost Estimate for the Patient Protection and Affordable Care Act," November 18, 2009, p. 18, at http://www.cbo.gov/ftpdocs/107xx/doc10731/Reid_letter_11_18_09.pdf.

[150] CBO, "CBO's Activities Under the Unfunded Mandates Reform Act," at https://www.cbo.gov/publication/51335.

problem it seeks to address, determining whether existing laws or regulations could be modified to address the problem, identifying alternatives, and designing regulations in the most cost-effective manner available;

- expand the scope of cost statements accompanying significant regulatory actions to include, among other requirements, a reasonably detailed description of the need for the proposed rulemaking or final rule and an explanation of how the proposed rulemaking or final rule will meet that need; an assessment of the potential costs and benefits of the proposed rulemaking or final rule; estimates of the mandate's future compliance costs and any disproportionate budgetary effects upon any particular regions of the nation or state, local, or tribal governments; a detailed description of the agency's consultation with the private sector or elected representatives of the affected state, local, or tribal governments; and a detailed summary of how the agency complied with each of the regulatory principles included in the bill;
- no longer allow a federal agency to forgo UMRA analysis because the agency published a rule without first issuing a notice of proposed rulemaking;
- require federal agencies to meet enhanced levels of consultation with state, local, and tribal governments and the private sector before issuing a notice of proposed rulemaking or a final rule; and
- require federal agencies to conduct a retrospective analysis of the costs and benefits of an existing regulation when requested by the chair or ranking member of a committee.

Advocates argue that these reforms will "improve the quality of congressional deliberations and... enhance the ability of Congress, federal agencies, and the public to identify federal mandates that may impose undue harm on state, local, and tribal governments and the private sector."[151] Opponents argue that these reforms are "an assault on the nation's health, safety, and environmental protections, would erect new barriers to unnecessarily slow down the regulatory process, and would give regulated industries an unfair advantage to water down consumer protections."[152]

Underlying disagreements over UMRA's future are fundamentally different values concerning American federalism. One view emphasizes the importance of freeing state and local government officials from the constraints brought about by the directives and costs associated with federal mandates so they can experiment with innovative ways to achieve results with greater efficiency and cost effectiveness. This view focuses on the positive effect active state and local governments can have in promoting a sense of state and community responsibility and self-reliance, encouraging participation and civic responsibility by allowing more people to become involved in public questions, adapting public programs to state and local needs and conditions, and reducing the political turmoil that sometimes results from single policies that govern the entire nation.[153]

Another view emphasizes the federal government's responsibility to ensure that all citizens are afforded minimum levels of essential government services. This view focuses on the propensity of states to restrict governmental services because they compete with one another for businesses and taxpaying residents; the variation in state fiscal capacities that makes it difficult for some states to provide certain governmental services even though they might have the political will to do so; and the propensity of states to have different views concerning what services are essential and what constitutes a sufficient level of essential government services.[154]

---

[151] U.S. Congress, House Committee on Oversight and Government Reform, *Unfunded Mandates Information and Transparency Act of 2015*, report to accompany H.R. 50, 114th Cong., 1st sess., February 2, 2015, H.Rept. 114-11 (Washington: GPO, 2015), p. 2.

[152] Ibid., p. 37.

[153] Thomas R. Dye, *Understanding Public Policy*, 6th edition (Englewood Cliffs, N.J.: Prentice-Hall, Inc., 1987), p. 301.

[154] Ibid., p. 300; ACIR, *Categorical Grants: Their Role and Design* (Washington, DC: ACIR, 1978), pp. 50-58; and Claude E. Barfield, *Rethinking Federalism: Block Grants and*

156 *Robert Jay Dilger*

Given these disagreements over fundamental values, it is perhaps not surprising that there are differences of opinion concerning UMRA's future. Using President Clinton's words, debates over UMRA's future are more than just arguments over who will pay for what; they are also about finding "the right balance" for American federalism in the 21st century.

APPENDIX A. THE RISE OF UNFUNDED MANDATES AS A NATIONAL ISSUE AND UMRA'S LEGISLATIVE HISTORY

Unfunded mandates became a national issue during the 1980s as state and local government officials and their affiliated public interest groups, led by the National League of Cities (NLC), U.S. Conference of Mayors (USCM), and National Association of Counties (NACO), began an intensive lobbying effort to limit unfunded intergovernmental mandates. Their efforts were supported by various business organizations, led by the U.S. Chamber of Commerce, which opposed the imposition of unfunded mandates on both state and local governments and the private sector, particularly mandates issued through federal rules.[155]

Increased Number and Cost of Unfunded Mandates

State and local government officials became involved in the issue of unfunded federal mandates during the 1980s primarily because the number and costs of unfunded intergovernmental mandates were increasing and, by

---

Federal, State, and Local Responsibilities (Washington, DC: American Enterprise Institute, 1981), pp. 4-8.

[155] Vernon Louviere, "The Strings Become a Noose," *Nation's Business*, vol. 69, no. 3 (March 1981), p. 64; Joan C. Szabo, "How Costly are Mandated Benefits?" *Nation's Business*, vol. 76, no. 4 (April 1988), p. 14; Mary McElvenn, "The Federal Impact on Business," *Nation's Business*, vol. 79, no. 1 (January 1991), pp. 23-26; David Warner, "Regulations' Staggering Costs," *Nation's Business*, vol. 80, no. 6 (June 1992), pp. 50-53; Michael Barrier, "Taxing the Man Behind the Tree," *Nation's Business*, vol. 81, no. 9 (September 1993), pp. 31, 32; and Michael Barrier, "Mandates Foes Smell a Victory," *Nation's Business*, vol. 82, no. 9 (September 1994), p. 50.

then, nearly every community in the nation had become subject to their effects. For example, ACIR reported that during the 1980s the costs of unfunded intergovernmental mandates were increasing at a rate faster than federal assistance. ACIR also identified 63 federal statutes as of 1990 that, in its view, imposed "major" restrictions or costs on state and local governments. Many of the statutes involved civil rights, consumer protection, improved health and safety, and environmental protection.[156] Only 2 of the 63 statutes it identified, the Davis-Bacon Act of 1931 and Hatch Act of 1940, were enacted prior to 1964, 9 were enacted during the 1960s, 25 during the 1970s, 21 during the 1980s, and 6 in 1990. A study completed by the Clinton Administration's National Performance Review identified 172 laws in force that imposed requirements (regardless of the magnitude of their impact) on state and local governments as of December 1992.[157]

Some of the major federal statutes adopted during the 1970s that imposed relatively costly federal mandates on state and local governments were the Equal Employment Opportunity Act of 1972, which extended the prohibitions against discrimination in employment contained in the Civil Rights Act of 1964 to state and local government employment; the Fair Labor Standards Act Amendments of 1974, which extended the prohibitions against age discrimination in the Age Discrimination in Employment Act of 1967 to state and local government employment; and the Public Utilities Regulatory Policy Act of 1978, which established federal requirements concerning the pricing of electricity and natural gas.[158] One of the more costly federal mandates enacted during the 1970s was Section 504 of the Rehabilitation Act of 1973. It prohibited discrimination against handicapped persons in federally assisted programs. CBO estimated that it would require states and localities to spend $6.8

---

[156] ACIR, *Regulatory Federalism: Policy, Process, Impact, and Reform*, A-95 (Washington, DC: ACIR, 1984), pp. 19- 21; and ACIR, *Federal Regulation of State and Local Governments: The Mixed Record of the 1980s*, A-126 (Washington, DC: ACIR, 1993), pp. 44, 45.

[157] Office of the Vice President, *Strengthening the Partnership in Intergovernmental Service Delivery, National Performance Review Accompanying Report* (Washington, DC: GPO, September 1993), http://govinfo.library.unt.edu/ npr/library/reports/isd.html.

[158] ACIR, *Regulatory Federalism: Policy, Process, Impact, and Reform*, A-95 (Washington, DC: ACIR, 1984), p. 88.

158 *Robert Jay Dilger*

billion over 30 years to equip buses with wheelchair lifts, to install elevators in subway systems, and to expand access to public transit systems for the physically disabled.[159]

Three of the more costly unfunded federal mandates adopted during the 1980s were the Safe Drinking Water Act Amendments of 1986 (which was estimated to impose an additional cost of between $2 billion and $3 billion on state and local governments to improve public water systems); the Asbestos Hazard Emergency Response Act of 1986 (which required schools to remove hazardous asbestos at an estimated cost of $3.15 billion over 30 years); and the Water Quality Act of 1987 (which was estimated to cost states and localities about $12 billion in capital costs for wastewater treatment).[160] ACIR estimated that new federal mandates adopted between 1983 and 1990 cost state and local governments between $8.9 billion and $12.7 billion, depending on the definition of mandate used; in FY1991, federal mandates imposed estimated costs of between $2.2 billion and $3.6 billion on state and local governments; and additional mandates, not included in these estimates, were scheduled to take effect in the years ahead.[161]

ACIR suggested that the expansion of federal intergovernmental mandates during the 1960s, 1970s, and 1980s fundamentally changed the nature of intergovernmental relations in the United States:

> During the 1960s and 1970s, state and local governments for the first time were brought under extensive federal regulatory controls… Over this period, national controls have been adopted affecting public functions and services ranging from automobile inspection, animal preservation and college athletics to waste treatment and waste disposal. In field after field

---

[159] ACIR, *Federal Regulation of State and Local Governments: The Mixed Record of the 1980s*, A-126 (Washington, DC: ACIR, 1993), p. 61.

[160] Ibid., p. 46; and Timothy J. Conlan and David R. Beam, "Federal Mandates: The Record of Reform and Future Prospects," *Intergovernmental Perspective,* vol. 18, no. 4 (Fall 1992), pp. 9, 10.

[161] Timothy J. Conlan and David R. Beam, "Federal Mandates: The Record of Reform and Future Prospects," *Intergovernmental Perspective,* vol. 18, no. 4 (Fall 1992), pp. 9, 10.

the power to set standards and determine methods of compliance has shifted from the states and localities to Washington.[162]

State and Local Governments Seek Relief from Unfunded Mandates

Edward I. Koch, then mayor of New York City and a former Member of Congress, was one of the first public officials to highlight the mandate issue. In 1980, he authored an article criticizing what he called "the mandate millstone."[163] He noted that as a Member of Congress he voted for many federal mandates "with every confidence that we were enacting sensible permanent solutions to critical problems" but now that he was a mayor he had come to realize that "over the past decade, a maze of complex statutory and administrative directives has come to threaten both the initiative and the financial health of local governments throughout the country."[164]

The continued growth in the number and cost of federal mandates during the 1980s and early 1990s generated renewed and heightened opposition from state and local government officials and their affiliated public interest groups. This opposition culminated in the National Unfunded Mandates (NUM) Day initiative, sponsored by the NLC, USCM, NACO, and International City/County Management Association. Held on October 27, 1993, local government officials across the nation held press conferences and public forums criticizing unfunded mandates, and released a study of the costs imposed by federal mandates on local governments. Over 300 cities and 128 counties participated in the study, which, when extrapolated nationally, estimated that federal mandates imposed additional

---

[162] ACIR, *Regulatory Federalism: Policy, Process, Impact, and Reform*, A-95 (Washington, DC: ACIR, 1984), p. 246.

[163] Edward I. Koch, "The Mandate Millstone," *The Public Interest*, no. 61 (Fall 1980), pp. 42-57.

[164] Ibid., p. 42.

160   *Robert Jay Dilger*

costs of $6.5 billion annually for cities and $4.8 billion annually for counties.[165]

The NUM Day methodology used to estimate the costs of unfunded federal mandates was later challenged because of the absence of independent validation of local government submissions and the nonrandom nature of the participating jurisdictions. However, politically, NUM Day was considered a success by its organizers for two reasons. First, it attracted unprecedented media attention to the issue of unfunded federal mandates. For example, the number of newspaper articles discussing unfunded federal mandates increased from 22 in 1992, to 179 in 1993, and to 836 in 1994.[166] Second, it increased congressional awareness of state and local government concerns about unfunded mandates. For example, on January 5, 1995, Senator John Glenn mentioned NUM Day as having an impact on congressional awareness of unfunded mandates at a Senate congressional hearing on S. 1—The Unfunded Mandate Reform Act:

> On October 27, 1993, State and local elected officials from all over the Nation came to Washington and declared that day—"National Unfunded Mandates Day." These officials conveyed a powerful message to Congress and the Clinton Administration on the need for Federal mandate reform and relief. They raised four major objections to unfunded Federal mandates.
>
> First, unfunded Federal mandates impose unreasonable fiscal burdens on their budgets;
>
> Second, they limit State and local government flexibility to address more pressing local problems like crime and education;

---

[165] Timothy J. Conlan, James D. Riggle, and Donna E. Schwartz, "Deregulating Federalism? The Politics of Mandate Reform in the 104th Congress," *Publius: The Journal of Federalism*, vol. 25, no. 3 (Summer 1995), p. 26; and Jeffrey L. Esser, "National Unfunded Mandates Day: An Idea Whose Time Has Come," *Government Finance Review*, vol. 9, no. 5 (October 1, 1993), p. 3, http://findarticles.com/p/articles/mi_hb6642/is_n5_v9/ai_n28629948/?tag=content.

[166] Timothy J. Conlan, James D. Riggle, and Donna E. Schwartz, "Deregulating Federalism? The Politics of Mandate Reform in the 104th Congress," *Publius: The Journal of Federalism*, vol. 25, no. 3 (Summer 1995), p. 27.

Unfunded Mandates Reform Act

Third, Federal mandates too often come in a "one-size-fits-all" box that stifles the development of more innovative local efforts—efforts that ultimately may be more effective in solving the problem the Federal Mandate is meant to address; and

Fourth, they allow Congress to get credit for passing some worthy mandate or program, while leaving State and local governments with the difficult tasks of cutting services or raising taxes in order to pay for it.[167]

State and local government officials continued to lobby Congress for mandate relief legislation and coordinated their efforts to increase public awareness of their concerns. For example, on March 21, 1994, state and local government officials across the nation held town hall meetings and their affiliated public interest groups sponsored a rally on the Capitol steps to draw media attention to their concerns about unfunded federal mandates. The NLC and state municipal leagues across the country also declared October 24-30, 1994, Unfunded Mandates Week, which also generated considerable media coverage.[168]

The Initial Congressional Response

The efforts of state and local government officials appeared to have an effect on congressional legislative activity concerning unfunded federal mandates. During the 102nd Congress (1991- 1992), 12 federal mandate relief bills were introduced in the House and 10 were introduced in the Senate. All of these bills failed to be reported out of committee, and only one had a congressional hearing. During the first session of the 103rd Congress (1993), 32 federal mandate relief bills were introduced and one of them, S. 993, the Federal Mandate Accountability and Reform Act of

---

[167] U.S. Congress, Senate Committee on Governmental Affairs, S. 1-*Unfunded Mandates*, 104th Cong., 1st sess., January 5, 1995, S.Hrg. 104-392 (Washington: GPO, 1995), p. 5.

[168] Mary-Margaret Lamouth, "Local and Congressional Leaders Talk Mandates," *Nation's Cities Weekly*, March 21, 1994, p. 3; Beverly Schlotterbeck, "Rally to Stop the Mandate Madness Galvanizes Anti-mandate Campaign," *County News*, vol. 26, March 21, 1994, pp. 2, 3; and "Cities Gearing Up For National Unfunded Mandates Week," *Illinois Municipal Review* (September 1994), p. 13.

1994 cosponsored by Senators John Glenn and Dirk Kempthorne, was reported by the Senate Governmental Affairs Committee on June 16, 1994. It contained several provisions that were later in UMRA, and included an amendment offered by Senator Byron Dorgan "to include the private sector under the CBO and Committee mandate cost analysis requirements of Title I of S. 993, and a Glenn amendment to allow CBO to waive the private-sector cost analysis if CBO cannot make a "reasonable estimate" of the bills cost."[169] The bill was considered by the Senate on October 6, 1994, without a time agreement. After the introduction of several amendments and some debate, the Senate proceeded to other issues and adjourned without voting on the measure.[170] The House Government Operations Committee also reported a bill, H.R. 5128, the Federal Mandates Relief for State and Local Government Act of 1994, sponsored by Representative John Conyers Jr., on October 5, 1994. It was similar to S. 993, but its approval was delayed, reportedly due to concerns raised by several senior Democratic Members worried that mandate legislation might make it more difficult to adopt laws to protect the environment and address social issues. Congress adjourned before the bill could move to the floor for consideration.[171]

Core Federalism Principles Debated during UMRA's Consideration

The Republican Party gained control of the House of Representatives for the first time in 40 years following the congressional elections held on November 8, 1994. They also achieved a slim majority in the Senate as

---

[169] U.S. Congress, Senate Committee on Governmental Affairs, *Unfunded Mandate Reform Act of 1995*, report to accompany S. 1, 104th Cong., 1st sess., January 11, 1995, S.Rept. 104-1 (Washington: GPO, 1995), p. 9.

[170] Ibid.

[171] Timothy J. Conlan, James D. Riggle, and Donna E. Schwartz, "Deregulating Federalism? The Politics of Mandate Reform in the 104th Congress," *Publius: The Journal of Federalism*, vol. 25, no. 3 (Summer 1995), pp. 28-31.

well.[172] Mandate reform was a key provision in the Republican Party's "Contract With America."[173] Perhaps reflecting its importance to the Republican leadership, the prospective Senate majority leader, Senator Robert Dole, designated a revised unfunded mandate relief bill, cosponsored by Senators Kempthorne and Glenn and introduced on January 4, 1995, the opening day of the new Congress, as S. 1, the Unfunded Mandates Reform Act of 1995. The Senate Governmental Affairs Committee and Senate Budget Committee held a joint hearing on the bill the following day and it was reported out of the Senate Governmental Affairs Committee with three amendments (9 to 4) on January 9, 1995, and out of the Senate Budget Committee with four amendments (21-0) also on January 9, 1995.

To expedite Senate floor consideration, neither committee filed a committee report. Instead, the committee chairs, Senator William Roth Jr. on behalf of the Senate Governmental Affairs Committee and Senator Pete Domenici on behalf of the Senate Budget Committee, each submitted a chairman's statement for insertion into the *Congressional Record*.[174] When Senate floor consideration commenced on January 12, 1995, Senator Robert Byrd objected to several features of the way the legislation was being handled, including the absence of a committee report and the pace of consideration. In addition, Senators introduced 228 amendments to the bill. Floor debate lasted for more than two weeks. During floor debate, Senator Kempthorne argued that the bill should be adopted out of a sense of

---

[172] Senator Richard Shelby of Alabama switched from the Democratic to the Republican Party on November 9, 1994, giving the Republican Party a majority of Senate seats.

[173] Representative Newt Gingrich, "Election of Speaker," remarks in the House, *Congressional Record*, vol. 141, part 1 (January 4, 1995), p. H444; Representative Dick Armey, "H. Res. 6, Title 1, Contract With America: A Bill of Accountability," House debate, *Congressional Record*, vol. 141, part 1 (January 4, 1995), pp. H662-H477; and U.S. Congress, House Committee on Ways and Means, *Contract With America-An Overview*, 104th Cong., 1st sess., January 5, 1995 (Washington: GPO, 1995), pp. 11-18.

[174] Senator William Roth Jr., "Statement of the Chairman on the Reporting By the Governmental Affairs Committee of S.1, Unfunded Mandate Reform Act of 1995," remarks in the Senate, *Congressional Record*, vol. 141, part 1 (January 9, 1995), pp. 891-898; and Senator Pete Domenici, "Statement of the Senate Committee on the Budget on S.1, Unfunded Mandate Reform Act of 1995," remarks in the Senate, *Congressional Record*, vol. 141, part 1 (January 11, 1995), pp. 1092-1099.

164 *Robert Jay Dilger*

fairness to state and local governments and as a commitment to federalism principles:

> Under this legislation, we are acknowledging for the first time, in a meaningful way, that there must be limits on the Federal Government's propensity to impose costly mandates on other levels of government. As the representatives of those governments have very effectively demonstrated, this is a real problem. Cities, for example, generally are fortunate if they have adequate resources just to meet their own local responsibilities. Unfunded Federal mandates have put a real strain on those resources. This has been the practice of the Federal Government for the past several decades, but in recent years it has mushroomed into an intolerable burden.
>
> This has been due, at least in part, to the Federal Government's own budget crisis. In the past, if Congress felt that a particular problem warranted a national solution, it would often fund that solution with Federal dollars. Mandates imposed on State and local governments could frequently be offset with generous Federal grants. But the Federal Government no longer has the money to fund the governmental actions it wishes to see accomplished throughout the country. In fact, it hasn't had the money to do this for many years. Instead, it borrowed for a long time, to cover those costs. But now the Federal deficit is so large, that the only alternative left for imposing so-called national solutions is to impose unfunded mandates....
>
> The State legislators and Governors know this. This is why they feel so strongly that legislation regarding this practice must first be in place, before they are asked to ratify a balanced budget amendment. Otherwise, in the drive to achieve a balance Federal budget, Congress might be tempted to mandate that State and local governments shall pick up many of the costs that were formerly Federal. This is why any effort to add a sunset provision to this bill ought to be opposed. Our commitment to protect federalism ought to be permanent.
>
> S. 1 is designed to put in place just such a mechanism. In this regard, it may truly be called balanced legislation. First of all, it helps bring our system of federalism back into balance, by serving as a check against the easy imposition of unfunded mandates. And, second, it does so in a way

Unfunded Mandates Reform Act

that strikes a balance between restraining the growth of mandates and recognizing that there may be legitimate exceptions.[175]

Senator Frank Lautenberg was among those opposing UMRA. He argued that the bill should be defeated because, among other things, the federal government has an obligation to set national standards to protect the environment and ensure the quality of life for all Americans:

> Halting interstate pollution is an important responsibility of the Federal Government. And I am concerned that this act may have a chilling effect on future Federal environmental legislation. Another issue that may get loss in this debate is the benefit that States and their citizens derive from Federal mandates—even those not fully funded. States may say, we know how best to care for our citizens; a program that may be good for New Jersey, may not be good for Idaho or Ohio. But, I would argue that there is a broader national interest in some very fundamental issues which transcend that premise. I would argue that historically, not all States have provided a floor of satisfactory minimum decency standards for their citizens and that, as a democratic and fair society, we should worry about that. Further, as a practical matter, I would argue that the policies of one State in a society such as ours will certainly affect citizens and taxpayers of another State just as certainly as unfunded mandates can.
>
> Let us look at our welfare system. There has been a lot of discussion about turning welfare over to the States, with few or virtually no Federal guidelines or requirements. What would happen if we do that? Would we see a movement of the disadvantaged between States, putting a heavier burden on the citizens of a State that provides more generous benefits?
>
> Let us look at occupational safety, or environmental regulation. With a patchwork of differing standards across the States, would we see a migration of factories and jobs to States with lower standards? I think so. But by mandating floors in environmental and workplace conditions, the Federal Government ensures that States will comply with minimal standards befitting a complex, interrelated, and decent society.

---

[175] Senator Dirk Kempthorne, "Unfunded Mandate Reform Act," remarks in the Senate, *Congressional Record*, vol. 141, part 1 (January 12, 1995), p. 1166.

166   *Robert Jay Dilger*

Or let us look at gun control. My State of New Jersey generally has strong controls on guns. But New Jerseyans still suffer from an epidemic of gun violence–in no small measure because firearms come into New Jersey from other States. Without strong national controls, this will remain a problem. That is why we passed a ban on all assault weapons and why we passed the Brady bill.

Currently the Federal Government discourages a scenario whereby a given State decides not to enforce some worker health and safety laws as a way of lowering costs and attracting industry. A State right next door might feel compelled to lower its standards in order to remain competitive. In the absence of a Federal Standard, we would likely see a bidding war that lowers the quality of life for all Americans.

These are some of a host of very fundamental, very basic, and even profound questions raised by the notion that we should never have unfunded mandates. These are questions each Member of the Senate should consider long and hard, before moving to drastically curtail—or make impossible—any unfunded mandates.[176]

After voting on 44 amendments and several cloture motions, the Senate approved S. 1 on January 27, 1995, 86-10.[177]

One of the amendments approved by the Senate was the "Byrd look-back amendment," which is the only provision in UMRA that allows for the regulation of any mandates based on actual rather than estimated costs.[178] It provided that legislation containing intergovernmental mandates would be considered funded, and hence not subject to a point of order, if it authorized appropriations to cover the estimated direct costs of the intergovernmental mandate and incorporated a prescribed mechanism requiring further review if, in any fiscal year, Congress did not appropriate

---

[176] Senator Frank Lautenberg, "Unfunded Mandate Reform Act," remarks in the Senate, *Congressional Record*, vol. 141, part 1 (January 12, 1995), p. 1193.

[177] Timothy J. Conlan, James D. Riggle, and Donna E. Schwartz, "Deregulating Federalism? The Politics of Mandate Reform in the 104th Congress," *Publius: The Journal of Federalism*, vol. 25, no. 3 (Summer 1995), pp. 31, 32; and "Consideration of S.1, Unfunded Mandate Reform Act, Senate Rollcall Vote No. 61," *Congressional Record*, vol. 141, part 2 (January 27, 1995), pp. 2750, 2751.

[178] Senator Robert Byrd, "Byrd Amendment No. 213," Amendments Submitted, Unfunded Mandate Reform Act of 1995," *Congressional Record*, vol. 141, part 2 (January 24, 1995), p. 2195. See 2 U.S.C. §658d(a)(B).

funds sufficient to cover those costs. Under this mechanism, if the responsible federal agency determines that the appropriation provided was insufficient to cover the estimated direct costs of the mandate it shall notify the appropriate authorizing committees not later than 30 days after the start of the fiscal year and submit recommendations for either implementing a less costly mandate or making the mandate ineffective for the fiscal year. The statutory mechanism must also include expedited procedures for the consideration of legislative recommendations to achieve these outcomes not later than 30 days after the recommendations are submitted to Congress. Finally, the mechanism must provide that the mandate "shall be ineffective until such time as Congress has completed action on the recommendations of the responsible federal agency."[179] After Senator Robert Byrd offered this amendment, the Senate adopted it on January 26, 1995, 100-0.[180]

The House companion bill to S. 1 was H.R. 5, the Unfunded Mandate Reform Act of 1995, which was cosponsored by Representatives William F. Clinger Jr., Rob Portman, Gary A. Condit, and Thomas M. Davis. It was reported by the House Government Reform and Oversight Committee, on January 13, 1995, by voice vote and without hearings.[181] Floor consideration began on January 20, 1995. Numerous amendments were introduced by Democratic Members to add various exemptions to the bill, such as the health of children and the disabled, the disposal of nuclear waste, and child support enforcement. These amendments were rejected on

---

[179] Ibid.

[180] "Consideration of S.1, Unfunded Mandate Reform Act, Senate Rollcall Vote No. 49," *Congressional Record*, vol. 141, part 2 (January 26, 1995), pp. 2606, 2607.

[181] Representative William F. Clinger Jr., Chair of the House Government Reform and Oversight Committee, indicated in the committee's report that hearings were not necessary because "the Committee held several hearings on this issue as well as on a similar bill last session." Members from the minority party argued in the committee's report that "The haste in which this bill was considered left a number of substantive issues unaddressed, which even the authors conceded at markup that they would like to address on the Floor. Most importantly, a ruling from the Chairman in the middle of the markup prohibited members from offering amendments to the operative sections of Title II and III." U.S. Congress, House Committee on Government Reform and Oversight, *Unfunded Mandate Reform Act of 1995*, report to accompany H.R. 5, 104th Cong., 1st sess., January 13, 1995, H.Rept. 104-1, Part 2 (Washington: GPO, 1995), pp. 53-56. Portions of the bill were also sequentially referred to and reported by the Committees on Rules, Budget, and Judiciary.

168   *Robert Jay Dilger*

party-line votes. On February 1, 1995, H.R. 5 was adopted, 360-74, inserted into S. 1 as a House substitute, and sent to conference.[182]

There were two major differences between the House and Senate versions of S. 1. The House version did not include the Byrd look-back amendment, and it permitted judicial review of federal agency compliance with the bill's provisions. Initially, House conferees refused to accept the Byrd look-back amendment and Senate conferees; worried that outside parties could delay regulations for years by filing lawsuits, refused to accept judicial review of federal agency compliance with the bill's provisions. Negotiations continued for six weeks. The deadlock over judicial review was ended by allowing judicial review of whether an appropriate analysis of mandate costs was done, but restricting the court's ability to second-guess the quality of the cost estimates. The deadlock over the Byrd look-back amendment ended when House conferees accepted its inclusion after being assured that its intent was to make certain that Congress, rather than an executive agency, retained responsibility for setting policy.[183]

The Senate adopted the conference report, which renamed the bill the Unfunded Mandates Reform Act of 1995, on March 15, 1995, 91-9, and the House adopted it the next day, 394-28. President Bill Clinton signed it on March 22, 1995.[184]

---

[182] "Consideration of H.R. 5, Unfunded Mandate Reform Act, House Roll No. 83," *Congressional Record*, vol. 141, part 3 (February 1, 1995), p. 3252, 3258; and Timothy J. Conlan, James D. Riggle, and Donna E. Schwartz, "Deregulating Federalism? The Politics of Mandate Reform in the 104th Congress," *Publius: The Journal of Federalism*, vol. 25, no. 3 (Summer 1995), pp. 33, 34.

[183] Timothy J. Conlan, James D. Riggle, and Donna E. Schwartz, "Deregulating Federalism? The Politics of Mandate Reform in the 104th Congress," *Publius: The Journal of Federalism*, vol. 25, no. 3 (Summer 1995), pp. 36, 37.

[184] "Unfunded Mandate Reform Act of 1995–Conference Report, Senate Rollcall Vote No. 104," *Congressional Record*, vol. 141, part 6 (March 15, 1995), p. 7876; "Conference Report on S.1, Unfunded Mandate Reform Act, House Roll No. 252," *Congressional Record*, vol. 141, part 6 (March 16, 1995), p. 8136; and President Bill Clinton, "Remarks on Signing the Unfunded Mandates Reform Act of 1995," *Weekly Compilation of Presidential Documents*, vol. 31, no. 12 (March 22, 1995), pp. 453-455.

Appendix B. UMRA Points of Order

1) Representative Bill Archer, "Contract With America Advancement Act of 1996," House debate on motion to recommit H.R. 3136, *Congressional Record*, vol. 142, part 5 (March 28, 1996), pp. 6931-6937.

2) Representative Rob Portman, "The Employee Commuting Act of 1996," House debate on H.R. 1227, *Congressional Record*, vol. 142, part 9 (May 23, 1996), pp. 12283-12287.

3) Representative Bill Orton, "The Welfare—Medicaid Reform Act of 1996," House debate on H.R. 3734, *Congressional Record*, vol. 142, part 13 (July 18, 1996), p. 17668.

4) Representative Melvin Watt, "The Housing Opportunity and Responsibility Act," House debate on H.R. 2, *Congressional Record*, vol. 143, part 5 (May 1, 1997), pp. 7006-7012.

5) Representative John Ensign, "The Nuclear Waste Policy Act of 1997," House debate on H.R. 1270, *Congressional Record*, vol. 143, no, 148 (October 29, 1997), pp. H9655-H9657.

6) Representative Gerald Soloman, "The Agricultural Research, Extension, and Education Reform Act of 1998," House debate on the conference report for S. 1150, *Congressional Record*, vol. 144, part 8 (June 4, 1998), pp. H9655-H9657.

7) Representative Jerrold Nadler, "The Bankruptcy Reform Act of 1998," House debate on H.R. 3150, *Congressional Record*, vol. 144, part 8 (June 10, 1998), pp. 11853-11857.

8) Representative Steve Largent, "The Minimum Wage Increase Act," House debate on H.R. 3846, *Congressional Record*, vol. 144, part 2 (March 9, 2000), pp. 2623- 2624.

9) Representative James Gibbons, "The Nuclear Waste Policy Amendments Act of 2000," House debate on S. 1287, *Congressional Record*, vol. 146, part 2 (March 22, 2000), pp. 3234-3236.

10) Representative John Conyers, "The Internet Nondiscrimination Act of 2000," House debate on H.R. 3709, *Congressional Record*, vol. 146, part 6 (May 10, 2000), pp. 7483-7485.

11) Representative Charles Stenholm, "The Medicare RX 2000 Act," House debate on H.R. 4680, *Congressional Record*, vol. 146, part 9 (June 28, 2000), pp. 12650- 12653.

12) Representative Jim Moran, "The Department of Transportation Appropriations Act, 2002," House debate on H.R. 2299, *Congressional Record*, vol. 147, part 9 (June 26, 2001), pp. 11906-11910.

13) Representative James Gibbons, "The Yucca Mountain Repository Site Approval Act," House debate on H.J.Res. 87, *Congressional Record*, vol. 148, part 5 (May 8, 2002), pp. 7145-7148.

14) Representative Sheila Jackson-Lee, "The Real ID Act of 2005," House debate on H.R. 418, *Congressional Record*, vol. 151, no. 13 (February 9, 2005), pp. H437- H442.

15) Representative James McGovern, "The Energy Policy Act of 2005," House debate on H.R. 6, *Congressional Record*, vol. 151, no. 48 (April 20, 2005), pp. H 2174-H2178.

16) Senator Kit Bond, "The Transportation, Treasury, HUD and Independent Agencies Appropriations Act, 2006," Senate debate on H.R. 3058, *Congressional Record*, vol. 151, no. 133 (October 19, 2005), p. S11547.

17) Senator Ted Kennedy, "The Transportation, Treasury, HUD and Independent Agencies Appropriations Act, 2006," Senate debate on H.R. 3058, *Congressional Record*, vol. 151, no. 133 (October 19, 2005), p. S11548.

18) Representative Jim McDermott, "The Deficit Reduction Act of 2005," House debate on H.R. 4241, *Congressional Record*, vol. 151, no. 152 (November 17, 2005), pp. H10531-H10534.

19) Representative Jim McDermott, "The Deficit Reduction Act of 2005," House debate on H.Res. 653, *Congressional Record*, vol. 152, no. 10 (February 1, 2006), pp. H37-H40.

20) Representative Tammy Baldwin, "The Communications Opportunity, Promotion, and Enhancement Act of 2006," House debate on H.R. 5252, *Congressional Record*, vol. 152, no. 72 (June 8, 2006), pp. H3506-H3510.

21) Representative Jim McDermott, "The Federal Election Integrity Act of 2006," House debate on H.R. 4844, *Congressional Record*, vol. 152, no. 118 (September 20, 2006), pp. H6742-H6745.

22) Representative Pete Sessions, "The Children's Health and Medicare Protections Act of 2007," House debate on H.R. 3162, *Congressional Record*, vol. 153, no. 124-125 (August 1, 2007), pp. H9288-H9290.

23) Representative Pete Sessions, "The Children's Health Insurance Program Reauthorization Act of 2007," House debate on H.R. 3963, *Congressional Record*, vol. 153, no. 163 (October 25, 2007), pp. H12027-H12029.

24) Representative Jeff Flake, "Senate Amendments to H.R. 6, Energy Independence and Security Act of 2007," House debate on H.R. 6, *Congressional Record*, vol. 153, no. 186 (December 6, 2007), pp. H4255-H4259.

25) Representative Mike Conaway, "The Renewable Energy and Energy Conservation Tax Act of 2008," House debate on H.R. 5351, *Congressional Record*, vol. 154, no. 32 (February 27, 2008), pp. H1079-H1082.

26) Representative Paul Broun, "The Paul Wellstone Mental Health and Addiction Equity Act of 2007," House debate on H.R. 1424, *Congressional Record*, vol. 154, no. 37 (March 5, 2008), pp. H1259-H1262.

27) Representative Jeff Flake, "The Food, Conservation, and Energy Act of 2008," House debate on H.R. 2419, *Congressional Record*, vol. 154, no. 79 (May 14, 2008), pp. H3784-H3789.

28) Representative Eric Cantor, "The Comprehensive American Energy Security and Consumer Protection Act," House debate on H.R. 6899, *Congressional Record*, vol. 154, no. 147 (September 16, 2008), pp. H8152-H8157.

29) Representative Jeff Flake, "The Consolidated Security, Disaster Assistance and Continuing Appropriations Act, 2009," House debate on H.R. 2638, *Congressional Record*, vol. 154, no. 152 (September 24, 2008), pp. H9218-H 9220.

30) Representative David Drier, "The American Recovery and Reinvestment Act," House debate on H.R. 1, *Congressional Record*, vol. 155, no. 30 (February 13, 2009), pp. H1524-H1536.
31) Representative Jeff Flake, "The Omnibus Appropriations Act, 2009," House debate on H.R. 1105, *Congressional Record*, vol. 155, no. 33 (February 25, 2009), pp. H2643-H2646.
32) Representative Jeff Flake, "The Agriculture, Rural Development, Food and Drug Administration Appropriations Act, 2010," House debate on H.R. 2997, *Congressional Record*, vol. 155, no. 101 (July 8, 2009), pp. H7783-H7786.
33) Representative Jeff Flake, "The Military Construction and Veteran's Affairs Appropriations Act, 2010," House debate on H.R. 3082, *Congressional Record*, vol. 155, no. 103 (July 10, 2009), pp. H7951-H7953.
34) Representative Jeff Flake, "The Energy and Water Development Appropriations Act, 2010," House debate on H.R. 3183, *Congressional Record*, vol. 155, no. 106 (July 15, 2009), pp. H8107-H8109.
35) Representative Jeff Flake, "The Financial Services and General Government Appropriations Act, 2010," House debate on H.R. 3170, *Congressional Record*, vol. 155, no. 107 (July 16, 2009), pp. H8191-H8193.
36) Representative Jeff Flake, "The Transportation, Housing and Urban Development Appropriations Act, 2010," House debate on H.R. 3288, *Congressional Record*, vol. 155, no. 112 (July 23, 2009), pp. H8593-H8594.
37) Representative Jeff Flake, "The Departments of Labor, Health, and Human Services, and Education Appropriations Act, 2010," House debate on H.R. 3293, *Congressional Record*, vol. 155, no. 113 (July 24, 2009), pp. H8593-H8594.
38) Representative Jeff Flake, "The Department of Defense Appropriations Act, 2010," House debate on H.R. 3326, *Congressional Record*, vol. 155, no. 116 (July 29, 2009), pp. H8977-H8978.

39) Senator Robert Corker, "H.R. 3590, the Service Members Home Ownership Act of 2009," remarks in the Senate, *Congressional Record*, daily edition, vol. 155, no. 199 (December 23, 2009), pp. S13803-S13804.

40) Representative Paul Ryan, "Providing for Consideration of Senate Amendments to H.R. 3590, Service Members Home Ownership Tax Act of 2009, and Providing for Consideration of H.R. 4872, Health Care and Education Reconciliation Act of 2010," House debate on H.Res. 1203, *Congressional Record*, daily edition, vol. 156, no. 43 (March 21, 2010), pp. H1825-H1828.

41) Representative Jeff Flake, "Providing For Consideration of H.R. 5822, Military Construction and Veterans Affairs and Related Agencies Appropriations Act, 2011," House debate on H.R. 5822, *Congressional Record*, vol. 156, no. 112 (July 28, 2010), pp. H6206-H6209.

42) Representative Jeff Flake, "Providing For Consideration of H.R. 5850, Transportation, Housing And Urban Development, and Related Agencies Appropriations Act, 2011," House debate on H.R. 5850, *Congressional Record*, vol. 156, no. 113 (July 29, 2010), pp. H6298-H6290.

43) Representative Jeff Flake, "Providing For Consideration of Senate Amendment to House Amendment to Senate Amendment to H.R. 4853, Tax Relief, Unemployment Insurance Reauthorization, and Job Creation Act of 2010," House debate on H.R. 4853, *Congressional Record*, vol. 156, no. 157 (December 16, 2010), pp. H8525-H8526.

44) Representative Keith Ellison, "Providing For Consideration of H.R. 1255, Government Shutdown Prevention Act of 2011," House debate on H.Res. 194, *Congressional Record*, vol. 157, no. 46 (April 1, 2011), pp. H2219-H2222.

45) Representative John Garamendi, "Providing For Further Consideration of H.R. 1540, National Defense Authorization Act for Fiscal Year 2012," House debate on H.R. 276, *Congressional Record*, vol. 157, no. 73 (May 25, 2011), pp. H3423- H3424.

174   *Robert Jay Dilger*

46) Representative Keith Ellison, "Providing For Consideration of H.R. 2017, Department of Homeland Security Appropriations Act, 2012," House debate on H.Res. 287, *Congressional Record*, vol. 157, no. 77 (June 1, 2011), pp. H3816-H 3818.

47) Representative John Garamendi, "Providing For Further Consideration of H.R. 2021, Jobs and Energy Permitting Act of 2011 and Providing for Consideration of H.R. 1249, America Invents Act," House debate on H.Res. 316, *Congressional Record*, vol. 157, no. 73 (June 22, 2011), pp. H4379-H.4380.

48) Representative Marcia Fudge, "Providing For Consideration of H.R. 1315, Consumer Financial Protection Safety and Soundness Improvement Act of 2011," House debate on H.Res. 358, *Congressional Record*, vol. 157, no. 110 (July 21, 2011), p. H5302.

49) Representative Gwen Moore, "Providing For Consideration of H.Res. 358, Protect Life Act," House debate on H.Res. 430, *Congressional Record*, vol. 157, no. 153 (October 13, 2011), pp. H6869, H6870.

50) Representative Gwen Moore, "Providing For Consideration of H.R. 3630: Middle Class Tax Relief and Job Creation Act of 2011," House debate on H.Res. 491, *Congressional Record*, vol. 157, no. 191 (December 13, 2011), pp. H8745-H 8748.

51) Representative Gwen Moore, "Providing For Consideration of H.R. 4089: Sportsmen's Heritage Act of 2012, and for Other Purposes," House debate on H.Res. 614, *Congressional Record*, vol. 158, no. 55 (April 17, 2012), pp. H1860- H1862.

52) Representative Gwen Moore, "Providing For Consideration of H.R. 4970, the Violence Against Women Reauthorization Act of 2012, and Providing For Consideration of H.R. 4310, the National Defense Authorization Act for Fiscal Year 2013," House debate on H.Res. 656, *Congressional Record*, vol. 158, no. 70 (May 16, 2012), pp. H2776-H2731.

53) Representative Gwen Moore, "Providing For Consideration of House Joint Resolution 118, Disapproving Rule Relating To Waiver and Expenditure Authority with Respect to the Temporary Assistance For Needy Families Program. Providing For Consideration of H.R. 3409,

the Stop The War On Coal Act of 2012; and Providing For Proceedings during the Period from September 22, 2012, through November 12, 2012," House debate on H.Res. 788, *Congressional Record*, vol. 158, no. 128 (September 20, 2012), pp. H6165-H 6173.

54) Representative Jared Polis, "Providing For Consideration of H.R. 273, Elimination of 2013 Pay Adjustment, and for Other Purposes," House debate on H.Res. 66, *Congressional Record*, vol. 159, no. 24 (February 14, 2013), pp. H 517-H519.

55) Representative Donna Edwards, "Providing For Consideration of H.R. 1947, Federal Agriculture Reform and Risk Management Act of 2013; and Providing for Consideration of H.R. 1797, Pain-Capable Unborn Child Protection Act," House debate on H.Res. 266, *Congressional Record*, vol. 159, no. 87 (June 18, 2013), pp. H3708-H3710.

56) Representative Jim McGovern, "Providing For Further Consideration of H.R. 1947, Federal Agriculture Reform and Risk Management Act of 2013," House debate on H.Res. 271, *Congressional Record*, vol. 159, no. 88 (June 19, 2013), pp. H3770-H3774.

57) Representative Jim McGovern, "Providing For Consideration of H.R. 7, No Taxpayer Funding for Abortion and Abortion Insurance Full Disclosure Act of 2014, and Providing for Consideration of Conference Report on H.R. 2642, Federal Agriculture Reform and Risk Management Act of 2013," House debate on H.Res. 465, *Congressional Record*, vol. 160, no.16 (January 28, 2014), pp. H1443-H1445.

58) Representative Danny Davis, "Providing For Consideration of H.R. 4438, American Research and Competitiveness Act of 2014," House debate on H.R. 4438, *Congressional Record*, vol. 160, no. 68 (May 7, 2014), pp. H3465-H3466.

59) Representative Jim McGovern, "Providing For Further Consideration of H.R. 4435, Howard P. "Buck" McKeon National Defense Authorization Act for Fiscal Year 2015; and Providing for Consideration of H.R. 3361, USA FREEDOM Act," House debate on

H.R. 4435, *Congressional Record*, vol. 160, no.77 (May 21, 2014), pp. H4699-H4701.

60) Representative Jared Polis, "Providing For Further Consideration of H.R. 5, Student Success Act," House debate on H.R. 5, *Congressional Record*, vol. 161, no.33 (February 26, 2015), pp. H1180-H1182.

61) Representative Bonnie Watson Coleman, "Providing For Consideration of H.R. 1732, Regulatory Integrity Protection Act of 2015; Providing for Consideration of Conference Report on S.Con.Res. 11, Concurrent Resolution on the Budget, Fiscal Year 2016; and Providing for Consideration of H.J.Res. 43, Disapproval of District of Columbia Reproductive Health Non-Discrimination Amendment Act of 2014," House debate on H.Res. 231, *Congressional Record*, vol. 161, no.64 (April 30, 2015), pp. H2672-H2674.

62) Representative Louise Slaughter, "Providing For Consideration of the Senate Amendment to H.R. 2146, Defending Public Safety Employees' Retirement Act," House debate on H.Res. 321, *Congressional Record*, vol. 161, no. 98 (June 18, 2015), pp. H4497-H4507.

63) Representative Elizabeth Esty, "Providing For Consideration of H.R. 2130, Red River Private Property Protection Act, and Providing for Consideration of Motions to Suspend the Rule," House debate on H.Res. 556, *Congressional Record*, vol. 161, no. 178 (December 9, 2015), pp. H9092-H9095.

64) Representative Joaquin Castro, "Providing For Consideration of H.R. 5325, Legislative Branch Appropriations Act, 2017," House debate on H.Res. 771, *Congressional Record*, vol. 162, no. 91 (June 9, 2016), pp. H3586-H3588.

65) Senator Bernie Sanders, "National Sea Grant College Program Amendments of 2015 (Puerto Rico Oversight, Management, and Economic Stability Act– PROMESA)," Senate debate on S. 2328, *Congressional Record*, vol. 162, no. 105 (June 29, 2016), pp. S4691-S4702.

66) Representative Jim McGovern "Providing For Consideration of H.R. 5698, Protect and Serve Act of 2018; Providing For Consideration of S. 2372, Veterans Cemetery Benefit Correction Act; and Providing For Consideration of H.R. 2, Agriculture and Nutrition Act of 2018," House debate on H.Res. 891, *Congressional Record*, vol. 164, no. 80 (May 16, 2018), pp. H3991-H3993.

In: Key Congressional Reports for May 2019   ISBN: 978-1-53616-382-7
Editor: Piotr Meza   © 2019 Nova Science Publishers, Inc.

Chapter 4

MILITARY PAY: KEY QUESTIONS
AND ANSWERS[*]

Lawrence Kapp and Barbara Salazar Torreon

ABSTRACT

From the earliest days of the republic, the federal government has
compensated members of the Armed Forces for their services. While the
original pay structure was fairly simple, over time a more complex
system of compensation has evolved. The current military compensation
system includes cash payments such as basic pay, special and incentive
pays, and various allowances. Servicemembers also receive noncash
benefits such as health care and access to commissaries and recreational
facilities, and may qualify for deferred compensation in the form of
retired pay and other retirement benefits. This chapter provides an
overview of military compensation generally, but focuses on cash
compensation for current servicemembers.

---

[*] This is an edited, reformatted and augmented version of Congressional Research Service,
Publication No. RL33446, dated May 6, 2019.

Since the advent of the all-volunteer force in 1973, Congress has used military compensation to improve recruiting, retention, and the overall quality of the force. Congressional interest in sustaining the all-volunteer force during a time of sustained combat operations led to substantial increases in compensation in the decade following the attacks of September 11, 2001.

Subsequently, in the earlier part of the 2010s, concerns over government spending generated congressional and executive branch interest in slowing the rate of growth in military compensation. Initiatives to slow compensation growth included presidentially directed increases in basic pay below the rate of increase for the Employment Cost Index (ECI) for 2014-2016 and statutory authority for the Department of Defense (DOD) to reduce Basic Allowance for Housing (BAH) payments by 1% of the national average monthly housing cost per year from 2015 to 2019 (for a maximum reduction of 5% under the national monthly average housing cost).

Some have raised concerns about the impact of personnel costs on the overall defense budget, arguing that they decrease the amount of funds available for modernizing equipment and sustaining readiness. Others argue that robust compensation is essential to maintaining a high-quality force that is vigorous, well-trained, experienced, and able to function effectively in austere and volatile environments. The availability of funding to prosecute contingency operations in Iraq and Afghanistan mitigated the pressure to trade off personnel, readiness, and equipment costs, but the current budgetary environment appears to have brought these trade-offs to the fore again.

DOD spends about $100,000-$110,000 per year to compensate the average active duty servicemember—to include cash, benefits, and contributions to retirement programs—although some estimates of compensation costs are substantially higher. However, gross compensation figures do not tell the full story, as military compensation *relative to* civilian compensation is a key factor in an individual's decision to join or stay in the military. Thus, the issue of comparability between military and civilian pay is an often-discussed topic. Some analysts and advocacy groups have argued that a substantial "pay gap" has existed for decades—with military personnel earning less than their civilian counterparts—although they generally concede that this gap is fairly small today.

Others argue that the methodology behind this "pay gap" is flawed and does not provide a suitable estimate of pay comparability. Still others believe that military personnel, in general, are better compensated than their civilian counterparts. The Department of Defense takes a different approach to pay comparability. The 9th Quadrennial Review of Military Compensation (QRMC), published in 2002, argued that compensation for servicemembers should be around the 70th percentile of wages for civilian employees with similar education and experience. According to the 11th QRMC, published in 2012, regular military compensation for officers was at the 83rd percentile of wages for civilian employees with similar education and experience, and at the 90th percentile for enlisted personnel. A 2018 RAND report concluded that these overall percentiles were nearly the same in 2016.

INTRODUCTION

The military compensation system is complex and includes an array of cash compensation elements, noncash compensation (benefits), deferred compensation (retirement pay, Thrift Savings Plan, retiree health care, and other retirement benefits), and tax advantages. This chapter focuses primarily on the cash compensation provided to members of the active component Armed Forces.[1]

This chapter uses a question and answer format to highlight key aspects of the military compensation system and to address topics of recurring congressional interest, including the following:

- Compensation elements and rates.
- Statutory formulas for increasing compensation elements.
- Historical increases in basic pay.
- Comparability with civilian pay.
- Additional compensation for those serving in Iraq or Afghanistan.

---

[1] Unless otherwise specified, the terms "member of the Armed Forces" or "servicemember" in this chapter refer to members of the active component. Members of the reserve component receive nearly identical compensation when they are ordered to active duty for over 30 days, but are compensated somewhat differently when on active duty for 30 days or less, and much differently when not on active duty. For more information on reserve component compensation see CRS Report RL30802, *Reserve Component Personnel Issues: Questions and Answers*, by Lawrence Kapp and Barbara Salazar Torreon.

KEY QUESTIONS AND ANSWERS

How Are Military Personnel Compensated?

There are three main ways in which military personnel are compensated: cash compensation, noncash compensation, and deferred compensation.

- Cash compensation takes a variety of forms and includes basic pay, housing and subsistence allowances, enlistment bonuses, skill proficiency pay, and additional pay for particularly demanding or dangerous duty.
- Noncash compensation includes various benefits such as medical and dental care, government-provided housing, educational benefits, space-available travel on military aircraft, and access to subsidized grocery stores (commissaries), retail stores (exchanges), and child care centers.[2]
- The main elements of deferred compensation are retired pay and retiree health care, but commissary and exchange access, space-available travel, and other benefits are also part of this. Servicemembers may also participate in the Thrift Savings Plan (TSP),[3] although until 2018 they generally did not receive matching contributions from the government.[4] However, recent changes to the military retirement system made matching

---

[2] The subsidies vary in type and amount. For example, the commissary system receives about $1.3 billion to $1.4 billion in appropriated funds per year. Exchanges do not receive appropriated funds, but DOD does provide exchanges with certain free services, including building maintenance, transportation of goods overseas, and utilities at overseas stores. See CRS In Focus IF11089, *Defense Primer: Military Commissaries and Exchanges*, by Kristy N. Kamarck and Barbara Salazar Torreon.

[3] The TSP is a defined contribution retirement plan similar to the 401(k) plans provided by many employers in the private sector.

[4] 37 U.S.C. 211(d) has authorized TSP matching contributions as a retention incentive since 1999, and as a recruiting incentive since 2006.

contributions to the Thrift Savings Plan a key component of many servicemembers' deferred compensation starting in 2018.[5]

The basic compensation package provided to all servicemembers includes basic pay, a housing allowance (or government-provided housing), a subsistence allowance (or government-provided meals), free medical and dental care for servicemembers, free or low-cost medical and dental care for dependents, paid annual leave, and certain other benefits. Table 1 summarizes the main elements of compensation provided to all servicemembers. Servicemembers may also receive additional cash compensation based on their occupational specialty, duty assignment, and other factors.

What Is Regular Military Compensation (RMC)? How Much Do Servicemembers Receive in RMC?

When people talk about military pay, they are often only referring to *basic pay*. Although basic pay is usually the largest component of cash compensation that a servicemember receives, there are other types of military pay that increase it significantly. There are tax benefits as well.

Regular Military Compensation is a statutorily defined measure of the cash or in-kind compensation elements that all servicemembers receive every payday. It is widely used as a basic measure of military cash compensation levels and for comparisons with civilian salary levels.

Regular Military Compensation (RMC)

RMC, as defined in law, is "the total of the following elements that a member of the uniformed services accrues or receives, directly or indirectly, in cash or in kind every payday: basic pay, basic allowance for housing, basic allowance for subsistence, and federal tax advantage accruing to the aforementioned allowances because they are not subject to

---

[5] For more information on these changes, see CRS Report RL34751, *Military Retirement: Background and Recent Developments*, by Kristy N. Kamarck.

federal income tax."[6] Though military compensation is structured much differently than civilian compensation, making comparison difficult, RMC provides a more complete understanding of the cash compensation provided to all servicemembers. Therefore, it is usually preferred over simple basic pay when comparing military with civilian compensation, analyzing the standards of living of military personnel, or studying military compensation trends over time.

Table 1. Major compensation elements provided to all active duty personnel

Name	Statutory Authority	Purpose[a]	Description
Basic Pay	37 U.S.C. 203-205, 1009	"Basic pay is the primary means of compensating members of the armed forces for their service to the country. Except during periods of unauthorized absence, excess leave, and confinement after an enlistment has expired, every member is entitled to basic pay while on active duty. Basic pay is paid to individual members on a regular basis; the amount of basic pay to which a particular member is entitled depends on the member's pay grade and length of service."	Provided to all servicemembers. Rate of payment varies based on rank and years of service. See 2019 Basic Pay Rates: https://www.dfas.mil/milita rymembers/payentitlement s/Pay-Tables.html.
Government-provided housing or Basic Allowance for Housing (BAH) Or Overseas Housing	37 U.S.C. 403 & 405	BAH and OHA "provide a cash allowance to military personnel not provided with government quarters adequate for themselves and their dependents to	The government provides housing to many servicemembers and their families, but the large majority live in civilian housing or in privatized military housing and

---

[6] Statutory definition contained in 37 U.S.C. 101(25).

Military Pay: Key Questions and Answers 185

Name	Statutory Authority	Purpose[a]	Description
Allowance (OHA)		enable such personnel to obtain civilian housing as a substitute."	receive BAH or OHA. Servicemembers based in the United States and not provided with government housing receive BAH; those based outside the United States receive OHA. Rates vary based on servicemember's rank, location, and whether or not the servicemember has dependents (see footnote 9 for the definition of "dependent"). See 2019 Basic Allowance for Housing Rates: http://www.defensetravel.dod.mil/site/bahCalc.cfm. See 2019 Overseas Housing Allowance Rates: http://www.defensetravel.dod.mil/site/ohaCalc.cfm.
Government-provided meals or Basic Allowance for Subsistence (BAS)	37 U.S.C. 402	"To provide a cash allowance to members of the armed forces to defray a portion of the cost of subsistence, such allowance being payable to all enlisted and officer personnel, with variations to account for the unavailability of adequate messing facilities at some duty stations."	All servicemembers receive BAS except in limited circumstances when they are required to eat government-provided meals (e.g., enlisted personnel in basic training). The BAS rate varies based on officer or enlisted status; enlisted receive higher BAS than do officers. For 2019, the BAS rate is $254.39 per month for officers and $369.39 for enlisted.
Medical and Dental Care	10 U.S.C. 1071-1110	"To make medical care available to members of the uniformed services and their dependents in order to help ensure the availability of physically acceptable and	All servicemembers and their family members are eligible for medical care under the TRICARE system. This system provides free medical and dental care to the

Table 1. (Continued)

Name	Statutory Authority	Purpose[a]	Description
		experienced personnel in time of national emergency; to provide incentives for armed forces personnel to undertake military service and remain in that service for a full career; and to provide military physicians and dentists exposure to the total spectrum of demographically diverse morbidity necessary to support professional training programs and ensure professional satisfaction for a medical service career."	servicemember, and free or low-cost medical and dental care to the servicemember's dependents.
Annual Leave	10 U.S.C. 701, 704; 37 U.S.C. 501	"To authorize members of the uniformed services to take a specified number of days of leave of absence, or vacation, for rest and relaxation away from their respective duty stations; to allow the accumulation for later use of earned leave that cannot be currently used because of military, or other, exigencies; and to authorize cash payments as reimbursement for accrued leave remaining unused at the expiration of a member's term of service."	All servicemembers are entitled to 30 days of annual leave per year (includes leave taken on weekends, holidays, or other regular days off). Typically, a maximum of 60 days may be accrued, although under certain circumstances up to 120 days may be accrued. Leave in excess of the allowable limit is forfeited at the end of the fiscal year. Under limited circumstances, servicemembers may receive a cash payment in lieu of their unused leave (see 37 U.S.C. 501).

Military Pay: Key Questions and Answers 187

Name	Statutory Authority	Purpose[a]	Description
Life Insurance	38 U.S.C. 1965-1980	"To make life insurance available to members of the uniformed services at a reasonable cost."	Servicemembers' Group Life Insurance (SGLI) is available to all servicemembers, though they may opt to not purchase it. Provides up to $400,000 in life insurance coverage and $100,000 traumatic injury coverage for the servicemember; up to $100,000 in coverage for spouse is also available. Servicemembers normally pay the costs for this coverage, but the government reimburses the premiums for those serving in an assignment outside the United States or its possessions in support of a contingency operation in an area that "has been designated a combat zone" or "is in direct support of an area that has been designated a combat zone" (37 U.S.C. 437). See current SGLI rates: http://benefits.va.gov/insurance/sgli.asp.
Commissary	10 U.S.C. 2481-85; 10 U.S.C. 1061- 64	"To allow items of convenience and necessity— especially items of subsistence—to be made available for purchase by military personnel at convenient locations and reasonable prices."	Subsidized grocery stores on military bases around the world. The Defense Commissary Agency estimates average savings of about 30% compared to commercial stores, though the savings would be less if compared only to discount chains.

Table 1. (Continued)

Name	Statutory Authority	Purpose[a]	Description
Exchange	10 U.S.C. 2481	"As a military resale and category C revenue-producing morale, welfare, and reaction [*sic*](MWR) activity, the armed services exchanges have the dual mission of providing authorized patrons with articles of merchandise and services and generating nonappropriated fund (NAF) earnings."	Retail stores (furniture, electronics, clothing, jewelry, etc.) on military bases around the world. They do not receive direct subsidies like commissaries, but do receive some indirect subsidies in the form of waived or reduced costs for utilities, rent, and base services.

Source: Congressional Research Service compilation from statutory authorities, *Military Compensation Background Papers*, government websites, and other data.

[a]All entries in the "Purpose" column are taken verbatim from *Military Compensation Background Papers*, 8th Edition, 2018, https://www.loc.gov/rr/frd/pdf-files/ Military_Comp-2018.pdf.

Basic Pay

For most servicemembers, basic pay is the largest element of the compensation they receive in their paycheck and typically accounts for about two-thirds of an individual's RMC. All members of the Armed Forces receive basic pay, although the amount varies by pay grade (rank) and years of service (also called longevity). Table 2 provides illustrative examples of basic pay rates.

Housing

All servicemembers are entitled to either government-provided housing or a housing allowance, known as basic allowance for housing (BAH) for those living within the United States or Overseas Housing Allowance (OHA) for those living outside of the United States. Roughly one- third of servicemembers receive government-provided housing (in the form of barracks, dormitories, ship berthing, or government-owned family housing), with the remainder receiving BAH or OHA to offset the costs of

Military Pay: Key Questions and Answers 189

the housing they rent or purchase in the civilian economy or the *privatized housing* they rent on or near military bases.[7]

The proportion of housing costs covered by housing allowances has varied over time. See the section entitled "Basic Allowance for Housing: Increases Are Linked to Increases in Housing Costs" later in this chapter for more information on this topic.

The amount of BAH a servicemember receives is based on three factors: paygrade (rank), geographic location, and whether the servicemember has dependents.[8] Paygrade and dependency status are used to determine the type of accommodation—or "housing profile"—that would be appropriate for the servicemember (for example, one-bedroom apartment, two-bedroom townhouse, or three-bedroom single family home). Geographic location is used to determine the median costs[9] associated with each of these housing profiles. The median costs of these housing profiles are the basis for BAH rates, with some additional adjustments made on the basis of paygrade (that is, an E-7 without

---

[7] In mid-1990s, the Department of Defense (DOD) was concerned that the poor quality of government provided housing on its bases was negatively affecting servicemembers' morale and readiness. According to a 2018 report from the Government Accountability Office (GAO), "the DOD estimated that it would need about $20 billion in appropriated funds and up to 40 years to eliminate the poor quality housing through new construction or renovation using the traditional military construction approach." See U.S. Government Accountability Office, *DOD Should Take Steps to Improve Monitoring, Reporting, and Risk Assessment*, GAO-18-218, March 2018, p. 1. The FY1996 National Defense Authorization Act established the Military Housing Privatization Initiative (MHPI). The MHPI allows the DOD to enter into agreements with private-sector developers to build and renovate military housing, in part through leasing or transferring land and/or housing units to developers. The developers renovate these units, and in some cases build new houses, which they subsequently manage. Rental rates for privatized housing are tied to the amount of BAH a servicemember is authorized. Servicemembers typically sign a lease for a privatized housing unit that includes an authorization for the property owner to receive rent via a direct allotment from servicemember pay. The Assistant Secretary of Defense for Sustainment maintains a list of frequently asked questions about MHPI here: https://www.acq.osd.mil/EIE/FIM/Housing/Housing_FAQs.html.

[8] A dependent is defined to include a spouse, unmarried children under 21 (or older in some circumstances), certain parents dependent on the servicemembers, and certain individuals placed in the legal custody of the servicemember. See 37 U.S.C. 401 for the complete definition. Note that for the purposes of BAH rates, no distinction is made between a servicemember with one dependent and a servicemember with multiple dependents. The only distinction is whether or not the servicemember has dependents.

[9] Prior to 2015, BAH rates factored in the average costs of rental housing rates, utilities, and renter's insurance in a wide array of housing markets. DOD eliminated the cost of renter's insurance from the calculation in 2015.

dependents will receive more than an E-6 without dependents, even though the appropriate housing profile for both of them is "two bedroom apartment"). As a result of this methodology, BAH rates are much higher in some areas than others, but servicemembers of similar paygrade and dependents status should be able to pay for roughly comparable housing regardless of their duty location.[10] BAH rates are paid to the servicemember at the specified rate, regardless of the actual housing expenses incurred. Table 2 provides illustrative examples of how much BAH servicemembers receive annually.

OHA is also based on paygrade, geographic location, and whether the servicemember has dependents, but the manner in which it is calculated is significantly different than BAH.[11] OHA is paid based on the servicemember's reported actual housing expenses, up to a maximum amount that varies by location, plus an allowance for utilities. The amount is reduced if the servicemember resides with one or more "sharers."[12] There is also a fixed one-time allowance to cover certain move-in expenses (such as real estate agents' fees, phone and utility connections, and security improvements).

---

[10] For a more detailed description of how BAH rates are calculated, see the Department of Defense's BAH Primer, at http://www.defensetravel.dod.mil/Docs/perdiem/BAH-Primer.pdf. For a complete listing of BAH rates, see these tables: http://www.defensetravel.dod.mil/site/pdcFiles.cfm?dir=/Allowances/BAH/PDF/.

[11] The Joint Travel Regulations describe the differences between BAH and OHA. BAH is "[p]aid for housing in the United States. The BAH rate is based on median housing costs and is paid independently of a Service member's actual housing costs." OHA is "[p]aid monthly to help offset housing expenses for a Service member or dependent authorized to live in private-sector leased or owned housing at an assigned overseas location outside the United States. OHA is based on cost reimbursement. The amount of OHA paid considers factors, such as whether the housing is shared, the appropriate utilities...and whether the Service member owns or rents the housing." Joint Travel Regulations (January 1, 2019), Chapter 10, Table 10-1, https://www.defensetravel.dod.mil/Docs/perdiem/JTR_Chapters(8-10).pdf.

[12] "Sharers" include other servicemembers authorized OHA, federal civilian employees authorized a Living Quarters Allowance or Cost of Living Allowance, and other persons (excluding the servicemembers dependents) who contribute towards the payment of rent, mortgage, and/or utilities. Those involved in a sharing arrangement have their proportional rent shares determined by dividing the total rent for the dwelling by the number of sharers. See Joint Travel Regulations (January 1, 2019), Chapter 10, paragraphs 100101 and 100502, https://www.defensetravel.dod.mil/ Docs/perdiem/JTR_Chapters(8-10).pdf.

Food

Table 2. Average regular military compensation for selected paygrades (2019 data; assumes BAH and BAS instead of government quarters and meals)

Pay Grade	Rank	Average Annual Basic Pay	Average Annual Housing Allowance	Average Annual Subsistence Allowance	Estimated Average Annual Federal Tax Advantage	Average Annual RMC
E-1	Private (Army and Marine Corps) Seaman Recruit (Navy) Airman Basic (Air Force)	$19,303	$14,020	$4,433	$2,528	$40,283
E-5	Sergeant (Army and Marine Corps) Petty Officer Second Class (Navy) Staff Sergeant (Air Force)	$35,785	$19,503	$4,433	$4,823	$64,544
E-8	Master Sergeant or First Sergeant (Army and Marine Corps) Senior Chief Petty Officer (Navy) Senior Master Sergeant or First Sergeant (Air Force)	$64,055	$24,069	$4,433	$4,189	$96,746
O-1	Second Lieutenant (Army, Air Force and Marine Corps) Ensign (Navy)	$39,210	$17,827	$3,053	$4,111	$64,200
O-4	Major (Army, Air Force and Marine Corps) Lieutenant Commander (Navy)	$91,706	$28,064	$3,053	$7,623	$130,446
O-6	Colonel (Army, Air Force and Marine Corps) Captain (Navy)	$135,118	$32,433	$3,053	$10,105	$180,709

Source: Department of Defense, Selected Military Compensation Tables, January 1, 2019, B3, https://militarypay.defense.gov/Portals/3/Documents/Reports/GreenBook%202019.pdf?ver=2019 -01-16-132128- 617. For the E-1 data above, CRS used the "ALL E-1" row of the referenced table; for the O-1 data, CRS used the "O-1" row, which excludes the higher rates for those in paygrade O-1 who formerly served as enlisted personnel. The tax advantage is computed "using the standard deduction and 2018 tax rates, including the earned income tax credit." Actual annual tax advantage of servicemembers will vary based on their unique tax situation.

Notes: BAH = Basic Allowance for Housing; BAS = Basic Allowance for Subsistence; RMC = Regular Military Compensation.

192 Lawrence Kapp and Barbara Salazar Torreon

Nearly all servicemembers receive a monthly payment to defray their personal food costs.[13] This is known as basic allowance for subsistence (BAS). BAS is provided at a flat rate: In 2019, enlisted personnel receive $369.39 a month, while officers receive $254.39 a month.[14] There have been calls in the past to merge BAS with basic pay to reduce the complexity of military compensation and the need for BAS computations each year.

Federal Tax Advantage

Certain types of military compensation are not subject to federal income tax, thus generating a tax benefit for servicemembers. The various types of military pay—basic pay, special pay, and incentive pay—are considered part of gross income and are usually subject to federal income tax.[15] Military allowances, on the other hand, are generally not considered part of gross income and are not subject to federal income tax; nor are the various in-kind benefits of the military—for example, government housing, health care, fitness centers, and subsidized grocery stores.[16,17] RMC

---

[13] Those who do not receive BAS—for example, enlisted personnel in basic training—receive government-provided meals. Historically, enlisted personnel did not receive BAS except in specific circumstances; rather, they were normally provided free meals in government dining facilities. This changed in 2002. Enlisted personnel now receive BAS except in limited circumstances. However, if a servicemember receiving BAS elects to eat in a government dining facility, he or she must pay for the meal. There are also circumstances, such as sea duty and field duty, in which a servicemember may be required to receive government meals and pay for them (essentially forfeiting their BAS in exchange for government provided meals). For more information on this topic, see the Department of Defense Financial Management Regulation, Volume 7A, Chapter 25, at http://comptroller.defense.gov/Portals/45/documents/fmr/current/ 07a/07a_25.pdf.

[14] Enlisted personnel receive a higher BAS than officers. Historically, the federal government always provided enlisted personnel with meals or a cash allowance to purchase suitable meals, but it did not always take that position with officers; sometimes they were given a subsistence allowance, sometimes they were expected to pay for their own meals out of their regular pay. Enlisted BAS, then, has historically been intended to cover the full cost of meals for the servicemember; officer BAS has not.

[15] These types of pay are exempt from federal taxation if earned in a combat zone by enlisted personnel and warrant officers; for officers, these types of pay are exempt from federal taxation up to the maximum amount of enlisted basic pay plus the amount of imminent danger pay.

[16] This exemption, which reflects the long-standing exclusion of certain military benefits from gross income, was codified in the Internal Revenue Code (26 U.S.C. 134) by the Tax Reform Act of 1986 (P.L. 99-514). For a detailed discussion on these topics, see the Military Compensation Background Papers, 8th edition, pages 169-182 and 873-883,

considers only the federal income tax advantage provided by the exemption of BAH and BAS from gross income. The precise value of the federal tax advantage for an individual servicemember will vary depending on his or her unique tax situation.

Compensation Elements Not Included in RMC

RMC *does not* include the full array of compensation elements (e.g., special pays and bonuses, reimbursements, educational assistance, deferred compensation, or any estimate of the cash value of nonmonetary benefits such as health care, child care, recreational facilities, commissaries, and exchanges). As the value of these forms of compensation can be very substantial, RMC should not be considered a measure of *total* military compensation.

How Are Each Year's Increases in Basic Pay, BAH, and BAS Computed?

Mentions of the "military pay raise" are almost always references to the annual increase in basic pay. The statutory formula for calculating each year's pay raise is discussed below, but basic pay is only one element of RMC. BAH and BAS are also subject to periodic adjustment, although they typically do not receive as much attention as increases in basic pay.

---

https://www.loc.gov/rr/frd/pdf-files/Military_Comp-2018.pdf. Table 2 of this IRS publication is also helpful: http://www.irs.gov/pub/irs-pdf/p3.pdf. The exception to the general nontaxability of allowances is the CONUS Cost of Living Allowance (COLA), since it was created after the 1986 Tax Reform Act.

[17] 26 U.S.C. 134 reads, *in part*, as follows:

§ *134. Certain military benefits.*

(a) General rule. Gross income shall not include any qualified military benefit.

(b) Qualified military benefit. For purposes of this section—

(1) In general. The term "qualified military benefit" means any allowance or in-kind benefit (other than personal use of a vehicle) which—

(A) is received by any member or former member of the uniformed services of the United States or any dependent of such member by reason of such member's status or service as a member of such uniformed services, and

(B) was excludable from gross income on September 9, 1986, under any provision of law, regulation, or administrative practice which was in effect on such date (other than a provision of this title).

Basic Pay: Increases Are Linked to Increases in the Employment Cost Index (ECI)

Section 1009 of Title 37 provides a permanent formula for an automatic annual increase in basic pay that is indexed to the annual increase in the Employment Cost Index (ECI) for "wages and salaries, private industry workers." For 2000-2006, the statute required the military raise to be equal to the ECI increase plus an additional one half percentage point (i.e., if the ECI annual increase were to be 3.0%, the military raise would be 3.5%). For 2007 and onward, the statute required the raise be equal to the ECI, although Congress continued to enact increases above the ECI through 2010.

Under subsection (e) of this statute, the President can specify an alternative pay adjustment that supersedes the automatic adjustment. President Obama invoked this option with regard to the 2014-2016 pay raises. Additionally, Congress can pass legislation to specify the annual pay raise which, if enacted, would supersede the automatic adjustment and/or any proposed presidential adjustment. The frequency of such congressional action is discussed below.

The automatic adjustment under 37 U.S.C. 1009 is tied to the increase in the ECI from the third quarter of the third preceding year to the third quarter of the second preceding year. For example, in the 12-month period between the quarter which ended in September 2015 and the quarter which ended in September 2016, the ECI increased by 2.4%. Hence the pay raise for 2018, as calculated by the statutory formula, was 2.4%. An illustration of how the formula operates is provided in Figure 1. This methodology results in a substantial lag between increases in the ECI and increases in basic pay; the lag appears to be related to the stages of the federal budget process.[18]

---

[18] In other words, the 2.4% increase described above informed the FY2018 budget request, which was being developed in the fall of 2016 and submitted to Congress in February of 2017. The FY2018 National Defense Authorization Act was enacted December 12, 2017, shortly before the day (January 1, 2018) that the 2018 pay raise would go into effect.

Source: Congressional Research Service.

Figure 1. How Increases in Basic Pay are Calculated under the Statutory Formula; In accordance with 37 U.S.C. 1009(c)(1).

Congress Has Frequently Waived the Automatic Adjustment and Specified the Amount of the Military Pay Raise, Although This Has Become Less Common In Recent Years

Despite the statutory formula, which could operate each year without any further action, Congress has frequently waived the automatic adjustment and legislated particular percentage increases.

For the pay raises effective in fiscal years 1981 and 1982 and calendar years 1984-2010, 2013, and 2017-2018[19] Congress specified the increase that was to take effect in the annual defense authorization act. Congress specified no percentage increase for 1983, 2011, 2012, 2014-2016,[20] or 2019, thereby allowing the statutory formula or the presidential alternative adjustment to go into effect. The statutory formula is important even when it does not go into effect, as it provides a benchmark around which alternatives are developed and debated.

Basic Allowance for Housing: Increases Are Linked to Increases in Housing Costs

Basic Allowance for Housing is paid to servicemembers living in the United States who do not choose or are not provided government

---

[19] Increases in basic pay became effective at the start of the calendar year, rather than the fiscal year, in 1984.
[20] While not specifying a specific increase for 2015 and 2016, Congress did stipulate in law that for those years there would be no increase for general and flag officers (those in paygrades O-7 and above) For a listing of increases in basic pay since 1994, see the later section of this chapter entitled "4. What Have Been the Annual Percentage Increases in Basic Pay Over the Past 20 Years? What Were Each Year's Major Executive and Legislative Branch Proposals and Actions on the Annual Percentage Increase in Military Basic Pay?"

quarters.[21] By law, the Secretary of Defense sets the BAH rates for localities, known as military housing areas (MHAs), throughout the United States.

However, the law requires the Secretary to set the rates "based on the costs of adequate housing determined for the area" and ties this determination to "the costs of adequate housing for civilians with comparable income levels in the same area."[22] As increases in BAH are tied to increases in local housing costs, they are not affected by the annual percentage increase in the ECI. Thus, the average increase in BAH almost always differs from the increase in basic pay.

To determine the cost of adequate housing, DOD conducts an annual[23] survey of rental costs in each of the MHAs.[24] DOD employs a contractor to collect rental costs for various types of housing, including apartments, townhouses, and single-family units of varying bedroom sizes. Costs for utilities are also collected.[25] DOD uses these annual surveys to determine how much housing costs have increased or decreased in each MHA. If costs in a given MHA increase, it adjusts BAH rates for that locality upward accordingly at the start of the next calendar year. If costs in a given MHA decrease, it adjusts the BAH rates downward. However, in the case of a downward adjustment, a "save pay" provision on the BAH statute prevents the decrease from applying to individuals currently assigned to that locality: "So long as a member of a uniformed service retains uninterrupted eligibility to receive a basic allowance for housing within an area of the United States, the monthly amount of the allowance for the member may not be reduced as a result of changes in housing costs in the

---

[21] Many servicemembers prefer to live off post and elect to receive BAH instead of government quarters; in other cases, there may not be a sufficient supply of government quarters to house all interested personnel. Those servicemembers living overseas and not provided with government quarters receive OHA. The adjustment mechanism for OHA is similar to that of BAH.

[22] 37 U.S.C. 403(b).

[23] There have been occasional proposals to survey the housing costs on which BAH is based more frequently than once a year. These proposals typically occur when housing costs or utility costs are rising rapidly.

[24] For more information on this process, see the Defense Travel Management Office's "A Primer on the Basic Allowance for Housing (BAH)," at http://www.defensetravel.dod.mil/Docs/perdiem/BAH-Primer.pdf.

[25] DOD eliminated the cost of renter's insurance from the calculation in 2015.

area or the promotion of the member."[26] Thus, only personnel newly assigned to the area receive the lower payment.

Congress has periodically changed the law with regard to the proportion of housing costs covered by BAH or its predecessor, known as Basic Allowance for Quarters (BAQ) and Variable Housing Allowance (VHA).[27] DOD estimated that BAQ+VHA covered about 80% of housing costs in 1996.[28] In 1997, Congress replaced BAQ+VHA with BAH, and subsequently raised BAH rates so that they covered 100% of the cost of adequate housing by 2005.[29]

More recently, the FY2015 National Defense Authorization Act allowed the Secretary of Defense to reduce BAH payments by 1% of the national average monthly housing cost,[30] and the FY2016 National Defense Authorization Act extended this authority, authorizing an additional 1% reduction per year through 2019 (for a maximum reduction of 5% under the national monthly average housing cost).[31] DOD has

---

[26] 37 U.S.C. 403(b)(6). An analogous provision for OHA is provided in 37 U.S.C. 403(c)(2).

[27] From 1980 to 1997, servicemembers not assigned to government quarters received BAQ and, depending on location, VHA. Congress revised this BAQ+VHA system in 1984 to set BAQ at 65% of the national median housing cost, with VHA provided when the local median housing cost in a given locality exceeded 80% of the national median housing cost. Except for those living in lower cost areas where the local median housing cost was below 80% of the national median housing cost—who therefore only received BAQ—servicemembers were expected to pay 15% of anticipated housing costs (this rate was also known as *absorption* or *out-of-pocket*). However, in subsequent years, congressionally approved increases to BAQ and VHA did not keep up with increases in civilian housing costs. Dissatisfaction with the BAQ+VHA system, including the persistent disparity between intended and actual out-of-pocket expenses, led Congress to replace it with BAH in 1997.

[28] "In creating the BAQ and the Variable Housing Allowance (VHA) [the predecessors to BAH], Congress intended to cover 85 percent of service members' housing costs. In reality though, housing allowances only covered approximately 80 percent of service members' total housing expenses in 1996. In an effort to close that gap, the Department funded a 3.0 percent increase in housing allowances in 1997, and Congress added an additional 1.6 percent. This will lower out- of-pocket housing costs to approximately 19% percent of a service member's total costs, the lowest percentage since before 1987." Testimony of Fred Pang, Assistant Secretary of Defense for Force Management Policy, before the House National Security Committee, Military Personnel Subcommittee, March 14, 1997.

[29] For more information on this topic, see Department of Defense, Military Compensation Background Papers, Eighth Edition, Washington, DC, July 2018, p. 136-139, https://www.loc.gov/rr/frd/pdf-files/Military_Comp-2018.pdf.

[30] Also, starting in 2015, the Department of Defense decided it would no longer consider renter's insurance in BAH calculations. This change effectively reduced BAH rates by an additional 1%.

[31] P.L. 113-291, §604 and P.L. 114-92, §603.

198   *Lawrence Kapp and Barbara Salazar Torreon*

indicated that a *save pay* provision, discussed above, will apply to these changes.[32]

Basic Allowance for Subsistence: Increases Are Linked to Increases in Food Costs

BAS is paid at a uniform rate to all eligible enlisted personnel, and at a uniform but lower rate for all eligible officers. By law, BAS is adjusted each year according to a formula that is linked to changes in food prices. The increase is identical to "the percentage increase in the monthly cost of a liberal food plan for a male in the United States who is between 20 and 50 years of age over the preceding fiscal year, as determined by the Secretary of Agriculture each October 1."[33]

What Have Been the Annual Percentage Increases in Basic Pay over the Past 20 Years? What Were Each Year's Major Executive and Legislative Branch Proposals and Actions on the Annual Percentage Increase in Military Basic Pay?

The following subsections itemize action on the basic pay increase going back to 1997. *Unless otherwise noted, all increases were proposed to be effective on January 1 of the year indicated in bold.* The public law number for each year's National Defense Authorization Act is included at the end of each section below, even for those years in which there was no statutory language relevant to the pay raise.

---

[32] "An integral part of the Basic Allowance for Housing program is the provision of individual rate protection to all members. No matter what happens to measured housing costs—including the out-of-pocket cost sharing adjustment noted above, an individual member who maintains uninterrupted Basic Allowance for Housing eligibility in a given location will not see his/her Basic Allowance for Housing rate decrease. This ensures that members who have made long-term commitments in the form of a lease or contract are not penalized if the area's housing costs decrease." DOD News Release, "DoD Releases 2016 Basic Allowance for Housing Rates," http://www.defense.gov/News/News-Releases/News-Release-View/Article/636341/dod-releases-2016-basic-allowance-for-housing-rates.

[33] 37 U.S.C. 402(b)(1)(B).

Military Pay: Key Questions and Answers 199

- **2019.** *Statutory Formula: 2.6%. Administration request: 2.6%.* The House-passed version of the FY2019 National Defense Authorization Act (NDAA) contained no provision to specify the rate of increase in basic pay. Section 601 of the Senate-passed version of the FY2019 NDAA waived the automatic increase in basic pay under the statutory formula of 37 U.S.C. §1009, and set the pay raise at 2.6%. The John S. McCain National Defense Authorization Act for FY 2019 (P.L. 115-232) contained no provision relating to a general increase in basic pay, thereby leaving the automatic adjustment of 37 U.S.C. 1009 in place. *Final increase: 2.6% across-the-board.*

- **2018.** *Statutory Formula: 2.4%. Administration request: 2.1%.* Section 601 of the House-passed version of the FY2018 National Defense Authorization Act (NDAA) required the statutory formula increase (2.4%) to go into effect, "notwithstanding any determination made by the President under subsection (e) of such section with respect to an alternative pay adjustment" Section 601 of the Senate-passed version of the FY2018 NDAA waived the automatic increase in basic pay under the statutory formula of 37 U.S.C. §1009, and set the pay raise at 2.1%. On August 31, 2017, President Trump sent a letter to congressional leaders invoking his authority under 37 U.S.C. 1009(e) to set the pay raise at 2.1%. However, Section 601 of the enacted version of the FY2018 NDAA (P.L. 115-91) specified the statutory formula increase (2.4%) would go into effect, superseding the President's alternative adjustment. Therefore, basic pay for all servicemembers increased by 2.4% on January 1, 2018. *Final increase: 2.4% across-the-board (P.L. 115-91).*

- **2017.** *Statutory Formula: 2.1%. Administration request: 1.6%.* Section 601 of the House version of the FY2017 NDAA (H.R. 4909) required the statutory formula increase (2.1%) to go into effect, "notwithstanding any determination made by the President under subsection (e) of such section with respect to an alternative pay adjustment" Section 601 of the Senate version of the FY2017

NDAA (S. 2943) waived the automatic increase in basic pay under the statutory formula of 37 U.S.C. §1009, and set the pay raise at 1.6%. On August 31, 2016, the President sent a letter to congressional leaders invoking his authority under 37 U.S.C. 1009(e) to set the pay raise at 1.6%. However, Section 601 of the final version of the FY2017 NDAA set the pay raise at 2.1%, and President Obama signed this bill into law on December 23, 2016. This statutory adjustment supplanted the President's alternative pay adjustment. Therefore, basic pay for all servicemembers increased by 2.1% on January 1, 2017. *Final increase: 2.1% across-the-board (P.L. 114-328).*

- **2016.** *Statutory Formula: 2.3%. Administration request: 1.3%.* The House version of the FY2016 NDAA (H.R. 1735) contained no provision to specify the rate of increase in basic pay, although the report accompanying it stated that the committee supported a 2.3% increase. The Senate version (H.R. 1735) contained a provision that waived the automatic adjustment of 37 U.S.C. §1009 and set the pay increase at 1.3%, but excluded generals and admirals. On August 28, the President exercised his authority to specify an alternative adjustment, setting the increase at 1.3%. No general pay raise provision was included in the final version of the NDAA, thereby leaving in place the 1.3% increase specified by President Obama. However, Section 601 of the FY2016 NDAA prevented the pay increase from applying to generals and admirals. *Final increase: 1.3% across-the-board, excluding generals and admirals (P.L. 114-92).*

- **2015.** *Statutory Formula: 1.8%. Administration request: 1.0%.* The House version of the FY2015 NDAA contained no statutory provision to specify the rate of increase in basic pay, although the report accompanying it stated that the committee supported a 1.8% increase; it also included a provision to prevent general and flag officers from receiving any increase in basic pay in 2015. The Senate committee-reported version contained a provision waiving the automatic adjustment of 37 U.S.C. 1009 and setting the pay increase at 1.0% for servicemembers, but excluded generals and admirals. On August 29, President Obama sent a letter to Congress invoking 37 U.S.C. 1009(e) to set the pay raise for 2015 at 1.0%. No general pay raise provision was included in the final version of the NDAA, thereby leaving in place the 1.0% increase specified by President Obama. However, Section 601 of the FY2015 NDAA prevented the pay increase from applying to generals and admirals. *Final increase: 1% across-the-board, excluding generals and admirals (P.L. 113-291).*

- **2014.** *Statutory Formula: 1.8%. Administration request: 1.0%.* The House version of the FY2014 NDAA contained no provision to specify the rate of increase in basic pay, while the Senate committee-reported bill specified an increase of 1.0%. On August 30, President Obama sent a letter to Congress invoking 37 U.S.C. 1009(e) to set the pay raise for 2014 at 1.0%. No provision was included in the final version of the NDAA, thereby leaving in place the 1.0% increase specified by the President. *Final increase: 1% across-the-board (P.L. 113-66).*

- **2013.** *Statutory Formula: 1.7%. Administration request: 1.7%.* The House version of the FY2013 NDAA supported a 1.7% across-the-board pay raise. The Senate bill contained no statutory language. The final bill specified a 1.7% increase. *Final increase: 1.7% across-the-board (P.L. 112-239).*

- **2012.** *Statutory Formula: 1.6%. Administration request: 1.6%.* The House version of the FY2012 NDAA supported a 1.6% across-the-board pay raise, equal to the ECI. Both the Senate-reported bill and the final version were silent on the pay raise issue. As a result, the statutory formula became operative with an automatic January 1, 2012, across-the-board raise equal to 1.6%. *Final increase: 1.6% across-the-board (P.L. 112-81).*

- **2011.** *Statutory formula: 1.4%. Administration request: 1.4%.* The House version of the FY2011 NDAA supported a 1.9% across-the-board pay raise, 0.5% above the ECI. Both the Senate- reported bill and the final bill were silent on the pay raise issue. As a result, the statutory formula became operative with an automatic across-the-board raise of 1.4%; equal to the ECI. *Final increase: 1.4% across-the-board (P.L. 111-383).*

- **2010.** *Statutory formula:* 2.9%. *Administration request:* 2.9%. The FY2010 NDAA specified a 3.4% increase. *Final increase: 3.4% across-the-board (P.L. 111-84).*

- **2009.** *Statutory formula:* 3.4%. *Administration request:* 3.4%. The FY2009 NDAA specified a 3.9% increase. *Final increase: 3.9% across-the-board (P.L. 110-417).*

- **2008.** *Statutory formula:* 3.0%. *Administration request:* 3.0% across-the-board. The presidential veto of the initial FY2008 NDAA resulted in a 3.0% pay raise taking effect on January 1, 2008 (statutory formula). The final version of the NDAA, signed into law on January 28, specified that basic pay be increased by 3.5% retroactive to January 1. *Final increase: 3.5% across-the-board (P.L. 110-181).*

- **2007.** *Statutory formula:* 2.2%. The statutory formula for 2007 was based solely on the ECI and not a rate 0.5% higher than the ECI that had been specified for 2000-2006. *Administration request:* 2.2%. The NDAA specified a minimum 2.2% increase, with greater increases for certain pay cells.[34] *Final increase: 2.2% across-the-board but with an additional April 1, 2007, targeted pay raise that would be as high as 8.3% for some warrant officers and range from 2.5% for E-5s to 5.5% for E-9s[35] (P.L. 109-364).*

- **2006.** *Statutory formula:* 3.1%. *Administration request:* 3.1% across-the-board. The NDAA specified a 3.1% increase. *Final increase: 3.1% across-the-board (P.L. 109-163).*

- **2005.** *Statutory formula:* 3.5%. *Administration request:* 3.5%. The NDAA specified a 3.5% increase. *Final increase: 3.5% across-the-board (P.L. 108-375).*

---

[34] The basic pay table is made up of various pay cells for specified combinations of pay grade and years of service.

[35] Maze, Rick, "DoD seeks targeted raises of up to 8.3 percent," *Army Times*, March 20, 2005.

Military Pay: Key Questions and Answers   203

- **2004.** *Statutory formula:* 3.7%. *Administration request:* Average 4.1%; minimum 2.0%; maximum of 6.5%. The NDAA specified a 3.7% minimum increase, with greater increases for certain pay cells. *Final increase: 3.7% minimum, 4.15% average, 6.25% maximum for some senior NCOs (P.L. 108-136).*
- **2003.** *Statutory formula:* 4.1%. *Administration request:* minimum 4.1%; average 4.8%; between 5.0% and 6.5% for some mid-level and senior noncommissioned officers, warrant officers, and mid-level commissioned officers. The NDAA specified increases identical to the Administration request. *Final increase: Identical to the Administration request (P.L. 107-314).*
- **2002.** *Statutory formula:* 4.6%. *Administration request:* numerous figures for the "Administration request" were mentioned in the pay raise debate, depending on when and which agency produced the figures. In general, however, they all proposed increases of at least 5% and no more than 15% (the latter applying only to a very few individuals), depending on pay grade and years of service; the average increase was 6.9%. The NDAA specified a 5% minimum increase, with greater increases for certain pay cells. *Final increase: Between 5 and 10%, depending on pay grade and years of service (P.L. 107-107).*[36]
- **2001.** *Statutory formula:* 3.7%. *Administration request:* 3.7%. The FY2001 NDAA specified a 3.7% minimum increase of 3.7%, with greater increases for certain pay cells. The NDAA specified a 3.7% minimum increase, with greater increases for certain pay cells. *Final increase: 3.7% across-the-board, effective January 1, 2001, plus additional raises of between 1.0 and 5.5% for mid-grade officer and enlisted personnel, to be effective July 1, 2001 (P.L. 106-398).*

---

[36] The 2002 increase remains the largest across-the-board percentage raises since that of FY1982, which took effect on October 1, 1981. The latter was a 14.3% across-the-board raise, which followed an 11.7% raise the previous year, FY1981, resulting in a two-year raise of almost 28%. This was principally in response to the high inflation of the late 1970s.

- **2000.** *Statutory formula:* 4.8% (based on the change to the statutory formula; the original statutory formula would have led to a proposed raise of 3.8%). *Administration request:* 4.4% on January 1, 2000, plus increases averaging an additional 1.4% for mid-grade officer and enlisted personnel, effective July 1, 2000. The NDAA specified a 4.8% minimum increase, with greater increases for certain pay cells. *Final increase: 4.8% on January 1, 2000, plus increases averaging an additional 1.4% for mid-grade officer and enlisted personnel, effective July 1, 2000 (P.L. 106-65).*
- **1999.** *Statutory formula*: 3.1%. *Administration request*: 3.6%. The House approved 3.6%, or whatever percentage increase was approved for federal GS civilians, whichever was higher. The Senate approved 3.6%. The final version accepted the House provision. *Final increase*: *3.6%, as GS civilians also received 3.6% (P.L. 105-261).*

What Is an "Adequate" Level of Military Pay?

Since the end of the draft in 1973, the "adequacy" of military pay has tended to become an issue for Congress if it appears that

- the military services are having trouble recruiting enough new personnel, or keeping sufficient career personnel, of requisite quality; or
- the standard of living of career personnel is perceived to be less fair or equitable than that of demographically comparable civilians (in terms of age, education, skills, responsibilities, and similar criteria).

The first issue is an economic inevitability in some periods. In the absence of a draft, the services must compete in the labor market for new military personnel, and—a fact often overlooked— have always had to compete in the labor market to retain the more experienced individuals who make up the career force.[37] When unemployment is low, employment opportunities in the civilian world abound and military recruiting is more difficult. When unemployment is high, military service becomes a more attractive alternative, and military recruiting is easier.

From 2010 to 2017, recruiting and retention in the Armed Forces were quite strong, hence weakening the case for compensation increases based on competition with the civilian economy and generating discussion of possible compensation cuts and/or restructuring. However, the strong recruiting and retention results in those years were due in part to a civilian economy still recovering from recession and to force reductions in the Air Force, Marine Corps, and Army, which generated lower recruiting and retention goals. Congress approved active duty end-strength increases for all four Services in FY2018. Subsequently, the Army did not meet its FY2018 recruiting goal[38] and senior defense officials have testified that a strong economy has made it more challenging for them to recruit new personnel.[39] If recruiting problems were to become more widespread, increased advocacy for compensation increases could well occur.

---

[37] Unlike civilian enterprises, the military services generally do not recruit mid- or senior-level personnel from outside the existing military workforce. Rather, they rely on promotions from within to fill these positions.

[38] The FY2018 NDAA approved an active duty end-strength of 483,500 for the Army. The Army fell short of this objective, ending FY2018 with a strength of 476,179 (nearly the same as its FY2017 end-strength of 476,245). The Army attributes its inability to meet the end-strength objective primarily to a shortfall in enlisted recruits: the Army set a goal of 76,500 new enlisted recruits (also referred to as non-prior service accessions) but brought in 69,972. The FY2019 NDAA authorized an active duty end-strength of 487,000 for the Army, but in its FY2020 budget request (submitted in March 2019), the Army proposed a revised end-strength goal: "Given the FY 2018 end strength outcome and a challenging labor market for military recruiting, the Army Active Component has decided to pursue a new end strength growth ramp. The Army has shifted to a more modest end strength growth ramp of 2,000 Soldiers per year, with end strength targets of 478,000 in FY 2019 and 480,000 in FY 2020." Despite a similarly challenging labor market, the Air Force was able to increase its active duty strength in FY2018 by about 3,000 (322,787 on September 30, 2017 vs. 325,880 on September 30, 2018) and the Navy increased by about 6,000 (323,933 on September 30, 2017 vs. 329,851 on September 30, 2018).

[39] See for example, U.S. Congress, House Committee on Appropriations, Subcommittee on Defense, *Army Fiscal 2020 Budget Request*, 116th Cong., April 9, 2019, testimony of the Honorable Mark Esper, Secretary of the Army ("...we face a difficult recruiting environment...you're doing it in a country that is facing one of the lowest unemployment rates in decades and American population is increasingly isolated form the Army that serves

The second situation is frequently stated in moral or ethical terms. Proponents of this viewpoint argue that, even if quantitative indexes of recruiting and retention appear to be satisfactory, the crucial character of the military's mission of national defense, and its acceptance of the professional ethic that places mission accomplishment above survival, demands certain enhanced levels of compensation. However, the compensation increases that occurred in the 2000s have led many analysts to conclude that military compensation is currently quite robust in comparison to civilian counterparts.

Is There a "Pay Gap" between Military and Civilian Pay? Do Military Personnel Make More or Less Than Their Civilian Counterparts?

The issue of a military-civilian "pay gap" raises several additional questions:

- How can the existence of a gap be determined and the gap be measured?
- Is there a gap and, if so, are civilians or military personnel being paid more? How much more?
- If there is a gap, does that in itself require action?

---

it.") and U.S. Congress, Senate Committee on Armed Services, Subcommittee on Personnel, *Military Personnel Policies and Military Family Readiness*, 116th Cong., 1st sess., February 27, 2019, Statement of Vice Admiral Robert P. Burke, Chief of Naval Personnel ("Under good economic conditions, America's youth have more options at their disposal, challenging Navy's ability to meet recruiting requirements as potential candidates explore alternative employment opportunities. This past year, the U.S. economy experienced its strongest growth since the recession of 2008, resulting in significant expansion of employment opportunity in an ever-tightening labor market.") Other factors that can affect recruiting and retention include the level of resources allocated to recruiting and retention and attitudes about military career prospects and job satisfaction. For more information on the recruiting and retention issues of the 1990s, see CRS Report RL31297, *Recruiting and Retention in the Active Component Military: Are There Problems?*, by Lawrence Kapp.

A wide range of studies over the past several decades have attempted to compare military and civilian (both federal civil service and private sector) compensation. In general, the markedly different ways in which civilian public and private sector compensation and benefit systems are structured, compared to those of the Armed Forces, make it difficult to validate any generalizations about whether there is a "gap" between military and civilian pay.[40]

Measuring and Confirming a "Gap"

It is difficult to find a common index or indicator to compare the dollar values of military and civilian compensation. First, military compensation includes numerous separate components, whose receiving population and taxability vary widely. Which of these, if any, should be included in a military-civilian pay comparison? Furthermore, total military compensation includes a wide range of noncash benefits—health care, commissary access, recreational facilities—as well as a unique deferred compensation package. Few civilians work in organizations where analogous benefits are provided. Attempts to facilitate a comparison by assigning a cash value to noncash benefits almost always founder on the large number of debatable assumptions that must be made to generate such an estimate.

Second, it is also difficult to establish a comparison between military ranks and pay grades on the one hand and civilian jobs on the other. The range of knowledge, supervision, and professional judgment required of military personnel and civilians performing similar duties in a standard peacetime industrial or office milieu may be roughly equivalent. However,

---

[40] Some advocates for federal civil servants argue that federal civilian pay lags behind private sector pay, which in turn leads some people to infer that military pay lags behind private sector pay (given the past linkage between civil service and military basic pay percentage increases). A separate debate, more common about a decade ago, was over "pay parity" between the percentage increases in military basic pay and federal civil service pay. The issue has been whether the civil service should get a percentage raise identical to that of the military, or whether the military should get a higher raise because of (1) the much greater degree of danger and hardship military service entails, compared to most civilian employment, especially in time of war, and (2) the need to cope with actual or forestall potential military recruiting and retention problems.

208 *Lawrence Kapp and Barbara Salazar Torreon*

when the same military member's job in the field and in combat is concerned, comparisons become difficult.

Third, generally speaking, the conditions of military service are frequently much more arduous than those of civilian employment, even in peacetime, for families as well as military personnel themselves. This aspect of military service is sometimes cited as a rationale for military compensation being at a higher level than it otherwise might be. On the other hand, the military services all mention travel and adventure in exotic places as a positive reason for enlistment and/or a military career, so it may be misleading to automatically assume that this is always a liability. Thus, it can be difficult to make direct comparisons between military and civilian occupations. As noted by the Congressional Budget Office:[41]

> Comparing compensation in the military and civilian sectors can be problematic. One obvious limitation is that such comparisons cannot easily account for different job characteristics. Many military jobs are more hazardous, require frequent moves, and are less flexible than civilian jobs in the same field. Members of the armed forces are subject to military discipline, are considered to be on duty at all times, and are unable to resign, change jobs at will or negotiate pay. Military personnel also receive extensive training, paid for by the government. Family support programs are generally more available in the military compared with civilian employers. Intangible rewards, such as a shared sense of purpose, may be higher among military personnel as well. Quantifying those elements among military and civilian personnel is extremely difficult.

Fourth, differing methodologies for calculating compensation can yield different results. For example, comparing the percentage increase in pay over different time periods can produce widely varying rates of increase. Likewise, when indexes of compensation include different elements (for example, basic pay versus RMC), the results will typically diverge as well.

Finally, the level of specificity used in a pay comparison can lead to differing results, especially when the comparison is between private sector

---

[41] "Evaluating Military Compensation", Congressional Budget Office, June, 2007, p. 2.

Military Pay: Key Questions and Answers

and federal pay, both civil service and military. For instance, Army colonels may, according to some indexes, be paid roughly as much as federal civil service GS-15s, or as much as private sector managers with certain responsibilities.

However, if the pay comparisons focus on those occupational specialties that are highly paid in the private sector—health care, information technology, and some other scientific and engineering skills are examples—the comparison may not be as favorable. Other common subcategories for comparison—such as age, gender, years in the labor force, and educational levels—can also produce differing results.

Estimates of a Military-Civilian Pay Gap

Various comparisons of military and civilian compensation exist which illustrate a gap that favors civilian pay levels, refute the existence of such a gap, or show that the pay gap favors the military. Some of these reports lack precision in identifying what aspects of military pay were compared with civilian pay, which indexes were used to make the comparison, or the length of time covered by the comparison.

One method of estimation, which indicates there is a pay gap in favor of civilians, asserts that rough pay parity existed between civilian and military personnel in 1982, but that increases since then in military basic pay have generally not kept up with increases in civilian pay (as measured by the ECI).[42] As a result, a pay gap of about 13% in 1999 was gradually eliminated by 2011 due to above-ECI increases in basic pay. It reappeared in 2014 with military pay estimated to be 2.6% lower than civilian pay in 2018.[43]

However, using the same starting date (1982) but considering RMC rather than just basic pay, the Congressional Budget Office (CBO) came to a much different conclusion in 2010. In congressional testimony, a CBO

---

[42] See, for example, Military Officers Association of America (MOAA), "Military Pay Comparability," http://takeaction.moaa.org/military_pay.

[43] "MOAA's 2019 Key Goals: Keep Pace with Private-Sector Pay," Military Officer's Association, December 20, 2018, http://www.moaa.org/Content/Publications-and-Media/News-Articles/2018-News-Articles/Advocacy/MOAA-s-2019-Key-Goals—Keep-Pace-with-Private-Sector-Pay.aspx.

210   *Lawrence Kapp and Barbara Salazar Torreon*

analyst answered the question "Is there a 'gap' between civilian and military pay raises over the past few decades," as follows:

> The answer depends on how narrowly military cash pay is defined. One common method of comparison is to calculate the cumulative difference between increases in military and civilian pay using military basic pay, a narrow measure of cash compensation that does not include, for example, tax-free allowances for housing and food. Applying that method would indicate that cumulatively, civilian pay rose by about 2 percent more than military pay between 1982 and the beginning of 2010. But that measure does not encompass the full scope of military cash compensation. Using a broader measure that includes cash allowances for housing and food indicates that the cumulative increase in military compensation has exceeded the cumulative increase in private-sector wages and salaries by 11 percent since 1982. That comparison excludes the value of noncash and deferred benefits, which would probably add to the cumulative difference, because benefits such as military health care have expanded more rapidly than corresponding benefits in the private sector.[44]

Another approach to estimating a pay gap attempts to compare actual compensation levels of military personnel to civilians with similar education and experience, rather than comparing rates of compensation increase over time. For example, the 9th Quadrennial Review of Military Compensation (QRMC), published in 2002, compared the RMC of junior enlisted personnel to the earnings of civilian high school graduates, middle grade NCOs with civilians with some college education, and senior enlisted personnel with civilians who are college graduates. It compared the RMC of officers to the earnings of civilians with bachelors or advanced degrees in professional or managerial occupations. Based on a separate body of research, it argued that "pay at around the 70th percentile of comparably educated civilians has been necessary to enable the military to

---

[44] Statement of Carla Tighe Murray, Senior Analyst for Military Compensation and Health Care, before the Subcommittee on Personnel Committee on Armed Services, U.S. Senate, "Evaluating Military Compensation," April 28, 2010, p. 2, http://www.cbo.gov/sites/default/files/04-28-MilitaryPay.pdf.

Military Pay: Key Questions and Answers
211

recruit and retain the quantity and quality of personnel it requires"[45] and pointed out those groups of military personnel that fell short of this compensation goal. Congress approved several rounds of pay table reform to address situations where servicemembers fell below the 70% mark. Additionally, general increases in basic pay higher than the rate of increase in the ECI (2000-2010) and the elimination of "out-of-pocket" housing expenses by 2005 pushed servicemember RMC up substantially in relation to civilian compensation. According to the 11th QRMC, by 2009 military compensation had substantially exceeded this goal:

> In 2009, average RMC for enlisted members exceeded the median wage for civilians in each relevant comparison group—those with a high school diploma, those with some college, and those with an associate's degree. Average RMC for the enlisted force corresponded to the 90th percentile of wages for civilians from the combined comparison groups. For officers, average RMC exceeded wages for civilians with a bachelor's or graduate-level degree. Average RMC for the officer force corresponded to the 83rd percentile of wages for the combined civilian comparison groups.[46]

Since that time, Congress and the executive branch have made efforts to slow the growth of military compensation. Recent initiatives have included presidentially directed increases in basic pay below the ECI for 2014-2016 and statutory authority for DOD to reduce BAH payments by 1% of the national average monthly housing cost per year from 2015 to 2019 (for a maximum reduction of 5% of the national monthly average housing cost).

In 2018, RAND published a report that compared RMC in 2016 to civilian pay levels, and compared those results to those generated by the 11th QRMC in 2009. Using a similar, though not identical, methodology

---

[45] Department of Defense, 9th Quadrennial Review of Military Compensation, March 2002, p. xxiii, http://militarypay.defense.gov/Portals/3/Documents/Reports/9th_QRMC_Report_Volumes_I_-_V.pdf.

[46] Department of Defense, 11th Quadrennial Review of Military Compensation, June 2012, p. xvii, http://militarypay.defense.gov/Portals/3/Documents/Reports/11th_QRMC_Main_Report_FINAL.pdf?ver=2016-11-06- 160559-590.

212 — Lawrence Kapp and Barbara Salazar Torreon

the RAND report found that RMC had remained well above the 70th percentile of comparability educated civilians:

> The 11th QRMC, using 2009 data, placed RMC at the 90th percentile of civilian pay for enlisted and the 83rd for officers. Our percentiles for 2016—the 84th for enlisted and 77th for officers—are somewhat lower than those of the 11th QRMC. Although the estimates differ, both estimates show relatively high percentiles, yet methodological differences contribute to the discrepancy.[47]

Taking into account the somewhat different methodology used by RAND in 2018, its authors conclude "overall RMC percentiles for 2016 for enlisted personnel and officers were virtually the same as for 2009."[48]

If There Is a Pay Gap, Does It Matter?

Some have suggested that the emphasis on a pay gap, whether real or not, is an inappropriate guide to arriving at sound policy. They argue that the key issue is, or should be, not *comparability* of military and civilian compensation, but the *competitiveness* of the former. Absent a draft, the Armed Forces must compete in the labor market for new enlisted and officer personnel. The career force by definition has always been a "volunteer force," and thus has always had to compete with civilian opportunities, real or perceived. Given these facts, some ask what difference it makes whether military pay is much lower, the same, or higher than that of civilians? If the services are having recruiting difficulties, then pay increases might be appropriate, even if the existing "gap" favors the military. Conversely, if military compensation is lower than equivalent civilian pay, and if the services are doing well in recruiting and retaining sufficient numbers of qualified personnel, then there might be no reason to raise military pay.

---

[47] James Hosek, Beth J. Asch, and Michael G. Mattock et al., *Military and Civilian Pay Levels, Trends, and Recruit Quality*, RAND Corporation, 2018, p. 28, https://www.rand.org/pubs/research_reports/RR2396.html.

[48] James Hosek, Beth J. Asch, and Michael G. Mattock, et al., *Military and Civilian Pay Levels, Trends, and Recruit Quality*, RAND Corporation, 2018, p. xiv, https://www.rand.org/pubs/research_reports/RR2396.html.Page xiv. See also pages 28-29.

Military Pay: Key Questions and Answers 213

The 11th QRMC voiced similar sentiments when it argued the following:

> A comparison between military and civilian wages does not, by itself, determine if military pay is at the optimal level. As previously noted, other factors are also at play including: recruiting and retention experiences and outlook; unemployment in the civilian economy; political factors, such as a wartime environment or risk of war; and the expected frequency and duration of overseas deployments. But the relative standing of military compensation provides context to help make decisions about RMC and other elements of the compensation system, such as those studied by the QRMC.[49]

What Additional Benefits Are Available for Military Personnel Serving in Iraq and Afghanistan?

Members of the Armed Forces serving in Iraq or Afghanistan are entitled to various additional forms of compensation, described below. Those serving in nearby countries are often eligible as well.

Hostile Fire/Imminent Danger Pay

Military personnel serving in Iraq or Afghanistan are eligible for Hostile Fire Pay (HFP) or Imminent Danger Pay (IDP).[50] HFP is paid at the rate of $225 per month; IDP is paid at an equivalent rate, but on a daily basis ($7.50 per day).[51] The purpose of this pay is to compensate

---

[49] Department of Defense, 11th Quadrennial Review of Military Compensation, June 2012, p. xvii, http://militarypay.defense.gov/Portals/3/Documents/Reports/11th_QRMC_Main_Report_FINAL.pdf?ver=2016-11-06- 160559-590.

[50] 37 U.S.C. 351 (previously 37 U.S.C. 310). Under 37 U.S.C. 351, HFP and IDP are types of hazardous duty pay. By law, the maximum amount of HFP is $450 per month and the maximum amount of IDP is $250 per month. However, these figures are caps; DOD has discretion to offer lesser amounts. See DOD Instruction 1340.09, Hazardous Pay Program, January 26, 2018, http://www.esd.whs.mil/Portals/54/Documents/DD/issuances/dodi/134 009p.PDF?ver=2018-01-30-123041-040.

[51] Servicemembers exposed to a hostile fire event receive the full $225 for the month in which the hostile fire event occurs. Those not exposed to hostile fire, but serving in an IDP location, receive IDP on a daily basis (i.e., $7.50 per day).

214 *Lawrence Kapp and Barbara Salazar Torreon*

servicemembers for physical danger. An individual can collect either Hostile Fire Pay or Imminent Danger Pay, not both simultaneously. Iraq and Afghanistan are designated imminent danger locations; any servicemember in these locations is entitled to IDP by virtue of their presence. Certain areas surrounding these countries were formerly designated as imminent danger locations, but DOD revoked this designation in 2014.[52] For a list of all imminent danger locations, see the DOD Financial Management Regulations.[53]

Hardship Duty Pay

Military personnel serving for over 30 days in Iraq, Afghanistan, and certain surrounding countries are eligible for Hardship Duty Pay (HDP).[54] HDP is compensation for the exceptional demands of certain duty. In the case of Iraq and Afghanistan, it is compensation for the austere living conditions of the location. The rate for HDP in Iraq and Afghanistan is $100 per month.[55]

Family Separation Allowance

Military personnel serving in Iraq, Afghanistan, and surrounding areas may be eligible for Family Separation Allowance (FSA).[56] FSA provides a special pay for those servicemembers *with dependents* who are separated from their families for more than 30 days. The purpose of this pay is to "partially reimburse, on average, members of the uniformed services involuntarily separated from their dependents for the reasonable amount of

---

[52] For example, DOD ended the imminent danger designation for Kuwait, Bahrain, Oman, Qatar, Saudi Arabia, United Arab Emirates, Kyrgyzstan, Tajikistan, Uzbekistan, and certain nearby bodies of water on May 31, 2014.

[53] DOD FMR, Chapter 10, Figure 10-1, available at http://comptroller.defense.gov/Portals/45/documents/fmr/ Volume_07a.pdf.

[54] 37 U.S.C. 351 (previously 37 U.S.C. 305). By law, the maximum amount of HDP is $1,500 per month. However, this figure is a cap; DOD has discretion to offer lesser amounts. DOD Instruction 1340.26, *Assignment and Special Duty Pays*, September 25, 2017, http://www.esd.whs.mil/Portals/54/Documents/DD/issuances/dodi/134026p.pdf?ver=2017-09-25-112849-877.

[55] For a complete listing of HDP locations, see Chapter 17, Figure 17-1 of this document: http://comptroller.defense.gov/Portals/45/documents/fmr/Volume_07a.pdf.

[56] 37 U.S.C. 427. See also DOD Financial Management Regulation, Volume 7A, Chapter 27, http://comptroller.defense.gov/Portals/45/documents/fmr/Volume_07a.pdf.

Military Pay: Key Questions and Answers 215

extra expenses that result from such separation, and to reimburse members who must maintain a home in the United States for their dependents and another home overseas for themselves for the average expenses of maintaining the overseas home."[57] To be eligible for this allowance, U.S. military personnel must be separated from their dependents for 30 continuous days or more; but once the 30-day threshold has been reached, the allowance is applied retroactively to the first day of separation. The authorizing statute for FSA sets the rate at $250 per month.

Per Diem for Incidental Expenses

Military personnel using military facilities and serving in Iraq and Afghanistan receive per diem equivalent to $105 per month to cover incidental expenses. The rate is the same for all personnel.

Combat Zone Tax Exclusion

One of the more generous benefits for many of those serving in Iraq or Afghanistan, and certain surrounding areas,[58] is the "combat zone tax exclusion."[59] Military personnel serving in direct support of operations in these combat zones are also eligible for the combat zone tax exclusion, as are those "hospitalized as a result of wounds, disease, or injury incurred while serving in a combat zone."[60] For enlisted personnel and warrant officers, this means that all compensation for active military service in a combat zone is free of federal income tax. For commissioned officers, their compensation is free of federal income tax up to the maximum amount of enlisted basic pay plus any imminent danger pay received. While this benefit applies only to federal income tax, almost all states have provisions extending the benefit to their state income tax as well.

In addition, military personnel who qualify for a reenlistment or retention bonus while stationed in a combat zone do not have to pay

---

[57] Department of Defense, *Military Compensation Background Papers*, 8th Edition, November 2018, p. 827, available at https://www.loc.gov/rr/frd/pdf-files/Military_Comp-2018.pdf.

[58] For a listing of areas that qualify for the combat zone tax exclusion, see http://www.irs.gov/uac/Combat-Zones.

[59] 26 U.S.C. 112.

[60] 26 U.S.C. 112; note that the hospitalization provision expires two years after the termination of combat activities in the designated combat zone.

216 *Lawrence Kapp and Barbara Salazar Torreon*

federal income tax on the bonus (though commissioned officers are still subject to the cap mentioned above).[61] The amounts involved can be substantial, often in the tens of thousands of dollars, and occasionally over $100,000.[62]

Savings Deposit Program

Another benefit available to those deployed to a combat zone[63] is eligibility for the Savings Deposit Program. This program allows servicemembers to earn a guaranteed rate of 10% interest on deposits of up to $10,000, which must have been earned in the designated areas. The deposit is normally returned to the servicemember, with interest, within 90 days after he or she leaves the eligible region, although earlier withdrawals can sometimes be made for emergency reasons.

What Benefits Are Available to the Survivors of Military Personnel Killed in Iraq or Afghanistan?

Currently, the survivors (typically, spouses and children) of military personnel who die on active duty, whether serving in combat zones or not, are eligible for a number of monetary and other benefits. These generally include the following:

- A death gratuity of $100,000, payable within a few days of the death to assist families in dealing with immediate expenses.

---

[61] See DOD Financial Management Regulation, Volume 7A, Chapter 44, Table 44-1, Rule 5: "a bonus entitlement (including installments)" is considered not taxable "if earned (reenlists, extends, signs agreement) in a month during which combat zone or qualified hazardous duty area exclusion applies, regardless if the act of earning the bonus takes place before entering or after returning from the combat zone or qualified hazardous duty area."

[62] Reenlistment or retention bonuses of $100,000 or more are unusual, but they do occur. For example, in 2008, certain special forces soldiers were eligible for a critical skills retention bonus of $150,000 upon reenlisting for six years. See this article: http://www.stripes.com/news/150-000-bonus-offered-for-some-special-forces-1.75636.

[63] For a listing of areas that qualify for the combat zone tax exclusion, see http://www.irs.gov/uac/Combat-Zones. For more information on the Savings Deposit Program, see DOD Financial Regulation, Volume 7A, Chapter 51, https://comptroller.defense.gov/Portals/45/documents/fmr/current/07a/07a_51.pdf.

Military Pay: Key Questions and Answers 217

- Servicemembers' Group Life Insurance (SGLI)[64] of up to $400,000.[65]
- Disbursement of unpaid pay and allowances.
- One year of government housing or BAH.
- Three years of TRICARE coverage at the active duty dependent rate, followed by coverage at the retiree dependent rate (children remain covered as active duty family members until age 21, or until age 23 if enrolled in school full-time).[66]
- Commissary and Exchange access.
- Burial expenses.
- One or more survivor benefit annuities (Social Security Survivor Benefits, DOD Survivor Benefit Plan[67], and/or Veterans Affairs Dependency and Indemnity Compensation; receipt of more than one annuity may require offsets between the annuities).

Note, however, that each type of benefit described above has its own eligibility criteria. Survivors may, or may not, qualify for a given benefit based on their unique circumstances. For more detailed information on who qualifies for a given benefit, see the Department of Defense's *A Survivor's Guide to Benefits*.[68]

---

[64] All servicemembers are automatically enrolled in this benefit, which is paid for by a $28 per month deduction from their pay. Members may opt out or reduce coverage.

[65] The death gratuity and the SGLI maximum amount were raised substantially by the FY2005 Supplemental Appropriations Act for Defense, the Global War on Terror, and Tsunami Relief (P.L. 109-13). The death gratuity was raised from $12,420 to $100,000; and the maximum SGLI coverage was raised from $250,000 to $400,000. The 2006 NDAA applied the $100,000 death gratuity to all active-duty deaths (not just those that were combat-related) and made the payments retroactive to October 7, 2001.

[66] After their eligibility as a family member ends, children of survivors may also purchase TRICARE Young Adult to extend coverage up to age 26.

[67] For more information on this program and its offsets, see CRS Report R45325, *Military Survivor Benefit Plan: Background and Issues for Congress*, by Kristy N. Kamarck and Barbara Salazar Torreon.

[68] http://www.militaryonesource.mil/survivorsguide. For the earlier legislative history of some of these benefits, see Department of Defense, *Military Compensation Background Papers*, 8th Edition, 2018, Appendix IX.

HOMELAND SECURITY

In: Key Congressional Reports for May 2019   ISBN: 978-1-53616-382-7
Editor: Piotr Meza   © 2019 Nova Science Publishers, Inc.

Chapter 5

"SANCTUARY" JURISDICTIONS: FEDERAL, STATE, AND LOCAL POLICIES AND RELATED LITIGATION*

Sarah Herman Peck

ABSTRACT

There is no official or agreed-upon definition of what constitutes a "sanctuary" jurisdiction, and there has been debate as to whether the term applies to particular states and localities. Moreover, state and local jurisdictions have varied reasons for opting not to cooperate with federal immigration enforcement efforts, including reasons not necessarily motivated by disagreement with federal policies, such as concern about potential civil liability or the costs associated with assisting federal efforts. But traditional sanctuary policies are often described as falling under one of three categories. First, so-called "don't enforce" policies generally bar state or local police from assisting federal immigration authorities. Second, "don't ask" policies generally bar certain state or local officials from inquiring into a person's immigration status. Third,

---

* This is an edited, reformatted and augmented version of Congressional Research Service, Publication No. R44795, dated May 3, 2019.

"don't tell" policies typically restrict information sharing between state or local law enforcement and federal immigration authorities.

One legal question relevant to sanctuary policies is the extent to which states, as sovereign entities, may decline to assist in federal immigration enforcement, and the degree to which the federal government can stop state measures that undermine federal objectives. The Tenth Amendment preserves the states' broad police powers, and states have frequently enacted measures that, directly or indirectly, address aliens residing in their communities. Under the doctrine of preemption—derived from the Supremacy Clause—Congress may displace many state or local laws pertaining to immigration. But not every state or local law touching on immigration matters is necessarily preempted; the measure must interfere with, or be contrary to, federal law to be rendered unenforceable. Further, the anti-commandeering doctrine, rooted in the Constitution's allocation of powers between the federal government and the states, prohibits Congress from forcing state entities to perform regulatory functions on the federal government's behalf, including in the context of immigration. A series of Supreme Court cases inform the boundaries of preemption and the anti-commandeering doctrine, with the Court most recently opining on the issue in *Murphy v. NCAA*.

These dueling federal and state interests are front and center in numerous lawsuits challenging actions taken by the Trump Administration to curb states and localities from implementing sanctuary-type policies. Notably, Section 9(a) of Executive Order 13768, "Enhancing Public Safety in the Interior of the United States," directs the Secretary of Homeland Security and the Attorney General to withhold federal grants from jurisdictions that willfully refuse to comply with 8 U.S.C. § 1373—a statute that bars states and localities from prohibiting their employees from sharing with federal immigration authorities certain immigration-related information. The executive order further directs the Attorney General to take "appropriate enforcement action" against jurisdictions that violate Section 1373 or have policies that "prevent or hinder the enforcement of federal law." To implement the executive order, the Department of Justice added new eligibility conditions to the Edward Byrne Memorial Justice Assistance Grant (Byrne JAG) Program and grants administered by the Justice Department's Office of Community Oriented Policing Services (COPS). These conditions tied eligibility to compliance with Section 1373 and other federal immigration priorities, like granting federal authorities access to state and local detention facilities housing aliens and giving immigration authorities notice before releasing from custody an alien wanted for removal.

Several lawsuits were filed challenging the constitutionality of the executive order and new grant conditions. So far the courts that have reviewed these challenges—principally contending that the executive order and grant conditions violate the separation of powers and anti-commandeering principles—generally agree that the Trump Administration acted unconstitutionally. For instance, the Ninth Circuit Court of Appeals upheld a permanent injunction blocking enforcement of Section 9(a) against California. Additionally, two separate district courts permanently enjoined the Byrne JAG conditions as applied to Chicago and Philadelphia. In doing so, these courts concluded that the Supreme Court's most recent formulation of the anti-commandeering doctrine in *Murphy* requires holding Section 1373 unconstitutional. These lawsuits notwithstanding, the courts still recognize the federal government's pervasive, nearly exclusive role in immigration enforcement. This can be seen in the federal government's lawsuit challenging three California measures governing the state's regulation of private and public actors' involvement in immigration enforcement within its border. Although a district court opined that several measures likely were lawful exercises of the state's police powers, it also concluded that two provisions regulating private employers are likely unlawful under the Supremacy Clause. This ruling was mostly upheld on appeal, in which the Ninth Circuit additionally opined that a provision requiring the California attorney general to review the circumstances surrounding detained aliens' apprehension and transfer to detention facilities within the state also violates the Supremacy Clause.

INTRODUCTION

The federal government is vested with the exclusive power to create rules governing alien entry and removal.[1] However, the impact of alien migration—whether lawful or unlawful—is arguably felt most directly in the communities where aliens reside. State and local responses to unlawfully present aliens within their jurisdictions have varied considerably, particularly in determining the role that state or local police should play in enforcing federal immigration law. At one end of the spectrum, some states and localities actively assist federal immigration

---

[1] *See, e.g.,* Arizona v. United States, 567 U.S. 387, 394 (2012) ("The Government of the United States has broad, undoubted power over the subject of immigration and status of aliens."); Toll v. Moreno, 458 U.S. 1, 10 (1982) ("Our cases have long recognized the preeminent role of the Federal Government with respect to the regulation of aliens within our borders."); Hampton v. Mow Sun Wong, 426 U.S. 88, 95 (1976) ("Congress and the President have broad power over immigration and naturalization which the States do not possess.").

authorities in identifying and apprehending aliens for removal.[2] For example, jurisdictions sometimes enter into "287(g) Agreements" with the federal government, in which state or local law enforcement are deputized to perform certain immigration enforcement activities.[3] Some states and localities have attempted to play an even greater role in immigration enforcement, in many cases because of perceptions that federal efforts have been inadequate.[4] In the past, some have adopted measures that criminally sanction conduct believed to facilitate the presence of unlawfully present aliens and have also instructed police to actively work to detect such aliens as part of their regular duties.[5] The adoption of these kinds of measures has waned considerably, though, after the Supreme Court's 2012 ruling in *Arizona v. United States* held that several provisions of one such enactment, Arizona's S.B. 1070, were preempted by federal immigration law.[6] Subsequent lower court decisions struck down many other state and local measures that imposed criminal or civil sanctions on immigration-related activity.[7]

---

[2] *See* Immigration Legal Resource Center, *National Map of 287(g) Agreements* (Nov. 6, 2018), https://www.ilrc.org/national-map-287g-agreements.

[3] *See* 8 U.S.C. § 1357(g) (authorizing the Department of Homeland Security (DHS) to enter into written agreements with state and local jurisdictions that enable specially trained state or local officers to perform specific functions related to the investigation, apprehension, or detention of aliens, while under federal supervision for a predetermined time); *see also* ICE, *Delegation of Immigration Authority Section 287(g) Immigration and Nationality Act*, https://www.ice.gov/287g (last visited Nov. 8, 2018); ICE, *Updated Facts on ICE's 287(g) Program*, https://www.ice.gov/factsheets/287g-reform (last visited Nov. 8, 2018).

[4] *See, e.g.,* Marisa S. Cianciarulo, *The "Arizonafication" of Immigration Law: Implications of* Chamber of Commerce v. Whiting *for State & Local Immigration Legislation*, 15 HARV. LATINO L. REV. 85, 88 (2012); Keith CunninghamParmeter, *Forced Federalism: States as Laboratories of Immigration Reform*, 62 HASTINGS L.J. 1673, 1674 (2011).

[5] Kevin J. Fandl, *Putting States out of the Immigration Law Enforcement Business*, 9 HARV. L. & POL'Y REV. 529, 533-35 (2015); Bianca Figueroa-Santana, Note, *Divided We Stand: Constitutionalizing Executive Immigration Reform through Subfederal Regulation*, 115 COLUM. L. REV. 2219, 2219-20 (2015).

[6] 567 U.S. 387 (2012); *see* Stella Burch Elias, *The New Immigration Federalism*, 74 OHIO ST. L.J. 703, 704 (2013).

[7] *See, e.g.,* Ariz. Dream Act Coal. v. Brewer, 855 F.3d 957 (9th Cir. 2017) (applying *Arizona*'s preemption principles to conclude that Arizona cannot independently classify persons as being without "authorized presence" in the United States because the federal government is vested with the exclusive authority to classify aliens); Valle del Sol Inc. v. Whiting, 732 F.3d 1006 (9th Cir. 2013) (upholding preliminary injunction barring enforcement of Arizona statute, which prohibited harboring unlawfully present aliens by certain persons, on preemption and vagueness grounds), *cert. denied*, 134 S. Ct. 1876 (2014); United States v. South Carolina, 720 F.3d 518 (4th Cir. 2013) (applying the Supreme Court's ruling in *Arizona*; affirming enjoinment of South Carolina criminal

At the other end of the spectrum, some states and localities have been less willing to assist the federal government with its immigration enforcement responsibilities. Often dubbed "sanctuary jurisdictions," some states and localities have adopted measures that limit their participation in enforcing federal immigration laws, including, for example, prohibiting police officers from assisting with federal efforts to identify and apprehend unlawfully present aliens within the state or locality's jurisdiction.[8] That said, there is debate over both the meaning and application of the term "sanctuary jurisdiction."[9] Additionally, state and local jurisdictions have varied reasons for choosing not to cooperate with federal immigration enforcement efforts, including reasons not necessarily motivated by disagreement with federal immigration enforcement policies, such as concern about potential civil liability or the availability of state or local resources to assist federal immigration enforcement efforts.[10] During

---

provisions for (1) an unlawful alien to conceal, harbor, or shelter him or herself from detection; (2) for a third party to conceal, shelter, or transport an unlawfully present person; (3) failing to carry an alien registration card; and (4) possessing a false identification card for proving lawful presence); United States v. Alabama, 691 F.3d 1269 (11th Cir. 2012) (enjoining several Alabama laws, including those that penalize (1) failing to carry registration documents; (2) working without authorization; (3) concealing, harboring, or shielding an unlawfully present alien from detection; (4) transporting an unlawfully present alien; (5) harboring an unlawfully present alien by entering into a rental agreement with that alien; and (6) deducting as a business expense on state tax filings any compensation paid to unauthorized aliens, based on the Supreme Court's ruling in *Arizona*), *cert. denied*, 133 S. Ct. 2022 (2013); Georgia Latino Alliance for Human Rights v. Governor of Georgia, 691 F.3d 1250 (11th Cir. 2012) (enjoining criminal provisions in Georgia for (1) transporting or moving an illegal alien; (2) concealing or harboring an illegal alien; and (3) inducing an illegal alien to enter Georgia, based on the Supreme Court's ruling in *Arizona*); Sol v. Whiting, No. CV-10-01061-PHX-SRB, 2015 WL 12030514, at *1 (D. Ariz. Sept. 4, 2015) (discussing the resolution of legal challenges to various provisions of Arizona immigration enforcement measure in the aftermath of *Arizona*).

[8] *See, e.g.,* Steven Papazian, Note, *Secure Communities, Sanctuary Laws, & Local Enforcement of Immigration Law: The Story of Los Angeles,* 21 S. CAL. REV. L. & SOC. JUST. 283, 290-91 (2012); Rose Cuison Villazor, *What is a "Sanctuary"?,* 61 SMU L. REV. 133, 147-48 & n.91 (2008).

[9] *See infra* section *What Is a Sanctuary Jurisdiction?*

[10] *See, e.g.,* Matthew Feeney, *Walling Off Liberty: How Strict Immigration Enforcement Threatens Privacy and Local Policing,* CATO INSTITUTE (Nov. 1, 2018), https://www.cato.org/publications/policy-analysis/walling-liberty-how-strictimmigration-enforcement-threatens-privacy#full ("But there are also sound law enforcement reasons for declining to enforce immigration law. Sanctuary policies help police, allowing them to secure cooperation from crime victims and witnesses who don't wish to disclose their immigration status or the immigration status of a friend, spouse, or family member."); Raina Bhatt, Note, *Pushing an End to Sanctuary Cities: Will it Happen,* MICH. J. RACE & L.

President Donald Trump's first month in office, he issued an executive order, "Enhancing Public Safety in the Interior of the United States," which, in part, seeks to encourage state and local cooperation with federal immigration enforcement and disincentivize state and local adoption of sanctuary policies.[11]

This chapter discusses legal issues related to state and local measures limiting law enforcement cooperation with federal immigration authorities, as well as the federal government's efforts to counter those measures. It begins by providing a general explanation of the term "sanctuary jurisdiction" for the purpose of this chapter. Next, it provides an overview of constitutional principles underlying the relationship between federal immigration laws and related state and local measures, namely, preemption and the anti-commandeering doctrine. Then, it discusses various types of laws and policies adopted by states and localities to limit their participation with federal immigration enforcement efforts, which may give rise to a label of "sanctuary jurisdiction," and federal efforts to counter those measures. Finally, the report concludes with a discussion of the lawsuits challenging the executive order targeting sanctuary jurisdictions and certain executive branch actions to implement the executive order.

WHAT IS A SANCTUARY JURISDICTION?

State or local measures limiting police participation in immigration enforcement are not a recent phenomenon.[12] Indeed, many of the recent

---

139, 144-45 (2016) (collecting various rationales for states and localities adoption of sanctuary policies).

[11] Exec. Order No. 13,768, 82 Fed. Reg. 8,799 (Jan. 30, 2017).

[12] For example, in 1979 the Los Angeles Police Department issued Special Order 40, which (1) barred police officers from arresting persons for suspected violations of the federal statute criminalizing illegal entry, (2) prohibited the initiation of police action "with the objective of discovering the alien status of a person," and (3) established a process and criteria for notifying federal immigration officials when an unlawfully present alien was arrested on criminal charges. OFFICE OF THE CHIEF OF POLICE, LOS ANGELES, SPECIAL ORDER 40: UNDOCUMENTED ALIENS (1979), [hereinafter LAPD ORDER], http://www.lapdonline.org/assets/pdf/SO_40.pdf; *see also* Doug Smith, *How LAPD's Law-and-Order Chief Revolutionized the Way Cops Treated Illegal Immigration,* LOS

"sanctuary"-type initiatives can be traced back to church activities designed to provide refuge—or "sanctuary"—to unauthorized Central American aliens fleeing civil unrest in the 1980s.[13] A number of states and municipalities issued declarations in support of these churches' actions.[14] Others went further and enacted more substantive measures intended to limit police involvement in federal immigration enforcement activities.[15] These measures have included, among other things, restricting state and local police from arresting persons for immigration violations, limiting the sharing of immigration-related information with federal authorities, and barring police from questioning a person about his or her immigration status.[16]

Still, there is no official definition of a "sanctuary" jurisdiction in federal statute or regulation.[17] Broadly speaking, sanctuary jurisdictions are

---

ANGELES TIMES (Feb. 5, 2017, 3:00 AM), http://www.latimes.com/local/lanow/la-me-ln-special-order-40-retrospective-20170205-story.html.

[13] *See, e.g.,* Susan Gzesh, *Central Americans & Asylum Policy in the Reagan Era,* MIGRATION POLICY INST. (Apr. 1, 2006), http://www.migrationpolicy.org/article/central-americans-and-asylum-policy-reagan-era (describing the "network of religious congregations that became known as the Sanctuary Movement" and that provided humanitarian assistance to foreign nationals from Central America fleeing civil unrest in the 1980s).

[14] *See generally* Jorge L. Carro, *Municipal & State Sanctuary Declarations: Innocuous Symbolism or Improper Dictates?,* 16 PEPP. L. REV. 297 (1989) (identifying and distinguishing various state and local responses in support of church actions).

[15] *See* Villazor, *supra* note 8 at 142 ("In due course, what originally began with churches as proactive efforts to provide shelter and food to immigrants led to state and local governmental efforts to assure immigrants that they too will be safe within their borders.").

[16] *See* Orde F. Kittrie, *Federalism, Deportation, & Crime Victims Afraid to Call the Police,* 91 IOWA L. REV. 1449, 1455 (2006) (surveying local sanctuary policies and describing them as doing "one or more of the following: (1) limit[ing] inquiries about a person's immigration status unless investigating illegal activity other than mere status as an unauthorized alien ('don't ask'); (2) limit[ing] arrests or detentions for violation of immigration laws ('don't enforce'); and (3) limit[ing] provision to federal authorities of immigration status information ('don't tell')").

[17] The term "sanctuary" jurisdiction is not defined by federal statute or regulation, though it has been used on occasion by federal agencies to refer to state or local entities that have particular types of immigration-related laws or policies. Most recently, in an executive order targeting public safety within the U.S. interior, President Trump referred to "sanctuary jurisdictions" as those that "willfully refuse to comply with 8 U.S.C. 1373," which, as discussed in great detail later in this chapter, imposes restrictions on state and local limitations on the sharing of certain information with immigration authorities. Exec. Order No. 13,768, 82 Fed. Reg. 8799 (Jan. 25, 2017). Before that, in a 2007 report by the Office of the Inspector General at the U.S. Department of Justice, the agency used the term "sanctuary" to reference "jurisdictions that may have state laws, local ordinances, or departmental policies limiting the role of local law enforcement agencies and officers in the

228   *Sarah Herman Peck*

commonly understood to be those that have laws or policies designed to substantially limit involvement in federal immigration enforcement activities,[18] though there is not necessarily a consensus as to the meaning of this term.[19] Some jurisdictions have self-identified as a sanctuary (or some other similar term).[20] For other jurisdictions, there might be disagreement regarding the accuracy of such a designation, particularly if state or local law enforcement cooperates with federal immigration authorities in some areas but not others.[21] Any reference by this chapter to a policy of a particular jurisdiction is intended only to provide an example of the type of measure occasionally referenced in discussions of "sanctuary" policies.[22] These references should not be taken to indicate CRS is of the view that a particular jurisdiction is a "sanctuary" for unlawfully present aliens.

---

enforcement of immigration laws." U.S. Dep't Of Justice, Office Of The Inspector General, Audit Division, Cooperation Of SCAAP Recipients In The Removal Of Criminal Aliens From The United States 7 N.44 (Jan. 2007), https://oig.justice.gov/reports/OJP/a0707/final.pdf (redacted public version).

[18] *See, e.g.*, H.B.C., *What are Sanctuary Cities*, THE ECONOMIST (Nov. 22, 2016), http://www.economist.com/blogs/   economist-explains/2016/11/economist-explains-13 ("There is no specific legal definition for what constitutes a sanctuary jurisdiction but the term is widely used to refer to American cities, counties or states that protect undocumented immigrants from deportation by limiting cooperation with federal immigration authorities."); Dr. Michael J. Davidson, *Sanctuary: A Modern Legal Anachronism*, 42 CAP. U. L. REV. 583, 610 (2014) ("The modern concept of sanctuary cities now refers to jurisdictions that have adopted formal or informal policies limiting cooperation with federal immigration authorities." (internal quotation marks, alteration, and citations omitted)).

[19] *See, e.g.*, Davidson, *supra* note 18, at 610.

[20] *See, e.g.*, S.F. CAL. ADMIN. CODE §§ 12H.1, 12H.2 (declaring San Francisco a "City and County of Refuge" and restricting cooperation with federal immigration enforcement efforts); *City of Philadelphia Action Guide: Immigration Policies*, CITY OF PHILADELPHIA (Jan. 8, 2018), https://www.phila.gov/2018-01-08-immigration-policies/ (describing Philadelphia as a "Welcoming City" in its policies toward immigrants); *see also* Ruairí Arrieta-Kenna, *Sanctuary Cities Stand Firm against Trump*, POLITICO (Dec. 12, 2016 5:14 AM), http://www.politico.com/story/2016/12/sanctuarycities-trump-immigration-232449 (listing cities where municipal and police leaders have publicly affirmed or reaffirmed sanctuary status).

[21] *See Sanctuary City? Not L.A.*, L.A. Times (Aug. 26, 2011), http://articles.latimes.com/2011/aug/26/opinion/la-edsanctuary-20110825 (disputing characterization of Los Angeles as a "sanctuary" jurisdiction and noting areas in which local police cooperate with federal immigration authorities); Villazor, *supra* note 8 at 154-56 (describing some jurisdictions' resistance to being labeled a "sanctuary").

[22] *See, e.g.*, Villazor, *supra* note 8 (discussing the term "sanctuary" as applied to contemporary immigration issues); Kittrie, *supra* note 16 (discussing and describing various state and local law enforcement "sanctuary" policies).

LEGAL BACKGROUND

The heart of the debate surrounding the permissible scope of sanctuary jurisdictions centers on the extent to which states, as sovereign entities, may decline to assist in federal efforts to enforce federal immigration law, and the degree to which the federal government can stop state action that undercuts federal objectives in a manner that is consistent with the Supremacy Clause and constitutional principles of federalism.

The Supremacy Clause and Preemption

The federal government's power to regulate immigration is both substantial and exclusive.[23] This authority derives from multiple sources, including Congress's Article I powers to "establish a uniform Rule of Naturalization"[24] and to "regulate commerce with foreign nations, and among the several states,"[25] as well as the federal government's "inherent power as sovereign to conduct relations with foreign nations."[26] Rules governing the admission and removal of aliens, along with conditions for aliens' continued presence within the United States, are primarily contained in the Immigration and Nationality Act of 1952, as amended

---

[23] *See, e.g.*, Arizona v. United States, 567 U.S. 387, 394 (2012) ("The Government of the United States has broad, undoubted power over the subject of immigration and status of aliens."); Toll v. Moreno, 458 U.S. 1, 10 (1982) ("Our cases have long recognized the preeminent role of the Federal Government with respect to the regulation of aliens within our borders."); De Canas v. Bica, 424 U.S. 351, 354 (1976) ("Power to regulate immigration is unquestionably exclusively a federal power."); Hampton v. Mow Sun Wong, 426 U.S. 88, 95 (1976) ("Congress and the President have broad power over immigration and naturalization which the States do not possess."); Sandoval-Luna v. Mukasey, 526 F.3d 1243, 1247 (9th Cir. 2008) ("Federal authority in the areas of immigration and naturalization is plenary." (internal quotation marks, alteration, and citation omitted)).

[24] U.S. CONST. art. I., § 8, cl. 4.

[25] U.S. CONST. art. I., § 8, cl. 3.

[26] *See Arizona*, 567 U.S. at 394-95; *see also Toll*, 458 U.S. at 10 (citing the Naturalization Clause and Commerce Clause, along with the federal government's broad authority over foreign affairs, as three of the primary sources for federal authority to regulate the status of aliens); *The Chinese Exclusion Case*, 130 U.S. 581, 604 (1889) (identifying the powers to "declare war, make treaties, suppress insurrection, repel invasion, regulate foreign commerce, secure republican governments to the States, and admit subjects of other nations to citizenship" as authorizing Congress to enact legislation barring certain aliens from admission).

(INA).[27] The INA further provides a comprehensive immigration enforcement regime that contains civil and criminal elements.[28]

Arizona v. United States reinforced the federal government's pervasive role in creating and enforcing the nation's immigration laws. The ruling invalidated several Arizona laws designed "to discourage and deter the unlawful entry and presence of aliens and economic activity by persons unlawfully present in the United States"[29] as preempted by federal law.[30] In doing so, the Court declared that "[t]he Government of the United States has broad, undoubted power over the subject of immigration and the status of aliens."[31]

As *Arizona* highlights, the doctrine of preemption is relevant in assessing state policies related to immigration. The preemption doctrine derives from the Constitution's Supremacy Clause, which states that the "Constitution, and the laws of the United States ... shall be the supreme law of the land."[32] Therefore, Congress, through legislation, can preempt (i.e., invalidate) state law.[33] Preemption can be express or implied. Express preemption occurs when Congress enacts a law that explicitly expresses the legislature's intent to preempt state law.[34] Preemption may be implied in two ways: (1) when Congress intends the federal government to govern exclusively, inferred from a federal interest that is "so dominant" and federal regulation that is "so pervasive" in a particular area (called "field preemption");[35] or (2) when state law conflicts with federal law so that it is impossible to comply with both sovereigns' regulations, or when the state

---

[27] 8 U.S.C. §§ 1101-1537.

[28] In some cases, criminal and civil enforcement measures may be relevant to similar activities. For instance, unlawful entry into the United States is a criminal offense subject to imprisonment. *See* 8 U.S.C. §§ 1325-1326. But the removal proceedings that may follow an unlawful entry (or any violation of U.S. immigration laws) are civil in nature, *see Arizona*, 567 U.S. at 396, designed "to put an end to a continuing violation of the immigration laws," rather than "to punish an unlawful entry," *see* INS v. Lopez-Mendoza, 468 U.S. 1032, 1038-39 (1984).

[29] *See* ARIZ. S.B. 1070 § 1, amended by H.B. 2162 (2010), http://www.azleg.gov/alispdfs/council/SB1070- HB2162.PDF.

[30] *Arizona*, 567 U.S. at 416.

[31] *Id.* at 394.

[32] U.S. CONST. art. VI, cl. 2.

[33] Oneok, Inc. v. Learjet, Inc., 135 S. Ct. 1591, 1595 (2015).

[34] *Id.* at 1595.

[35] *Arizona*, 567 U.S. at 399 (internal quotation marks and citations omitted).

law prevents the "accomplishment and execution" of Congress's objectives (called "conflict preemption").[36] Accordingly, any preemption analysis of the relationship between a federal statute and a state measure must be viewed through the lens of congressional intent.

The Supremacy Clause establishes that lawful assertions of federal authority may preempt state and local laws, even in areas that are traditionally reserved to the states via the Tenth Amendment.[37] One notable power reserved to the states is the "police power" to promote and regulate public health and safety, the general welfare, and economic activity within a state's jurisdiction.[38] Using their police powers, states and municipalities have frequently enacted measures that, directly or indirectly, address aliens residing in their communities.[39]

Yet despite the federal government's sweeping authority over immigration, the Supreme Court has cautioned that not "every state enactment which in any way deals with aliens is a regulation of immigration and thus *per se* preempted" by the federal government's

---

[36] *Id.*

[37] U.S. CONST. amend. X ("The powers not delegated to the United States by the Constitution, nor prohibited by it to the States, are reserved to the States respectively, or to the people."). For example, Congress, acting under its Commerce Clause power, may displace state and local laws that were enacted under their police powers. *See, e.g.,* Hodel v. Va. Surface Mining & Reclamation Ass'n, 452 U.S. 264, 291-92 (1981) ("The Court long ago rejected the suggestion that Congress invades areas reserved to the States by the Tenth Amendment simply because it exercises its authority under the Commerce Clause in a manner that displaces the States' exercise of their police powers.").

[38] *See, e.g.,* Bond v. United States, 572 U.S. 844, 854 (2014) ("The States have broad authority to enact legislation for the public good—what we have often called a 'police power.'"); Kelley v. Johnson, 425 U.S. 238, 247 (1976) ("The promotion of safety of persons and property is unquestionably at the core of the State's police power."); City of New Orleans v. Dukes, 427 U.S. 297, 303 (1976) ("States are accorded wide latitude in the regulation of their local economies under their police powers."); Western Turf Ass'n v. Greenberg, 204 U.S. 359, 363 (1907) ("Decisions of this court ... recognize the possession, by each state, of powers never surrendered to the general government; which powers the state, except as restrained by its own Constitution or the Constitution of the United States, may exert not only for the public health, the public morals, and the public safety, but for the general or common good, for the wellbeing, comfort, and good order of the people.").

[39] *See* NAT'L CONFERENCE OF STATE LEGISLATORS, IMMIGRANT POLICY PROJECT, REPORT ON 2015 STATE IMMIGRATION LAWS [hereinafter NCSL 2015 REPORT], http://www.ncsl.org/research/immigration/report-on-2015-state-immigration-laws.aspx (discussing state legislation enacted in 2015 concerning non-U.S. citizens).

232   *Sarah Herman Peck*

exclusive power over immigration.[40] Accordingly, in *Arizona* the Supreme
Court reiterated that, "[i]n preemption analysis, courts should assume that
the historic police powers of the States are not superseded unless that was
the clear and manifest purpose of Congress."[41] For example, in *Chamber of
Commerce of the United States v. Whiting,* the Supreme Court upheld an
Arizona law—related to the states' "broad authority under their police
powers to regulate the employment relationship to protect workers within
the State"[42]—that authorized the revocation of licenses held by state
employers that knowingly or intentionally employ unauthorized aliens.[43]
Even though the Immigration Reform and Control Act of 1986 (IRCA)
expressly preempted "any State or local law imposing civil or criminal
sanctions ... upon those who employ, or recruit or refer for a fee for
employment, unauthorized aliens," the Supreme Court concluded that
Arizona's law fit within IRCA's savings clause for state licensing regimes
and thus was not preempted.[44]

The Anti-Commandeering Doctrine

Although the federal government's power to preempt state or local
activity touching on immigration matters is extensive, this power is not
absolute. The U.S. Constitution establishes a system of dual sovereignty

---

[40] De Canas v. Bica, 424 U.S. 351, 355 (1976) (holding—before the INA was amended to
comprehensively regulate alien employment and expressly preempt most state sanctions for
unauthorized alien employment—that a state law regulating employment of unauthorized
aliens was not preempted by federal law); *see also Arizona,* 567 U.S. at 407-16 (finding
many provisions of an Arizona immigration enforcement law preempted but rejecting facial
preemption challenge to provision requiring police to verify immigration status of lawfully
stopped persons who were suspected of unlawful status); Chamber of Commerce of the
United States v. Whiting, 563 U.S. 582 (2011) (holding that federal law did not preempt an
Arizona law that authorized or required the suspension or termination of business licenses
for employers that knowingly or intentionally hired unauthorized aliens); Lopez-Valenzuela
v. Cty. of Maricopa, 719 F.3d 1054, 1070-73 (9th Cir. 2013) (upholding Arizona law that
barred state courts from setting bail for unlawfully present aliens charged with certain
felonies).
[41] *Arizona,* 567 U.S. at 400 (internal quotation marks and citations omitted).
[42] *Whiting,* 563 U.S. at 588 (quoting *De Canas,* 424 U.S. at 356).
[43] *Id.* at 611.
[44] 8 U.S.C. § 1324(a)(h)(2); *Whiting,* 563 U.S. at 587.

between the federal government and the states, including by creating a national legislature with enumerated powers and reserving most other legislative powers to the states by way of the Tenth Amendment.[45] The anti-commandeering doctrine derives from this structural allocation of power, which "withholds from Congress the power to issue orders directly to the [s]tates"[46] and prevents Congress from directly compelling states "to enact and enforce a federal regulatory program."[47] Thus, the federal government cannot "issue directives requiring the [s]tates to address particular problems, nor command the [s]tates' officers, or those of their political subdivisions, to administer or enforce a federal regulatory program."[48]

Several Supreme Court rulings inform the boundaries of the anti-commandeering doctrine. First, in *New York v. United States*, the Court reviewed a constitutional challenge to provisions of a federal law that created a series of incentives for states to dispose of radioactive waste.[49] The statute provided states the option of (1) regulating according to Congress's direction, or (2) taking title to, and possession of, the low-level radioactive waste generated within their borders and becoming liable for all damages suffered by waste generators resulting from the state's failure to timely do so.[50] The law, in the Court's view, gave states a "choice" between two options concerning their maintenance of radioactive waste disposal, neither of which the Constitution authorized Congress, on its own, to impose on the states.[51] By offering this "choice," Congress had, in the Court's view, "crossed the line distinguishing encouragement from coercion," and in doing so acted "inconsistent[ly] with the federal structure of our Government established by the Constitution."[52] In so holding, the

---

[45] *See generally* CRS Report R45323, *Federalism-Based Limitations on Congressional Power: An Overview*, coordinated by Andrew Nolan and Kevin M. Lewis.

[46] Murphy v. NCAA, 138 S. Ct. 1461, 1475 (2018).

[47] New York v. United States, 505 U.S. 144, 175, 176-78 (1992).

[48] *See* Printz v. United States, 521 U.S. 898, 935 (1997).

[49] *New York,* 505 U.S. at 149-51, 169-77 (discussing the Low-Level Radioactive Waste Policy Amendments Act of 1985, P.L. 99-240, 99 Stat. 1842).

[50] *New York,* 505 U.S. at 174-175.

[51] *Id.* at 174-76 ("A choice between two unconstitutionally coercive regulatory techniques is no choice at all.").

[52] *Id.* at 177.

234   *Sarah Herman Peck*

Court declared that "[t]he Federal Government may not *compel* the States to enact or administer a federal regulatory program."[53]

Then, in *Printz v. United States,* the Supreme Court reviewed whether certain interim provisions of the Brady Handgun Violence Prevention Act (Brady Act)[54] violated the anti-commandeering doctrine.[55] The relevant provisions required state and local law enforcement officers to conduct background checks (and other related tasks) on prospective handgun purchasers.[56] The Court rejected the government's position that the challenged Brady provisions—which directed states to implement federal law—were distinguishable from the law at issue in *New York*—which directed states to create a policy—and thus was constitutionally permissible.[57] Rather, the Court concluded that a federal mandate requiring state and local law enforcement to perform background checks on prospective handgun purchasers violated the anti-commandeering doctrine.[58] Accordingly, the Court announced that "Congress cannot circumvent" the Constitution's prohibition against compelling states to enact or enforce a federal regulatory scheme "by conscripting the State's officers directly."[59]

But not every federal requirement imposed on the states necessarily violates the anti-commandeering principles identified in *Printz* and *New York*. A number of federal statutes provide that certain information collected by state entities must be reported to federal agencies.[60] And the Court in *Printz* expressly declined to consider whether these kinds of requirements were constitutionally impermissible, distinguishing reporting requirements from the case before it, which involved "the forced

---

[53] *Id.* at 188 (emphasis added).
[54] P.L. 103-159, 107 Stat. 1536 (1993).
[55] Printz v. United States, 521 U.S. 898 (1997).
[56] *Id.* at 902-04.
[57] *Id.* at 926-30.
[58] *Id.* at 933.
[59] *Id.* at 935.
[60] *See, e.g.,* 42 U.S.C. § 5779 (providing that, when a missing child report is submitted to state or local law enforcement, the agency shall report the case to the National Crime Information Center of the Department of Justice). For discussion of various federal reporting requirements applicable to states, see Robert A. Mikos, *Can States Keep Secrets from the Federal Government?*, 161 U. PA. L. REV. 103 (2012).

participation of the States ... in the actual administration of a federal program."[61]

Additionally, in *Reno v. Condon*, the Supreme Court unanimously rejected an anti-commandeering challenge to the Driver's Privacy Protection Act (DPPA),[62] which barred states from disclosing or sharing a driver's personal information without the driver's consent, subject to specific exceptions.[63] The Court distinguished the DPPA from the federal laws struck down in *New York* and *Printz* because, in the Court's view, the DPPA sought to regulate states "as owners of databases" and did not "require the States in their sovereign capacity to regulate their own citizens ... [or] enact any laws or regulations ... [or] require state officials to assist in the enforcement of federal statutes regulating private individuals."[64] The Court declined to address the state's argument that Congress may only regulate the states through generally applicable laws that apply to individuals as well as states, given that the Court deemed the DPPA to be a generally applicable law.[65]

The Supreme Court recently clarified the scope of the anti-commandeering doctrine in its 2018 ruling, *Murphy v. National Collegiate Athletic Association.*[66] *Murphy* involved a challenge under the anti-commandeering doctrine to the Professional and Amateur Sports

---

[61] *Printz*, 521 U.S. at 918; *see also id.* at 936 (O'Connor, J., concurring) (describing the Court as having refrained "from deciding whether other purely ministerial reporting requirements imposed by Congress on state and local authorities pursuant to its Commerce Clause powers are similarly invalid"). For criticism of the distinction made in *Printz* between reporting requirements and situations where the federal government directly compels states to administer federal regulatory programs, see generally Mikos, *supra* note 60.

[62] 18 U.S.C. §§ 2721 to 2725.

[63] Reno v. Condon, 528 U.S. 141, 143-45 & n.1 (2000).

[64] *Reno*, 528 U.S. at 151.The Court also noted that, even though compliance with the DPPA would require "time and effort" by state officials, this did not mean that the law violated anti-commandeering principles. *Id.* at 150. "That a State wishing to engage in certain activity must take administrative and sometimes legislative action to comply with federal standards regulating that activity is a commonplace [situation] that presents no constitutional defect." *Id.* at 150- 51 (quoting South Carolina v. Baker, 485 U.S. 505, 514- 515 (1988) (upholding federal prohibition on states' issuance of unregistered bonds in the face of a Tenth Amendment challenge)); *see also* Garcia v. San Antonio Metro. Transit Auth., 469 U.S. 528 (1985) (holding that extending overtime and minimum wage requirements of the Fair Labor Standards Act to public transit authority did not violate the Tenth Amendment).

[65] *Reno*, 528 U.S. at 151.

[66] 138 S. Ct. 1461 (2018).

Protection Act (PASPA), which, as relevant here, prohibited states from "authorizing" sports gambling "by law."[67] (This is sometimes referred to as PASPA's "anti-authorization" provision.[68]) In 2012—20 years after PASPA's enactment—New Jersey eliminated its constitutional ban on sports gambling and then, two years later, repealed state laws that prohibited certain sports gambling.[69] Invoking PASPA's civil-suit provision, several sports leagues sued to enjoin New Jersey from enforcing its new law, arguing that it violated PASPA.[70] The Third Circuit Court of Appeals, sitting en banc, agreed.[71] Further, the Third Circuit rejected New Jersey's counterargument that PASPA unlawfully commandeered state legislatures.[72]

The Supreme Court concluded otherwise, holding that PASPA's anti-authorization provision violated the anti-commandeering doctrine.[73] The sports leagues (and the United States, which appeared as *amicus curiae*) had argued that under the anti-commandeering doctrine, Congress cannot compel states to enact certain measures, but it *can* prohibit states from enacting new laws, as PASPA does.[74] The Court described this distinction as "empty," emphasizing that "[t]he basic principle—that Congress cannot issue direct orders to state legislatures—applies in either event."[75] Further, the Court elucidated two situations in which the anti-commandeering doctrine is not implicated. First, the doctrine does not apply "when Congress evenhandedly regulates an activity in which both States and private actors engage" (as the Court characterized the situation in *Reno*).[76] Second, the federal government does not commandeer states when it enacts

---

[67] Professional and Amateur Sports Protection Act, P.L. 102-559, 106 Stat. 4227 (Oct. 28, 1992); *Murphy,* 138 S Ct. at 1468.

[68] *See Murphy*, 138 S. Ct. at 1473.

[69] *Id*. at 1471-72. The law does not permit placing bets on a New Jersey college team of a college event taking place in New Jersey. 2014 N.J. Laws p. 602.

[70] *Murphy*, 138 S. Ct. at 1471-72; 28 U.S.C. § 3703.

[71] NCAA v. Governor of N.J., 832 F.3d 389, 395-98 (3d Cir. 2016).

[72] *Id*. at 398-402.

[73] *Murphy,* 138 S. Ct. at 1478.

[74] *Id*. The sports leagues and the United States also unsuccessfully argued that the anti-authorization provision was a valid preemption provision under the Constitution's Supremacy Clause. *See id*. at 1479.

[75] *Id*. at 1478.

[76] *Id*. at 1478-79.

a scheme involving "cooperative federalism," in which a state is given a choice either to implement, on its own, a federal program, or opt-out and yield to the federal government's administration of that program.[77]

Finally, the Court rejected the sports leagues and the government's contention that PASPA validly preempts state and local gambling laws.[78] The Court announced that "regardless of the language sometimes used by Congress and this Court, every form of preemption is based on a federal law that regulates the conduct of private actors, *not the States*."[79] But PASPA neither imposes federal restrictions, nor confers federal rights, on private actors, and so, the Court concluded, PASPA can be construed only as a law that regulates state actors and not as a valid preemption provision.[80]

Congress's Spending Powers and the Anti-Commandeering Doctrine

Congress does not violate the Tenth Amendment or anti-commandeering principles more generally when it uses its broad authority to enact legislation for the "general welfare" through its spending power,[81] including by placing conditions on funds distributed to the states that require those accepting the funds to take certain actions that Congress otherwise could not directly compel the states to perform.[82] However,

---

[77] *Id.* at 1479 (relying on Hodel v. Va. Surface Mining & Reclamation Ass'n, 452 U.S. 264 (1981)).

[78] *Id.* at 1479-81.

[79] *Id.* at 1481 (emphasis added).

[80] *Id.*

[81] *See* U.S. CONST. art. I, § 8, cl. 1 ("The Congress shall have power to lay and collect taxes, duties, imposts and excises, to pay debts and provide for the common defense and general welfare of the United States."); Agency for Int'l Dev. v. All. for Open Society Int'l, Inc., 570 U.S. 205, 213 (2013) (noting that the Spending Clause "provides Congress broad discretion to tax and spend for the 'general Welfare,' including by funding particular state or private programs or activities"); Nat'l Fed'n of Indep. Bus. v. Sebelius [NFIB], 567 U.S. 519, 579 (2012) ("Congress may attach appropriate conditions to federal taxing and spending programs to preserve its control over the use of federal funds."); Arlington Cent. Sch. Dist. Bd. of Educ. v. Murphy, 548 U.S. 291, 296 (2006) ("Congress has broad power to set the terms on which it disburses federal money to the States."); Sabri v. United States, 541 U.S. 600, 605 (1941) ("Congress has authority under the Spending Clause to appropriate federal moneys to promote the general welfare.").

[82] *See NFIB,* 657 U.S. at 536 ("[I]n exercising its spending power, Congress may offer funds to the States, and may condition those offers on compliance with specified conditions," which

238   *Sarah Herman Peck*

Congress cannot impose a financial condition that is "so coercive as to pass the point at which 'pressure turns into compulsion.'"[83] For example, in *National Federation of Independent Business v. Sebelius*, the Supreme Court struck down a provision of the Patient Protection and Affordable Care Act of 2010 (ACA) that purported to withhold Medicaid funding to states that did not expand their Medicaid programs.[84] The Court found that the financial conditions placed on the states in the ACA (withholding all federal Medicaid funding, which, according to the Court, typically totals about 20% of a state's entire budget) were akin to "a gun to the head" and thus unlawfully coercive.[85]

SELECT STATE AND LOCAL LIMITATIONS ON IMMIGRATION ENFORCEMENT ACTIVITY

Several states and municipalities have adopted measures intended to limit their participation in federal immigration enforcement efforts. These limitations take several forms.[86] For example, some states and localities have sought to restrict police cooperation with federal immigration authorities' efforts to apprehend removable aliens, sometimes called "don't enforce" policies.[87] Other measures may restrict certain state officials from

---

"may well induce the state to adopt policies that the federal Government itself could not impose"); *see also* South Dakota v. Dole, 483 U.S. 203, 201-11 (1987).

[83] *See Dole,* 483 U.S. at 211 (quoting Steward Mach. Co. v. Davis, 301 U.S. 548, 590 (1937)).

[84] *NFIB,* 567 U.S. at 588.

[85] *NFIB,* 132 S. Ct. at 2604.

[86] *See, e.g.,* Tal Kopan, *What are Sanctuary Cities, & Can They be Defunded?,* CNN POLITICS (Jan. 25, 2017, 5:09 PM), http://www.cnn.com/2017/01/25/politics/sanctuary-cities-explained/; Immigrant Legal Resource Ctr., Searching For Sanctuary: An Analysis Of America's Counties & Their Voluntary Assistance With Deportations (Dec. 2016), https://www.ilrc.org/sites/default/files/resources/sanctuary_report_final_1-min.pdf; Nat'l Council Of State Legislatures, What's A Sanctuary Policy? FAQ on Federal, State, And Local Action On Immigration Enforcement (July 28, 2017), http://www.ncsl.org/research/immigration/sanctuary-policyfaq635991795.aspx; NCSL 2015 REPORT, *supra* note 39; CTR. For Immigration Studies, *Maps: Sanctuary Cities, Counties and State* (last updated May 30, 2018), http://cis.org/Sanctuary-Cities-Map.

[87] *See, e.g.,* Jessica Saunders, Nelson Lim & Don Prosnitz, Enforcing Immigration Law At The State And Local Levels: A Public Policy Dilemma, Rand Ctr. Of Quality Policing (2010),

inquiring about a person's immigration status, sometimes referred to as "don't ask" policies.[88] Still others restrict information sharing between local law enforcement and federal immigration authorities, sometimes described as "don't tell" policies.[89] The following sections discuss some state and local restrictions on law enforcement activity in the field of immigration enforcement along those lines, including the relationship between these restrictions and federal law.

Limiting Arrests for Federal Immigration Violations

Violations of federal immigration law may be criminal or civil in nature. Removal proceedings are civil,[90] although some conduct that makes an alien removable may also warrant criminal prosecution.[91] For example, an alien who knowingly enters the United States without authorization is not only potentially removable,[92] but could also be charged with the criminal offense of unlawful entry.[93] Other violations of the INA are exclusively criminal or civil in nature. Notably, an alien's unauthorized immigration status makes him or her removable but, absent additional factors (e.g., having reentered the United States after being formally removed),[94] unlawful presence on its own is not a criminal offense.

Some jurisdictions have adopted measures that restrict its police officers from making arrests for violations of federal immigration law. In some jurisdictions restrictions prohibit police from detaining or arresting

---

https://www.rand.org/content/dam/rand/pubs/occasional_papers/2010/RAND_OP273.pdf (describing types of limited-cooperation policies); Kittrie, *supra* note 16, at 1455.

[88] Kittrie, *supra* note 16, at 1455.

[89] *See id.*

[90] *See* Padilla v. Kentucky, 559 U.S. 356, 365 (2010); INS v. Lopez-Mendoza, 468 U.S. 1032, 1038-39 (1984).

[91] For more information on criminal grounds for removal, see CRS Report R45151, *Immigration Consequences of Criminal Activity*, by Sarah Herman Peck and Hillel R. Smith.

[92] *See* INA § 212(a)(6)(A)(i); 8 U.S.C. §1182(a)(6)(A)(i) (providing that an alien is inadmissible and subject to removal if present in the United States without have been admitted or paroled, or if the alien arrives in the United States at any time or place other than as designated).

[93] 8 U.S.C. § 1325.

[94] 8 U.S.C. § 1326.

240 *Sarah Herman Peck*

aliens for civil violations of federal immigration law, like unlawful presence.[95] Other jurisdictions prohibit police from making arrests for some criminal violations of federal immigration law, like unlawful entry.[96] Still others prohibit law enforcement from assisting federal immigration authorities with investigating or arresting persons for civil *or* criminal violations of U.S. immigration laws.[97] And some other jurisdictions have prohibitions that are broader in scope, such as a general statement that immigration enforcement is the province of federal immigration authorities, rather than that of local law enforcement.[98]

State or local restrictions on police authority to arrest persons for federal immigration law violations do not appear to raise significant legal issues. Even though the INA expressly allows state and local law enforcement to engage in specified immigration enforcement activities,[99] nothing in the INA *compels* such participation. Indeed, any such requirement likely would raise anti-commandeering issues.[100] Moreover, after *Arizona*, it appears that states and localities are generally preempted from making arrests for civil violations of the INA in the absence of a

---

[95] *See, e.g.*, SAN JOSE, CA, Police Dep't Duty Manual 581 (2018) (public version) ("Officers will not detain or arrest any person on the basis of the person's citizenship or status under civil immigration laws."), http://www.sjpd.org/ Records/DutyManual.asp; Washington, DC, Mayor's Order 2011-174 (Oct. 19, 2011) (hereinafter "DC Mayor's Order") ("No person shall be detained solely on the belief that he or she is not present legally in the United States or that he or she has committed a civil immigration violation."), http://www.dclc.org/ docs/10-18- 2011%20Mayors%20oder.pdf; OR. REV. STAT. §181A.820 ("No law enforcement agency of the State of Oregon or of any political subdivision of the state shall use agency moneys, equipment or personnel for the purpose of detecting or apprehending persons whose only violation of law is that they are persons of foreign citizenship present in the United States in violation of federal immigration laws.").

[96] *See, e.g.*, LAPD ORDER, *supra* note 12 (barring arrests for federal crime of unlawful entry).

[97] Takoma Park, MD MUN. CODE § 9.04.010 ("No agent, officer or employee of the City, in the performance of official duties, shall assist the United States Bureau of Immigration and Customs Enforcement in the investigation or arrest of any persons for civil or criminal violation of the immigration and nationality laws of the United States.").

[98] Phoenix, AZ Police Dep't Operations Order Manual 1.4 (rev. 2015) ("The investigation and enforcement of federal laws relating to illegal entry and residence in the United States is specifically assigned to [Homeland Security Investigations]"), https://www.phoenix.gov/ policesite/Documents/operations_orders.pdf.

[99] *See e.g.*, INA § 287(g); 8 U.S.C. § 1357(g).

[100] *See supra* section "The Anti-Commandeering Doctrine."

"Sanctuary" Jurisdictions   241

specific federal statutory authorization or the "request, approval, or other instruction from the Federal Government."[101]

Limiting Police Inquiries into Immigration Status

Many sanctuary-type policies place restrictions on police inquiries or investigations into a person's immigration status.[102] Some policies provide that police may not question a person about his or her immigration status except as part of a criminal investigation.[103] Others bar law enforcement from initiating police activity with an individual for the sole purpose of

---

[101] Arizona v. United States, 567 U.S. 387, 410 (2012); *see also* Santos v. Frederick Cty. Bd. of Comm'rs, 725 F.3d 451, 464 (4th Cir. 2013) ("Lower federal courts have universally—and we think correctly—interpreted *Arizona v. United States* as precluding local law enforcement officers from arresting individuals solely based on known or suspected civil immigration violations."). *Arizona*'s discussion of state authority to enforce federal immigration law was related to arrests for noncriminal, immigration status violations. *Arizona*, 567 U.S. at 407-11. The Supreme Court did not opine on whether state law enforcement agencies are also precluded from making arrests for criminal violations of federal immigration law. However, some lower courts have generally recognized that state and local police are not constitutionally forbidden from making such arrests. *See, e.g.,* United States v. Argueta-Mejia, 615 F. App'x 485, 488 (10th Cir. 2015) ("The federal constitution allows a state law enforcement officer to make an arrest for any crime, including federal immigration offenses."); Villas at Parkside Partners v. City of Farmers Branch, Tex., 726 F.3d 524, 530-31 (5th Cir. 2013) (observing that 8 U.S.C. § 1324(c), a federal statute that criminalizes harboring unlawfully present aliens, permits state and local law enforcement to make arrests for criminal violations); Gonzales v. City of Peoria, 722 F.2d 468, (9th Cir. 1983) ("We therefore hold that federal law does not preclude local enforcement of the criminal provisions of the [Immigration and Nationality] Act."), *overruled on other grounds in* Hodgers-Durgin v. de la Vina, 199 F.3d 1037, 1040 n.1 (9th Cir. 1999); United States v. Vasquez-Alvarez, 176 F.3d 1294, 1299 n.4 (10th Cir. 1999) ("[S]tate law-enforcement officers have the general authority to investigate and make arrests for criminal violations of federal immigration laws.").

[102] *See, e.g., City of Philadelphia Action Guide: Immigration Policies*, City of Philadelphia (Jan. 8, 2018), https://www.phila.gov/2018-01-08-immigration-policies/ ("We do not allow our City employees, including police officers, to ask about the documentation status of people they encounter."); Christina M. Rodriguez, *The Significance of the Local in Immigration Regulation,* 106 MICH. L. REV. 567, 602 (2008) (describing New York City's sanctuary policies).

[103] DC Mayor's Order, *supra* note 95 (declaring that public safety employees "shall not inquire about a person's immigration status ... for the purpose of initiating civil enforcement of immigration proceedings that have no nexus to a criminal investigation"); N.Y.C. Exec Order No. 34, http://www1.nyc.gov/site/immigrants/about/local-laws-executiveorders.page ("Law enforcement officers shall not inquire about a person's immigration status unless investigating illegal activity other than mere status as an undocumented alien.").

242 *Sarah Herman Peck*

discovering immigration status.[104] And other policies prohibit law enforcement from questioning crime victims and witnesses about their immigration status.[105] Still other policies more broadly limit officials from gathering information about persons' immigration status, except as required by law.[106]

Restricting the authority of police to question a person about his or her immigration status helps ensure that law enforcement lacks any information that could be shared with federal immigration authorities. As explained in the "PRWORA and IIRIRA" section below, two federal laws prevent state or local restrictions on sharing information about a person's immigration status with federal immigration authorities, but the provisions do not require state or local police to actually collect such information.[107] *Murphy* has raised questions, though, about the continuing constitutional viability of these statutes.[108]

Limiting Information Sharing with Federal Immigration Authorities

Some states and localities have restricted government agencies or employees from sharing information with federal immigration

---

[104] *See, e.g.,* LAPD ORDER, *supra* note 12 ("Officers shall not initiate police action with the objective of discovering the alien status of a person.").

[105] *See, e.g.,* DC Mayor's Order, *supra* note 92 ("It shall be the policy of Public Safety Agencies not to inquire about the immigration status of crime victims, witnesses, or others who call or approach the police seeking assistance."); New Haven Dep't of Police Service General Order 06-2 (2006) ("Police officers shall not inquire about a person's immigration status unless investigation criminal activity."), https://www.newhavenct.gov/gov/depts/nhpd/ division/ internal_affairs/general_orders.htminternal_affairs/general_orders.htm; N.Y.C. Exec Order No. 34, *supra* note 103 ("It shall be the policy of the Police Department not to inquire about the immigration status of crime victims, witnesses, or others who call or approach the police seeking assistance.").

[106] *See, e.g.,* CHI., ILL. MUN. CODE ch. 2-173-020 (declaring that "[n]o agent or agency shall request information about or otherwise investigate or assist in the investigation of the citizenship or immigration status of any person," subject to exceptions, including as required by law).

[107] *See* 8 U.S.C. §1373(b) (barring state or local restrictions on sending, maintaining, or exchanging immigration status information with federal immigration authorities).

[108] *See supra* notes 62 to 72 and accompanying text.

authorities.[109] For instance, some jurisdictions prohibit law enforcement from notifying federal immigration authorities about the release status of incarcerated aliens, unless the alien has been convicted of certain felonies.[110] Similarly, other jurisdictions prohibit their employees from disclosing information about an individual's immigration status unless the alien is suspected of engaging in illegal activity that is separate from unlawful immigration status.[111] Some jurisdictions restrict disclosing information except as required by federal law[112]—sometimes referred to as a "savings clause"—although it appears that the Department of Justice has interpreted those provisions as conflicting with federal information-sharing provisions.[113]

---

[109] *See, e.g.*, S.F. ADMIN CODE § 12H.2 ("No department, agency, commission, officer, or employee of the City and County of San Francisco shall use City funds or resources to assist in the enforcement of Federal immigration law or to gather or disseminate information regarding release status of individuals or any such personal information . . . unless such assistance is required by Federal or State statute, regulation, or court decision."); N.Y.C. Executive Order 124 (Aug. 7, 1989) [hereinafter 1989 New York City Order] (limiting transmission of information about an alien to federal immigration authorities except in certain circumstances, including when the alien was suspected of criminal activity), http://www.nycourts.gov/library/queens/PDF_files/Orders/ord124.pdf (revoked and replaced in 2003 by N.Y.C. Executive Order 34, as amended by N.Y.C. Executive Order 41, to permit information sharing in a broader range of circumstances, but not on the basis of alien's unlawful immigration status); Governor of Maine Executive Order 13 FY 04/05, Concerning Access to State Services By All Entitled Maine Residents (Apr. 9, 2004) (limiting the sharing of information about aliens with federal immigration authorities, except when an alien is involved in illegal activity other than unlawful status; rescinded by Exec. Order 08 FY 11/12 (Jan. 6, 2011)).

[110] *See, e.g.*, S.F. ADMIN CODE §§ 12H.2, 12I.3.

[111] *See, e.g.*, N.Y.C. Exec Order No. 41 (Sept. 17, 2003), http://www1.nyc.gov/site/immigrants/about/local-laws- executive-orders.page.

[112] CHI., ILL. MUN. CODE ch. 2-173-030 ("Except as otherwise provided under applicable federal law, no agent or agency shall disclose information regarding the citizenship or immigration status of any person unless required to do so by legal process or such disclosure has been authorized in writing by the individual to whom such information pertains, or if such individual is a minor or is otherwise not legally competent, by such individual's parent or guardian.").

[113] *See* Michael R. Horowitz, Inspector General, Dep't of Justice Referral of Allegations of Potential Violations of 8 U.S.C. § 1373 By Grant Recipients (May 31, 2016), https://oig.justice.gov/reports/2016/1607.pdf.

FEDERAL MEASURES TO COUNTERACT SANCTUARY POLICIES

Over the years the federal government has enacted measures designed to counter certain sanctuary policies. Notably, in 1996 Congress enacted Section 434 of the Personal Responsibility and Work Opportunity Reconciliation Act (PRWORA), and Section 642 of the Illegal Immigration Reform and Immigrant Responsibility Act (IIRIRA), to curb state and local restrictions on information sharing. Most recently, the President issued Executive Order 13768, "Enhancing Public Safety in the Interior of the United States," which, as relevant here, seeks to encourage state and local cooperation with federal immigration enforcement and disincentivize state and local adoption of sanctuary policies that hinder federal immigration enforcement. These federal initiatives—and related legal issues—are described below.

PRWORA and IIRIRA

In 1996 Congress sought to end state and local restrictions on information sharing through provisions in PRWORA[114] and IIRIRA.[115] Neither PRWORA nor IIRIRA *requires* state or local government entities to share immigration-related information with federal authorities.[116] Instead, these provisions bar restrictions that prevent state or local government entities or officials from voluntarily communicating with federal immigration authorities regarding a person's immigration status.[117]

---

[114] P.L. 104-193, §434 (1996); 8 U.S.C. § 1644.

[115] P.L. 104-208, §642 (1996); 8 U.S.C. § 1373.

[116] Whether Congress could permissibly *require* states and localities to submit collected information to federal immigration authorities is an open question. As previously noted, the Supreme Court in *Printz* distinguished federal laws requiring states to report certain information to federal agencies from those that compel state authorities to administer a federal regulatory program as to private parties, and declined to opine on whether reporting requirements violated the anti-commandeering doctrine. *See* Printz v. United States, 521 U.S. 898, 918 (1997).

[117] 8 U.S.C. §§ 1373, 1644.

IIRIRA § 642, codified at 8 U.S.C. § 1373, bars any restriction on a federal, state, or local governmental entity or official's ability to send or receive information regarding "citizenship or immigration status" to or from federal immigration authorities.[118] It further provides that no person or agency may prohibit a federal, state, or local government entity from (1) sending information regarding immigration status to, or requesting information from, federal immigration authorities; (2) maintaining information regarding immigration status; or (3) exchanging such information with any other federal, state, or local government entity.[119] PRWORA § 434, codified at 8 U.S.C. § 1644, similarly bars state and local governments from prohibiting or restricting state or local government entities from sending or receiving information, to or from federal immigration authorities, regarding the "immigration status" of an individual.[120]

Related Litigation

Shortly after Congress enacted these information-sharing restrictions, New York City, which had a policy limiting information sharing with federal immigration authorities,[121] brought suit challenging the constitutionality of Sections 1373 and 1644. Among other things,[122] New York City alleged that the provisions facially violated the Tenth Amendment by barring states and localities from controlling the degree to which their officials may cooperate with federal immigration authorities.[123]

---

[118] 8 U.S.C. § 1373(a).

[119] *Id.* § 1373(b). Federal immigration authorities are also required to respond to immigration status or citizenship verification requests made by state or local authorities pertaining to persons within their jurisdiction. Id. § 1373(c).

[120] *Id.* § 1644.

[121] 1989 New York City Order, *supra* note 109.

[122] New York City also unsuccessfully argued that the information-sharing provisions in PRWORA and IIRIRA violated the Guarantee Clause of the Constitution, U.S. CONST. art. IV, § 4, by interfering with the city's oversight of its employees, City of New York v. United States [City of New York I], 971 F. Supp. 789 (S.D.N.Y. 1997) (holding that Guarantee-Clause claim was nonjusticiable); City of New York v. United States [City of New York II], 179 F.3d 29 (2d Cir. 1999) (assuming that Guarantee-Clause claim was justiciable and concluding that PRWORA and IIRIRA information-sharing provisions were permissible).

[123] *City of New York I*, 971 F. Supp. at 791.

246 *Sarah Herman Peck*

A federal district court dismissed this claim in *City of New York v. United States*,[124] and the U.S. Court of Appeals for the Second Circuit affirmed the judgment.[125]

The Second Circuit observed that, unlike the statutes struck down on anti-commandeering grounds in *New York* and *Printz*, the information-sharing provisions in PRWORA and IIRIRA did not directly compel state authorities to administer and enforce a federal regulatory program.[126] Instead, the court reasoned, these provisions prohibited state and local governments from restricting "the voluntary exchange" of immigration information between federal and state authorities.[127] Further, the court added, "informed, extensive, and cooperative interaction of a voluntary nature" between states and federal authorities is an integral feature of the American system of dual sovereignty, and, in any event, the Supremacy Clause "bars states from taking actions that frustrate federal laws and regulatory schemes."[128] Accordingly, the Second Circuit concluded that the Tenth Amendment does not provide states and municipalities with the "untrammeled right to forbid all voluntary cooperation by state or local officials with particular federal programs."[129] The court therefore rejected New York City's constitutional challenge to the information-sharing provisions of PRWORA and IIRIRA, holding that that they did not violate the Tenth Amendment or principles of federalism.[130]

New York City sought to appeal the decision to the Supreme Court, but its petition for certiorari was denied.[131] A few months later, though, the Court handed down *Reno*, which, as explained earlier, held that the DPPA (a federal statute regulating the dissemination of certain personal information collected by state authorities) did not violate federalism principles embodied in the Tenth Amendment.[132]

---

[124] *Id.* at 789.
[125] *City of New York II*, 179 F.3d 29 (2d Cir. 1999).
[126] *See id.* at 34-35.
[127] *Id.* at 35.
[128] *Id.*
[129] *Id.*
[130] *Id.* at 31.
[131] 528 U.S. 1115 (2000).
[132] 528 U.S. 141 (2000).

Since the Second Circuit's ruling, questions about Section 1373's constitutionality remained relatively quiet until President Trump issued the executive order targeting jurisdictions that do not comply with Section 1373. This sparked new litigation challenging Section 1373, some of which invoked *Murphy* after the ruling came down.

EXECUTIVE ORDER 13768 AND RELATED LITIGATION

Shortly after taking office, President Trump issued Executive Order (EO) 13768, "Enhancing Public Safety in the Interior of the United States,"[133] which, in Section 9, addresses sanctuary jurisdictions. Specifically, Section 9(a) of the EO seeks to encourage state and local cooperation with federal immigration enforcement and disincentivize—by threatening to withhold federal grant money—state and local adoption of sanctuary policies.[134] Although EO 13768 did not explicitly define "sanctuary jurisdiction," later interpretive guidance from the Department of Justice (DOJ or Justice Department) defined the term, as it is used in the executive order, as a jurisdiction that willfully refuses to comply with 8 U.S.C. § 1373 (IIRIRA § 642).[135]

This section discusses recent litigation concerning efforts by the Trump Administration to deter the implementation of state or local "sanctuary" policies. It begins by providing a brief description of Section 9(a) of EO 13768 and the DOJ's implementation of its requirements. Next, it discusses ongoing litigation involving challenges to Section 9(a). Several of these cases involve direct challenges to the executive order. Other lawsuits involve challenges to the Justice Department's decision, in implementing the executive order, to attach new conditions for grant eligibility under the Edward Byrne Memorial Justice Assistance Grant (Byrne JAG) program and Community Oriented Policing Services (COPS)

---

[133] Exec. Order No. 13,768, 82 Fed. Reg. 8,799 (Jan. 30, 2017).
[134] *Id.*
[135] Memorandum from Att'y Gen. Jeff Sessions, *Implementation of Executive Order 13768, "Enhancing Pub. Safety in the Interior of the U.S."* (May 22, 2017) [hereinafter DOJ Implementation Memo], https://www.justice.gov/opa/pressrelease/file/968146/download.

program,[136] all of which are designed to encourage state and local law enforcement cooperation with federal immigration enforcement. Finally, this section discusses a lawsuit filed by the United States against California, claiming that three new state laws obstruct the federal government's immigration enforcement efforts and, as a result, violate the Constitution's Supremacy Clause.[137]

Section 9 of Executive Order 13768

On January 25, 2017, the President signed EO 13768, "Enhancing Public Safety in the Interior of the United States."[138] Section 9 of the executive order seeks to encourage state and local cooperation with federal immigration enforcement and disincentivize state and local adoption of sanctuary policies.[139] In particular, Section 9 declares that "[i]t is the policy of the executive branch to ensure, to the fullest extent of the law, that a State, or political subdivision of a State, shall comply with 8 U.S.C. 1373."[140]

To implement the policy set forth in the executive order, the President instructs the Attorney General and the Secretary of the Department of Homeland Security (DHS) under Section 9(a) to ensure that jurisdictions that "willfully refuse to comply with 8 U.S.C. 1373 (sanctuary jurisdictions) are not eligible to receive Federal grants," subject to limited exception.[141] The executive order authorizes the DHS Secretary to designate a jurisdiction she determines to be a "sanctuary," and directs the Attorney General to take "appropriate enforcement actions" against "any entity" that violates Section 1373 or that "has in effect a statute, policy, or

---

[136] *See* Dep't of Justice, Office of Justice Programs, *Edward Byrne Memorial Justice Assistance Grant Program*, https://www.bja.gov/jag/ (last visited Nov. 7, 2018); CRS In Focus IF10691, *The Edward Byrne Memorial Justice Assistance Grant (JAG) Program*, by Nathan James.

[137] "This Constitution, and the laws of the United States . . . shall be the supreme Law of the Land . . . ." U.S. CONST. art. VI.

[138] Exec. Order No. 13,768, 82 Fed. Reg. 8,799 (Jan. 30, 2017).

[139] *Id.* at 8,801.

[140] *Id.*

[141] Exec. Order No. 13,768, 82 Fed. Reg. 8,799 (Jan. 30, 2017).

practice that prevents or hinders the enforcement of Federal law."[142] Under Section 9(b), the President directs the DHS Secretary to publish, weekly, a list of jurisdictions that ignore or fail to honor detainer requests for incarcerated aliens, "[t]o better inform the public regarding the public safety threats associated with sanctuary jurisdictions."[143]

DOJ Implementation of EO 13768

A few months later, on May 22, 2017, Attorney General Sessions issued a memorandum interpreting EO 13768.[144] First, he announced that "sanctuary jurisdictions," for the purposes of enforcing the executive order, are "jurisdictions that 'willfully refuse to comply with 8 U.S.C. 1373.'"[145] Further, the Attorney General stated that the executive order applies only to grants that the DOJ or DHS administer. As a result, the Attorney General announced that the DOJ would "require jurisdictions applying for certain Department grants to certify their compliance with federal law, including 8 U.S.C. § 1373, as a condition for receiving an award."[146] In addition, the certification requirement would apply to all existing grants administered by the DOJ's Office of Justice Programs and Office of Community Oriented Policing Services (COPS) that expressly contain the certification condition, and to future grants for which the DOJ has statutory authority to impose such conditions.[147] Further, the Attorney General added that "[s]eparate and apart from the Executive Order, statutes may authorize the Department to tailor grants or to impose additional conditions on grantees to advance the Department's law enforcement priorities."[148] Accordingly, "[g]oing forward," the Attorney General announced, "the Department, where authorized, may seek to tailor grants to promote a lawful system of immigration."[149]

---

[142] *Id.*
[143] *Id.*
[144] DOJ Implementation Memo, *supra* note 135; 8 U.S.C. § 1373.
[145] *Id.* (quoting Exec. Order No. 13,768, 82 Fed. Reg. 8,799 (Jan. 30, 2017)).
[146] *Id.*
[147] *Id.*
[148] *Id.*
[149] *Id.*

250   *Sarah Herman Peck*

As a follow up to that interpretive memorandum, two months later on July 25, 2017, the DOJ issued a press release and accompanying background document announcing new conditions for recipients of the Byrne JAG program.[150] The Byrne JAG program provides federal funds to the states, District of Columbia, Puerto Rico, and other territories for various nonfederal criminal justice initiatives.[151] The press release announced three new conditions:

1. Compliance Condition.[152] Byrne JAG program grant recipients must certify compliance with Section 1373, which would notify the federal government that the jurisdiction does not restrict its offices and personnel from sending or receiving citizenship or immigration status to or from federal immigration authorities.[153]

2. Access Condition. Grant recipients that have detention facilities housing aliens (e.g., local jails or state prisons where aliens may be confined) must permit DHS immigration enforcement personnel (i.e., enforcement officers with DHS's U.S. Immigration and Customs Enforcement [ICE]) to access those facilities to meet with housed aliens and inquire into their eligibility to remain in the country.

3. Notice Condition. When DHS believes that an alien in state or local custody is removable from the United States for a violation of federal immigration law, ICE officers may issue a "detainer"

---

[150] Press Release, Dep't of Justice, *Attorney General Sessions Announces Immigration Compliance Requirements for Edward Byrne Memorial Justice Assistance Grant Programs* (July 25, 2017), https://www.justice.gov/opa/pr/attorneygeneral-sessions-announces-immigration-compliance-requirements-edward-byrne-memorial.

[151] *See* CRS In Focus IF10691, *The Edward Byrne Memorial Justice Assistance Grant (JAG) Program*, by Nathan James.

[152] For the sake of brevity and clarity, throughout the memorandum the conditions will be referred to as the "compliance condition," the "access condition," and the "notice condition."

[153] 8 U.S.C. § 1373(a). In March 2016, the DOJ had previously notified grant recipients under the Byrne JAG program that they had an obligation to comply with Section 1373, but the agency did not establish a formal certification requirement. *See* Dep't of Justice, *Backgrounder on Grant Requirements* (attached to July 25, 2017 press release) https://www.justice.gov/opa/press-release/file/984346/download [hereinafter Grant Requirement Backgrounder].

requesting that the state or local entity give notice of the alien's pending release from custody so that ICE may take control of the alien for possible removal proceedings.[154] To be eligible for grants under the Byrne JAG program, DOJ announced that recipients generally must give DHS 48 hours' advance notice before releasing from custody an alien wanted for removal.[155]

These requirements were made applicable to Byrne JAG applications that were due six weeks later, on September 5, 2017, meaning that applying jurisdictions would need to be in compliance with all three conditions within six weeks.

Additionally, the Justice Department announced a requirement for applicants seeking grants administered by the COPS Office to certify compliance with Section 1373.[156] COPS grants are used to advance community policing, for example, through training, technical assistance, and developing "innovative policing strategies"[157] in a number of "topic areas" selected by the DOJ.[158] For FY2018, in the topic area for "Field Initiated Law Enforcement," priority consideration could be given to applicants that cooperate with federal immigration authorities "to address illegal immigration."[159] Further, the COPS Office notified potential applicants that additional consideration would be given to applicants that partner with federal law enforcement to combat illegal immigration.[160] To obtain that special consideration, applicants could sign a form certifying

---

[154] U.S. Immigration & Customs Enforcement, *Detainer Policy,* https://www.ice.gov/detainer-policy (last visited Nov. 8, 2018).

[155] Grant Requirement Backgrounder, *supra* note 153.

[156] *See* Dep't of Justice, Office of Community Oriented Policing Services, *Certification of Compliance with 8 U.S.C. 1373,* https://cops.usdoj.gov/pdf/2017AwardDocs/cpd/Certification_of_Compliance.pdf.

[157] *See* Dep't of Justice, *Grants,* https://www.justice.gov/grants (last visited Nov. 8, 2018).

[158] *See* U.S. Dep't Of Justice, Office Of Community Oriented Policing Services, Fy 2018 Community Policing Development (Cpd) Application Guide 2, 67, https://cops.usdoj.gov/pdf/2018AwardDocs/cpd/App_Guide.pdf (2018) (listing topic areas).

[159] *See id.* at 2, 67. Application solicitations for the Field-Initiated Law Enforcement Microgrants topic area is currently on hold, however, on account of ongoing litigation. *Id.* at 2; *see also* U.S. Dep't Of Justice, *Community Policing Development (CPD),* https://cops.usdoj.gov/cpd (last visited Nov. 8, 2018).

[160] *See* City of Los Angeles v. Sessions, 293 F. Supp. 3d 1087, 1093 (C.D. Cal. 2018).

that they follow practices mirroring those of the notice and access conditions of Byrne JAG program: (1) allowing federal immigration authorities to access detention facilities where they may question known or suspected aliens about their immigration status; and (2) providing at least 48 hours' notice of those persons' expected custodial release.[161]

Litigation Challenging EO 13768 and its Implementation

The lawsuits challenging Section 9(a) of EO 13768 and its implementation came in two waves. The first wave came shortly after President Trump signed the executive order, when several jurisdictions sued for injunctive relief. The second, larger wave of litigation came after the DOJ announced the new Byrne JAG and COPS conditions. In the litigation challenging the EO's implementation, the various challengers have brought arguments raising similar statutory and constitutional concerns, chiefly

- the DOJ lacked statutory authority to impose the new conditions;
- the DOJ imposed the conditions arbitrarily and capriciously in violation of the Administrative Procedure Act;
- the executive branch violated principles of separation of powers by usurping the legislature's spending power; and
- the government violated the anti-commandeering doctrine by unconstitutionally conscripting the states into federal immigration enforcement.

The County and City of San Francisco and the County of Santa Clara (collectively, the "Counties"), for example, filed suit within days of each other, and those lawsuits were considered jointly by a district judge in the

---

[161] *Id.*

"Sanctuary" Jurisdictions 253

Northern District of California.[162] The district court presiding over the Counties' challenges ultimately issued an injunction blocking nationwide enforcement of Section 9(a).[163] The Ninth Circuit agreed with the lower court that Section 9(a) violates the Constitution's principles of separation of powers.[164] However, while agreeing that the injunction was appropriate to prevent Section 9(a) from having effect in California, the appellate court concluded that the current factual record was insufficient to support a nationwide injunction and remanded the case to the district court for further factfinding.[165]

As for the litigation challenging new Byrne JAG and COPS conditions, in one case, the U.S. District Court of the Northern District of Illinois enjoined the Byrne JAG conditions as applied to Chicago.[166] The court held that, in imposing those conditions, the DOJ exceeded the statutory authority Congress delegated to implement the Byrne JAG program.[167] In another case, the U.S. District Court for the Eastern District of Pennsylvania enjoined the federal government from enforcing the three Byrne JAG conditions against Philadelphia.[168] The district court concluded, among other things, that the conditions were imposed arbitrarily and capriciously in violation of the Administrative Procedure Act (APA) because the government had failed to adequately justify imposing the new conditions.[169] For reasons similar to the federal district courts in Chicago and Pennsylvania, a district court in New York enjoined the government from enforcing the new conditions against the City of New York and the

---

[162] Complaint, City & Cty. Of San Francisco v. Trump, No. 3:17-cv-00485-WHO (N.D. Cal. Jan. 31, 2017); Complaint, Cty. of Santa Clara v. Trump, No. 3:17-cv-00574-WHO, (N.D. Cal. Feb. 3, 2017).

[163] Order Granting Motion for Summary Judgment, City & Cty. of San Francisco v. Trump, No. 3:17-cv-00485-WHO & Cty. Of Santa Clara v. Trump, No. 17-cv-00574-WHO (N.D. Cal. Nov. 20, 2017).

[164] City & Cty. of San Francisco v. Trump, 897 F.3d 1225, 1231-35 (9th Cir. 2018).

[165] Id. at 1245.

[166] City of Chicago v. Sessions, 321 F. Supp. 3d 855 (E.D. Ill. 2018). The district court technically issued a nationwide injunction but stayed its nationwide effect until the Seventh Circuit rules. Id. at 880.

[167] Id. at 873-76.

[168] City of Philadelphia v. Sessions, 309 F. Supp. 3d 289, 296 (E.D. Pa. 2018).

[169] Id. at 323-25. Under the Administrative Procedure Act, a court may set aside executive actions that are "arbitrary, capricious, an abuse of discretion, or otherwise not in accordance with law." 5 U.S.C. § 706(2).

States of New York, Connecticut, New Jersey, Rhode Island, Washington, Massachusetts, and Virginia (the collective plaintiffs in that case).[170] Notably, all of the district judges held, post-*Murphy*, that Section 1373 violates the anti-commandeering doctrine.[171] Finally, in another lawsuit brought by the City of Los Angeles, California, a district judge permanently enjoined the new considerations for COPS grant selections, concluding that they were imposed without statutory authority, violated the Spending Clause, and were arbitrarily and capriciously imposed in violation of the APA.[172]

City & Cty. of San Francisco v. Trump and Cty. of Santa Clara v. Trump

Shortly after President Trump issued EO 13768, the City and County of San Francisco and the County of Santa Clara, California, filed suit, asking a federal court to enjoin Section 9(a) of the order.[173] The Counties principally argued that Section 9(a) is unconstitutional in three ways.[174] First, the Counties contended that the funding restrictions, by purporting to withhold, or impose new eligibility conditions on, congressional appropriations, violated the separation of powers by usurping the legislature's spending power granted in Article I, Section 8 of the Constitution.[175] Alternatively, even assuming that the President had lawful authority to withhold, or impose conditions on, congressionally appropriated funds, the Counties argued that Section 9(a) would still

---

[170] States of New York v. Dep't of Justice, 343 F.Supp.3d 213, 245-46 (S.D.N.Y. 2018).

[171] *City of Philadelphia*, 309 F. Supp. 3d at 329-31; *City of Chicago*, 321 F. Supp. 3d at 872; *States of New York*, 343 F.Supp.3d at 234-38.

[172] City of Los Angeles v. Sessions, 293 F. Supp. 3d. 1087, 1095-1100 (C.D. Cal. 2018).

[173] Complaint, City & Cty. Of San Francisco v. Trump, No. 3:17-cv-00485-WHO (N.D. Cal. Jan. 31, 2017); Complaint, Cty. of Santa Clara v. Trump, No. 3:17-cv-00574-WHO, (N.D. Cal. Feb. 3, 2017). These cases were filed separately but considered together.

[174] Motion for Summary Judgment, City & Cty. of San Francisco v. Trump, No. 3:17-cv-00485-WHO (N.D. Cal. Aug. 30, 2017); Motion for Summary Judgment, Cty. of Santa Clara v. Trump, No. 3:17-cv-00574-WHO (N.D. Cal. Aug. 30, 2017).

[175] Motion for Summary Judgment at 12-13, City & Cty. Of San Francisco v. Trump, No. 3:17-cv-00485-WHO (N.D. Cal. Aug. 30, 2017) ("The Constitution grants *Congress*—not the President—the federal spending power, including the power to impose conditions on federal funds."). The **Spending Clause** states that "[t]he Congress shall have Power To lay and collect Taxes, Duties, Imposts and Excises, to pay the Debts and provide for the common Defence and general Welfare of the United States ...." U.S. CONST. art I, § 8, cl. 1.

violate the Spending Clause because it surpasses the constitutional limits of the Spending Clause set forth by the Supreme Court.[176] Finally, the Counties argued that Section 9(a) violates the anti-commandeering doctrine, contending, for instance, that Section 9(a) coerces jurisdictions into complying with ICE-issued immigration detainers by threatening to withhold federal funding and take unspecified enforcement action against jurisdictions that "'hinder the enforcement of federal law.'"[177]

The district judge ultimately agreed with all three arguments and permanently enjoined— nationwide—Section 9(a) of the executive order.[178] The Ninth Circuit, in a 2-1 ruling, affirmed the district court's judgment on the ground that Section 9(a) violates the separation of powers by usurping Congress's spending power.[179] The Ninth Circuit vacated the injunction's nationwide application, however, and remanded for further factfinding on whether the injunction ought to be nationwide in scope.[180]

In holding that EO Section 9(a) violates the separation of powers, the Ninth Circuit recounted that "when it comes to spending, the President has none of his own constitutional powers to rely upon."[181] That power, the court explained, is exclusively Congress's domain, subject to delegation.[182] Yet, the court opined, Congress had not authorized the executive branch "to withdraw federal grant moneys from jurisdictions that do not agree with the current Administration's immigration strategies."[183] Further, the court pointed to nearly a dozen failed congressional proposals to do just that during the 114th Congress.[184] Thus, the Ninth Circuit concluded,

---

[176] Motion for Summary Judgment at 13-17, City & Cty. Of San Francisco v. Trump, No. 3:17-cv-00485-WHO (N.D. Cal. Aug. 30, 2017).

[177] *Id.* at 18-20 (quoting Section 9(a) of EO 13768).

[178] Cty. of Santa Clara v. Trump, 275 F. Supp. 3d 1196 (N.D. Cal. 2017).

[179] City & Cty. of San Francisco v. Trump, 897 F.3d 1225, 1231-35 (9th Cir. 2018). In dissent, Judge Fernandez disagreed with the majority's characterization of Section 9(a)'s savings clause—directing the Attorney General or Secretary of Homeland Security to take actions "consistent with law" to ensure compliance with Section 1373—as "implausible, or boilerplate." *Id.* at 1249-50 (Fernandez, J., dissenting). Judge Fernandez also contended that the plaintiffs' claims were not ripe for review. *Id.* at 1247-48.

[180] *Id.* at 1231.

[181] *Id.* at 1233-34 (internal quotation marks and citation omitted).

[182] *Id.* at 1233.

[183] *Id.* at 1234.

[184] *Id.* at 1234 & n.4.

"[n]ot only has the Administration claimed for itself Congress's exclusive spending power, it also attempted to coopt Congress's power to legislate."[185]

City of Richmond v. Trump

Another California city unsuccessfully tried to challenge EO 13768 as it relates to sanctuary jurisdictions. Richmond, California, like Santa Clara and San Francisco, argued that (1) the President exceeded his constitutional authority by purporting to appropriate federal funds; (2) even assuming that the President has such spending authority, the conditions set forth in the executive order violate the Spending Clause's lawful parameters; and (3) the executive order unlawfully commandeers the states.[186] The district court denied Richmond's request for injunctive relief, however, after concluding that the city could not establish pre-enforcement standing to challenge the executive order.[187]

In dismissing Richmond's suit, the district court applied the framework that the Supreme Court set forth in *Babbitt v. Farm Workers National Union* to determine whether a plaintiff has standing to challenge a statute *before* it is enforced against the plaintiff.[188] Under *Babbitt,* the plaintiff must demonstrate "an intention to engage in a course of conduct arguably affected with a constitutional interest, but proscribed by a statute, and there exists a credible threat of prosecution thereunder."[189] The district court assumed without deciding that Richmond had policies proscribed by the executive order, could lose federal funding if the order was enforced against it, and put forward claims that implicated constitutional interests. So the ruling on whether Richmond had pre-enforcement standing ultimately hinged on whether Richmond had demonstrated a "well-founded

---

[185] *Id.* at 1234.

[186] Complaint for Injunctive & Declaratory Relief at 18-21, City of Richmond v. Trump, No. 3:17-cv-01535 (N.D. Cal. Mar. 21, 2017). The same judge presided over this case and the lawsuits brought by San Francisco and Santa Clara. The Richmond lawsuit was resolved after the judge issued a preliminary injunction in the cases brought by San Francisco and Santa Clara but before the permanent injunction was issued in that case.

[187] Order Granting Motion to Dismiss at 1, City of Richmond v. Trump, No. 3:17-cv-01535 (N.D. Cal. Aug. 21, 2017).

[188] *Id.* at 4.

[189] Babbitt v. United Farm Workers Nat'l Union, 442 U.S. 289, 298 (1979).

fear" that the executive order would be enforced against it, and the court concluded the city had not.[190] The court opined that "[t]he likely targets of enforcement under the [Executive] Order are jurisdictions that have actually refused to cooperate with ICE and that ICE believes are hindering its immigration enforcement efforts."[191] But according to Richmond's own complaint, the court found, the federal government had never asked Richmond to assist in enforcing immigration policy, nor had it been identified as a locality that restricts cooperation with ICE or regularly declines immigration detainers.[192] Thus, the court decided that Richmond had "no real-world friction with ICE or the defendants over its policies" and thus was unlikely to be subjected to the executive order's funding restrictions.[193]

City of Seattle & City of Portland v. Trump

The Cities of Seattle, Washington, and Portland, Oregon, jointly challenged President Trump's executive order.[194] The cities asked a district court to declare that Section 9(a) of EO 13768 is unconstitutional under the Tenth Amendment, the Spending Clause, and separation-of-power principles, principally for the same reasons as the other jurisdictions challenging the executive order.[195] Soon after the plaintiffs brought suit, though, the district court stayed the case, pending the resolution of the appeal in the Ninth Circuit of the injunction issued in the Santa Clara/San Francisco litigation.[196] After the Ninth Circuit concluded that Section 9(a) was unconstitutional, the district judge in this case also ruled that Section 9(a) unconstitutionally violated the separation of powers.[197]

---

[190] Order Granting Motion to Dismiss at 4, City of Richmond v. Trump, No. 3:17-cv-01535 (N.D. Cal. Aug. 21, 2017).

[191] *Id.* at 5.

[192] *Id.*

[193] *Id.* at 6.

[194] First Amended Complaint, City of Seattle v. Trump & City of Portland v. Trump, No. 2:17-cv-00497-RAJ (W.D. Wash. June 26, 2017).

[195] *Id.* at 37-49.

[196] Order, City of Seattle v. Trump & City of Portland v. Trump, No. 2:17-cv-00497-RAJ (W.D. Wash. Oct. 31, 2017).

[197] Order & Judgment Granting Declaratory Relief, City of Seattle v. Trump & City of Portland v. Trump, No. 2:17-cv00497-RAJ (W.D. Wash. Oct. 24, 2018). The parties stipulated to this result. Stipulation & Proposed Order & Judgment Granting Declaratory Relief, City of

City of Chelsea & City of Lawrence v. Trump

Two cities in Massachusetts, Chelsea and Lawrence, also filed suit shortly after President Trump issued EO 13768, challenging Section 9(a). Chelsea and Lawrence principally argued that that Section 9(a) violates the Tenth Amendment and the Constitution's separation-of-power principles, for reasons substantially similar to those argued by Santa Clara, San Francisco, and Richmond.[198] However, after the district court in the Santa Clara/San Francisco litigation issued a nationwide preliminary injunction blocking the executive order, the parties agreed to stay the proceedings unless and until the injunction is lifted.[199]

City of Chicago v. Sessions

After the Justice Department announced the new Byrne JAG conditions, the City of Chicago, Illinois, sued, asking a district court to enjoin the Attorney General from imposing them.[200] Chicago's suit challenged each of the three conditions that the Justice Department imposed for grant eligibility (compliance with the information-sharing requirements of Section 1373, DHS access to state and local detention facilities, and providing notice to DHS when an alien wanted for removal is released from custody).[201]

First, Chicago argued that the DOJ lacked statutory authority to impose the new conditions because the Byrne JAG statute does not confer agency discretion to add substantive conditions to the receipt of those federal funds.[202] And even though the Byrne JAG statute requires that recipients

---

Seattle v. Trump & City of Portland v. Trump, No. 2:17-cv-00497-RAJ (W.D. Wash. Oct. 19, 2018).

[198] Complaint at 38-41, City of Chelsea & City of Lawrence v. Trump, No. 1:17-cv-10214-GAO (D. Mass. Feb. 8, 2017).

[199] Plaintiff's Unopposed Motion to Stay Proceedings, City of Chelsea & City of Lawrence v. Trump, No. 1:17-cv10214-GAO (D. Mass. May 2, 2017). The case was administratively closed on December 29, 2017. Order, City of Chelsea & City of Lawrence v. Trump, No. 1:17-cv-10214-GAO (D. Mass. Dec. 29, 2017).

[200] Complaint at 1, City of Chicago v. Sessions, No. 1:17-cv-05720 (N.D. Ill. Aug. 7, 2017).

[201] *Id.* at 19-23.

[202] Memorandum of Law in Support of Plaintiff's Motion for Preliminary Injunction at 10-13, City of Chicago v. Sessions, No. 1:17-cv-05720 (N.D. Ill. Aug. 10, 2017) (citing 42 U.S.C. § 3752(a), subsequently reclassified as 34 U.S.C. § 10153(a)).

certify compliance with "all other applicable Federal laws,"[203] Chicago contended that conditioning the receipt of the grant on state and local compliance with Section 1373 is a new condition nevertheless.[204] This is so because, Chicago asserted, Section 1373 is not an "applicable" law as intended by the JAG statute; rather, Chicago argued that the word "applicable" necessarily narrows the phrase from one that includes the entire body of federal law, to one that includes a subset of laws that "make[s] clear to grant recipients that their receipt of money is conditioned on compliance."[205] In Chicago's view, the correct set of "applicable" laws is "the specialized body of statutes that govern federal grantmaking."[206]

Second, Chicago argued that the notice and access conditions violate the Constitution's separation-of-power principles because the DOJ—an executive branch agency—unlawfully exercised the spending authority exclusively granted to the legislative branch.[207] Third, Chicago asserted that, even if the DOJ had been given the discretion to condition grant eligibility, the notice and access conditions exceeded constitutional spending authority.[208] According to Chicago, the new conditions (1) are not germane to the federal interest in the Byrne JAG funds Chicago receives,[209] and (2) by requiring grant recipients to provide immigration authorities with 48 hours' notice before releasing an alien in custody, would induce Chicago to engage in activities that violate the Fourth Amendment because, in practice, Chicago would have to hold detainees longer than constitutionally permitted.[210] Finally, Chicago alleged that Section 1373,

---

[203] 34 U.S.C. § 10153(a)(5)(D).

[204] Memorandum of Law in Support of Plaintiff's Motion for Preliminary Injunction at 19, City of Chicago v. Sessions, No. 1:17-cv-05720 (N.D. Ill. Aug. 10, 2017).

[205] *Id.*

[206] *Id.*

[207] *Id.* at 17-18.

[208] Id. at 13-17. For more information on the Spending Clause, see CRS Report R44797, *The Federal Government's Authority to Impose Conditions on Grant Funds*, by Brian T. Yeh.

[209] Memorandum of Law in Support of Plaintiff's Motion for Preliminary Injunction at 13-14, City of Chicago v. Sessions, No. 1:17-cv-05720 (N.D. Ill. Aug. 10, 2017). In particular, Chicago asserted that "the sweeping tools for federal immigration enforcement imposed by the new conditions are not reasonably relevant to the objectives of the Byrne JAG program." *Id.* at 14.

[210] *Id.* at 14-17. For instance, Chicago asserted that "[a] warrantless arrest initially reasonable for Fourth Amendment purposes becomes unreasonable once the 'mission' that occasioned the original seizure is complete." *Id.* at 16 (citing Illinois v. Caballes, 543 U.S. 405, 407

on its face, violates the Tenth Amendment, and thus the DOJ cannot condition the receipt of federal funds on state and local compliance with it.[211]

The district court initially granted a nationwide, preliminary injunction concerning the notice and access conditions.[212] The Seventh Circuit upheld this ruling on interlocutory appeal[213] but stayed its nationwide effect,[214] making the injunction applicable to only Chicago.[215] Before the district court made its final ruling, the Supreme Court issued *Murphy*, prompting the court to reconsider its earlier conclusion that the compliance condition was lawful.[216] Ultimately, the court issued a nationwide, permanent injunction, holding that Section 1373 is unconstitutional on its face and blocking the enforcement of all three Byrne JAG conditions.[217] However, because the en banc Seventh Circuit previously had stayed the nationwide effect of the preliminary injunction, the district court stayed the nationwide effect of the permanent injunction, pending appeal, in deference to the Seventh Circuit's earlier order.[218]

Turning to the merits of the district court's order, the court first concluded that Section 1373 violates the anti-commandeering doctrine.[219] The court recounted that in *Murphy,* the Supreme Court held that, under the anti-commandeering doctrine, "Congress cannot issue direct orders to state legislatures" through a federal law that compels state action or that prohibits state action.[220] Thus, because Section 1373 *prohibits* state

---

(2005)). Chicago declared that those subject to a warrantless arrest are usually released from custody within 24 hours. *Id*. at 15. Accordingly, Chicago argued that holding warrantless arrestees longer than necessary to complete the "mission" of the original arrest to allow DHS to investigate unrelated immigration violations would violate the arrestee's Fourth Amendment rights. *Id*. at 15-16.

[211] *Id*. at 20-21. Chicago argued that "Section 1373 is particularly problematic because it prohibits state and local governments from engaging in a core aspect of governing: controlling the actions of their employees." *Id*. at 20.

[212] City of Chicago v. Sessions [City of Chicago I], 264 F. Supp. 3d 933 (N.D. Ill. 2017).

[213] City of Chicago v. Sessions [City of Chicago II], 888 F.3d 272 (7th Cir. 2018).

[214] City of Chicago v. Sessions, No. 17-2991, 2018 WL 4268817 (7th Cir. June 4, 2018).

[215] City of Chicago v. Sessions [City of Chicago III], 321 F. Supp. 3d 855, 880 (N.D. Ill. 2018).

[216] *Id*. at 866-67.

[217] *Id*. at 882.

[218] *Id*. at 881-82.

[219] *Id*. at 872.

[220] *Id*. at 867 (quoting Murphy v. NCAA, 138 S. Ct. 1461, 1478 (2018)).

policymakers from forbidding its employees to share immigration-status information with immigration authorities, the court concluded that this federal prohibition on state action runs afoul of the anticommandeering doctrine.[221] The court further rejected the government's request to carve out an exception to the anti-commandeering doctrine for laws requiring states to share information with the federal government "in the face of clear guidance from *Murphy*" and without the Supreme Court ever creating such an exception.[222] Next, the district court concluded that the notice, access, and compliance conditions were imposed without statutory authority and thus unlawful.[223] The court's conclusion that Section 1373 is unconstitutional doomed the compliance condition. The Byrne JAG statute requires compliance with "all other applicable Federal laws."[224] But, "[a]s an unconstitutional law," the court explained, "Section 1373 automatically drops out of the possible pool of 'applicable Federal laws.'"[225]

For the notice and access conditions, the court principally relied on the Seventh Circuit's reasoning in its order affirming the preliminary injunction, adding that "the Attorney General ha[d] not mustered any other convincing argument in support of greater statutory authority" and that "nothing ha[d] shaken this Court from the opinion it expressed at the preliminary injunction stage."[226] For instance, the Seventh Circuit had rejected the government's contention that the conditions are authorized by 34 U.S.C. § 10102(a)(6), which sets forth the duties and functions of the *Assistant* Attorney General (AAG) in running the Office of Justice Programs, which administers the Byrne JAG program.[227] The government had pointed to the statutory text granting the AAG the authority to exercise "powers and functions as may be vested in the Assistant Attorney General

---

[221] *Id*. at 869. The court further described Section 1373 as a "federally-imposed restructuring of power within state government" because, according to the court, it "redistributes local decision-making power by stripping it from local policymakers and installing it instead in line-level employees who may decide whether or not to communicate with [immigration authorities]." *Id*. at 870.

[222] *Id*. at 871-72.

[223] *Id*. at 873-76.

[224] 34 U.S.C. § 10153(a)(5)(D).

[225] *City of Chicago III*, 321 F. Supp. 3d at 875.

[226] *Id*. at 874.

[227] City of Chicago v. Sessions, 888 F.3d 272, 284-85 (7th Cir. 2018).

262   *Sarah Herman Peck*

pursuant to this chapter or by delegation of the Attorney General, including placing special conditions on all grants, and determining priority purposes for formula grants."[228] But, according to the Seventh Circuit, "[t]he inescapable problem here is that the Attorney General does not even claim that the power exercised here is authorized anywhere in the chapter, nor that the Attorney General possesses that authority and therefore can delegate it to the Assistant Attorney General."[229]

City of Evanston v. Sessions

The City of Evanston, Illinois (City), and the United States Conference of Mayors (Conference),[230] together, brought a lawsuit that mirrored Chicago's and requested preliminary injunctive relief.[231] The case was assigned to the same district judge who had presided over Chicago's lawsuit.[232] For that reason, when considering whether the plaintiffs were likely to succeed on the merits of their claims, the district court relied on its earlier opinions and those of the Seventh Circuit.[233] The district judge observed that, "though the plaintiffs at bar have changed, the legislation proscribing which conditions the Attorney General may attach has not."[234] Accordingly, because the Seventh Circuit described as "untenable" the government's arguments for its statutory authority to impose the Byrne JAG conditions, the district court concluded that the City and Conference were likely to prevail.[235] Consequently, the district court enjoined the government from enforcing the conditions against the plaintiffs.[236]

---

[228] City of Chicago II, 888 F.3d 272, 284 (7th Cir. 2018) (emphasis in original omitted) (quoting 34 U.S.C. § 10102(a)(6)).

[229] *Id.* at 285.

[230] The United States Conference of Mayors is "a non-partisan organization of cities with populations of 30,000 or more, with each city being represented by its mayor. *See* The U.S. Conference of Mayors, *About the Conference*, https://www.usmayors.org/the-conference/about/ (last visited Jan. 11, 2019)

[231] Order at 1-2, City of Evanston & the U.S. Conference of Mayors v. Sessions, 1:18-cv-04853 (N.D. Ill. Aug. 9, 2018).

[232] *Id.* at 2.

[233] *Id.* at 8.

[234] *Id.*

[235] *Id.*

[236] *Id.* at 1. The district court initially stayed the application of the preliminary injunction as it applied to the Conference. *Id.* at 11-12. The court reasoned that "[e]ven in its most limited form, any injunction issued in their favor will have the effects throughout the country and

"Sanctuary" Jurisdictions   263

City of Philadelphia v. Sessions

The City of Philadelphia, Pennsylvania, also sued to stop the Attorney General from imposing the new Byrne JAG conditions.[237] Like Chicago, Philadelphia argued that the DOJ lacked statutory authority to impose the new conditions, violated constitutional principles of separation of powers, violated the Spending Clause, and unconstitutionally conscripted the states into federal immigration enforcement.[238] Philadelphia also argued that the conditions were arbitrarily and capriciously imposed in violation of the APA.[239]

Initially, the district court found that all three of the conditions were unlawfully imposed and preliminarily blocked their enforcement against Philadelphia.[240] Then, after a bench trial, the court permanently enjoined the DOJ from enforcing against Philadelphia the three new Byrne JAG conditions.[241] The district court concluded that the Byrne JAG Statute contained no explicit authority for the notice and access conditions.[242] The court further held that the Justice Department's decision to impose all three

---

certainly far beyond the border of the Seventh Circuit, which, the court continued, "engenders many of the same concerns that agitated against entering a nationwide injunction in the *Chicago* case." *Id.* at 9-10. The Conference then filed an emergency motion with the Seventh Circuit asking it to lift the stay of injunctive relief. Emergency Motion, U.S. Conference of Mayors v. Sessions, 18-2734 (7th Cir. Aug. 10, 2018). The Seventh Circuit granted the motion and lifted the stay. Order at 2, U.S. Conference of Mayors v. Sessions, 18-2734 (7th Cir. Aug. 29, 2018). The Seventh Circuit reasoned that, unlike in the Chicago case, applying the injunction to the Conference in this case would be appropriate because the injunction would still be "limited to the parties actually before the court who have demonstrated a right to relief." *Id.*

[237] Complaint, City of Philadelphia v. Sessions, 2:17-cv-03894-MMB (E.D. Pa. Aug. 30, 2017).

[238] Amended Complaint at 43-44, City of Philadelphia v. Sessions, 2:17-cv-03894-MMB (E.D. Pa. Jan. 8, 2018).

[239] Complaint at 40, City of Philadelphia v. Sessions, 2:17-cv-03894-MMB (E.D. Pa. Aug. 30, 2017).

[240] Memorandum Re: Motion for Preliminary Injunction, at 52-58, 126-28, City of Philadelphia v. Sessions, 2:17-cv03894-MMB (E.D. Pa. Nov. 15, 2017).

[241] City of Philadelphia v. Sessions [City of Philadelphia II], 309 F. Supp. 3d 289, 296 (E.D. Pa. 2018).

[242] In holding that the notice and access conditions were imposed without statutory authority, the district court relied on its reasoning for granting a preliminary injunction. *Id.* at 321 ("Because the DOJ has presented no argument, beyond those previously considered by the Court at the Preliminary Injunction stage, which dictates a different result, the Court reaches the same result now: the Access and Notice Conditions exceed the authority delegated by Congress in 34 U.S.C. § 10102(a)(6).").

264   *Sarah Herman Peck*

conditions was arbitrary and capricious in violation of the APA.[243] The court reasoned that the DOJ did not adequately justify imposing the new conditions.[244] For instance, the court found that, before imposing the certification condition, the government had not "assess[ed] the benefits or drawbacks of imposing a condition, but instead merely assessed whether jurisdictions would be compliant were such a condition imposed."[245] Finally, the district court in Philadelphia concluded that *Murphy* mandates holding Section 1373 unconstitutional.[246]

The Third Circuit affirmed the district court's ruling but on narrower grounds: The court held that the conditions were imposed without statutory authority and thus are unlawful.[247] The circuit court first concluded that the JAG statute did not authorize any of the challenged conditions. In support of the notice and access conditions, the government pointed to two provisions of the statute requiring the Attorney General to direct grant applicants (1) to report "data, records, and information (programmatic and financial)" that he may "reasonably require," and (2) to certify that "there

---

[243] *Id.* at 323-25. In so holding, the court principally relied on its analysis in its preliminary injunction order. *Id* at 323 ("Given the nearly perfect overlap between the items considered at the two stages, it should come as no surprise to the litigants that the Court's opinion at the Summary Judgment stage closely aligns with its opinion from the Preliminary Injunction stage, as to the arbitrary and capricious nature of the Challenged Conditions. There is no need to fully reproduce the Court's prior opinion on this point, which is extensively discussed in 280 F.Supp.3d at 619-625.").

[244] City of Philadelphia v. Sessions [City of Philadelphia I], 280 F. Supp. 3d 579, 621, 625 (E.D. Pa. 2017).

[245] *Id.* at 624.

[246] City of Philadelphia II, 309 F. Supp. 3d 289, 329-31 (E.D. Pa. 2018). The district court here further concluded that the certification condition, *itself*, is unconstitutional because it requires compliance with an unconstitutional statute. *Id.* at 329. The court did not explain the constitutional underpinnings for this conclusion (or provide supporting case law), but contended that Congress cannot "pass blatantly unconstitutional statutes—including statutes already struck down as unconstitutional by court—but essentially require state and localities to adhere to those statutes by tying a 'certification' of compliance" with that statute to federal grants. *Id.* The veracity of this conclusion is unclear, given that, had the Byrne JAG statute given the DOJ discretion to add substantive conditions to the receipt of federal funds, the Spending Clause likely would have permitted the DOJ to independently require recipients to share immigration-related information with federal authorities. *See* NFIB v. Sebelius, 657 U.S. 519, 536 (2012) ("[I]n exercising its spending power, Congress may offer funds to the States, and may condition those offers on compliance with specified conditions," which "may well induce the state to adopt policies that the federal Government itself could not impose").

[247] City of Philadelphia v. Attorney General of the U.S. [City of Philadelphia III], 916 F.3d 276, 279 (3d Cir. 2019).

has been appropriate coordination with affected agencies."[248] In the government's view, "information" the Attorney General may "reasonably require" includes notification of an alien's release from custody from law-enforcement and corrections programs funded by the JAG grant.[249] But the court disagreed, explaining that JAG statute explicitly limits information to programmatic and financial information, meaning "information regarding the handling of federal funds and the programs to which those funds are directed" and not "priorities unrelated to the grant program."[250]

The court also rejected the government's argument that the coordination provision authorizes access to aliens in Philadelphia's custody because that would amount to "appropriate coordination" with immigration authorities affected by those same JAG-funded law-enforcement and corrections programs.[251] Because the statute refers to instances where "there *has been*" coordination, which the court understood to reference past coordination, the court concluded that the statutory language "does not serve as a basis to impose an *ongoing* requirement to coordinate."[252] As for the lawfulness of the compliance condition, the government invoked another JAG statute provision, this one requiring applicants to certify compliance with "all other applicable Federal laws."[253] The government contended that Section 1373 is an applicable federal law. The court rejected the government's expansive view of the term, however. The court reasoned, for instance, that if the Attorney General could condition funds based on compliance with any law in the *U.S. Code*, this practice would essentially turn the JAG formula grant—which is awarded to a jurisdiction through a formula that considers only population and violent crime statistics—into a discretionary grant.[254]

Next, the court rejected the government's other asserted source of statutory authority for imposing the conditions: the provision establishing

---

[248] *Id.* at 285 (quoting 34 U.S.C. § 10153(a)(4), (a)(5)(C) (emphasis added)).

[249] Brief for Appellant at 34, City of Philadelphia III, 916 F.3d 276 (3d Cir. 2019).

[250] *City of Philadelphia III*, 916 F.3d at 285.

[251] Brief for Appellant at 34, City of Philadelphia III, 916 F.3d 276 (3d Cir. 2019); *City of Philadelphia III*, 916 F.3d at 285.

[252] *City of Philadelphia III*, 916 F.3d at 285.

[253] *Id.* at 288.

[254] *Id.* at 290.

the duties and functions of the AAG in 34 U.S.C. § 10102.[255] This statute directs the AAG to "exercise such other powers and functions as may be vested in the [AAG] pursuant to this chapter or by delegation of the Attorney General, including placing special conditions on all grants."[256] The court emphasized, however, that this provision authorizes the AAG to place conditions on grants *only if* that power has been vested by Title 34 of the *U.S. Code* or delegated by the Attorney General, and neither of those predicates had occurred.[257] All told, based on the sole ground that the Attorney General lacked statutory authority to impose the notice, access, and compliance conditions, the Third Circuit affirmed the district court's order enjoining those conditions as applied to Philadelphia, and declined to address Philadelphia's additional arguments.[258]

City & Cty. of San Francisco v. Sessions

In separate lawsuits considered together, the State of California and the City and County of San Francisco sued the Justice Department seeking to block the three new Byrne JAG conditions.[259] The California plaintiffs argued that the notice and access conditions were imposed without statutory authority and, thus, violate the separation of powers, invoking the conclusions reached by the district courts who had enjoined those conditions.[260] The plaintiffs further argued that, post-*Murphy*, Section 1373 is constitutionally unenforceable against the states.[261] They contended that Section 1373 "dictates what a state legislature may and may not do," and *Murphy* forecloses Congress's ability to do that.[262]

The district court concluded that the Byrne JAG conditions violate the separation of powers and that Section 1373 is unconstitutional, declaring that he is "[i]n agreement with every court that has looked at these

---

[255] *Id.* at 287-88.

[256] 34 U.S.C. § 10102(a)(6).

[257] *City of Philadelphia III*, 916 F.3d at 257.

[258] *Id.* at 291.

[259] City & Cty. of San Francisco v. Sessions, 349 F. Supp. 3d 924, 934 (N.D. Cal. 2018).

[260] California's Motion for Summary Judgment at 11-14, Becerra v. Sessions, 17-cv-04701 (N.D. Cal. July 9, 2018).

[261] *Id.* at 19-20.

[262] California's Motion for Summary Judgment at 19, Becerra v. Sessions, 17-cv-04701 (N.D. Cal. July 9, 2018) (quoting Murphy v. NCAA, 138 S. Ct. 1461, 1478 (2018)).

issues."[263] And "follow[ing] the lead of the district court in *City of Chicago*," the district judge entered a nationwide injunction, staying the nationwide aspect until the Ninth Circuit has an opportunity to review the order on appeal.[264] Like the district courts in Chicago and Philadelphia, the district court here concluded that the Byrne JAG statute does not authorize the Justice Department to impose the notice and access conditions, given the sparse, inapplicable discretion the statute delegates.[265] Without that delegated authority, the court continued, the Justice Department unlawfully exercised Congress's exclusive Spending Power and violated the separation of powers.[266] Next, the court held that Section 1373 violates principles of federalism.[267] The court explained that post-*Murphy*, "[t]here is no distinction for anti-commandeering purposes . . . between a federal law that affirmatively commands States to enact new laws and one that prohibits States from doing the same."[268] And even if the Supreme Court eventually were to carve out an exception for federally required information-sharing, the district court opined that Section 1373 impacts jurisdictions much more than "a ministerial information-sharing statute."[269] For example, the court found that Section 1373 "takes control over the State's ability to command its own law enforcement."[270]

States of New York v. Department of Justice

The States of New York, Connecticut, New Jersey, Rhode Island, Washington, Massachusetts, and Virginia and the City of New York (collectively, the "States and City") sued the DOJ, challenging the three new Byrne JAG conditions.[271] Like other jurisdictions, these plaintiffs contended that the conditions violate the separation of powers and the APA, and, further, that Section 1373 violates the anti-commandeering

---

[263] *City & Cty. of San Francisco*, 349 F. Supp. 3d at 934.
[264] *Id.*
[265] *Id.* at 945-47.
[266] *Id.* at 944.
[267] *Id.* at *949-53.
[268] *Id.* at *953.
[269] *Id.*
[270] *Id.*
[271] States of New York v. Dep't of Justice, 343 F.Supp.3d 213, 225 (S.D.N.Y. 2018).

268 *Sarah Herman Peck*

doctrine.[272] A district judge in the Southern District of New York enjoined the Justice Department from imposing the notice, access, and compliance conditions on the States and City.[273]

The court first concluded that the conditions were imposed without statutory authority and thus, as the APA directs, must be set aside.[274] Agreeing with the other courts, the district judge rejected the government's arguments that the statutory provision authorizing the Assistant Attorney General to exercise powers delegated by the Attorney General to impose grant conditions. Specifically, the government had contended that 34 U.S.C. § 10102(a)(6) authorizes the imposition of the conditions, and Department's compliance condition is authorized by the Byrne JAG statute's requirement, under 34 U.S.C. § 10153(a)(5)(D), to certify compliance with "all other applicable Federal laws."[275] Concerning § 10102(a)(6), the district court concluded that the Assistant Attorney General could not impose the conditions because the Attorney General had no statutory authority to do so, and thus had no authority to delegate.[276] As for § 10153(a)(5)(D), the court concluded that the term "all other *applicable* Federal laws" is ambiguous and thus violates the tenet that "if Congress intends to impose a condition on the grant of federal moneys, it must do so unambiguously."[277] Accordingly, the court viewed the language "'from the perspective of a state official who is engaged in the process of deciding whether the State should accept [the] funds and the obligations that go with those funds,' and 'must ask whether such a state official would clearly understand that one of the obligations of the Act is the [purported] obligation.'"[278] From that perspective, the court concluded that the applicable federal laws are limited to those applicable grant, given that the

---

[272] *See id.*

[273] *Id.* at 245.

[274] *Id.* at 227-232.

[275] *See id.* at 229-231 (quoting 34 U.S.C. § 10153(a)(5)(D)).

[276] *See id.* at 230-31.

[277] *See id.* at 231 (emphasis added) (quoting Pennhurst State Sch. & Hosp. v. Halderman, 451 U.S. 1, 17 (1981)).

[278] *Id.* (alteration in original) (quoting Arlington Cent. Sch. Dist. Bd. of Educ. v. Murphy, 548 U.S. 291, 296 (2006)).

rest of § 10153 concerns requirements for the application and grant itself.[279]

Additionally, the district court concluded that the conditions constitute arbitrary and capricious agency action in violation of the APA.[280] The court reasoned that, notwithstanding the government's evidence in support of the benefits of withholding Byrne JAG funds from jurisdictions that fail to comply with the three conditions, "[c]onspicuously absent" from the government's evidence "is any discussion of the negative impacts that may result from imposing the conditions, and the record is devoid of any analysis that the perceived benefits outweigh these drawbacks."[281]

Next, the district court concluded that Section 1373 violates the anti-commandeering doctrine and thus is unconstitutional.[282] The court acknowledged that the Second Circuit—whose opinions are binding precedent on the Southern District of New York—held that Section 1373 is constitutional in *City of New York v. United States*.[283] But the court concluded that the Second Circuit's earlier ruling "cannot survive the Supreme Court's decision in *Murphy*."[284] *City of New York*, the court explained, had relied on a distinction between affirmative commands, which were considered unconstitutional, and affirmative prohibitions, which the circuit court had considered permissible. But, the Second Circuit continued, the Supreme Court in *Murphy* described that distinction as "empty."[285] Because *Murphy* concluded that the anti-commandeering doctrine forbids the federal government from imposing a direct prohibition on state legislatures, the district court held that Section 1373—by dictating what a state legislature may not do—is unconstitutional.[286]

---

[279] *Id.*

[280] *Id.* at 239-41.

[281] *Id.* at 240.

[282] *Id.* at 233-38. Based on this conclusion, the court additionally opined that Section 1373 could not be an "applicable federal law" for the purposes of complying with Section 10153. *Id.* at 231.

[283] *Id.* at 233-34. For a discussion of *City of New York v. United States*, see *supra* Subsection "Related Litigation" under Section "Federal Measures to Counteract Sanctuary Policies."

[284] *States of New York*, 343 F.Supp.3d 213, 234.

[285] *Id.* (quoting *Murphy v. NCAA*, 138 S. Ct. 1461, 1478 (2018)).

[286] *Id.*

270   *Sarah Herman Peck*

The district court additionally held that the three Byrne JAG conditions violate the separation of powers.[287] Harking back to its earlier analysis of the Byrne JAG statute provisions, the court explained that when Congress delegated spending authority to the executive branch in the statute, it did not delegate the authority to impose the new conditions.[288] The Byrne JAG statute, the court continued, authorizes the distribution of funds "according to statutorily prescribed criteria" that the executive branch is powerless to disturb.[289]

City of Los Angeles v. Sessions

The City of Los Angeles, California, separately challenged the new conditions attached to the Byrne JAG program and the additional consideration factors for the COPS program.[290] Initially focusing on the COPS program, Los Angeles first asked the U.S. District Court for the Central District of California to enjoin the DOJ from implementing the new COPS considerations in any future grant solicitations, contending, among other things, that they were imposed without statutory authority, violate the Spending Clause, and are invalid under the APA.[291]

The district court agreed with Los Angeles and granted a permanent injunction.[292] The court first concluded that the DOJ lacked statutory authority to consider the degree to which applying jurisdictions cooperate with federal immigration enforcement when assessing applications.[293] The

---

[287] *Id.* at 238.

[288] *Id.*

[289] *Id.*

[290] Complaint, City of Los Angeles v. Sessions, 2:17-cv-07215-R-JC (C.D. Cal. Sept. 29, 2017).

[291] Memorandum in Support of Motion for Partial Summary Judgment, City of Los Angeles v. Sessions, 2:17-cv07215-R-JC (C.D. Cal. Nov. 21, 2017). Initially, Los Angeles had sought to preliminarily enjoin the DOJ from implementing the new considerations during the grant application cycle for the 2017 fiscal year. City of Los Angeles v. Sessions, 293 F. Supp. 3d 1087, 1093 (C.D. Cal. 2018). But less than two weeks later, the DOJ notified Los Angeles that it had already selected the recipients, that Los Angeles was not one of them, and that the City would not have received a grant even had it received the extra consideration for certifying that it provided the requested notice and access to federal immigration authorities. *Id.* at 1093-94. Los Angeles then withdrew its motion for preliminary relief and, instead, asked the district court to enjoin the DOJ from implementing the new consideration factors in future grant cycles. *Id.* at 1094.

[292] *City of Los Angeles*, 293 F. Supp. at 1095-1101.

[293] *Id.* at 1095-98.

court pointed to 34 U.S.C. § 10381(c)—the statute authorizing the COPS program for community-policing grants—which identifies when the DOJ "may give preferential consideration" to applicants, and explained that none of the scenarios listed apply to federal immigration enforcement.[294]

Next, the court concluded that the challenged COPS considerations violate the Spending Clause.[295] The federal government had contended that the challenged "considerations" on grant funding were not subject to the same Spending Clause requirements as grant "conditions" because compliance with the considerations was not required to receive the grant.[296] But the court found no meaningful distinction between grant "conditions" and the challenged "considerations," declaring that "compliance *is* required in order for applicants to compete on a level playing field."[297] Further, the court remarked, if the government's assertion were correct, "it would be simple for federal agencies to avert Spending Clause requirements by labeling all considerations 'plus factors.'"[298] And because the COPS *statute* does not identify as a factor for preferential treatment a jurisdiction's cooperation with federal immigration enforcement, the court concluded that Congress did not, as the Spending Clause requires, "unambiguously condition" the receipt of funds on the recipients' compliance with federal authorities.[299] "It is irrelevant" that the DOJ's COPS Office was forthcoming about the conditions because, the court added, it is Congress—not the agency—that "must be clear in its directives."[300] Additionally, the added considerations violate the Spending Clause because, the court concluded, they are not germane to the goals of the COPS program: "[C]ommunity policing is about developing partnerships between local authorities and the community," and, in the court's view,

---

[294] *Id.* at 1096-97 ("In the Court's view, subsection (c) does not plainly or even arguably authorize the Attorney General to give preferential treatment to competitors based on compliance with the Challenged Considerations.").

[295] *Id.* at 1098-99.

[296] *Id.* at 1098.

[297] *Id.* at 1098-99 (emphasis added) (noting that 80% of selected recipients complied with the added conditions).

[298] *Id.* at 1099.

[299] *Id.*

[300] *Id.*

272   *Sarah Herman Peck*

"there is no relationship between local police partnerships with federal authorities and *community* policing."[301]

Finally, the district court concluded that the added considerations are arbitrary and capricious in violation of the APA because the government put forth no evidence, nor did it argue, that its explanation for adding the considerations—that "'[c]ities and states that cooperate with federal law enforcement make all of us safer by helping remove dangerous criminals from our communities,' including by ending 'violent crime stemming from illegal immigration'"—was based on any findings or data.[302] Thus the court concluded that the government had no reasonable basis for adding the new conditions.[303]

Concerning the Byrne JAG notice and access conditions, the district court later entered a preliminary injunction blocking the government from enforcing those conditions against Los Angeles. In doing so, the court pointed to the text of the Byrne JAG statute, explaining that "[t]he authority explicitly granted to the Attorney General . . . is limited."[304] That limited authority, the court concluded, does not include requiring states or localities to assist in immigration enforcement.[305]

Justice Department Lawsuit Against California

On the other side of the coin, the Justice Department has sued California, seeking to invalidate three laws governing the state's regulation of private and public actors' involvement in immigration enforcement within its border.[306] The government contends that these laws "reflect a deliberate effort by California to obstruct the United States' enforcement of federal immigration law, to regulate private entities that seek to cooperate with federal authorities consistent with their obligations under federal law,

---

[301] *Id.*

[302] *Id.* at 1099-1100 (alteration in original).

[303] *Id.*

[304] Order Granting Plaintiff's Application for Preliminary Injunction at 2, City of Los Angeles v. Sessions, 2:17-cv07215 (C.D. Cal. Sept. 13, 2018).

[305] *Id.* at 3.

[306] Complaint, United States v. California, 2:18-cv-00490-JAM-KJN (E.D. Cal. Mar. 6, 2018).

"Sanctuary" Jurisdictions 273

and to impede consultation and communication between federal and state law enforcement officials," and, thus, violate the Supremacy Clause.[307] The government is challenging parts of the following three California laws: (1) The Immigrant Worker Protection Act, Assembly Bill 450 (AB 450); (2) Section 12 of Assembly Bill 103 (AB 103); and (3) the California Values Act, Section 3 of Senate Bill 54 (SB 54).[308] In particular, the federal government principally contends that these laws violate the Supremacy Clause in two ways. First, the DOJ argues that the state measures violate the doctrine of intergovernmental immunity—a doctrine that derives from the Supremacy Clause and provides that "a State may not regulate the United States directly or discriminate against the Federal Government or those with whom it deals."[309] Second, the government asserts that the California laws are preempted because they create an obstacle for the federal government's enforcement of certain immigration laws.[310]

The Challenged California Laws

The Immigrant Worker Protection Act (AB 450)

AB 450 imposes on public and private employers in California several requirements related to federal immigration enforcement actions taking place at the worksite.[311] First, AB 450 prohibits an employer from allowing an immigration enforcement officer to enter any nonpublic areas of a worksite, unless the officer has a judicial warrant or "as otherwise required by federal law."[312] Second, AB 450 bars employers from permitting immigration enforcement officers to access, review, or obtain employee records without a subpoena or judicial warrant, or "as otherwise required

---

[307] *Id.* at 2.

[308] *Id.*

[309] United States v. California, 314 F. Supp. 3d 1077, 1088 (E.D. Cal. 2018) (citing North Dakota v. United States, 495 U.S. 423, 435 (1990) (plurality op.)).

[310] Plaintiff's Motion for Preliminary Injunction & Memorandum of Law in Support at 9-18, United States v. California, No. 2:18-cv-00490-JAM-KJN, 2018 WL 1473199 (E.D. Cal. Mar. 6, 2018).

[311] A.B. 450, 2017-2018 Cal. State Assembly (Cal. 2017), https://leginfo.legislature.ca.gov/faces/billNavClient.xhtml?bill_id=201720180AB450.

[312] *Id.* § 1(a).

274   *Sarah Herman Peck*

by federal law" (together, the "consent" provisions).[313] Third, "[e]xcept as otherwise required by federal law," AB 450 requires employers to provide employees with written notice of any I-9 employment eligibility inspection[314] (or other employment record inspections) within 72 hours after receiving notice of the inspection (the "notice" provision).[315] Fourth, AB 450 prohibits an employer (or a person acting on the employer's behalf) from reverifying the employment eligibility of a current employee unless as required by 8 U.S.C. § 1324a(b)[316] or "as otherwise required by federal law" (the "reverification" provision).[317]

Section 12 of AB 103

Section 12 of AB 103—part of California's omnibus budget bill— requires, for the next 10 years, the California Attorney General (or a designee) to review and report on county, local, and private detention facilities that house aliens in immigration proceedings, including those housing minors on behalf of, or by contract with, the U.S. Office of Refugee Resettlement or ICE.[318] The review must include the conditions of confinement, standard of care, due process provided, and the circumstances surrounding the aliens' apprehension and transfer to the facility.[319]

California Values Act (Section 3 of SB 54)

SB 54 enacts the California Values Act, which regulates to California's participation in federal immigration enforcement.[320] As relevant here, the

---

[313] *Id.* § 2(a). However, this section of AB 450 does not apply to the federal I-9 Employment Eligibility Verification forms and other documents for which a notice of inspection has been provided. *Id.*

[314] All employers within the U.S. must complete an I-9 form for every person they hire—U.S. citizens and noncitizens alike—to verify the identity and employment authorization for each hired person. U.S. Citizenship & Immigration Servs., *I-9, Employment Eligibility Verification*, https://www.uscis.gov/i-9 (last visited Nov. 8, 2018).

[315] A.B. 450, § 4; Complaint, United States v. California, No. 2:18-cv-00490-JAM-KJN (E.D. Cal. Mar. 6, 2018).

[316] Section 1321a(b) lays out the process for verifying the employment eligibility for persons hired by agricultural employers or farm laborer contractors. 8 U.S.C. § 1324a(a)(1)(B), (b).

[317] A.B. 450, § 5.

[318] A.B. 103, § 12(a), 2017-2018 Cal. State Assembly (Cal. 2017), https://leginfo.legislature. ca.gov/faces/billTextClient.xhtml?bill_id=201720180AB103.

[319] A.B. 103 § 12(b)(1).

[320] S.B. 54, § 3, 2017-2018 Cal. Senate (Cal. 2017).

California Values Act generally prohibits law enforcement agencies from using agency money or personnel to investigate, interrogate, detain, detect, or arrest persons for the purpose of immigration enforcement, including

- inquiring into immigration status;
- detaining a person subject to a hold request;
- providing information about a person's release date;
- providing personal information such as a person's home or work address, unless it is publicly available;
- making or participating in arrests based on civil immigration warrants; or
- performing any functions of an immigration officer.[321]

The Act also prohibits California law enforcement agencies from placing their officers under the supervision of federal agencies or employing officers who are deputized as special federal officer for purposes of immigration enforcement.[322] Further, under the Act, California law enforcement agencies may not use immigration authorities as "interpreters" for law enforcement matters relating to persons in custody.[323] Nor may California law enforcement agencies transfer a person to immigration authorities unless authorized to do so by judicial warrant, a judicial probable cause determination, or otherwise in accordance with California law.[324] Additionally, subject to limited exception, the agencies may not contract with the federal government to use California law enforcement facilities to house federal detainees.[325]

However, the Act specifies that it does not prevent California law enforcement from enforcing violations of 8 U.S.C. § 1326, which makes it a criminal offense to unlawfully enter the United States after being denied admission to, or being removed from, the United States.[326] Nor does the

---

[321] *Id.*
[322] *Id.*
[323] *Id.*
[324] *Id.*
[325] *Id.*
[326] *Id.*

276 *Sarah Herman Peck*

Act prevent California law enforcement from responding to requests for information about a person's criminal history.[327] Further, the Act does not prevent California law enforcement from engaging in certain joint law enforcement task force activities.[328] Additionally, California law enforcement may still give immigration authorities access to interview an individual in custody, in compliance with California law, and to make inquiries related to determining whether a person is a potential crime or trafficking victim and thus eligible for certain visas.[329]

United States v. California

On March 6, 2018, the United States sued California, requesting an injunction to preliminarily block the three California laws described above.[330] In particular, the government contends that the contested California laws violate the Supremacy Clause.[331] The government asserts that the California laws "reflect a deliberate effort by California to obstruct the United States' enforcement of federal immigration law, to regulate private entities that seek to cooperate with federal authorities consistent with their obligations under federal law, and to impede consultation and communication between federal and state law enforcement officials."[332] Further, the United States contends that the California laws "have the purpose and effect of making it more difficult for federal immigration officers to carry out their responsibilities in California," and "[t]he Supremacy Clause does not allow California to obstruct the United States' ability to enforce laws that Congress has enacted or to take actions entrusted to it by the Constitution."[333] The district court granted the government's request, in part, concluding only that parts of California's Immigrant Worker Protection Act (AB 450), as applied to private

---

[327] S.B. 54 § 3.

[328] *Id.*

[329] *Id.*

[330] Complaint, United States v. California, No. 2:18-cv-00490-JAM-KJN (E.D. Cal. Mar. 6, 2018); Plaintiff's Motion for Preliminary Injunction & Memorandum of Law in Support, United States v. California, No. 2:18-cv-00490-JAMKJN, 2018 WL 1473199 (E.D. Cal. Mar. 6, 2018).

[331] Complaint at 16-17, No. 2:18-cv-00490-JAM-KJN (E.D. Cal. Mar. 6, 2018).

[332] *Id.* at 2.

[333] *Id.* at 3.

employers,[334] violates the Supremacy Clause.[335] The government appealed, arguing that the other challenged California provisions, too, likely are unconstitutional. But the Ninth Circuit sustained all but one of the district court's rulings, concluding that one subsection within Section 12 of AB 103 violates the doctrine of intergovernmental immunity.[336]

AB 450

The district court concluded that the United States was likely to succeed on its claim challenging AB 450's consent and reverification provisions. The court concluded that consent provision violates the doctrine of intergovernmental immunity because it imposes monetary penalties on employers for voluntarily consenting to immigration officers entering nonpublic areas of the worksite and to access employment records, and thus, the provision "impermissibly discriminates against those who choose to deal with the Federal Government."[337] Concerning the reverification provision, the court reasoned that the government was likely to succeed on the merits of its claim that the provision is preempted by IRCA. The court concluded that the reverification provision likely stands as an obstacle to enforcing IRCA's continuing obligation imposed on employers to avoid knowingly employing an unauthorized alien.[338]

But the court concluded that the government was unlikely to succeed on its claim that AB 450's notice provision violates the Supremacy Clause.[339] The court first concluded that this provision does not violate the intergovernmental immunity doctrine because, the court explained, it punishes employers for failing to communicate with its employees and not for choosing to deal with the federal government.[340] The Ninth Circuit agreed, adding that "intergovernmental immunity attaches only to state

---

[334] The government did not challenge AB 450 as applied to public employers. United States v. California, 314 F. Supp. 3d 1077, 1094 (E.D. Cal. 2018).

[335] *Id.* at 1086.

[336] United States v. California, —F.3d—, No. 18-16496, 2019 WL 1717075, at *2 (9th Cir. Apr. 18, 2019).

[337] United States v. California, 314 F. Supp. 3d 1077, 1096 (E.D. Cal. 2018).

[338] *Id.* at 1098.

[339] *Id.* at 1096-97.

[340] *Id.* at 1097.

laws that discriminate against the federal government *and burden it in some way*."[341] And the Ninth Circuit accepted California's contention that "[t]he mere fact that those notices" required by AB 450 "contain information about federal inspections does not convert them into a burden on those inspections."[342]

The district court also rejected the government's argument that the notice provision prevents an obstacle to enforcing IRCA's prohibition on employing unauthorized aliens because, the government asserted, if investigation targets are warned, investigations will be less effective.[343] But the court opined that IRCA imposes obligations and penalties on *employers*, not employees, and so the "target" of any investigation is the *employer*, not the employee.[344] Likewise, the Ninth Circuit concluded that AB 450's notice requirement does not impose "additional or contrary obligations that undermine or disrupt the activities of federal immigration authorities" in implementing IRCA.[345]

AB 103

The district court declined to preliminarily enjoin Section 12 of AB 103. The government had argued that California's "efforts to assess the process afforded to immigrant detainees" through the review and reporting requirements in AB 103, create an obstacle to administering the federal government's exclusive discretion in deciding whether and how to pursue an alien's removal.[346] The court disagreed, though, opining that the California Attorney General's review would not give the state a role in determining whether an alien should be detained or removed from the United States.[347] Rather, the court characterized the provision as one that

---

[341] United States v. California, —F.3d—, No. 18-16496, 2019 WL 1717075, at *8-9 (9th Cir. Apr. 18, 2019) (emphasis added).

[342] *Id.* at *8.

[343] *California,* 314 F. Supp. 3d at 1097; Plaintiff's Motion for Preliminary Injunction & Memorandum of Law in Support at 9-10, United States v. California, 18-cv-00490, 2018 WL 1473199 (E.D. Cal. Mar. 6, 2018).

[344] *California,* 314 F. Supp. 3d at 1097.

[345] United States v. California, —F.3d—, No. 18-16496, 2019 WL 1717075, at *9 (9th Cir. Apr. 18, 2019).

[346] *California,* 314 F. Supp. 3d at 1091.

[347] *Id.* at 1091.

harnesses power California's Attorney General lawfully possesses to investigate matters related to state law enforcement.[348]

Nor, the court concluded, would the government likely succeed on its claim Section 12 of AB 103 violates the doctrine of intergovernmental immunity.[349] The court recognized that the law imposes inspections only on facilities that contract with the federal government.[350] But the court opined that the burden imposed on the federal contractors is minimal, and the government had not shown that the burden imposed under AB 103 is higher than burdens imposed under independent California laws governing inspections of other detention facilities within the state.[351]

On appeal, however, the Ninth Circuit concluded that part of Section 12 of AB 103 (the requirement for the California Attorney General to review the circumstances surrounding detained aliens' apprehension and transfer to each facility) violates the doctrine of intergovernmental immunity.[352] The Ninth Circuit characterized the district court's ruling as creating a "de minimis exception" to the doctrine of intergovernmental immunity.[353] But the Ninth Circuit rejected this new exception, opining that "[a]ny economic burden that is discriminatorily imposed on the federal government is unlawful." [354] Still, the court decided that only the provision requiring state inspectors to examine the circumstances surrounding the immigration detainees' apprehension and transfer to the facility likely violates the doctrine of intergovernmental immunity.[355] In the Ninth Circuit's view, this "unique" requirement appeared distinct from any other inspection imposed under California law, and, thus, the Ninth Circuit concluded that the district court erred in finding that the review appears no more burdensome than other legally mandated inspections.[356]

---

[348] *Id.* at 1091-92.
[349] *Id.* at 1093.
[350] *Id.*
[351] *Id.*
[352] United States v. California, —F.3d—, No. 18-16496, 2019 WL 1717075, at *10 (9th Cir. Apr. 18, 2019).
[353] *Id.* at *11.
[354] *Id.*
[355] *Id.* at *12.
[356] *Id.*

SB 54

Finally, the district court rejected the government's argument that SB 54 acts as an obstacle to immigration enforcement and, thus, is preempted.[357] The government had asserted that SB 54's limitations on information sharing and transferring to federal custody certain alien inmates "impede immigration enforcement from fulfilling its responsibilities regarding detention and removal because officers cannot arrest an immigrant upon the immigrant's release from custody and have a more difficult time finding immigrants after the fact without access to address information."[358] The court opined, however, that "refusing to help is not the same as impeding."[359] A state's refusal to help with federal immigration enforcement will always make obtaining the federal objective more difficult than if the state voluntarily assists, but, the court explained, "[s]tanding aside does not equate to standing in the way."[360]

The Ninth Circuit upheld the district court's ruling.[361] First, the court concluded that SB 54 does not obstruct the government's implementation of the INA.[362] The court reasoned that the INA (with the exception of Section 1373) "provides state and localities the *option*, not the *requirement*, of assisting federal immigration authorities," and "SB 54 simply makes that choice for California law enforcement agencies."[363] Further, invoking the Supreme Court's ruling in *Murphy*, the Ninth Circuit opined that invalidating SB 54 under the principles of conflict preemption "would, in effect, 'dictate[] what a state legislature may and may not do,' because it would imply that a state's otherwise lawful decision *not* to assist federal authorities is made unlawful when it is codified as state law."[364] Nor does Section 1373 preempt the information-sharing provisions of SB 54 because, the court concluded, the state measure expressly permits the

---

[357] United States v. California, 314 F. Supp. 3d 1077, 1104 (E.D. Cal. 2018).

[358] *Id.* at 1104.

[359] *Id.*

[360] *Id.* at 1104-05.

[361] United States v. California, —F.3d—, No. 18-16496, 2019 WL 1717075, at *13-19 (9th Cir. Apr. 18, 2019).

[362] *Id.* at *13-17.

[363] *Id.* at *16.

[364] *Id.* (quoting Murphy v. NCAA, 138 S. Ct. 1461, 1478 (2018)).

type of information required by Section 1373, specifically, citizenship or information status.[365] Moreover, the Ninth Circuit, again relying on *Murphy*, concluded that anti-commandeering principles likely precluded a preemption challenge to the information-sharing provisions.[366] The court described the exception to the anti-commandeering doctrine for reporting requirements as existing only when the "Congress evenhandedly regulates an activity in which both States and private actors engage."[367] But here, Section 1373 regulates only state actors, and therefore anti-commandeering principles preclude the government from requiring California to exchange information with it.[368]

CONCLUSION

Ongoing lawsuits concerning sanctuary jurisdictions may offer clarity on some unsettled and cross-cutting issues involving immigration and federalism. The Tenth Amendment reserves for the states the "police power" to regulate and protect the health, safety, and welfare of the public,[369] and, in adopting sanctuary policies, jurisdictions have sometimes invoked public safety concerns as a justification for enacting those measures.[370] But the federal government's power to regulate immigration-related matters is substantial and exclusive,[371] and on occasion the exercise

---

[365] *Id.* at *17.

[366] *Id.*

[367] *Id.* (quoting *Murphy*, 138 S. Ct. at 1478).

[368] *Id.*

[369] *See* Ndioba Niang v. Carroll, 879 F.3d 870, 873-74 (8th Cir. 2018); Siena Corp. v. Mayor & City Council of Rockville, Md., 873 F.3d 456, 464 (4th Cir. 2017); Anaya v. Crossroads Managed Care Sys., Inc., 195 F.3d 584, 591 (10th Cir. 1999); Sinclair Refining Co. v. City of Chicago, 178 F.2d 214, 216 (7th Cir. 1949).

[370] For example, the California Values Act begins by declaring that "[a] relationship of trust between California's immigrant community and state and local agencies is central to *the public safety* of the people of California. S.B. 54 § 3, 2017-2018 Cal. Senate (Cal. 2017) (emphasis added).

[371] *See, e.g.*, Arizona v. United States, 567 U.S. 387, 394 (2012) ("The Government of the United States has broad, undoubted power over the subject of immigration and status of aliens."); Toll v. Moreno, 458 U.S. 1, 10 (1982) ("Our cases have long recognized the preeminent role of the Federal Government with respect to the regulation of aliens within our borders."); De Canas v. Bica, 424 U.S. 351, 354 (1976) ("Power to regulate immigration is

282   *Sarah Herman Peck*

of this power has been found to render unenforceable state or local initiatives that conflict with federal immigration enforcement priorities.[372] Additionally, Congress generally may condition the receipt of federal funds on compliance with specific conditions that achieve federal goals.[373] Still, the anti-commandeering doctrine restricts the federal government from compelling the states to administer or enforce a federal regulatory program,[374] like the immigration laws, whether through direct compulsion or prohibition, or indirectly, through monetary incentives that are unduly coercive.

With that background, the heart of the debate in the lawsuits challenging EO 13768 and its implementation has principally centered on what constitutionally permissible methods are available to the federal government to stop or deter state and local adoption of sanctuary policies, which the government views as hindering federal immigration enforcement objectives, and, on the flip side, whether and when state and local sanctuary policies do, in fact, undercut federal immigration enforcement efforts in a manner that contravenes the Supremacy Clause.

In *City & County of San Francisco v. Trump* and *County of Santa Clara v. Trump*, for example, the district court's ruling that enjoined Section 9(a) hinged, in part, on its conclusion that the executive branch lacked statutory authority from Congress to withhold and create new conditions for federal grants, and that purporting to withhold all federal grants from what it labeled as sanctuary jurisdictions was unconstitutionally coercive, given the sheer amount of money a sanctuary jurisdiction would stand to lose if it didn't dispense with its policies.[375]

---

unquestionably exclusively a federal power."); Hampton v. Mow Sun Wong, 426 U.S. 88, 95 (1976) ("Congress and the President have broad power over immigration and naturalization which the States do not possess.")

[372] *See Arizona*, 567 U.S. at 416 (holding the many provisions of an Arizona statute aimed at deterring the presence of aliens in the state who committed violations of federal immigration laws were preempted).

[373] *See* NFIB v. Sebelius, 567 U.S. 519, 579 (2012) ("Congress may attach appropriate conditions to federal . . . spending programs to preserve its control over the use of federal funds."); CRS Report R44797, *The Federal Government's Authority to Impose Conditions on Grant Funds*, by Brian T. Yeh.

[374] Printz v. United States, 521 U.S. 898, 935 (1997).

[375] *See supra* section *City & Cty. of San Francisco v. Trump and Cty. of Santa Clara v. Trump*.

Congress could step in to ratify Section 9(a), at least in part, using its spending power to incentivize states to cooperate with immigration enforcement, so long as it doesn't threaten to withhold an amount of money that could be deemed coercive. And in *City of Chicago v. Sessions* and *City of Philadelphia v. Sessions,* the district courts and one appellate court concluded that the executive branch lacked statutory authority to impose some of the spending conditions that the DOJ attached to the Byrne JAG program.[376] Likewise, Congress could amend the Byrne JAG statute to give the Attorney General, as it has done for other grant programs, the discretion to impose conditions on the receipt of the federal grant.

Moreover, since *Murphy,* the courts considering the challenges to Section 1373 have concluded that the statute is no longer constitutionally viable, given the Supreme Court's application of the anti-commandeering doctrine to a federal statute that prohibits states from enacting certain kinds of laws.[377] Accordingly, to achieve Section 1373's goals, Congress may consider using its power of the purse to incentivize states and localities to share immigration-related information with federal immigration authorities.

---

[376] *See supra* sections *City of Chicago v. Sessions* and *City of Philadelphia v. Sessions.*

[377] *See* Murphy v. NCAA, 138 S. Ct. 1461, 1478 (2018); City of Chicago v. Sessions, 321 F. Supp. 3d 855, 872 (N.D. Ill. 2018) (holding Section 1373 unconstitutional); City of Philadelphia v. Sessions, 309 F. Supp. 3d 289, 329-31 (E.D. Pa. 2018) (same); City & Cty. of San Francisco v. Sessions, Nos. 17-cv-04642-WHO & 17-cv-04701-WHO, 2018 WL 4859528, at *1 (N.D. Cal. Oct. 5, 2018) (same).

In: Key Congressional Reports for May 2019   ISBN: 978-1-53616-382-7
Editor: Piotr Meza   © 2019 Nova Science Publishers, Inc.

Chapter 6

THE H-2B VISA AND THE STATUTORY CAP: IN BRIEF (UPDATED)*

Andorra Bruno

ABSTRACT

The Immigration and Nationality Act (INA) of 1952, as amended, enumerates categories of foreign nationals, known as nonimmigrants, who are admitted to the United States for a temporary period of time and a specific purpose. One of these nonimmigrant visa categories— known as the H-2B visa—is for temporary nonagricultural workers.

The H-2B visa allows for the temporary admission of foreign workers to the United States to perform nonagricultural labor or services of a temporary nature if unemployed U.S. workers are not available. Common H-2B occupations include landscape laborer, housekeeper, and amusement park worker.

The H-2B program is administered by the U.S. Department of Homeland Security's (DHS's) U.S. Citizenship and Immigration Services (USCIS) and the U.S. Department of Labor's (DOL's) Employment and Training Administration. DOL's Wage and Hour Division also has

---

* This is an edited, reformatted and augmented version of Congressional Research Service, Publication No. R44306, dated May 14, 2019.

certain concurrent enforcement responsibilities. The H-2B program currently operates under regulations issued by DHS in 2008 on H-2B requirements, by DHS and DOL jointly in 2015 on H-2B employment, and by DHS and DOL jointly in 2015 on H-2B wages.

Bringing workers into the United States under the H-2B program is a multiagency process involving DOL, DHS, and the Department of State (DOS). A prospective H-2B employer must apply to DOL for labor certification. Approval of a labor certification application reflects a finding by DOL that there are not sufficient U.S. workers who are qualified and available to perform the work and that the employment of foreign workers will not adversely affect the wages and working conditions of U.S. workers who are similarly employed.

If granted labor certification, an employer can file a petition with DHS to bring in the approved number of H-2B workers. If the petition is approved, a foreign worker overseas who the employer wants to employ can go to a U.S. embassy or consulate to apply for an H-2B nonimmigrant visa from DOS. If the visa application is approved, the worker is issued a visa that he or she can use to apply for admission to the United States at a port of entry. H-2B workers can be accompanied by eligible spouses and children.

By law, the H-2B visa is subject to an annual numerical cap. Under the INA, the total number of individuals who may be issued H-2B visas or otherwise provided with H-2B nonimmigrant status in any fiscal year may not exceed 66,000. USCIS is responsible for implementing the H-2B cap, which it does at the petition receipt stage. Spouses and children accompanying H-2B workers are not counted against the H-2B cap. In addition, certain categories of H-2B workers are exempt from the cap. Among these categories are current H-2B workers who are seeking an extension of stay, change of employer, or change in the terms of their employment.

Employer demand for H-2B workers has varied over the years. In recent years, demand has exceeded supply, and special provisions have been enacted to make additional H-2B visas available. For FY2016, a temporary statutory provision exempted certain H-2B workers from the cap. It applied to H-2B workers who had been counted against the cap in any one of the three prior fiscal years and would be returning as H-2B workers in FY2016. For FY2017, FY2018, and FY2019, a different type of H-2B cap-related provision authorized DHS to issue additional H-2B visas (above the cap) subject to specified conditions.

INTRODUCTION

FY2019 is the fourth year in a row that Congress has enacted a special provision to allow for the issuance of H-2B visas beyond the annual statutory cap of 66,000 in response to high levels of demand for the visa. For FY2016, Congress exempted certain H-2B workers from the statutory cap. For the three past fiscal years, Congress has authorized the Department of Homeland Security (DHS) to make additional H-2B visas available subject to certain conditions. For FY2017 and FY2018, DHS used this authority to make an additional 15,000 H-2B visas available each year. For FY2019, DHS is making an additional 30,000 H-2B visas available.

H-2B NONAGRICULTURAL WORKER VISA

The Immigration and Nationality Act (INA) of 1952, as amended,[1] enumerates categories of aliens,[2] known as nonimmigrants, who are admitted to the United States for a temporary period of time and a specific purpose. Nonimmigrant visa categories are identified by letters and numbers, based on the sections of the INA that established them. Among the major nonimmigrant visa categories is the "H" category for temporary workers. Included in this category is the H-2B visa for temporary nonagricultural workers.[3]

The H-2B program allows for the temporary admission of foreign workers to the United States to perform nonagricultural labor or services of a temporary nature if unemployed U.S. workers are not available. H-2B workers perform a wide variety of jobs. Top H-2B occupations in recent years have included landscape laborer, groundskeeper, forest worker, housekeeper, and amusement park worker. By regulation, participation in

---

[1] Act of June 27, 1952, ch. 477, codified at 8 U.S.C. §1101 *et seq.* The INA is the basis of current immigration law.

[2] *Alien* is the term used in the INA to describe any person who is not a U.S. citizen or national.

[3] INA §101(a)(15)(H)(ii)(b), 8 U.S.C. §1101(a)(15)(H)(ii)(b).

288 *Andorra Bruno*

the H-2B program is limited to designated countries, and DHS publishes a list of eligible countries each year.[4]

Bringing workers into the United States under the H-2B program is a multiagency process involving the U.S. Department of Labor (DOL), DHS, and the Department of State (DOS). The program itself is administered by DHS's U.S. Citizenship and Immigration Services (USCIS) and DOL's Employment and Training Administration (ETA). DOL's Wage and Hour Division (WHD) also has certain concurrent enforcement responsibilities. The H-2B program currently operates under regulations issued by DHS in 2008 on H-2B requirements, DHS and DOL jointly in 2015 on H-2B employment, and DHS and DOL jointly in 2015 on H-2B wages.[5]

For work to qualify as temporary under the H-2B visa, the employer's need for the duties to be performed by the worker must "end in the near, definable future" and must be a one-time occurrence, a seasonal need, a peak load need, or an intermittent need.[6] The employer's need for workers generally must be for a period of one year or less, but in the case of a one-time occurrence, can be for up to three years.

In order to bring H-2B workers into the United States, an employer must first receive labor certification from DOL. An interim final rule on H-2B employment that was issued jointly by DHS and DOL in April 2015 establishes a new registration requirement as a preliminary step in the labor certification process; once it is implemented, prospective H-2B employers would demonstrate their temporary need to DOL through this registration process before submitting a labor certification application. (As of the date

---

[4] For 2019, nationals of 81 countries are eligible to participate in the H-2B program. For a list of these countries, see U.S. Department of Homeland Security, "Identification of Foreign Countries Whose Nationals Are Eligible To Participate in the H–2A and H–2B Nonimmigrant Worker Programs," 84 *Federal Register* 133, January 18, 2019.

[5] U.S. Department of Homeland Security, "Changes to Requirements Affecting H-2B Nonimmigrants and Their Employers," 73 *Federal Register* 78104, December 19, 2008; U.S. Department of Homeland Security and U.S. Department of Labor, Employment and Training Administration, "Temporary Non-Agricultural Employment of H–2B Aliens in the United States," 80 *Federal Register* 24042-24144, April 29, 2015 (hereinafter cited as the 2015 DHS- DOL rule on H-2B employment); U.S. Department of Homeland Security and U.S. Department of Labor, Employment and Training Administration, "Wage Methodology for the Temporary Non-Agricultural Employment H–2B Program," 80 *Federal Register* 24146-24190, April 29, 2015.

[6] 8 C.F.R. §214.2(h)(6)(ii)(B).

The H-2B Visa and the Statutory Cap: In Brief (Updated) 289

of this chapter, however, DOL continues to make determinations about temporary need during the processing of labor certification applications.).[7]

At the same time that the employer submits the labor certification application to DOL, the employer must submit a job order to the state workforce agency (SWA) serving the area of intended employment. The job order is used to recruit U.S. workers. The employer also must conduct its own recruitment.

In order to grant labor certification to an employer, DOL must determine that (1) there are not sufficient U.S. workers who are qualified and available to perform the work, and (2) the employment of foreign workers will not adversely affect the wages and working conditions of U.S. workers who are similarly employed. To prevent an adverse effect on U.S. workers, H-2B employers must offer and provide required wages and benefits to H-2B workers and workers in "corresponding employment."[8] H-2B employers must pay their workers the highest of the prevailing wage rate or the federal, state, or local minimum wage. They must provide a "three- fourths guarantee"; that is, they must guarantee to offer workers employment for at least three- fourths of the contract period.[9] H-2B employers also must pay worker visa fees and certain worker transportation costs. H-2B employers are not required to provide health insurance coverage.[10]

---

[7] According to the supplementary information to the 2015 rule, a future "announcement in the Federal Register ... will provide the public with notice of when DOL will initiate the registration process." 2015 DHS-DOL rule on H-2B employment, p. 24052.

[8] "Corresponding employment" is defined in regulation as "the employment of workers who are not H–2B workers by an employer that has a certified H–2B Application for Temporary Employment Certification when those workers are performing either substantially the same work included in the job order or substantially the same work performed by the H–2B workers," with exceptions for certain incumbent workers. 20 C.F.R. §655.5. Language included in DOL appropriations acts since FY2016 prohibits the use of funds to enforce this definition of corresponding employment. P.L. 114-113, Div. H, Title I, §113; P.L. 115-31, Div. H, Title I, §113; P.L. 115-141, Div. H, Title I, §113; P.L. 115-245, Div. B, Title I, §112.

[9] Language included in DOL appropriations acts since FY2016 prohibits the use of funds to enforce the three-fourths guarantee rule. P.L. 114-113, Div. H, Title I, §113; P.L. 115-31, Div. H, Title I, §113; P.L. 115-141, Div. H, Title I, §113; P.L. 115-245, Div. B, Title I, §112.

[10] H-2B workers, like nonimmigrants generally, are not eligible for federally funded public assistance, with the exception of Medicaid emergency services. See CRS Report RL33809, *Noncitizen Eligibility for Federal Public Assistance: Policy Overview*. Nonetheless, they

After receiving labor certification, a prospective H-2B employer can submit an application, known as a petition, to DHS to bring in foreign workers. If the foreign workers are already in the United States, the employer can request a change of status to H-2B status on the petition. In the typical case, however, the workers are abroad. If the petition is approved, they can visit a U.S. embassy or consulate to apply for H-2B nonimmigrant visas from DOS. If the visa applications are approved, the workers are issued visas that they can use to apply for admission to the United States at a port of entry. H-2B workers can be accompanied by eligible spouses and children, who are issued H-4 visas.

An alien's total period of stay as an H-2B worker may not exceed three consecutive years. An H-2B alien who has spent three years in the United States may not seek an extension of stay or be readmitted to the United States as an H-2B worker until he or she has been outside the country for at least three months.

The INA grants enforcement authority with respect to the H-2B program to DHS, but allows for the delegation of that authority to DOL.[11] DHS has delegated that authority to DOL, and now DOL's WHD has responsibility for enforcing compliance with the conditions of an H-2B petition and temporary labor certification.

Seafood Industry Staggered Entry Provision

As part of the labor certification process, prospective H-2B employers must accurately indicate the starting and ending dates of their period of need for H-2B workers. According to the supplementary information to the 2015 DHS-DOL interim final rule on H-2B employment: "An application with an accurate date of need will be more likely to attract qualified U.S. workers to fill those open positions, especially when the employer

---

may be eligible for coverage through a health insurance exchange. See archived CRS Report R43561, *Treatment of Noncitizens Under the Affordable Care Act.*

[11] INA §214(c)(14), 8 U.S.C. §1184(c)(14).

conducts recruitment closer to the actual date of need."[12] If within a season an employer has more than one date of need for workers to perform the same job, the employer must file a separate labor certification application for each date of need. The employer is not allowed to stagger the entry of H-2B workers based on one date of need.

There is an exception to this prohibition on the staggered entry of H-2B workers, however, that applies to employers in the seafood industry. First enacted as part of the Consolidated Appropriations Act, 2014,[13] and subsequently incorporated into the 2015 DHS-DOL interim final rule on H-2B employment,[14] this provision permits an employer with an approved H-2B petition to bring in the H-2B workers under that petition any time during the 120 days beginning on the employer's starting date of need. In order to bring in the workers between day 90 and day 120, though, the employer must conduct additional U.S. worker recruitment. This provision has been reenacted in DOL appropriations acts for each year from FY2015 through FY2019.[15]

NUMERICAL LIMITATIONS

The H-2B program is subject to an annual statutory numerical limit. Under the INA, as amended by the Immigration Act of 1990, the total number of aliens who may be issued H-2B visas or otherwise provided with H-2B nonimmigrant status in any fiscal year may not exceed 66,000.[16] Also, since FY2006 there has been a cap of 33,000 on the number of aliens subject to H-2B numerical limits who may enter the United States on an H-2B visa or be granted H-2B status during the first six months of a fiscal year.[17] This INA amendment, enacted as part of the REAL ID Act of 2005,

---

[12] 2015 DHS-DOL rule on H-2B employment, p. 24060.

[13] P.L. 113-76, Div. H, Title I, §113.

[14] See 20 C.F.R. §655.15(f).

[15] P.L. 113-235, Div. G, Title I, §108; P.L. 114-113, Div. H, Title I, §111; P.L. 115-31, Div. H, Title I, §111; P.L. 115-141, Div. H, Title I, §111; P.L. 115-245, Div. B, Title I, §110.

[16] INA §214(g)(1)(B), 8 U.S.C. §1184(g)(1)(B). The Immigration Act of 1990 is P.L. 101-649. Section 205(a) of that law established the H-2B cap of 66,000.

[17] INA §214(g)(10), 8 U.S.C. §1184(g)(10).

effectively divided the annual H-2B cap of 66,000 into two semiannual caps of 33,000, respectively covering work in the first and second halves of the fiscal year.[18]

Certain categories of H-2B workers are exempt from the cap, including the following:

- current H-2B workers seeking an extension of stay, change of employer, or change in the terms of employment;
- H-2B workers previously counted toward the cap in the same fiscal year;
- fish roe processors, fish roe technicians, and/or supervisors of fish roe processing;[19] and
- H-2B workers performing labor in the U.S. territories of the Commonwealth of the Northern Mariana Islands (CNMI) and/or Guam until December 31, 2029.

As noted, spouses and children who are accompanying H-2B workers are issued H-4 visas and, as such, are not counted against the H-2B cap.

Special H-2B Cap-Related Provisions

Legislation has been regularly introduced in Congress concerning the H-2B cap.[20] Several measures have been enacted since 2005 to provide for the issuance of H-2B visas, or the granting of H-2B status, beyond the statutory cap. The enacted provisions have been of two main types.

Returning Worker Exemption

The INA was amended during the 109th Congress to add a provision establishing a temporary exemption from the H-2B statutory cap for certain

---

[18] The REAL ID Act of 2005 is Division B of P.L. 109-13. The provision establishing the 33,000 semiannual cap is Div. B, Title IV, §405.

[19] P.L. 108-287, Title X, Chap. 4, §14006.

[20] H-2B cap-related bills introduced in the 116th Congress include H.R. 798 and S. 135.

The H-2B Visa and the Statutory Cap: In Brief (Updated)   293

H-2B returning workers. The provision, initially in effect for FY2005 and FY2006, exempted from the cap H-2B returning workers who had been counted against the cap in any one of the three prior fiscal years.[21] This H-2B returning worker provision was subsequently extended for FY2007,[22] and expired at the end of that fiscal year.[23] An H-2B returning worker exemption of the same type was reinstated for FY2016. It provided that an H-2B returning worker who had been counted against the statutory cap in FY2013, FY2014, or FY2015 would not be counted again in FY2016.[24] Multiple bills were introduced in the 115th Congress to enact temporary or permanent H-2B returning worker exemptions from the statutory cap.[25] At least one H-2B returning worker bill has been introduced in the 116th Congress as of the date of this chapter.[26]

Provision Authorizing Additional H-2B Visas

For FY2017 and FY2018, a different type of H-2B cap-related provision was enacted by the 115th Congress. For each of these years, provisions in year-end omnibus appropriations laws authorized DHS to make additional H-2B visas available beyond the statutory cap after consultation with DOL and "upon the determination that the needs of American businesses cannot be satisfied" with available U.S. workers. Under these provisions, the number of additional aliens who could receive H-2B visas each year was limited to "not more than the highest number of H–2B nonimmigrants who participated in the H–2B returning worker program in any fiscal year in which returning workers were exempt from such numerical limitation."[27]

The FY2019 Consolidated Appropriations Act includes a provision of the same type for FY2019. Using the same language as the FY2017 and

---

[21] P.L. 109-13, Div. B, Title IV, §402.

[22] P.L. 109-364, Div. A, Title X, §1074.

[23] For a discussion of legislative efforts to reenact an H-2B returning worker exemption in the 110th Congress, see archived CRS Report RL34204, *Immigration Legislation and Issues in the 110th Congress* (available to congressional clients upon request).

[24] P.L. 114-113, Div. F, Title V, §565.

[25] There were a variety of proposals. See, for example, H.R. 1941, H.R. 2004, H.R. 4207, S. 792, and S. 3125, as introduced in the 115th Congress.

[26] See H.R. 798, as introduced in the 116th Congress.

[27] P.L. 115-31, Div. F, Title V, §543; P.L. 115-141, Div. M, Title II, §205.

FY2018 provisions, the FY2019 provision authorizes DHS, after consultation with DOL and "upon the determination that the needs of American businesses cannot be satisfied" with available U.S. workers, to make additional H-2B visas available for FY2019 up to a maximum of "the highest number of H–2B nonimmigrants who participated in the H–2B returning worker program in any fiscal year in which returning workers were exempt from such numerical limitation."[28] As discussed below, the DHS-DOL rule implementing this provision limits the additional visas to H-2B returning workers.

FY2017 Provision

In July 2017, DHS and DOL jointly published a final rule to implement the FY2017 provision.[29] The rule temporarily amended DHS regulations on the H-2B visa to state that for FY2017, DHS "has authorized up to an additional 15,000 aliens who may receive H–2B nonimmigrant visas."[30] In the supplementary information to the rule, DHS explained that the statutory provision applied only to H-2B workers entering the United States on visas and not to aliens in the United States who were seeking a change of status to H-2B status.[31]

The statutory definition of the maximum authorized number (i.e., "the highest number of H–2B nonimmigrants who participated in the H–2B returning worker program in any fiscal year") can be interpreted in different ways, as DHS acknowledged in the supplementary information to the rule. However, the agency determined that 64,716 was the most appropriate maximum number of additional H-2B visas authorized under the special FY2017 provision, this being "the number of beneficiaries

---

[28] P.L. 116-6, Div. H, Title I, §105.
[29] U.S. Department of Homeland Security and U.S. Department of Labor, Employment and Training Administration, "Exercise of Time-Limited Authority To Increase the Fiscal Year 2017 Numerical Limitation for the H–2B Temporary Nonagricultural Worker Program," 82 *Federal Register* 32987, July 19, 2017.
[30] See 8 C.F.R. §214.2 (h)(6)(x)(A) (effective July 19, 2017, through September 30, 2017) in ibid. p. 32998.
[31] Ibid. p. 32989 (footnote 11).

The H-2B Visa and the Statutory Cap: In Brief (Updated)   295

covered by H–2B returning worker petitions that were approved for FY 2007."[32]

The supplementary information to the rule included the following explanation for limiting the FY2017 numerical increase to 15,000:

> Most recently, in FY 2016, 18,090 returning workers were approved for H–2B petitions, despite Congress having reauthorized the returning worker program with more than three- quarters of the fiscal year remaining. Of those 18,090 workers authorized for admission, 13,382 were admitted into the United States or otherwise acquired H–2B status [T]he Secretary, in consideration of the statute's reference to returning workers, determined that it would be appropriate to use these recent figures as a basis for the maximum numerical limitation under section 543. This rule therefore authorizes up to 15,000 additional H–2B visas (rounded up from 13,382) for FY 2017.[33]

In addition, in implementing the statutory provision, DHS decided to limit eligibility for the additional H-2B workers to certain U.S. businesses. Under the FY2017 rule, the prospective H- 2B employer must submit to DHS, along with the H-2B petition, a new attestation form

> evidencing that without the ability to employ all of the H–2B workers requested on the petition its business is likely to suffer irreparable harm (that is, permanent and severe financial loss).[34]

FY2018 Provision

In May 2018, DHS and DOL jointly published a final rule to implement the FY2018 H-2B cap- related provision.[35] The FY2018 rule, which is similar to the FY2017 rule, temporarily amended DHS H-2B

---

[32] Ibid. p. 32988 (footnote 4).

[33] Ibid. p. 32990.

[34] See 8 C.F.R. §214.2 (h)(6)(x)(B)(2) (effective July 19, 2017, through September 30, 2017) in ibid. p. 32998.

[35] U.S. Department of Homeland Security and U.S. Department of Labor, Employment and Training Administration, "Exercise of Time-Limited Authority To Increase the Fiscal Year 2018 Numerical Limitation for the H–2B Temporary Nonagricultural Worker Program," 83 *Federal Register* 24905, May 31, 2018.

296 *Andorra Bruno*

regulations to state that for FY2018, DHS had authorized the issuance of up to 15,000 additional H–2B visas.[36] In supplementary information to the FY2018 rule, DHS explained its decision to authorize up to 15,000 additional visas despite the fact that all 15,000 additional visas authorized in FY2017 were not used.

> Out of a maximum of 15,000 supplemental H–2B visas for FY 2017, a total of 12,294 beneficiaries were approved for H–2B classification [T]he Secretary has determined that it is appropriate to authorize 15,000 additional visas again, as employers will have a longer period in which to submit their petitions due to the earlier publication date of this rule, thereby allowing for the possibility of more petitions being filed this fiscal year than in FY 2017.[37]

The FY2018 rule also included the same language as the FY2017 rule requiring an employer petitioning for supplemental visas to submit an attestation along with the H-2B petition evidencing that without the ability to employ all the requested H–2B workers the employer's business would likely suffer irreparable harm.

FY2019 Provision

In May 2019, DHS and DOL jointly published a final rule to implement the FY2019 provision.[38] The FY2019 rule temporarily amends DHS H-2B regulations to state that for FY2019, DHS has authorized the issuance of up to 30,000 additional H–2B visas. As it did in the supplementary information to the FY2017 and FY2018 rules, DHS clarifies in the supplementary information to the FY2019 rule that the

---

[36] See temporary 8 C.F.R. §214.2 (h)(6)(x)(A) (effective May 31, 2018, through September 30, 2018) in ibid. p. 24917. In the supplementary information to the FY2018 rule, DHS explained that the statutory provision applied only to H-2B workers entering the United States on visas and not to aliens in the United States who were seeking a change of status to H-2B status. Ibid. p. 24908 (footnote 14).

[37] Ibid. p. 24908.

[38] U.S. Department of Homeland Security and U.S. Department of Labor, Employment and Training Administration, "Exercise of Time-Limited Authority To Increase the Fiscal Year 2019 Numerical Limitation for the H–2B Temporary Nonagricultural Worker Program," 84 *Federal Register* 20005, May 8, 2019.

FY2019 provision only authorizes DHS to increase the number of H-2B visas; it does not cover individuals in the United States who change to H-2B status. As a result, DHS states that the supplemental cap is limited to workers who obtain visas abroad and then seek admission to the United States.[39]

The supplementary information to the FY2019 rule, consistent with the supplementary information to the FY2017 and FY2018 rules, indicates that the most appropriate maximum number of additional H-2B visas authorized under the statutory provision is 64,716.[40] DHS explains its decision to allow 30,000 supplemental visas as follows:

> In setting the number of additional H–2B visas to be made available during FY 2019, DHS considered this number [i.e., 64,716], overall indications of increased need, and the time remaining in FY 2019, and determined that it would be appropriate to limit the supplemental cap to approximately half of the highest number for returning workers, or up to 30,000.[41]

Like its FY2017 and FY2018 predecessors, the FY2019 rule requires an employer petitioning for supplemental visas to submit an attestation along with the H-2B petition evidencing that without the ability to employ all the requested H–2B workers the employer's business would likely suffer irreparable harm.

In addition, the FY2019 rule imposes a limitation not applicable under the FY2017 and FY2018 rules. Under the FY2019 rule, an employer may request supplemental visas only for H-2B workers "who have been issued an H–2B visa or otherwise granted H–2B status in Fiscal Years 2016, 2017, or 2018."[42] DHS offers the following rationale for limiting the additional visas to H- 2B returning workers:

---

[39] See ibid. p. 20009 (footnote 17).

[40] The supplementary information to the FY2019 rule states, "The highest number of H–2B returning workers approved was 64,716 in FY2007." Ibid. p. 20009.

[41] Ibid. p. 20009.

[42] See 8 C.F.R. §214.2 (h)(6)(x)(B)(2)(*ii*)) (effective May 8, 2017, through September 30, 2019) in ibid. p. 20020. This language does not require the workers to have been counted against

298 *Andorra Bruno*

Such workers (i.e., those who recently participated in the H–2B program) have previously obtained H– 2B visas and therefore been vetted by DOS, would have departed the United States after their authorized period of stay as generally required by the terms of their nonimmigrant admission, and therefore may obtain their new visas through DOS and begin work more expeditiously.[43]

The supplementary information to the rule highlights the importance, in particular, of returning workers' proven "willingness to return home after they have completed their temporary labor or services or their period of authorized stay."[44] It states:

The returning workers condition therefore provides a basis to believe that H–2B workers under this cap increase will likely return home again after another temporary stay in the United States. That same basis does not exist for non-returning workers, not all of whom have a track record of returning home. Although the returning worker requirement limits the flexibility of employers, the requirement provides an important safeguard, which DHS deems paramount.[45]

Implementation of H-2B Numerical Limits

USCIS is responsible for implementing numerical limits on temporary worker visas (including the H-2B visa), which it does at the petition receipt stage. Under DHS regulations:

When calculating the numerical limitations ... USCIS will make numbers available to petitions in the order in which the petitions are filed. USCIS will make projections of the number of petitions necessary to achieve the numerical limit of approvals, taking into account historical data related to approvals, denials, revocations, and other relevant factors.

---

the H-2B cap in any of the three years, unlike the previous statutory returning worker provisions (see "Returning Worker Exemption"). See ibid. p. 20007 (footnote 11).

[43] Ibid. p. 20008.

[44] Ibid.

[45] Ibid.

The H-2B Visa and the Statutory Cap: In Brief (Updated)   299

USCIS will monitor the number of petitions (including the number of beneficiaries requested when necessary) received and will notify the public of the date that USCIS has received the necessary number of petitions (the "final receipt date") If the final receipt date is any of the first five business days on which petitions subject to the applicable numerical limit may be received (i.e., if the numerical limit is reached on any one of the first five business days that filings can be made), USCIS will randomly apply all of the numbers among the petitions received on any of those five business days.[46]

In one recent fiscal year, the final receipt date announced by USCIS ended up being too early. For FY2015, USCIS announced on April 2, 2015, that March 26, 2015, was the final receipt date for new H-2B petitions. The agency had accepted about 3,900 H-2B petitions for FY2015 through March 26, 2015, which it believed was sufficient to reach the annual 66,000 cap. In early June 2015, however, USCIS announced that it would reopen the H-2B cap for the second half of FY2015 and accept additional petitions for new H-2B workers. It offered the following public explanation:

> USCIS continues to work in collaboration with DOS to monitor the issuance of H-2B visas and has determined that as of June 5, 2015, DOS received fewer than the expected number of requests for H-2B visas. A recent analysis of DOS H-2B visa issuance and USCIS petition data reveals that the number of actual H-2B visas issued by DOS is substantially less than the number of H-2B beneficiaries seeking consular notification listed on cap- subject H-2B petitions approved by USCIS. In light of this new information, USCIS has determined that there are still available H-2B visa numbers remaining for the second half of the FY15 cap.[47]

---

[46] 8 C.F. R. §214.2(h)(8)(ii)(B). For a discussion of USCIS implementation of the H-2B cap over the years, see U.S. Department of Homeland Security, U.S. Citizenship and Immigration Services, *H-2B Usage and Recommendations*, Fiscal Year 2016 Report to Congress, July 22, 2016, https://www.dhs.gov/sites/default/files/publications/ U.S.%20Citizenship%20and %20Immigration%20Services%20-%20H-2B%20Usage%20and%20Recommendations.pdf.

[47] U.S. Department of Homeland Security, U.S. Citizenship and Immigration Services, "USCIS to Reopen H-2B Cap for the Second Half of Fiscal Year 2015," news alert, June 5, 2015, http://www.uscis.gov/news/alerts/uscis-reopen-h-2b-cap-second-half-fiscal-year-2015.

300 *Andorra Bruno*

Following a brief reopening, USCIS announced that June 11, 2015, was the final receipt date for new H-2B worker petitions for FY2015.

FY2018

Until FY2018, the final receipt date for H-2B petitions had never fallen within the first five days of filing and, thus, the random selection process (lottery) described in the regulatory provision in the preceding section had never been required.[48] As described below, that changed with petition filings by employers seeking to hire H-2B workers for the second half of FY2018, which began on April 1, 2018. DOL was also impacted by the high level of employer demand for H-2B workers for the second half of FY2018 since an employer must receive labor certification from DOL before filing an H-2B petition.

DOL Labor Certification Applications

In accordance with H-2B regulations, January 1, 2018, was the first date that employers could submit H-2B temporary labor certifications to DOL requesting a work start date of April 1, 2018. On January 1, 2018, DOL received about 4,498 applications requesting an April 1, 2018, start date; those applications covered 81,008 workers. In response, DOL announced a process change.

It indicated in a *Federal Register* notice that it would not begin releasing certified H–2B applications, which employers need in order to petition USCIS for H-2B workers (see "H-2B Nonagricultural Worker Visa"), until February 20, 2018, and on that date, it would issue such certified applications in order of receipt.[49] DOL offered the following explanation for adopting this procedure:

---

[48] By contrast, lotteries have been regularly held under the separate H-1B visa for professional specialty workers. For information about the H-1B visa, see CRS Report R43735, *Temporary Professional, Managerial, and Skilled Foreign Workers: Policy and Trends.*

[49] U.S. Department of Labor, Employment and Training Administration, "Labor Certification Process for the Temporary Employment of Aliens in Non-Agricultural Employment in the United States," 83 *Federal Register* 3189, January 23, 2018.

The H-2B Visa and the Statutory Cap: In Brief (Updated)   301

This process change will allow employers who filed promptly on January 1, 2018, sufficient time to meet regulatory requirements, including the recruitment and hiring of qualified and available U.S. workers, thus preserving the sequential order of filing that took place on January 1, 2018, to the extent possible.[50]

DHS Petitions

On March 1, 2018, USCIS announced that in the first five business days of accepting H-2B petitions for the second half of FY2018, it had received petitions requesting about 47,000 H-2B workers subject to the statutory cap. It further reported that it had conducted a lottery on February 28, 2018, to randomly select a sufficient number of these petitions to meet the statutory cap.[51]

As discussed, on May 31, 2018, USCIS published a final rule authorizing the issuance of up to 15,000 additional H–2B visas for FY2018. In the first five business days of accepting petitions under this supplemental cap, USCIS received petitions for more beneficiaries than the number of H-2B visas available. As a result, it conducted a second FY2018 H-2B lottery on June 7, 2018, to randomly select a sufficient number of petitions to meet the supplemental cap.[52]

FY2019

Employer demand for H-2B visas and associated temporary labor certifications for the second half of FY2019 reached new heights.

DOL Labor Certification Applications

January 1, 2019, was the first day that employers could file H-2B labor certification applications for the second half of FY2019. On January 2,

---

[50] Ibid. p. 3190.

[51] U.S. Department of Homeland Security, U.S. Citizenship and Immigration Services, "USCIS Completes Random Selection Process for H-2B Visa Cap for Second Half of FY 2018," news release, March 1, 2018, https://www.uscis.gov/news/news-releases/uscis-completes-random-selection-process-h-2b-visa-cap-second-half-fy- 2018-0.

[52] U.S. Department of Homeland Security, U.S. Citizenship and Immigration Services, "USCIS Completes Lottery for Temporary Increase in FY 2018 H-2B Cap," news alert, June 11, 2018, https://www.uscis.gov/news/alerts/uscis- completes-lottery-temporary-increase-fy-2018-h-2b-cap.

2019, DOL announced that due to high demand its iCERT online application filing system had "experienced a system disruption" on January 1, 2019, that prevented some employers from submitting their H-2B certification applications: "Within the first five minutes of opening the semi-annual H-2B certification process on January 1, 2019, the U.S. Department of Labor iCERT system had an unprecedented demand for H-2B certifications with more than 97,800 workers requested in pending applications for the 33,000 available visas."[53] When the system re-opened on January 7, 2019, it "handled the submission of approximately 4,749 H-2B applications covering more than 87,900 workers positions for an April 1, 2019, start date of work within the first one hour of operation."[54] This experience led DOL to announce additional process changes for FY2020, as described below.

DHS Petitions

On February 19, 2019, the first day of accepting H-2B petitions for the second half of FY2019, USCIS announced that it had received petitions for more H-2B workers than there were remaining H-2B numbers under the FY2019 cap. On February 21, 2019, USCIS conducted a lottery to randomly select a sufficient number of petitions to meet the cap.

FY2020

In February 2019, in light of its experience with H-2B submissions in January 2019 and the unanticipated "burdens" placed on "its electronic filing system, network infrastructure, and staff resources," DOL announced new H-2B temporary labor certification application processing changes for FY2020.[55] It indicated that beginning with H-2B certification applications

---

[53] U.S. Department of Labor, Employment and Training Administration, Office of Foreign Labor Certification, Announcements, "January 2, 2019. Important Announcement Regarding the Availability of the iCERT System for H- 2B Program Filings," available at https://www.foreignlaborcert.doleta.gov/.

[54] U.S. Department of Labor, Employment and Training Administration, Office of Foreign Labor Certification, Announcements, "January 7, 2019. OFLC Issues Status Update on the iCERT System," available at https://www.foreignlaborcert.doleta.gov/.

[55] U.S. Department of Labor, Employment and Training Administration, "Selection Procedures for Reviewing Applications Filed by Employers Seeking Temporary Employment of H-2B Foreign Workers in the United States," 84 *Federal Register* 7399, 7401, March 4, 2019.

for the first half of FY2020, it would randomly order and assign for processing all applications submitted within designated groups. The first group would consist of applications requesting the earliest start date of work (e.g., October 1, 2019, for the first half of FY2020) and filed during the first three calendar days of the filing period (which begins on July 3, 2019, for the first half of FY2020). DOL maintains that this new process "balances employers' interest in utilizing the H- 2B program with OFLC's [DOL's Office of Foreign Labor Certification's] interest in ensuring that access to its filing system is equitable and occurs with no user disruption."[56] DOL is seeking comments on these changes and plans for the new procedures to take effect on July 3, 2019.

Numbers Granted H-2B Status

In any year, most, but not all, foreign nationals who obtain H-2B status acquire that status through admission to the United States on H-2B visas. Those who obtain H-2B status but are not issued visas include H-2B workers who are admitted to the United States without visas (mostly Canadians) and individuals who change to H-2B status while in the United States. USCIS data are available on the latter group. These data show that between FY2009 and FY2017, the number of individuals who were approved for a change of status to H-2B status ranged from about 110 (in FY2017) to about 470 (in FY2010).[57]

H-2B Visa Issuances

Figure 1 provides data on H-2B visa issuances from FY1992 through FY2018. These data offer one way to measure the growth of the H-2B program over the years. As explained above, the visa application and

---

[56] Ibid. p. 7401-7402.

[57] U.S. Department of Homeland Security, U.S. Citizenship and Immigration Services, *Characteristics of H-2B Nonagricultural Temporary Workers* ..., FY2009-FY2016; U.S. Department of Homeland Security, U.S. Citizenship and Immigration Services, *H-2B Nonagricultural Temporary Worker Visa and Status* ..., FY2009-FY2017. Reports available from USCIS at https://www.uscis.gov/tools/reports-studies/reports-and-studies.

issuance process occurs after DOL has granted labor certification and DHS has approved the visa petition.

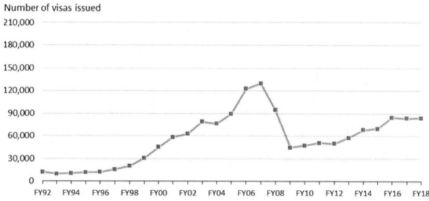

Source: CRS presentation of data from U.S. Department of State, Bureau of Consular Affairs.

Figure 1. H-2B Visas Issued, FY1992-FY2018.

As illustrated in Figure 1, the number of H-2B visas issued generally increased from FY1992 until FY2007, when H-2B visa issuances reached a highpoint of 129,547 (see the Appendix for yearly visa issuance data). H-2B visa issuances fell after FY2007 with the start of the economic recession, but, as shown in Figure 1, they have generally been increasing since FY2009.

In FY2005-FY2007 and FY2016-FY2018, as discussed, temporary provisions established exceptions to the statutory annual cap of 66,000. In some other years in which visa issuances surpassed 66,000, it seems reasonable to assume that the H-2B cap was exceeded given the magnitude of the numbers.[58]

---

[58] It should be noted, however, that for various reasons not all visas issued during a fiscal year necessarily count against that year's cap or, in some cases, any year's cap.

CONCLUSION

With employer demand for H-2B visas exceeding supply, H-2B admissions and the statutory cap are once again receiving attention from policymakers. While previous Congresses considered broad immigration reform bills that included proposals for new temporary worker programs to address any perceived shortfalls in the supply of foreign workers, any legislative efforts to address the numerical limitations on nonagricultural guest workers in the near term seem likely to be focused on the existing H-2B program.

APPENDIX. H-2B VISA ISSUANCES

Table A-1. Number of H-2B Visas Issued, FY1992-FY2018

Fiscal Year	H-2B Visas Issued
1992	12,552
1993	9,691
1994	10,400
1995	11,737
1996	12,200
1997	15,706
1998	20,192
1999	30,642
2000	45,037
2001	58,215
2002	62,591
2003	78,955
2004	76,169
2005	89,135
2006	122,541
2007	129,547
2008	94,304
2009	44,847
2010	47,403
2011	50,826
2012	50,009
2013	57,600

Table A-1. (Continued)

Fiscal Year	H-2B Visas Issued
2014	68,102
2015	69,684
2016	84,627
2017	83,600
2018	83,774

Source: CRS presentation of data from U.S. Department of State, Bureau of Consular Affairs.

INDEX

#

9/11, 79, 127
9/11 Commission, 127

A

access, xii, xv, 61, 108, 158, 179, 182, 207, 217, 222, 250, 252, 258, 259, 260, 261, 263, 264, 265, 266, 267, 268, 270, 272, 273, 276, 277, 280, 303
accessions, 205
accountability, 81, 86, 124, 137
accounting, xi, 29, 30, 72, 92, 98, 112
adequate housing, 196, 197
adjustment, 193, 194, 195, 196, 198, 199, 200
administrators, 28, 29, 60, 63
advancement, 53, 68
affirmative action, 77, 79
Afghanistan, xiii, 180, 181, 213, 214, 215, 216
age, 54, 65, 67, 112, 157, 198, 204, 209, 217

agencies, xi, xii, 11, 27, 39, 60, 66, 91, 92, 97, 98, 103, 109, 110, 130, 132, 133, 134, 135, 136, 139, 143, 144, 145, 146, 147, 149, 150, 151, 152, 153, 154, 227, 234, 241, 242, 244, 265, 271, 275, 280, 281
agency actions, 93
all-volunteer force, xii, 180
American public, x, 24, 26, 36
American Recovery and Reinvestment Act, 30, 35, 172
amusement park worker, xvi, 285, 287
appropriations, 9, 76, 110, 114, 119, 121, 123, 130, 166, 254, 289, 291, 293
Appropriations Act, 108, 123, 125, 170, 171, 172, 173, 174, 176, 217
armed forces, xii, 43, 179, 181, 184, 185, 186, 188, 205, 207, 208, 212, 213
arrest, 79, 240, 241, 259, 275, 280
assessment, x, 24, 27, 52, 133, 154
Attorney General, xv, 222, 248, 249, 250, 255, 258, 261, 262, 263, 264, 265, 266, 268, 271, 272, 274, 278, 279, 283
audit, xi, 53, 64, 92, 98, 112
authorities, xiv, xv, 188, 221, 222, 224, 226, 227, 228, 238, 240, 242, 243, 244, 245,

308 *Index*

246, 250, 251, 259, 261, 265, 270, 272, 275, 276, 278, 280, 283

awareness, x, 24, 26, 56, 160

B

balanced budget, 51, 164

ban, 166, 236

banking, 46

Basic Allowance for Housing (BAH), xiii, 180, 184, 185, 188, 189, 190, 191, 193, 195, 196, 197, 198, 211, 217

beneficiaries, 36, 294, 296, 299, 301

benefits, xii, xiii, 35, 36, 62, 66, 98, 101, 115, 132, 133, 134, 137, 144, 150, 154, 165, 179, 180, 181, 182, 183, 187, 192, 193, 207, 210, 215, 216, 217, 264, 269, 289

bonuses, 182, 193, 216

budget committee, ix, 5, 18, 163

Budget Committee, ix, 5, 18, 163

Bush, President George Walker, 79, 81, 106, 144

businesses, xi, 91, 130, 155, 293, 294, 295

C

canals, 44

cash, xii, xiii, 37, 43, 44, 45, 46, 48, 49, 179, 180, 181, 182, 183, 184, 185, 186, 192, 193, 207, 210

cash payments, xii, 179, 186

Catalog of Federal Domestic Assistance, 36, 38, 82

categorical grants, 27, 28, 30, 36, 40, 58, 59, 60, 61, 63, 64, 65, 67, 70, 72, 77, 78, 80, 82, 88

certification, xvi, xvii, 249, 250, 264, 286, 288, 289, 290, 300, 301, 302, 304

challenges, xv, 82, 84, 120, 148, 222, 225, 247, 253, 283

Chamber of Commerce, 131, 148, 156, 224, 232

Chicago, xv, 41, 45, 47, 48, 223, 253, 254, 258, 259, 260, 261, 262, 263, 267, 281, 283

Chief Justice, 43, 101

children, xvii, 53, 63, 65, 167, 189, 216, 217, 286, 290, 292

cities, 60, 159, 228, 238, 257, 258, 262

citizens, 47, 62, 105, 155, 165, 231, 235, 274

civil liability, xiv, 221, 225

civil rights, 40, 42, 47, 48, 51, 55, 56, 62, 74, 112, 157

civil service, 207, 209

Civil War, 41, 46, 47

civilian compensation, xiii, 180, 184, 207, 209, 211, 212

civilian employees, xiii, 181, 190

clients, 72, 102, 293

climate, 20

Clinton Administration, 157, 160

Clinton, President William Jefferson (, 156

coercion, 54, 233

collaboration, 54, 145, 299

colleges, 47, 48, 49

commerce, 43, 47, 48, 54, 108, 229

commercial, 46, 54, 187

commissaries, xii, 179, 182, 188, 193

committee chair term limits, vii, 4

committee markup meetings, viii, 4, 10

Committee on Education and Labor, viii, 4, 15, 16

Committee on Education and the Workforce, viii, 4, 15

Committee on Ethics, viii, 4, 10, 16, 17, 18

Committee on Financial Services, ix, 5, 19

Committee on Oversight and Government Reform, viii, 4, 11, 13, 148, 155

Committee on Oversight and Reform, viii, 4, 11, 12, 13, 14, 15

committee procedure, v, vii, 3, 5, 6

Committees on Appropriations, 119
Commonwealth of the Northern Mariana
  Islands, 292
communication, 273, 276
community, ix, 23, 25, 33, 57, 62, 64, 72,
  73, 79, 152, 155, 157, 251, 271, 281
community development, ix, 23, 25, 64, 70,
  71, 72, 79, 82, 84, 86
Community Oriented Policing Services
  (COPS), xv, 222, 226, 247, 249, 251,
  252, 253, 270, 271
compensation package, 183, 207
compliance, xv, 67, 94, 99, 110, 134, 142,
  144, 150, 154, 159, 168, 222, 235, 237,
  249, 250, 251, 255, 258, 259, 260, 261,
  264, 265, 266, 268, 271, 276, 282, 290
compulsion, 95, 101, 238, 282
conference, 7, 76, 116, 117, 118, 119, 121,
  125, 129, 168, 169, 262
Conference Report, 77, 168, 175, 176
congressional behavior, x, 24, 26
Congressional Budget Office, xi, 75, 91, 93,
  116, 148, 208, 209
congressional hearings, 104
congressional procedures, x, 24, 26, 51
consent, 121, 235, 274, 277
Consolidated Appropriations Act, 291, 293
Constitution, xiv, 6, 41, 43, 44, 45, 47, 53,
  222, 230, 231, 232, 233, 234, 236, 245,
  248, 253, 254, 258, 259, 276
constitutional principles, 226, 229, 263
construction, 44, 50, 52, 54, 55, 149, 189
consumer protection, 155, 157
consumers, xi, 92, 132, 146, 153
cooperation, 25, 68, 95, 225, 226, 228, 238,
  239, 244, 246, 247, 248, 257, 271
cooperative agreements, 39
cost effectiveness, 155
Court of Appeals, xv, 223, 236, 246
criminal activity, 242, 243
criminal justice system, 35
cultural norms, x, 24, 26, 41

D

danger, 192, 207, 214, 215
decentralization, 77, 78, 88
decoupling, 109, 110
defense budget, xiii, 180
deferred compensation, xii, 179, 181, 182,
  193, 207
delegates, viii, 4, 5, 7, 10, 13, 17, 18, 20, 21,
  267
democracy, 26
Democratic Party, 51, 88
demographic change, 40
Department of Defense (DOD), xiii, 172,
  180, 182, 189, 190, 191, 192, 196, 197,
  198, 211, 213, 214, 215, 216, 217
Department of Health and Human Services,
  141, 142
Department of Homeland Security, xvi, 83,
  127, 142, 174, 224, 248, 285, 287, 288,
  294, 295, 296, 299, 301, 303
Department of Justice, xv, 222, 227, 234,
  243, 247, 267
Department of Labor (DOL), viii, xvi, 4, 16,
  142, 285, 286, 288, 289, 290, 291, 293,
  294, 295, 296, 300, 301, 302, 304
depositions, viii, 4, 13, 14, 20
detainees, 259, 275, 278, 279
detention, xv, xvi, 222, 223, 224, 250, 252,
  258, 274, 279, 280
direct cost, xi, 75, 91, 93, 110, 113, 114,
  115, 119, 120, 130, 132, 136, 146, 153,
  166
directives, 114, 128, 155, 159, 233, 271
discrimination, xi, 55, 66, 67, 76, 92, 98,
  104, 112, 131, 149, 157
district courts, xv, 223, 253, 266, 267, 283
domestic affairs, x, 24, 26, 41, 42, 43, 44,
  47, 52, 53, 69
domestic policy, ix, 24, 43, 46, 47, 49, 51,
  53

310 *Index*

E

earnings, 188, 210

economic activity, 230, 231

economic interdependencies, x, 24, 26

education, viii, ix, xiii, 4, 15, 16, 23, 25, 30, 32, 33, 35, 39, 42, 44, 48, 50, 52, 57, 58, 61, 64, 67, 70, 72, 73, 80, 81, 83, 125, 145, 160, 169, 172, 173, 181, 204, 210

Edward Byrne Memorial Justice Assistance Grant (Byrne JAG), xv, 222, 223, 247, 248, 250, 251, 252, 253, 258, 259, 260, 261, 262, 263, 264, 266, 267, 268, 269, 270, 272, 283

election, 50, 55, 69, 81

electricity, 67, 157

emergency, xi, 9, 52, 80, 92, 98, 112, 216, 263, 289

emergency management, 80

employees, xiii, xv, 53, 105, 113, 134, 181, 190, 222, 241, 242, 245, 260, 261, 274, 277, 278

employers, xvi, 54, 127, 182, 208, 223, 232, 273, 274, 277, 278, 288, 289, 290, 291, 296, 298, 300, 301, 303

Employment and Training Administration, xvi, 285, 288, 294, 295, 296, 300, 302

Employment Cost Index (ECI), xiii, 180, 194, 196, 201, 202, 209, 211

employment opportunities, 62, 205, 206

employment relationship, 232

Energy Efficiency and Conservation Block Grant, 82

Energy Independence and Security Act, 171

Energy Policy Act, 170

enforcement, xiv, xv, xvi, 105, 112, 118, 121, 147, 167, 221, 222, 223, 224, 225, 226, 228, 230, 232, 234, 235, 238, 240, 241, 242, 243, 244, 247, 248, 250, 251, 252, 253, 255, 256, 259, 260, 263, 265,

270, 271, 272, 273, 274, 275, 276, 280, 282, 283, 286, 288, 290

enlisted personnel, xiv, 181, 185, 191, 192, 198, 203, 204, 210, 212, 215

environment, xiii, 56, 57, 62, 67, 76, 104, 151, 162, 165, 180, 205, 213

environmental protection, ix, 23, 25, 58, 88, 131, 135, 140, 145, 149, 152, 155, 157

Environmental Protection Agency, 135, 140, 145

equal opportunity, 113

equipment, xiii, 36, 180, 240

evidence, ix, 5, 17, 49, 74, 89, 122, 269, 272

executive branch, x, xii, 24, 26, 134, 180, 211, 226, 248, 252, 255, 259, 270, 282

executive branch officials, x, 24, 26

exercise, 43, 231, 261, 266, 268, 281

expenditures, 13, 22, 35, 49, 52, 53, 69, 102, 135, 136, 146

exposure, 186

F

factories, 165

Fair Labor Standards Act, 67, 157, 235

families, 65, 184, 208, 214, 216

family members, 185, 217

federal agency, 27, 28, 99, 144, 145, 146, 148, 149, 152, 154, 167, 168

federal aid, 74, 85, 103

federal assistance, xi, 52, 66, 68, 73, 82, 92, 98, 101, 112, 135, 143, 152, 153, 157

federal authorities, xv, 222, 227, 244, 246, 264, 271, 272, 276, 280

federal courts, 66, 241

Federal Emergency Management Agency, 84

federal employment, 36

federal funds, 52, 53, 74, 101, 237, 250, 254, 256, 258, 260, 264, 265, 282

Federal funds, 112

Federal Government, 45, 96, 151, 164, 165, 166, 223, 229, 234, 241, 259, 273, 277, 281, 282

federal government intervention, x, 24

federal grants, v, ix, xv, 23, 24, 25, 26, 27, 30, 31, 32, 33, 34, 35, 36, 38, 39, 40, 41, 48, 49, 50, 52, 54, 57, 58, 59, 65, 66, 68, 69, 71, 73, 74, 79, 80, 83, 86, 87, 88, 102, 103, 110, 130, 164, 222, 248, 264, 282

Federal Highway Administration, 45

federal immigration authorities, xiv, 221, 222, 224, 226, 228, 238, 240, 242, 243, 244, 245, 250, 251, 270, 278, 280, 283

federal immigration enforcement, xiv, 221, 222, 225, 226, 227, 228, 238, 244, 247, 248, 252, 259, 263, 270, 271, 273, 274, 280, 282

federal law, xiv, xv, 11, 130, 222, 230, 232, 233, 234, 235, 237, 239, 240, 241, 242, 243, 244, 246, 249, 251, 255, 259, 260, 265, 267, 268, 269, 272, 273, 276

federal mandates, x, 25, 66, 67, 69, 74, 75, 76, 77, 78, 80, 87, 88, 91, 92, 93, 95, 96, 97, 99, 103, 104, 105, 106, 109, 111, 112, 113, 119, 122, 124, 130, 132, 136, 137, 145, 146, 149, 152, 154, 155, 156, 157, 158, 159, 160, 161, 164, 165

federal regulations, 95

federalism, x, 24, 25, 26, 35, 38, 41, 43, 46, 47, 48, 50, 52, 54, 55, 56, 58, 59, 62, 63, 64, 65, 66, 67, 69, 70, 71, 72, 73, 74, 76, 77, 78, 79, 80, 81, 82, 87, 88, 95, 99, 100, 101, 104, 105, 106, 107, 108, 109, 122, 125, 152, 155, 156, 157, 159, 160, 162, 164, 166, 168, 224, 227, 229, 233, 237, 246, 267, 281

federalism scholars, ix, 24, 25, 26, 35, 41, 52, 63, 66, 67, 68, 71, 72, 79, 100, 104, 106, 107, 109, 152

felony offenses, viii, 4

financial, xi, xii, 66, 88, 92, 93, 95, 101, 110, 111, 113, 131, 132, 145, 147, 153, 159, 238, 264, 295

financial assistance, xi, 66, 88, 92, 132, 147, 153

financial condition, 238

fiscal year, xvii, 33, 34, 75, 76, 98, 110, 114, 118, 119, 126, 166, 186, 195, 198, 270, 286, 287, 291, 292, 293, 294, 295, 296, 299, 304

flexibility, 19, 52, 60, 70, 78, 79, 84, 85, 111, 153, 160, 298

food, 70, 72, 73, 125, 127, 192, 198, 210, 227

Food and Drug Administration, 172

Food, Conservation, and Energy Act of 2008, 171

force, xii, xiii, 5, 15, 68, 121, 157, 180, 205, 211, 212, 276

Ford, Gerald Rudolph, 60

foreign affairs, 112, 229

foreign nationals, xvi, 227, 285, 303

foreign workers, xvi, 285, 286, 287, 289, 290, 300, 302, 305

formula, 25, 27, 29, 30, 36, 39, 52, 59, 63, 64, 65, 193, 194, 195, 198, 199, 201, 202, 203, 204, 262, 265

formula-project, 25, 27, 36

funding, ix, xiii, 23, 24, 25, 28, 29, 30, 31, 35, 40, 48, 49, 52, 58, 61, 62, 64, 70, 71, 72, 73, 75, 76, 78, 81, 82, 84, 85, 86, 87, 88, 93, 94, 96, 97, 99, 101, 104, 106, 109, 110, 111, 112, 115, 125, 130, 136, 153, 180, 237, 238, 254, 256, 271

G

gambling, 236, 237

General Accounting Office, 37, 113, 125, 135, 136, 137, 143, 145

General Services Administration (GSA), 36

312 *Index*

Georgia, 225
global economy, x, 24, 26
governance, 24, 41, 152
government operations, v, vii, 1, 14, 33, 39, 41, 162
government spending, xii, 180
governments, ix, xi, 24, 25, 30, 31, 34, 35, 36, 37, 39, 40, 41, 42, 50, 52, 54, 57, 58, 60, 61, 62, 68, 71, 73, 74, 78, 79, 80, 82, 85, 86, 87, 88, 91, 92, 93, 94, 95, 96, 97, 101, 104, 107, 108, 109, 112, 113, 114, 116, 125, 126, 127, 129, 130, 133, 134, 137, 138, 142, 143, 144, 148, 149, 150, 153, 154, 155, 156, 157, 158, 159, 164, 229, 245
governor, 69
grades, 207
grant programs, 25, 36, 37, 49, 53, 64, 65, 72, 83, 85, 101, 107, 111, 283
grants-in-aid system, ix, 24, 27, 40
Great Britain, 42
Great Depression, 39

H

H-2B visa, vi, xvi, 285, 286, 287, 288, 291, 292, 293, 294, 297, 298, 299, 301, 303, 304, 305, 306
H-2B workers, xvii, 286, 287, 288, 289, 290, 291, 292, 294, 295, 296, 297, 299, 300, 301, 302, 303
health, ix, xii, 23, 25, 33, 35, 43, 52, 53, 57, 59, 61, 63, 72, 73, 74, 76, 82, 84, 85, 105, 111, 123, 127, 135, 152, 153, 155, 157, 159, 166, 167, 179, 181, 182, 192, 193, 207, 209, 210, 281, 289, 290
Health and Human Services, 70, 150
health care, ix, xii, 23, 25, 33, 35, 52, 57, 59, 61, 73, 74, 82, 85, 111, 123, 128, 152, 153, 173, 179, 181, 182, 192, 193, 207, 209, 210

health care programs, 57, 85
health insurance, 127, 289, 290
health services, 63
high school, 210, 211
high school diploma, 211
higher education, 39
history, xii, 15, 40, 44, 92, 96, 112, 124, 151, 217, 276
Homeland Security, v, vii, xv, xvi, 83, 120, 127, 142, 145, 147, 174, 219, 222, 224, 240, 248, 255, 285, 287, 288, 294, 295, 296, 299, 301, 303
House Manual, 6, 7, 8, 10, 11, 15, 18, 19
House of Representatives, vii, 3, 5, 6, 7, 8, 10, 12, 15, 16, 17, 19, 56, 79, 96, 97, 107, 162
housekeeper, xvi, 285, 287
housing, xiii, xv, 35, 56, 57, 70, 180, 182, 183, 184, 185, 188, 189, 190, 192, 196, 197, 198, 210, 211, 217, 222, 250, 274
Housing and Urban Development, 123, 172

I

identification, 126, 149, 225
immigrants, 227, 228, 241, 243, 280
immigration, xiv, xv, xvi, 221, 222, 223, 225, 226, 227, 228, 229, 230, 231, 232, 238, 239, 240, 241, 242, 243, 244, 245, 246, 247, 248, 249, 250, 251, 252, 255, 257, 259, 260, 261, 263, 264, 265, 270, 271, 272, 273, 274, 275, 276, 277, 278, 279, 280, 281, 282, 283, 287, 305
Immigration Act, 291
Immigration and Customs Enforcement, 240, 250
Immigration and Nationality Act (INA), xvi, 224, 229, 232, 239, 240, 280, 285, 286, 287, 290, 291, 292

Index

immigration status, xiv, 221, 225, 227, 232, 239, 241, 242, 243, 244, 245, 250, 252, 275

immunity, 273, 277, 279

improvements, 21, 33, 44, 45, 47, 190

inadmissible, 239

income, ix, 23, 25, 33, 35, 48, 49, 57, 65, 70, 73, 79, 103, 108, 110, 184, 191, 192, 193, 196, 215, 216

income security, ix, 23, 25, 33, 57, 73

income tax, 49, 103, 108, 110, 184, 191, 192, 215, 216

individuals, xvii, 7, 33, 35, 36, 37, 39, 58, 112, 130, 135, 189, 196, 203, 205, 235, 241, 243, 286, 297, 303

Individuals with Disabilities Education Act, 30

industrialization, x, 24, 26

inflation, 33, 35, 75, 98, 114, 133, 135, 142, 203

information sharing, xiv, 222, 239, 242, 243, 244, 245, 280

information technology, 209

infrastructure, 80, 84, 86, 302

insane, 45

insertion, 163

Intelligence Reform and Terrorism Prevention Act, 126

interest groups, x, 24, 26, 64, 128

Interstate Commerce Commission, 48

intervention, x, 24, 56

Iraq, xiii, 125, 180, 181, 213, 214, 215, 216

issues, x, 24, 26, 27, 40, 43, 54, 63, 78, 99, 137, 162, 165, 167, 206, 228, 240, 267, 281

J

Jackson, Andrew, 46

job training, ix, 23, 25, 57, 70, 72

job training programs, 57

Johnson, Lyndon Baines, 57

Johnson, President Lyndon B., 57

jurisdiction, vii, viii, xiv, 3, 4, 6, 10, 16, 17, 20, 22, 50, 71, 101, 221, 225, 226, 227, 228, 231, 245, 247, 248, 250, 265, 271, 282

K

Kennedy, John Fitzgerald, 55

L

labor market, 204, 205, 206, 212

law enforcement, xiv, 64, 222, 224, 225, 226, 227, 228, 234, 239, 240, 241, 242, 243, 248, 249, 267, 273, 275, 276, 279, 280

laws, xiv, 54, 55, 56, 80, 103, 105, 112, 125, 128, 129, 150, 154, 157, 162, 166, 222, 225, 226, 227, 228, 230, 231, 235, 236, 237, 240, 241, 243, 248, 259, 261, 265, 267, 268, 272, 276, 279, 282, 283, 293

lead, 19, 60, 63, 79, 153, 208, 267

legislation, viii, xi, xii, 4, 7, 9, 10, 25, 28, 29, 30, 42, 43, 45, 46, 51, 53, 56, 60, 63, 75, 88, 91, 92, 93, 95, 96, 97, 98, 99, 103, 104, 105, 106, 107, 109, 110, 111, 112, 113, 114, 115, 118, 119, 121, 123, 124, 130, 131, 132, 133, 137, 147, 152, 161, 162, 163,164, 165, 166, 194, 229, 230, 231, 237, 262

legislative proposals, xi, 57, 91

liberalism, 56

liberty, 225

litigation, 99, 247, 251, 252, 253, 257, 258

living conditions, 214

local community, 60, 62

local government, ix, x, xi, 23, 25, 27, 28, 30, 31, 33, 34, 35, 36, 37, 39, 40, 41, 43, 49, 50, 51, 52, 53, 54, 57, 58, 59, 60, 61,

62, 65, 66, 67, 69, 71, 73, 74, 75, 78, 79, 80, 81, 82, 83, 84, 85, 86, 87, 88, 91, 92, 94, 95, 96, 98, 99, 100, 102, 103, 104, 105, 106, 107, 108, 109, 110, 124, 125, 126, 127, 128, 129, 130, 132, 135, 136, 137, 142, 145, 146, 147, 149, 152, 153, 155, 156, 157, 158, 159, 160, 161, 164, 227, 244, 245, 246, 260

M

magnitude, 34, 157, 304
majority, 6, 12, 14, 50, 51, 56, 69, 74, 79, 107, 120, 121, 162, 163, 184, 255
management, viii, 4, 16, 28, 86
Marshall, John, 43
Maryland, 43
masking, 62
materialism, 56, 68
maternal care, 50
median, 28, 189, 190, 197, 211
Medicaid, 30, 31, 33, 35, 40, 57, 70, 72, 73, 76, 77, 79, 80, 82, 83, 84, 85, 107, 111, 130, 152, 169, 238, 289
medical, 182, 183, 185, 186
member, vii, xi, 4, 6, 7, 8, 10, 11, 13, 14, 16, 17, 18, 22, 63, 88, 92, 107, 113, 120, 123, 132, 143, 147, 153, 154, 159, 166, 181, 183, 184, 186, 190, 193, 196, 197, 198, 208, 217, 225
Member Day Hearing, viii, 4, 10
membership, vii, ix, 4, 5, 6, 7, 20, 21
methodology, xiii, 37, 39, 87, 160, 180, 190, 194, 211, 212
metropolitan areas, 58, 62
migration, 43, 165, 223
military, xii, xiii, 42, 44, 47, 56, 179, 180, 181, 182, 183, 184, 186, 187, 188, 189, 191, 192, 193, 194, 196, 204, 205, 206, 207, 208, 209, 210, 211, 212, 213, 215, 216

military compensation, xii, 179, 180, 181, 183, 184, 188, 191, 192, 193, 197, 206, 207, 208, 210, 211, 212, 213, 215, 217
military compensation system, xii, 179, 181
minimum wage, 76, 121, 122, 123, 125, 235, 289
Minneapolis, 42, 45
minorities, 56
mission, 188, 206, 259
modifications, vii, 3, 6
monetary policy, 147
morale, 188, 189
moratorium, 108, 126

N

National Crime Information Center, 234
national debt, 44
National Defense Authorization Act, 173, 174, 175, 189, 194, 197, 198, 199
national emergency, 186
national origin, 55, 66, 104
national policy, 41
National School Lunch Program, 33
national security, xi, 76, 92, 98, 112
nationality, 240
New Deal, 50, 53, 54
New England, 75
Nixon, Richard, 60
No Child Left Behind, 79, 81
nonagricultural worker, xvi, 285, 287, 294, 295, 296, 300
noncash benefits, xii, 179, 207
nonenforcement, 103, 109
nonimmigrant status, xvii, 286, 291
nonimmigrant visa, xvi, 285, 286, 287, 290, 294
nonprofit organizations, 58

Index

O

Obama Administration, 82

Obama, President Barack, 80, 82, 194, 200, 201

Office of Justice Programs, 248, 249, 261

Office of Management and Budget, 25, 27, 31, 32, 34, 134, 135, 139, 148, 150

Office of the Inspector General, 227

officials, x, xi, xiv, 24, 26, 41, 58, 59, 60, 66, 69, 74, 91, 92, 94, 95, 97, 100, 103, 104, 105, 106, 107, 109, 124, 129, 130, 134, 145, 149, 152, 155, 156, 159, 160, 161, 205, 221, 226, 235, 238, 242, 244, 245, 246, 273, 276

Omnibus Appropriations Act, 172

operations, xii, xiii, 14, 33, 39, 60, 106, 180, 215, 240

opportunities, 63, 212

opportunity costs, 132

opt out, 105, 107, 217

organized interest groups, x, 24, 26

oversight, viii, x, 4, 6, 11, 12, 14, 24, 27, 45, 53, 64, 84, 86, 87, 128, 245

P

participants, 131, 145, 149

pay gap, xiii, 180, 206, 209, 210, 212

penalties, 94, 100, 101, 277, 278

per capita income, 28, 63

percentile, xiii, 180, 210, 211, 212

permit, 134, 236, 243, 250

personnel, xiii, 44, 180, 181, 182, 184, 185, 186, 187, 192, 196, 197, 204, 205, 206, 207, 208, 209, 210, 212, 213, 214, 215, 216, 240, 250, 275

personnel costs, xiii, 180

Philadelphia, xv, 42, 223, 228, 241, 253, 254, 263, 264, 265, 266, 267, 283

police, xiv, xvi, 43, 46, 55, 221, 222, 223, 225, 226, 228, 231, 232, 238, 239, 240, 241, 242, 272, 281

policy, ix, 5, 9, 21, 22, 25, 28, 36, 38, 40, 41, 49, 52, 53, 55, 58, 59, 60, 63, 64, 65, 66, 67, 68, 74, 79, 80, 88, 100, 101, 102, 105, 107, 127, 147, 149, 151, 152, 153, 168, 212, 225, 227, 228, 234, 242, 245, 248, 251, 257

policymakers, 74, 78, 105, 124, 261, 305

political opposition, 47

political parties, 51, 88

pollution, 20, 62, 74, 165

population, 28, 42, 63, 205, 207, 265

port of entry, xvii, 286, 290

poverty, 28, 40, 52, 56, 57

preferential treatment, 271

presidency, 52, 69, 72, 79, 81

president, viii, x, 4, 14, 24, 26, 40, 45, 46, 52, 53, 54, 55, 57, 60, 64, 65, 69, 70, 71, 72, 78, 79, 80, 81, 82, 86, 88, 112, 151, 156, 157, 168, 194, 199, 200, 201, 223, 226, 227, 229, 244, 247, 248, 252, 254, 255, 256, 257, 258, 282

presidential veto, 77, 202

press conferences, 159

principles, xv, 88, 102, 153, 154, 164, 223, 224, 234, 235, 237, 246, 252, 253, 257, 258, 259, 267, 280

Privacy Protection Act, 235

private sector, xi, 75, 78, 91, 93, 95, 96, 97, 98, 100, 110, 113, 115, 116, 125, 129, 131, 133, 134, 135, 136, 137, 138, 142, 143, 144, 153, 154, 155, 156, 162, 182, 207, 208, 209, 210

project, 25, 27, 28, 30, 36, 39, 45, 52, 58, 59, 60, 62, 65

proliferation, 107

proposed regulations, xi, 91, 97

protection, 43, 47, 62, 105, 112, 198

public assistance, ix, 23, 25, 57, 58, 65, 70, 79, 289

316   *Index*

public awareness, 161
public education, 35, 42, 44, 82
public health, 50, 84, 105, 131, 149, 152, 231
public housing, 76
public interest, 58, 130, 131, 146, 147, 149, 156, 159, 161
public safety, 43, 227, 231, 241, 249, 281
public schools, 42, 48
public support, 58
Public Utilities Regulatory Policy Act, 67, 157

Q

Quadrennial Review of Military Compensation (QRMC), xiii, 180, 210, 211, 212, 213
quality of life, 165, 166
questioning, 227, 242

R

race, 55, 66, 104
radioactive waste, 233
ramp, 205
ratification, 41, 49
Reagan, Ronald, 40, 69, 72
reality, 103, 197
reasoning, 112, 261, 263
recession, 42, 46, 205, 206, 304
recipient discretion, 29
recommendations, ix, 5, 11, 12, 20, 21, 22, 80, 87, 99, 167
recovery, 30
recreational, xii, 179, 193, 207
recreational facilities, xii, 179, 193, 207
recruiting, xii, 180, 182, 204, 205, 206, 207, 212, 213

reform, 35, 62, 71, 76, 78, 95, 111, 123, 136, 137, 138, 152, 160, 163, 211, 224, 305
regulations, xi, xvi, 11, 13, 28, 41, 45, 69, 74, 75, 79, 91, 93, 94, 95, 97, 104, 127, 133, 135, 136, 138, 144, 146, 148, 153, 168, 230, 235, 286, 288, 294, 296, 298, 300
regulatory agencies, xi, 92, 98, 135, 147, 152, 153
regulatory controls, 67, 158
regulatory requirements, 134, 135, 301
reimburse, 214
rejection, 77
relaxation, 186
relief, 52, 60, 68, 69, 75, 88, 95, 105, 160, 161, 163, 252, 256, 262, 263, 270
Republican Conference, ix, 5, 8
Republican Party, 6, 14, 50, 69, 74, 79, 88, 162, 163
requirements, xi, xvi, 5, 36, 49, 53, 58, 59, 60, 62, 64, 66, 67, 76, 79, 92, 93, 94, 98, 100, 102, 103, 107, 111, 112, 113, 118, 119, 127, 130, 131, 133, 135, 142, 143, 146, 149, 150, 151, 153, 154, 157, 162, 165, 206, 234, 235, 244, 247, 250, 251, 258, 269, 271, 273, 278, 281, 286, 288
resale, 188
researchers, 152
reserves, 281
Resident Commissioner, vii, 4, 7, 8, 10, 13, 16, 17, 18, 20, 21
resistance, 55, 65, 228
resolution, vii, 3, 5, 8, 9, 12, 114, 119, 121, 225, 257
resources, 48, 61, 62, 106, 107, 136, 164, 206, 225, 238, 243, 302
response, 17, 40, 94, 203, 287, 300
restrictions, 46, 47, 80, 100, 107, 130, 157, 227, 237, 239, 240, 241, 242, 244, 245, 254, 257
restructuring, 205, 261

Index

retirement, xii, xiii, 105, 179, 180, 181, 182

retirement benefits, xii, 179, 181

revenue, 25, 27, 29, 38, 41, 44, 60, 61, 62, 63, 64, 65, 69, 72, 73, 88, 102, 108, 126, 136, 188

rights, xi, 44, 45, 48, 50, 51, 55, 56, 68, 76, 92, 98, 104, 105, 112, 131, 135, 149, 152, 237, 260

Roosevelt, Franklin Delano, 52

Rule XXIII, vii, 4, 7, 8

rules, vii, viii, ix, xi, xii, 3, 4, 5, 6, 7, 8, 9, 10, 11, 12, 13, 14, 15, 16, 18, 19, 20, 21, 71, 76, 92, 98, 101, 103, 105, 109, 110, 112, 120, 132, 134, 135, 136, 137, 138, 139, 140, 142, 143, 144, 146, 147, 149, 152, 156, 223, 253, 296, 297

Rules Committee, viii, 4, 5, 8, 9, 10, 13, 14, 16, 18, 19, 56

rural areas, 63

S

safety, 76, 105, 131, 149, 152, 155, 157, 165, 166, 231, 281

sanctions, 94, 100, 102, 224, 232

sanctuary policies, xiv, 221, 222, 225, 226, 227, 241, 244, 247, 248, 269, 281, 282

Saudi Arabia, 214

savings, 187, 232, 243, 255

school, 42, 81, 127, 158, 217

scope, ix, x, 24, 25, 26, 27, 43, 53, 54, 93, 131, 150, 151, 153, 154, 210, 229, 235, 240, 255

search terms, 39

secondary education, 30, 81

Secretary of Defense, 189, 196, 197

Secretary of Homeland Security, xv, 222, 255

Secretary of the Treasury, 50

security, ix, 23, 25, 33, 57, 73, 142, 190

Select Committee on the Climate Crisis, ix, 5, 20

Select Committee on the Modernization of Congres, ix, 5, 21

Senate, xii, 41, 45, 46, 51, 56, 69, 74, 76, 77, 79, 92, 96, 97, 99, 103, 104, 105, 107, 111, 112, 113, 119, 120, 121, 122, 123, 132, 137, 143, 145, 147, 160, 161, 162, 163, 165, 166, 167, 168, 170, 171, 173, 176, 199, 200, 201, 204, 206, 210, 273, 274, 281

September 11, xii, 180

servicemembers, xii, 179, 180, 182, 183, 184, 185, 186, 187, 188, 189, 190, 191, 192, 195, 196, 197, 199, 200, 201, 211, 213, 214, 216, 217

services, iv, xii, xvi, 36, 37, 39, 59, 61, 62, 67, 69, 71, 72, 94, 110, 111, 126, 155, 158, 161, 179, 182, 183, 185, 186, 187, 188, 193, 204, 205, 208, 212, 214, 285, 287, 289, 298

shelter, 225, 227

Sixteenth Amendment, 49

slavery, 42, 47

social group, 103, 148, 152

social movements, 40, 56

Social Security, xi, 40, 53, 54, 65, 76, 92, 98, 112, 217

social services, ix, 23, 25, 32, 33, 35, 57, 64, 70, 73, 84

social welfare, 35, 53

societal problems, x, 24, 26

society, x, 24, 26, 40, 41, 53, 68, 135, 165

South Dakota, 101, 238

sovereignty, 232, 246

spending, 41, 42, 50, 53, 69, 83, 84, 85, 87, 103, 105, 110, 114, 126, 130, 237, 252, 254, 255, 256, 259, 264, 270, 282, 283

spillover effects, 62

standard of living, 61, 204

standing committees, viii, 4, 5, 7, 10, 11, 20, 21, 22

318 *Index*

state authorities, 244, 246

state government funding, ix, 23, 25

state laws, 47, 78, 107, 130, 227, 236, 248, 278

states, xiv, xv, 8, 14, 19, 28, 38, 41, 42, 43, 44, 45, 46, 47, 48, 49, 50, 51, 52, 54, 56, 58, 60, 62, 65, 67, 72, 78, 81, 85, 94, 101, 102, 105, 108, 111, 125, 126, 130, 144, 150, 152, 155, 157, 158, 159, 215, 221, 222, 223, 225, 226, 227, 228, 229, 230, 231, 232, 233, 234, 235, 236, 237, 238, 240, 242, 244, 245, 246, 250, 252, 254, 256, 261, 263, 266, 272, 281, 283, 297, 298

statutes, 97, 106, 144, 157, 234, 235, 242, 246, 249, 259, 264

statutory authority, xiii, 180, 211, 249, 252, 253, 258, 261, 262, 263, 264, 265, 266, 268, 270, 282

structure, xii, 26, 46, 63, 87, 179, 233

subcommittee, ix, 4, 6, 7, 9, 16, 17, 19, 20, 26, 41, 56, 124, 139, 144, 145, 147, 148, 197, 205, 210

subpoena, 13, 20, 22, 273

subsistence, 182, 183, 185, 187, 192

Superfund, 77, 103

supervision, 207, 224, 275

Supplemental Nutrition Assistance Program, 70, 72, 84, 86, 125

Supreme Court, x, xiv, xv, 24, 26, 43, 47, 48, 50, 53, 54, 101, 111, 153, 222, 223, 224, 231, 233, 234, 235, 236, 238, 241, 244, 246, 255, 256, 260, 267, 269, 280, 283

survivors, 112, 216, 217

tax cuts, 108

tax policy, 86, 108

tax rates, 191

taxation, 46, 108, 192

taxes, 41, 43, 49, 55, 72, 78, 102, 108, 126, 161, 237

taxpayers, 62, 165

technical assistance, 134, 251

Tenth Amendment, xiv, 44, 53, 111, 222, 231, 233, 235, 237, 245, 246, 257, 258, 260, 281

territorial, 42

territory, 42, 128

Title I, 21, 98, 109, 112, 113, 115, 118, 125, 129, 132, 133, 135, 136, 137, 143, 144, 145, 146, 147, 149, 150, 162, 167, 289, 291, 292, 293, 294

Title II, 21, 98, 109, 133, 135, 136, 137, 143, 144, 145, 146, 147, 149, 150, 167, 293

Title IV, 99, 132, 147, 292, 293

Title V, 66, 293

total costs, 197

trade, xiii, 132, 180

trade-off, xiii, 132, 180

training, 5, 33, 36, 57, 64, 72, 73, 77, 185, 186, 192, 208, 251

training programs, 72, 77, 186

transportation, ix, 23, 25, 32, 33, 44, 45, 55, 57, 64, 72, 73, 77, 83, 123, 170, 172, 173, 182, 289

Treasury, 46, 61, 123, 151, 170

treatment, 58, 68, 88, 113, 158

trial, ix, 5, 17, 263

tribal officials, 135, 150

trust fund, 72, 73

T

Task Force, 108

tax base, 66, 108

tax collection, 80

Index

U

U.S. Citizenship and Immigration Services (USCIS), xvi, 285, 286, 288, 298, 299, 300, 301, 302, 303
U.S. Department of Agriculture, 142
U.S. Department of Commerce, 32, 57
U.S. Department of Labor, xvi, 142, 285, 288, 294, 295, 296, 300, 302
U.S. economy, 206
U.S. immigration law, 230, 240
unemployment rate, 205
Unfunded Mandates Information and Transparency Act, xi, 92, 132, 133, 146, 147, 151, 153, 155
Unfunded Mandates Reform Act, v, x, 75, 76, 81, 88, 91, 93, 112, 116, 117, 124, 125, 128, 129, 138, 139, 141, 142, 144, 145, 147, 148, 150, 151, 153, 163, 168
uniform, 61, 62, 112, 146, 198, 229
urban areas, 54, 56, 58
urban renewal, 55, 58
utility costs, 196

V

validation, 160
veto, 46
victims, 225, 242
Vietnam, 40, 56
violent crime, 265, 272
vocational education, 50
volatile environment, xiii, 180
vote, 8, 18, 56, 71, 87, 96, 97, 99, 120, 121, 167
voter constituencies, x, 24, 26
voting, 18, 47, 55, 120, 122, 162, 166
Voting Rights Act, 55, 112

W

wage and hour division, xvi, 285, 288
wage rate, 289
wages, xiii, xvi, xvii, 113, 180, 194, 210, 211, 213, 286, 288, 289
waiver, 107
war, 43, 47, 54, 79, 166, 207, 213, 229
War on Terror, 217
Washington, 6, 8, 14, 29, 37, 45, 46, 55, 56, 58, 59, 62, 64, 65, 66, 67, 71, 72, 73, 76, 95, 99, 101, 102, 103, 104, 105, 107, 108, 111, 113, 124, 132, 137, 139, 144, 145, 147, 148, 155, 157, 158, 159, 160, 161, 162, 163, 167, 197, 240, 254, 257, 267
waste, 67, 112, 158, 167, 233
waste disposal, 67, 158, 233
water, 44, 58, 62, 155, 158, 214
welfare, 43, 53, 54, 77, 165, 188, 231, 237, 281
welfare system, 165
White House, 57
Wisconsin, 44
withdrawal, 111
workers, xvi, xvii, 55, 127, 131, 149, 152, 194, 232, 285, 286, 287, 288, 289, 290, 291, 292, 293, 294, 295, 296, 297, 298, 299, 300, 301, 302, 303, 305
working conditions, xvii, 286, 289
working groups, 57
World War I, 54, 66, 71

Y

Yale University, 51
young people, 56

Related Nova Publications

KEY CONGRESSIONAL REPORTS FOR FEBRUARY 2019. PART III

EDITOR: Mandy Todd

SERIES: Congressional Policies, Practices and Procedures

BOOK DESCRIPTION: This book is a comprehensive compilation of all reports, testimony, correspondence and other publications issued by the Congressional Research Service during the month of March, grouped according to topics.

HARDCOVER ISBN: 978-1-53615-997-4
RETAIL PRICE: $230

KEY CONGRESSIONAL REPORTS FOR MARCH 2019. PART I

EDITOR: Sergio Frank

SERIES: Congressional Policies, Practices and Procedures

BOOK DESCRIPTION: This book is a comprehensive compilation of all reports, testimony, correspondence and other publications issued by the Congressional Research Service during the month of March, grouped according to topics. This book is focused on the following topics:
· Information Security & Technology
· Military Technology

HARDCOVER ISBN: 978-1-53615-976-9
RETAIL PRICE: $160

To see a complete list of Nova publications, please visit our website at www.novapublishers.com

Related Nova Publications

Key Congressional Reports for February 2019. Part II

Editor: Mandy Todd

Series: Congressional Policies, Practices and Procedures

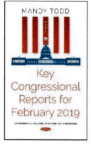

Book Description: This book is a comprehensive compilation of all reports, testimony, correspondence and other publications issued by the Congressional Research Service during the month of February, grouped according to topics. This book is focused on the following topics:
- Business
- Finance

Hardcover ISBN: 978-1-53615-737-6
Retail Price: $195

Key Congressional Reports on International Affairs

Editor: Hattie Ross

Series: Congressional Policies, Practices and Procedures

Book Description: This book is a comprehensive compilation of all reports, testimony, correspondence and other publications issued by the Congressional Research Service on U.S. International Relations during the month of February.

Hardcover ISBN: 978-1-53615-733-8
Retail Price: $230

To see a complete list of Nova publications, please visit our website at www.novapublishers.com